# Relationship Enhancement

~~~~~~~~~~~~~~~~~~~~~~~~~~~~

*Skill-Training Programs
for Therapy,
Problem Prevention,
and Enrichment*

# Bernard G. Guerney, Jr.

*With Chapters Contributed by*

Jerry D. Collins

Barry G. Ginsberg

Edward Vogelsong

# Relationship Enhancement

Jossey-Bass Publishers

San Francisco • Washington • London • 1982

RELATIONSHIP ENHANCEMENT
*Skill-Training Programs for Therapy, Problem Prevention, and Enrichment*
by Bernard G. Guerney, Jr.

Copyright © 1977 by: Jossey-Bass, Inc., Publishers
433 California Street
San Francisco, California 94104
&
Jossey-Bass Limited
28 Banner Street
London EC1Y 8QE

Library of Congress Catalogue Card Number LC 76-11884

International Standard Book Number ISBN 0-87589-310-4

Manufactured in the United States of America


JACKET DESIGN BY WILLI BAUM


FIRST EDITION
First printing: April 1977
Second printing: October 1979
Third printing: September 1982

Code 7709

*The Jossey-Bass*
*Behavioral Science Series*

*To Louise Fisher Guerney*

# Preface

∿∿∿∿∿∿∿∿∿∿∿∿∿∿

There is an apocryphal story about an old-fashioned sanity test, the "water-bucket test," which Eli Bower told many years ago. The person to be tested is brought into an otherwise bare room containing a faucet with a bucket under it, a small ladle near the bucket, and a sink several feet away. The examiner, saying nothing, turns on the faucet full force and leaves the room to observe through a window in the door. If the person races between the bucket and the sink with ladles full of water trying vainly to keep the bucket from overflowing, he is judged insane. If he turns off the water at the faucet before the bucket overflows, he is judged sane.

We seriously question whether the mental health professions could pass a similar test in their approach to the mental health problem. We question whether traditional methods of delivering services can adequately meet mental health needs. One reason we undertook the writing of this book is that we

believe the best approach to helping the public escape emotional and interpersonal pain is to try to cut it off at the source. We believe that one important way for mental health professionals to do this is to educate people in concepts and behavioral skills that will allow them to solve family conflicts reasonably and harmoniously without recourse to behaviors that are destructive to the self-concepts of other family members. Further, we believe that an educational method for changing interpersonal behavior, one which encompasses the most significant principles of both relationship therapy and behavior modification, can serve not only as the most powerful means for *preventing* personal and interpersonal problems but as the most powerful means of *treating* such problems if individuals already suffer them.

The type of education we describe in the book is one that takes full account of the importance and complexity of significant, intimate human relationships. It is a type of education in which emotion is regarded not only as worthy of careful attention but as the powerhouse from which behavior derives it energy. It is a type of education based on the premise that individuals should be provided with as much knowledge and skill as experts can give them and then encouarged to make their own decisions, including decisions in solving emotional, interpersonal, and social problems. We believe that solutions based on such self-applied knowledge and skills are likely to be the most satisfying and viable ones.

The type of education espoused here is built on the realization that clearly specified goals and highly specific methods and techniques of reaching them are powerful tools for building new attitudes and behaviors. These are methods of education that recognize the great utility of laws of learning and behavior modification to human problems and aspirations; methods that are replicable and relatively easy to test and refine by one of the most powerful and revealing methods of investigation psychological science can provide—controlled comparison between different experimental conditions with large numbers of subjects.

These beliefs led to the development of the Relationship Enhancement (RE) approach, and to this book.

The book is intended for all mental health and kindred professionals—anyone actively engaged in helping others to function in more satisfying ways emotionally and socially. One objective of the book is to stimulate the reader to a fuller consideration of the potential advantages of the educational model in general. But the major intent of the book is to present the Relationship Enhancement method in particular. Our objective is to present and illustrate the RE method at a level of specificity that will enable an experienced professional to incorporate it immediately into his professional practice. At the same time, we wanted to familiarize the reader with the scientific studies we have conducted on the RE method and with the theoretical and empirical background to this research. In a sense, we saw the task as involving a good bit of bridge building: bridging relationship therapy and behavior modification, and also bridging research and clinical practice.

Thus, the motivation underlying the work described in this book is an amalgam of strongly humanistic, reformist aspirations and a desire to build on the work of others in a scientific manner. Although we see no inherent contradiction in these two motivations, the blend makes for a certain amount of awkwardness in presenting the work. Should the style be broad, provocative and polemic; or should it be circumspect, cautious and scholarly? The choice was made to take different approaches in different sections of the book. We have already published articles of a more scholarly nature dealing with some of the themes underlying the rationale for our educational approach (Authier, Gustafson, Guerney, and Kasdorf, 1975; Guerney, Guerney, and Stollak, 1971/1972; Guerney, Stollak, and Guerney, 1970; Guerney, Stollak, and Guerney, 1971). Thus, in the chapters providing the rationale and description of Relationship Enhancement programs, we chose not to restrict ourselves to opinions already documented by empirical research or to slow down the flow of our presentation with documentations and citations, even where it would have been possible to provide them. On the other hand, in those chapters written by Jerry Collins, Barry Ginsberg and Edward Vogelsong, which include presentations of research on Relationship Enhancement

methods, we have cited a good deal of pertinent previous literature and research.

Throughout the book, we have tried to be specific and
thorough in describing our methods and the rationale underlying them. We believe that many mental health workers have the
skills and experience to succeed in applying our methods if the
techniques are presented in explicit detail. One of our major
goals was to make such success possible. Such a high level of
explicitness, however, entails the risk that some professionals
might regard a few sections as condescending or as belaboring
the obvious. It is a price we are willing to pay in order to avoid
gaps that would be highly frustrating to readers who would welcome a very comprehensive and detailed exposition.

## Acknowledgments

The work described in this book represents a truly broad-
based, collaborative effort. The methods were developed not
only with the help of the chapter contributors but with the help
of Louise Guerney, Lillian Stover, Michael Andronico, and
many students who worked with the method in early, less re-
fined stages. It would not be possible to acknowledge all of
these students, but those who made special contributions include Austin Ely, Nicholas Armenti, Barry Ginsberg, Roy
Grando, Gary Gruber, Stephen Schlein, Charles Figley, Jean-
nette Coufal, and Edward Vogelsong. Edward Vogelsong has
also been especially helpful in providing critical editorial assistance. Others who have been helpful editorially are: Dee Vogelsong, Carol Hatch, Diane Munson, Mary O'Connell, and Gary
Stollak. Margaret Lakatos and Diane Bernd have been most
helpful and patient in all stages of manuscript preparation.

The author is also very grateful to the National Institute
of Mental Health for the support it has provided over the years
for research projects involving the new methods of providing
mental health services described in this volume.

Certain colleagues who have been very generous with
their encouragement and help in the course of the development
of the Relationship Enhancement programs also deserve special

gratitude: Jay Fidler, Donald Ford, and my wife, Louise Guerney. Louise Guerney also deserves special thanks for the encouragement she provided throughout the writing of this book. Chapter contributors also express appreciation for the encouragement and support provided by their wives, Mindy Ginsberg and Dee Vogelsong.

*University Park, Pennsylvania*          Bernard G. Guerney, Jr.
*February 1977*

# Contents

~~~~~~~~~~~~~~~~~~~~~~~~~~~~

xv

# Contents

# The Author
# and Chapter Contributors

▸▸▸▸▸▸▸▸▸▸▸▸▸▸▸▸▸▸▸▸▸▸▸▸▸▸▸

Bernard G. Guerney, Jr., is professor of human development and head of the Individual and Family Consultation Center of The Pennsylvania State University. An American Board of Examiners in Professional Psychology (ABPP) diplomate in clinical psychology, he received his Ph.D. in clinical psychology from The Pennsylvania State University in 1956, worked as a psychologist at the Lafayette Clinic in Detroit, Michigan, for a year, and was a professor in the Clinical Psychology Graduate Program at Rutgers University, where he directed the Psychological Clinic for twelve years before returning to The Pennsylvania State University in 1969.

Bernard Guerney, Jr., is well known for his pioneering work on the use of parents and paraprofessionals as psychotherapeutic agents and for his research in individual and family psychotherapy. He has published articles and monographs on psychotherapy, interpersonal behavior, family relationships, education, and professional training in some thirty different scientific and professional journals. He also serves as a consulting editorial reviewer for several publishing firms and journals,

including *Science.* In addition, he has co-edited *Psychotherapy Research: Selected Readings* (1966); was a co-author of *Families of the Slums: An Explanation of Their Structure and Treatment* (1967); and has edited *Psychotherapeutic Agents: New Roles for Nonprofessionals, Parents, and Teachers* (1969).

Bernard Guerney, Jr., is founder and president of the Institute for the Development of Emotional and Life Skills (IDEALS), a multidisciplinary nonprofit organization that offers in-service staff training workshops to agencies interested in using the skill-training approach to prevention and treatment and that also offers consultation on the evaluation of mental health services.

He is married to Louise Fisher Guerney, who is a professional colleague as well as the mother of his three teenage children, Janis, Bruce, and Robert.

Jerry D. Collins is a licensed clinical psychologist in both Pennsylvania and Virginia and a clinical member of the American Association of Marriage and Family Counselors. After receiving his doctorate in Human Development and Family Studies at The Pennsylvania State University in 1971, he spent a year on a postdoctoral fellowship at St. Christopher's Hospital for Children in Philadelphia. From 1972 to 1976, he worked in a private residential school and treatment center with learning disabled and emotionally disturbed children, adolescents, and their families. Collins is now working with adolescent inpatients suffering from schizophrenia or severe character disorders in individual, group, and family therapy at the Dominion Psychiatric Treatment Center in Falls Church, Virginia.

Barry G. Ginsberg, father of three boys, is a community clinical psychologist. He is presently Director of Community Services and formerly Director of Child and Family Outpatient Services at the Lenape Valley Foundation, Chalfont, Pennsylvania. He has been a teacher, guidance counselor, and school psychologist in the New York City public schools. He received his Ph.D. in Human Development and Family Studies at The Pennsylvania State University in 1971. Ginsberg is a clinical

supervisor of the American Association of Marriage and Family Counselors and has worked and published in family therapy, parent-child relations, and marital interaction. He has had extensive experience in child development, dysfunction, and therapy. Ginsberg is presently involved in education as therapy and preventive mental health programs in the community and has considerable experience in training and consultation. He is an adjunct faculty member of The Pennsylvania State University and Rutgers Graduate School of Professional Psychology. Ginsberg is also Director of In-service Training for IDEALS, Inc.

Edward Vogelsong is assistant professor of human development at The Pennsylvania State University, where he does research on interpersonal relationships. He was awarded his Ph.D. in Human Development and Family Studies at The Pennsylvania State University in 1975. A clinical member of the American Association of Marriage and Family Counselors, he has maintained a private practice in marriage and family therapy. Vogelsong has trained many professionals in the use of Relationship Enhancement methods, including psychotherapists, counselors, case workers, school personnel, clergy, and nurses. He has also worked extensively, in both a training and supervisory capacity, with graduate students and paraprofessionals in Relationship Enhancement. He is the Executive Director of the Institute for the Development of Emotional And Life Skills, Inc. (IDEALS). Vogelsong lives with his wife and four children near State College, Pennsylvania.

# Relationship Enhancement

~~~~~~~~~~~~~~~~~~~~~~~~~~~~~~~~~~

*Skill-Training Programs
for Therapy,
Problem Prevention,
and Enrichment*

# Chapter 1

# Rationale of Relationship Enhancement Therapy and Programs

Relationship Enhancement (RE) therapy and programs are educational services designed to enhance relationships between intimates, especially between family members. RE programs can be conducted with individuals, with dyads, or with larger groups. The purpose of the programs is to increase the psychological and emotional satisfactions that can be derived from such intimate relationships and, in addition, to thereby increase the psychological and emotional well-being of the individual participants.

RE programs involve the sort of learning that one usually associates with educational programs; that is, they include intellectual explanation and discussion and deal on a cognitive level with concepts and ideas. However, expansion and change of ideas and attitudes, which is the end point of most educational experiences, is only the beginning phase of an RE program. The major goal of RE programs is the teaching of specific interpersonal behavioral skills—the modification of behavior.

The participants are given the rationale and the skills that enable them to meet communications from their intimates with empathic acceptance; to recognize and accept their own feelings

1

and those of others; to recognize that their view of inter-personal issues is necessarily subjective rather than objective and to express their viewpoint accordingly; to help others under-stand and formulate their own motivations more clearly and thus to develop their personalities more fully; and to express interpersonal messages—disappointments, expectations and wishes—in highly specific behavioral terms. The participants are also taught how to use these and other skills that are taught in the program in systematic ways to enable them to resolve rela-tionship problems (or, if there are no problems, to bring per-sonal and interpersonal satisfactions to higher levels) and as a method for continuous use in conflict resolution.

Many of these principles were derived from the theories and psychotherapeutic techniques developed by Carl Rogers; others are more related to the therapeutic principles developed by the behavior modification practitioners following Skinner; still others to the theories of Harry Stack Sullivan as these have been further developed by Timothy Leary. The methods em-ployed to teach the skills to the participants rely on the princi-ples of social learning as explicated by Bandura and others, and on principles of reinforcement as developed by Skinner and others, although reinforcement is used in a free-flowing fashion that many behavior modifiers would consider very loose. (This looseness is deliberate, and is related to our own particular view on the functions performed by reinforcement in this context.)

The programs, some of which we have been developing and researching since 1962, are highly structured, the training is very detailed and systematic, and the flow of emotion and com-munication is channeled in carefully defined ways. Participants benefit from this careful definition of skills and systematic method of teaching because they know exactly what they are being asked to do. RE leaders like the structure since it keeps the group task-oriented and prevents nonproductive digres-sions.

We believe that RE programs can have a very important impact on participants. This impact, of course, will be experi-enced primarily within the relationship itself. However, we also believe that the application of skills learned by the individuals

to their intimate and other relationships will result in an increase in the *general* psychological and emotional well-being of the participants. We believe these programs will have great impact on the psychological well-being of the participants as individuals because, like Sullivan, Leary, Schutz, and many others, we believe that the strength and stability of an individual's intrapsychic life is largely determined by the quality of his interpersonal relationships with significant others, particularly his family and other intimates. In addition, when intimates learn skills that are therapeutic in nature, we believe they can have extremely beneficial effects in helping each other to work through intrapsychic conflicts as well.

The same general RE principles are taught to clients in separate programs specifically aimed at different types of family-oriented relationships, for example, marital, premarital, parent-adolescent, and so on. The basic dyadic model can be adapted for use with larger groups (for example, with an entire family working together) or for use with a single person (for example, with a wife whose husband is not willing to come for marital therapy, or a mother whose adolescent will not enter treatment). RE methods also can be adapted for use with non-family relationships as these exist, for example, in hospitals, industry, and schools, such as psychiatric nurse-patient, supervisor-supervisee, student-teacher, administrator-staff, coworker, and peer relationships. We will elaborate on the use of modified RE methods in a later chapter.

### Interpersonal Relations and Mental Illness

We believe that there are people who are truly mentally ill. By this we mean that some people's mental functions, and therefore interpersonal relations, are deranged, disequilibriated because of biochemical factors. We do not doubt for a moment that life-styles—particularly ones ill-suited to avoiding and handling anxiety and stress—also play a definite role even for those individuals whose central difficulties developed from, or into, biochemical imbalances. Nevertheless, we accept the view that genetic predispositions and biochemical factors can play a cen-

tral role in certain types of schizophrenia and some other psychoses. It seems likely that the major breakthroughs toward helping individuals so afflicted will come from biochemical research.

We also have little doubt that individual differences in genetics and biochemistry will be found to play some sort of role in the development of psychological life-styles of people in general. It is our view, however, that genetic and biochemical forces are not the major determining factors in the problems of the overwhelming majority of people who see themselves, or are seen by others, as requiring the services of mental health professionals.

Always for this larger group, and at pre- and postcrisis points for the much smaller, truly ill group, the role of interpersonal relations is central to the problem and to the solution. Such a conclusion seems inescapable when we consider that relationships with other people are at the heart of everything we do and are virtually inseparable from all the stresses and anxieties of life.

### *Interpersonal Relations and the Mental Health Worker*

For the last half-century, mental health workers have tended to view as "sick" all people with interpersonal thought and behavior patterns that the client, others around him, or the professional himself considered undesirable. Even unsatisfying or troubled *relationships* between people came to be regarded as sick. Conceptual distinctions between biochemically mediated versus socially and interpersonally mediated determinants of unsatisfying or socially disapproved life-styles became very blurred. In our view, that was unfortunate. Medical terminology should have been reserved for difficulties in which the biochemical factors predominated.

Mental health professionals often fail to be sufficiently conscious of the fact that they are not in the business of "curing" people, or helping them to become "better" people. Rather, they are trying to change people in order to achieve an ideal or objective of the client, or the professional, or both.

Unless the client is suffering a biochemical deficiency or imbalance, he is no more sick than someone who wants to play tennis and does not know how, and the professional is no more providing "therapy" or "curing" his or her client than a tennis coach is "curing" his clients.

## Therapy or Education?

To adopt a realistic approach for helping people achieve lives more satisfying to themselves and others, mental health professionals should shed the protective cloak borrowed from medical practitioners, who do offer people cures via therapy. Instead, when not prescribing biochemical remedies, mental health professionals should offer new educational and reeducational services that reshape behavior and life-styles.

We do not mean that the goals of such new educational services should be different from the goals of what is now known as *psychotherapy* or *counseling*. The new services differ from traditional ways of delivering traditional relationship therapy and behavior modification services not as much in goals as in philosophy, conception, organization, and efficiency. We also do not mean to imply that the changes in a client's attitudes, behaviors, character, or life-styles to be sought via this new type of educational service would be any less deep, pervasive, or permanent than those that psychotherapists have sought. Quite the contrary. We believe that an ideological fog has enveloped many psychotherapists because of their long exposure to medically oriented theoreticians and work settings. Once this fog is lifted and the practitioners can see their role clearly as that of educators, they will be in a much *better* position to offer more meaningful, deeper, longer-lasting psychological, behavioral, and interpersonal benefits to more clients, and to clients of more types, than has hitherto been possible. Viewing psychotherapy as a type of education also makes it easier, in concept and in practice, to develop primary prevention programs that have hitherto been given the best possible lip service and have achieved the least possible realization.

The various Relationship Enhancement programs offered

here are also called parent-adolescent therapy, conjugal therapy, and so forth, in order to convey their nature to the many professionals and clients who would be unlikely to fully consider the potential of the program for drastically and permanently changing severe personal and interpersonal difficulties were the word *therapy* not used. It would be our preference to avoid the term *therapy* for *all* "psychotherapies" because use of the term tends to perpetuate confusion in the minds of both the public and professionals themselves about the kinds of services that mental health practitioners provide when they are not dispensing drugs. At this time, however, we fear that failing to label as *psychotherapy* the type of programs we are describing in this book (in addition to the other names given to the programs), would create more confusion than it would eliminate. It is our hope that the methods described here, along with others that are being developed now all across the country, will help to eliminate such semantic confusion and eventually make the term *psychotherapy* an archaic one.

Nonbiochemical techniques that have usually gone under the name of *psychotherapy* are in reality highly unstructured, unsystematic education. Because such methods do not necessarily deal with illness, or even abnormality, it is inappropriate to call them *therapeutic*. On the other hand, most of these methods are so unsystematic and unstructured that they do not deserve to be called *educational*, either. It is hoped that such techniques will evolve into, or give way to, new methods that will be more overt and specific in their educational intent and more systematic in their execution, and, thereby, will justify the use of the term *educational*.

One further comment seems necessary to clarify this issue. It is not necessary to give up the major contributions to understanding basic psychodynamics that Freud and other great psychotherapists have contributed in order to use an educational paradigm. In fact, it will eventually be necessary to add all the valid insights of the great psychologists, Freud as well as Skinner, to the insights of educational philosophers, theorists, and researchers if we are to build a network of educational pro-

grams geared to the scale of humanity's psychological and interpersonal aspirations.

## Cost-Benefit Factors

We believe the cost-benefit ratio is significantly better in
RE programs than in traditional methods that deal with relationship problems. This general hypothesis is based on a number
of reasons and subhypotheses.

First, we believe the RE approach resolves relationship
problems more quickly than traditional approaches because the
RE approach: (1) reduces client defensiveness related to the
therapist; (2) reduces rivalry between the members of the family by minimizing the clients' needs to prove themselves correct
in the eyes of the therapist and to fix the blame on others; (3)
focuses efficiently on fundamental relationship issues by using a
structured, systematic method designed to bring these issues to
the forefront as soon as clients are ready and able to discuss
them; and (4) consistently encourages clients to resolve their
own problems, rather than indirectly and inadvertently encouraging them to expect that the therapist will somehow provide
resolutions.

Second, although we have not yet exploited this potential
systematically, the RE approach makes it feasible: (1) to use the
principals in the relationship as psychotherapeutic and relationship change agents for each other, and (2) to use other nonprofessionals as change agents. The method lends itself to using
nonprofessionals (for example, successful clients who then receive additional training) as group leaders or assistant group
leaders. Also, the group members are systematically trained to
help one another in the same way the leader has been providing
help. Therefore, with long-running groups (for example, six
months or a year) it should prove feasible for the leader to first
provide special instruction and supervision in certain additional
aspects of the leader's role and then wean the group to relatively independent functioning. During the weaning period, one
leader might supervise several advanced groups in the same

amount of time it previously took to lead one. It may even be possible to do such multigroup supervision via tape recordings and occasional meetings with the groups. Still later, it may be feasible to have the group continue with the leader available only on special request.

Third, efficient use of professional time, space, and equipment results from using a group format whenever feasible in RE programs.

Fourth, the development of teaching aids is more feasible with an approach based on an educational model. We have found it relatively easy to develop written instructions, training films and tapes, and practice materials. The use of these instructional aids can be helpful in facilitating learning.

Fifth, the use of home assignments speeds progress. Our goal is to teach participants skills which they can use in their daily lives. By setting aside time to practice at home regularly, participants work on increasing their skill proficiency and learn to use their skills in their homes.

Sixth, RE programs are designed to increase affection and friendship bonds existing in natural relationships. This reduces the probability that clients will rely on the therapist to satisfy needs that are best satisfied outside a professional relationship. The inclination of clients to satisfy affectional needs through a relationship with a therapist rather than in their ordinary social environment is further reduced by the predesignation of points in time at which program phases terminate and clients and leader reassess whether a new phase should be undertaken.

Seventh, and last, problem resolution will be more stable and durable than in traditional approaches because RE programs emphasize continued use of problem-resolution and problem-prevention skills in the natural environment.

## Moral Values

It is also well to bear in mind that the building of such a massive network of educational programs as we propose will never be finished. Can you imagine a fixed, never-changing college, or even elementary school, curriculum? So it is with

personal and interpersonal skills. As knowledge grows, as technology changes, as patterns of wealth and work change, personal and interpersonal needs, and the kinds of experiences that can satisfy those needs, also change. Because of differences in cultures or subcultures, and at different stages of history, people's needs and desires differ. Variation is as characteristic of interpersonal wishes and expectations as it is, for example, of food preferences. Eating something with nutritive value is necessary to sustain physical life. Similarly, everyone also has needs that, in the last analysis, involve relationships with other people. Eating certain substances will kill you. Certain kinds of interpersonal relations would drive anyone crazy. But within those limits there is room for a very wide variety of choice based on cultural and individual needs and preferences.

We don't want the waiter, or even the chef, to tell us what to eat or to decide what's best for us; but they do know a great deal more than we do about the food and how it has been prepared and about what most people prefer to eat. For that reason, we should seek out their advice and guidance, but we want the choices to be ours and the judgment to be according to our own palate. We ourselves are the indisputable experts on that score. So it is with respect to "mental health" professionals, who are the presumed experts in interpersonal relations. The professional can provide a kind of "means-ends" analysis. He can tell us something about what the usual effects of our behavior are on others; how they are likely to respond to certain behaviors on our part; whether most people end up more or less content when they behave in certain ways toward people in general or toward certain types of people. He should be able to describe the kind of behavior that is likely to satisfy a given need in a given situation. If a client is uncomfortable about behaving accordingly, but wishes to do so, he can outline what steps the client should take to become comfortable. Ideally speaking, that is what his professional training and experience should have taught him to do for his clients. But it is the client who should choose which goals he will try to achieve—*what kind of a person he will try to become.*

The view espoused here is that the goals of the client and

his professional helper are not based on any inherent rightness or wrongness, but are very much a product of moral values held by the client and the professional, which in turn reflect the society in which they live. Science does not provide an escape from this conclusion. Science can only help us to say that if clients behave in way A, rather than way B, in a given set of circumstances, then X will happen instead of Y. Scientific methods cannot help to determine whether X is more desirable than Y. Scientific methods cannot set the goals, but only help us to establish whether certain behaviors are more likely to realize those goals than others. There is no scientific way to decide what clients' behaviors *should* be like, independent of a specified objective.

It is important that both the professional helper and his client recognize that they are engaged in learning to implement certain values. No behavioral practices can be divorced from the question of the personal and social values that they serve to implement. Helping professionals should face up to the cultural relativity of their position and the need to define clearly their objectives and their strategies for meeting these objectives.

For the sake of fairness and honesty, helping professionals also need to face up· to the task of trying to define the *cost* of meeting these objectives in terms of sacrificing the fulfillment of competing needs. One must sacrifice gustatory satisfaction to be slimmer, just as years of life may be sacrificed by not losing weight. To be more assertive costs something in terms of an increased risk of hostility from others, just as continued submissiveness may carry the cost of pain from tension headaches. Goals (such as how thin a person wants to be, or how assertive) should be decided by the client after he understands the probable positive consequences of achieving a particular goal and the probable costs of reaching them (financial, physical, psychological, emotional, interpersonal, and so on). It is knowledge along these lines that research in therapy and behavior modification should be providing. The search for a universal *set* of criteria of "success" in psychotherapy or behavior modification is as doomed as was the search for a *single* universal criterion. Each therapeutic or educational endeavor should

be assessed in terms of whether it reaches the specified goals balanced against the costs of reaching them. If it is an open and honest type of therapy or behavior modification program, the goals will be known to participating clients, and the costs judged worthwhile, before it is begun. Under these circumstances (barring consequences unforeseen by all concerned) if the goals are reached, the program may be counted a successful one. The assessment of goals, and of costs, always depends on one's moral and social values. Therefore, the general usefulness of any method designed to change the nature of interpersonal relationships ultimately depends on (1) how important and widely held are the values which it seeks to implement and (2) how well, in fact, it does implement them.

## *Moral Values Underlying RE*

Are there apostles of any psychotherapeutic creed amongst us who wish to suggest a universal primary value? No, not while warriors and dictators have so many admirers; not while survival itself can take second place to many other interpersonally based values such as pride, honor, loyalty, and justice. Individual "happiness," "satisfaction," and "pleasure" do not even come close to being universally valued: Many people value the goal of ending social injustices ahead of fulfilling their personal needs. How about the need to end social injustice, then? No, too many of us value our own need for personal satisfaction more than we value the goal of ending social injustice.

However, without claiming universal primacy, we do claim a very wide support base for the values on which the RE programs are based. Indeed, we believe the values on which RE programs are based always have had, and will continue to have, a base of support about as wide as almost any other program would have. In part, this is because the survival of the human race depends on support for the values underlying RE programs; and the value judgment that the human race should survive is, in turn, perhaps the most widely held of all.

The major value judgment underlying the RE programs is that lack of understanding or, worse, misunderstanding, of self

and one's intimates is bad and understanding is good. The fundamental goal of the program is to increase understanding of one's self and one's partner along dimensions directly pertinent to the relationship.

Many would readily agree with the desirability of such goals. There are some, however, who would not consider such a goal to be of primary importance. It must be recognized that this value does not necessarily coincide with other values that are also widely held and may, in certain particular relationships, actually conflict with them. It is possible that in some instances a fuller understanding of this type would lead to drastic changes in a relationship that would meet with the disapproval of many, for example, to a divorce. We think that better understanding of the type described would not actually *cause* a divorce in more than one case in a thousand. But even if it did, by our values the relationship would be considered improved, and the program successful, for that couple. By our definition, then, "enhanced" relationships are those in which the participants have developed a greater capacity, within and by virtue of the relationship, to better understand themselves and each other.

The use of the word *capacity* requires some clarification. It is meant to convey the idea that the increased honesty and understanding do not apply only to the past or present, but have the power to continue in the future. In an enhanced relationship as we define it, not only has a *condition* been changed but a capability has also been achieved for *doing* things differently: habitual processes have been altered.

The term *understand* as used here also requires clarification. It does not necessarily refer to any analytical kind of knowledge but to *the capacity and willingness to appreciate relationship-relevant needs, desires, preferences, aspirations, values, motivations, and emotions of one's own self and one's partners*. We refer here to relationships with a high degree of such understanding as being *empathic relationships*. This kind of understanding is facilitated by the view that whether one likes or hates what one sees in oneself or in others, there is *no reason to blame* anyone for the needs and feelings that they possess—or, perhaps more accurately, that possess them. The

components of interpersonal understanding, then, by our definition, are *honesty* and *compassion*. Both of these qualities are
highly valued by our civilization.

Honesty is a particularly important quality because it is a
necessary condition for the attainment of many other goals of
most people in most societies. For example, the ability to predict what is going to happen around us is one of the strongest of
our needs. Honesty allows us to know what others are going to
do. It is not without good reason that being told a lie infuriates
most people. If we could not rely on being told the truth nearly
all of the time, we would soon go mad. One's own honesty
toward others has tremendous survival value to them, and in the
long run is vitally important to one's own survival. To become
known as dishonest or inaccurate in one's interpersonal relations considerably reduces the chances of securing a friend, a
mate, or a satisfactory job. Without these, there are few other
values that can be implemented successfully.

As is the case with honesty, compassion (by which we
mean sympathy, mercy, tenderness toward another, and the
willingness to try to protect others from distress) is probably
close to being universally valued. Humans are social animals and
need the intelligence that growing up in a human group provides. Because of this need to grow up within a group, compassion assumes great importance and permits the implementation
of many other values. Without the compassion of other group
members, few children would survive; many adults would perish
from illnesses; the old would be discarded. Young adults, antici-
pating their discard, would tend to fend for themselves at the
expense of the welfare of the group, weakening a group in the
presence of enemies and catastrophes. Thus, compassion too is
part of the fabric of human survival, and the survival of the
fittest cultures has tended to foster its growth. Thus, like the
liar, although not nearly to the same degree, the person with
little compassion will also tend to find himself lacking in the
opportunities to implement many other values that hinge on
trust and friendship. A person discovered to be ruthless might
find that a few goals become easier to achieve but that many
others will be frustrated. The more compassionate person will

find greater opportunity to achieve his goals with respect to implementing a broader range of social, and often even material, values.

We are not saying, however, that everyone will profit in all ways from being interpersonally honest and compassionate. For example, a person who values power a great deal might sacrifice the attainment of his goals if he invests himself very much in being understanding toward others. Those who greatly value the ability to control others, perhaps "for their own good"—such as a parent who simply wants to implement his own values in his relationship with his child—would, at least initially, find the goals of RE difficult to accept.

It is time that professional helpers stopped thinking that everyone else holds—or should hold—the same values as they do. If the helper himself wishes to be thoroughly honest, the value judgments underlying a program should be made clear to clients before they embark on it. That is the reason we have taken pains to spell out the fact that honesty and compassion are the major values fostered and implemented by the RE programs. Certain other values, such as egalitarianism, tend also to be implemented to a greater extent when honesty and compassion are strengthened.

We do believe it is as appropriate for a professional helper as it is for anyone else to try to change the values of other people if he disagrees with them. We believe that educational programs openly seeking to influence the moral philosophies or attitudes of others should continue to exist and, in fact, should be multiplied. This should be done openly, not in the guise of helping others solve other problems. Prior to undertaking any psychotherapy, counseling, or educational program, the leaders and the participants should be aware of the underlying value judgments implicit in the approach so that clients may be in a position to make appropriate choices before they embark on it.

### When Is an Empathic Relationship a "Better" Relationship?

The empathic relationship has been defined as one wherein the participants more frequently exercise compassionate understanding of their own and the other's thoughts, needs,

wishes, and feelings. In an empathic relationship, each person can view and express the issues and emotions in their relationship more openly: with relatively little defensiveness, guilt, and blame. Each of them is more in touch with his own values, needs, and feelings regarding the relationship so that he engages in fewer self-deceptions and employs fewer psychological defense mechanisms. Each of them relates to the other his values, needs, and feelings regarding the relationship with greater clarity and directness. Each of them does this in such a manner as to reduce as much as possible the other's psychological pain and the other's tendency to respond to such communication with defensiveness or counterattack.

Is a relationship that is more empathic a "better" relationship? If we take people from a low to a high level of empathy in their relationship, have we "improved" their relationship? As we already have indicated, the answers to such questions ultimately are value judgments. Such questions cannot be answered through reason or science; each person must consider the probable consequences of low and high empathy among people and answer the questions in terms of his own values. Clearly there is immediate and direct value in establishing a more empathic relationship for the many, many people who value truth and compassion, who dislike verbal as well as physical violence, and who dislike deceit and oppression.

We believe that an empathic relationship also promotes and helps to sustain other qualities and feelings that many people value highly. These would include the feeling of being secure in the relationship and being relatively free of anxiety due to the fear of loss of love or fear of the termination of the relationship. We believe that having an empathic relationship with someone also promotes a feeling of general well-being, happiness, and confidence. It seems to raise a person's self-esteem and ego-strength, and to promote confidence in his ability to earn the respect and affection of other people in general. This in turn seems to make it much easier for people either to live with, or to overcome, what they may previously have regarded as serious deficiencies in their personal make-up.

At this point, it is well to recall that the empathic responsiveness that is one of the key components of RE programs was

derived from the attitudinal orientation and interpersonal behavior of Rogerian psychotherapists. One of the few fairly solid findings determined by decades of research in relationship-oriented psychotherapy is that a therapist's ability to show genuine empathic acceptance is a key determinant of his ability to help his client.

Such research probably offers only a minimum estimate of the power of an empathic relationship. We believe that the beneficial effects of empathy coming from a paid professional or paraprofessional is much weaker than the effects of empathy from someone, such as a friend, a parent, or a spouse, with whom one has a more natural, genuine, important, constant, and enduring relationship. Thus, what is often referred to as *personal* or *interpersonal growth* in psychotherapy has the potential for developing even more fully in an empathic relationship with someone who is naturally close and important to the individual—someone who is already in a symbiotic relationship with that individual.

Greater ability to resolve relationship problems seems to us to be another benefit of achieving a more empathic relationship. When an unresolved conflict bedevils a relationship, it is often because not *all* opinions, needs, and feelings pertinent to the conflict have been perceived accurately by one or both parties. In a marital relationship, for example, problems of control, dominance, freedom, or respect may never enter a discussion of who should be spending money and for what purpose; yet these issues may be the most pertinent ones involved in such a conflict. Also, once such problems have reached the chronic problem stage, they have become ensnared in nets of pseudo-opinion and pseudo-needs, and have become heavily encrusted with feelings of defensiveness, frustration, and anger. The result is that honesty, understanding, and problem resolution become still more difficult to achieve. If, instead, the individuals become skilled in creating an interpersonal climate between them that will allow them to face their true thoughts and feelings with relative calm and ease, the stage becomes set for effective problem solving and for maximizing their potential for satisfaction and "growth."

Given the above considerations, another consequence of establishing a more empathic relationship is that the relationship will probably be a more enduring one—and enduring relationships are still highly valued by many people. We would hypothesize, for example, that parents and children who had a more empathic relationship would tend to remain in more frequent contact over more years; and that marriages or other cohabiting relationships characterized by greater empathy would remain intact longer.

We do not say that an empathic relationship is always sufficient in and of itself to resolve any problem. We believe that it is highly useful to continue to develop other educational programs that deal with specific areas (for example, Masters' and Johnson's program in the area of sex). However, we do believe that an RE program of sufficient duration usually will be as efficient, or more so, than any other type of therapy in resolving relationship difficulties of almost any variety because it teaches a process that can be applied to any type of content. Where it proves insufficient, we believe that it can at least facilitate problem resolution by clarifying the nature of the problem, enhancing mutual respect, and increasing the motivation necessary to undertake additional steps toward resolving the difficulty. The research reported in this book takes a first step toward testing these views.

There are, however, certain consequences of establishing more empathic relationships that may conflict with certain values. We believe that a more empathic relationship is likely to lead to a more egalitarian relationship. When a relationship is more empathic, conflict resolution is more likely to be based on negotiation and compromise than on the wielding of power. Some parents, for example, those whose religious beliefs are more in accord with a paternalistic family philosophy, would find this basis to be in conflict with other important values. Similarly, in a society that strongly reinforces male dominance in the marital relationship, establishing a more empathic relationship might solve certain kinds of problems, but also create others via retaliation because of the violation of cultural norms —such as loss of social position and, as a result, even reduction of employment opportunities, income, and so on.

Complete spontaneity is a value held by increasing numbers of people that conflicts with the values fostered by a more empathic relationship. Although in most cases the skills taught by RE programs promote spontaneity far, far beyond what existed before, an empathic relationship presupposes some concern about how and when one expresses one's feelings. Instant, direct expression of one's feelings, uninhibited by forethought about the impact of such expression on the other's emotions and psyche, becomes difficult when empathy is strong. RE programs foster the attitude that when spontaneity is tempered by empathic relationships and social adjustments, the individual's own life satisfactions are enhanced.

In considering the costs of an educational or therapeutic program, including RE programs, one must also bear in mind that attentiveness to one's own and others' needs and feelings, like any other activity, consumes time. To the extent that one spends time engaged in this kind of activity, there is less time for other activities. We believe that in most instances the positive advantages of empathic communication will result in a net increase of time available for recreation and work because of the reduction of angry disputes, sulking, psychosomatic illness, and so forth. Situations are very rare where people are so concerned about how they and those around them feel, or how they perceive each other, that work or play goes begging. But we have seen that sort of thing happen at professional "workshops": participants getting so involved in their own feelings and interpersonal relationships that the educational purpose of the group is forgotten. Thus, it is not inconceivable that nonprofessionals, too, might find that they had ignored or sacrificed other values because of preoccupation with discussing their feelings and the status of their relationship.

Sometimes it may be better to forget about needs and feelings in the interest of either having fun or of getting a job done. In relationships that are *strictly* for fun or *strictly* for work, care might need to be exercised about how *much* time should be devoted to empathic communication.

Finally, it should be pointed out that there are some types of relationships that are best served not by maximizing

the empathic quality of the relationship but by minimizing it. We refer to relationships that by their very nature are adversary relationships: where one party's gain is the other party's loss. Examples would be: district attorney against public defender; tackle against guard; prize fight contenders; litigants; and business competitors. Even in these sorts of relationships, a greater degree of empathy might help in special circumstances or issues. Generally, however, more empathy within these relationships would interfere with the roles society has assigned them and they have accepted. Perhaps there are very good reasons, from the point of view of the general social good, for having such adversary relationships and perhaps not. At any rate, as long as the participants accept such roles as valid, promoting empathy within such relationships seems ill advised.

## The Educational Model

In Relationship Enhancement programs, as in any non-medical psychotherapeutic program, we are dealing with the implementation of values, not with illness. We are not so much doing something to people that changes them as giving them a skill that they may use or not use as they see fit to *change themselves*. These viewpoints cast RE in an educational rather than a medical mold.

*Providing skills to be used adaptively.* The purpose of RE programs is to give the participants skills that will allow them to be empathic when they want to be and to encourage them to try to use these skills at a variety of times and in a variety of situations. The extent to which the participants actually do exercise these skills after the program is completed will depend on the balance of satisfaction derived from these skills as opposed to satisfaction derived from alternative activities and alternate ways of relating to others.

The purpose of an RE program is to *add* a set of skills to the participants' behavioral repertoires that we believe they will come to value highly and use frequently, but that they are also perfectly free to use as seldom as they wish. Our purpose is not to make relationships more rigid but to add a new degree of

flexibility. Couples who vary in such dimensions as work orientation and spontaneity may adjust the frequencies and occasions of their use of empathic understanding according to its
importance in relation to other activities and values. A proper
fit may be established partly through deliberation and partly
through trial and error, and no doubt the use of the skills will
vary greatly from week to week and year to year depending on
a host of circumstances.

    *Not "what's wrong?" but "what's right!"* As we view it,
most difficulties and inabilities to achieve relationship goals that
are chronic and essentially interpersonal in nature stem from:
(1) lack of appropriate knowledge, training, and prior experience; (2) prior experiences that have led to unrealistic expectations; and/or (3) behaviors that produce unintended effects on
others.

    Viewing matters in this light, essentially as matters for
educational effort, it seems far less important for the helper to
discover what is wrong in a relationship, or why it went wrong,
than to provide clients with appropriate knowledge, training,
and experience aimed at the future—that is, aimed at overcoming the difficulties or accomplishing the relationship goals in
question. Usually, once one knows what the clients wish to
accomplish, not much time needs to be spent in finding out
what makes them behave the way they do (diagnosis) and still
less in finding out how they got the way they are (genesis).
Rather, it is assumed that by far the most expeditious approach
is immediately to begin: (1) teaching them what it is they need
to know (providing the rationale); (2) establishing the appropriate life experience they need to elicit such behavior (providing practice); (3) helping them perfect their skills (providing
supervision); and (4) increasing the use of skills in appropriate
everyday life situations (fostering generalization).

    If the pair does *not know what they want*, beyond ac-
cepting the general values of the program, then the first step
should be something more akin to educational guidance than to
diagnosis as it has been employed in the mental health field.
Alternatively, having the couple use goal-clarification skills,
such as those taught in RE programs, to *find out* what relation-

ship goals they truly wish to achieve may simply be the first thing to be accomplished.

In any case, although remediation may be the expected outcome, the orientation of the professional employing the educational model is not toward finding out more about *deficiencies* or poor habits and *remedying* them; rather, it is toward *setting goals* and *reaching* them. There may be a thousand reasons why a person has never learned to ski or to speak a foreign language. But with relatively minor variations (for those who may have had traumatic experiences in previous attempts), there is no need to approach the aspirant as if he were unique. Any good method of instruction follows essentially the same procedures with all who wish to learn—partly because any good method of instruction allows for a fairly broad range of individual differences in learning aptitude, prior conditioning, and so forth. Variations in assigned exercises, auxiliary courses in certain cases, and adjusting task assignments to learning speed can take care of nearly all individual differences. In the rare cases where these variations do not work, the educational model provides for individual tutoring. We look at the teaching of relationship skills in the same way.

*Programatic instructions to serve the widest range of needs.* An educational model encourages one to think in terms of designing programs that help large numbers of individuals to resolve their interpersonal difficulties and/or reach their interpersonal aspirations. Once an area of widespread interest (communication, sex, financial management, child rearing, or whatever) is identified, a particular educational program can be drawn up to teach the appropriate principles and skills in a systematic way. In conducting such a course, the professional does not view or present himself as treating illness nor present his programs to the public as "cures" even though they may be intended to be more "therapeutic" than traditional forms of therapy. Also, because the program (or a graded series of programs) is likely to meet the needs of a very wide range of individuals, the professional can and should open his course to the general public as well as to people referred for "treatment."

Of course, different programs may be offered for differ-

ent types of groups. Courses might differ according to age, for example. Also, in some instances it may be advisable to offer different courses (or different course sequences) for people who regard themselves as having serious problems as contrasted with people who wish to enhance an already satisfactory relationship or life-style.

It is our view that the educational methods exemplified by the RE programs would be far more beneficial in the majority of cases than traditional individual or group psychotherapy. However, we do not in any sense see such programs as being *incompatible*, concurrently or sequentially, with psychotherapy or other forms of psychiatric treatment. The instructor of a program designed to enhance personal and interpersonal skills should freely recommend courses other than his own and should likewise recommend psychotherapy or psychiatric help whenever he deems that to be appropriate.

*Economy in professional manpower and cost.* For the RE programs, and for most other interpersonal skill programs that we can envisage, class enrollment would be small relative to most mass education courses (at present we work in groups of 6 to 8). However, the development of appropriate instructional materials and the training of assistant teachers might permit much larger groups. Thus, a further advantage of the programatic approach is that it offers promise of conserving professional manpower, allowing the most highly trained professionals to function as program developers and as supervisors of those who have less extensive training. Of course, if we are correct in our observations that such courses offer faster and more efficient improvement in interpersonal functioning and psychological "adjustment" than does traditional individual or group psychotherapy, then low cost may be considered a significant advantage of the educational approach even without the benefits of programatic materials and assistant teachers.

*Reaching more people.* An additional advantage afforded by the educational model is that it seems to eliminate, or at least sharply reduce, the reluctance of people to take advantage of the resources offered. A class or program designed to teach

specific skills does not carry the stigma that has been associated with "mental illness." Participants are not asked to admit that there is something "wrong" with them; they come rather because they want to learn. Because these programs are designed to appeal to a wide audience, many people might avail themselves of this type of help who otherwise would not receive any.

*Reducing the obstacle of defensiveness.* One of the fundamental facts of psychological life that must be kept in the forefront of the professional's mind is the ever-present threat that psychological defense mechanisms present to effective learning. It has been our observation that the educational model, in comparison with traditional psychotherapeutic and counseling approaches, reduces psychological defensiveness to minimal levels. The lack of threat and defensiveness seems to be caused in large part by the task orientation of the group and the lack of attempt to trace the genesis of problems, to analyze behavior, or to uncover deficiencies. Also, defensiveness seems to be reduced because of the ever-present evidence in RE programs that the professional shows great respect for the client and confidence in his capacity to master the requisite skills for good interpersonal functioning. Finally, the fact that the leader minimizes criticism and maximizes social reinforcement in the teaching process serves to reduce defensiveness and quickly builds rapport, trust, and confidence.

*Preventative functions.* In the case of traditional methods of providing help, the participants are dependent on the skill of the professional to solve their problems. Since the clients with his help have merely solved one set of relationship problems rather than acquired problem-solving *skills*, they are likely to be dependent on a professional to help them resolve any future problems that develop. They have not necessarily learned much that will help them to prevent conflicts and problems from arising again or how to resolve the problems themselves if they do arise again. One of the most significant advantages of an educational approach is that it imparts a skill to the participants that they can continue to use for a lifetime. Thus, a skill-training program of the sort exemplified by an RE program may be con-

sidered simultaneously a remedial program and a program of primary, secondary, or tertiary prevention. For individuals who have problems, such a program has a remedial, secondary, or tertiary prevention function, and for those who do not have any problems, it has the function of primary prevention.

# Chapter 2

# Basic Skills of Relationship Enhancement Programs

**∾∾∾∾∾∾∾∾∾∾∾∾∾∾∾∾∾∾∾∾∾∾∾∾∾**

The goal of RE programs is to teach attitudes and skills that will enable the participants to relate to significant others in ways that will maximize satisfaction of emotional and functional needs. To do this, we explain the rationale for using the skills to begin the process of attitude change, then demonstrate the skills, and then coach the participants as they practice the skills. There are four basic sets of skills or behaviors. Two of these are specific types of communication. The third is the ability to use the first two effectively in an interpersonal dialog. The fourth is the ability to help others learn the other skills and use them appropriately and effectively.

The term *mode* is generally used to denote the basic sets of communication skills. It is used in preference to *role* because *mode* connotes only a set of behaviors instead of being associated, as *role* often is, with artificiality, acting, and insincerity.

One set of behavioral skills is called the *expressive* mode. This mode of communication is designed to enable the individual to express his emotions, thoughts, and desires clearly and honestly without generating unnecessary hostility and defensiveness in the recipient of the communication. When using this set of skills, the speaker is referred to as the *expresser*.

The second basic set of skills is called the *empathic* mode. When using this set of skills, the speaker is referred to as the *empathic responder*. This mode of communicating is designed to convey acceptance of another's communication and the ability to identify with another's perceptions, thoughts, and feelings. This response is the classic therapeutic response of client-centered therapists (Rogers, 1951). It is not essentially different from what is sometimes called *reflective listening*. In our view, however, the term *empathic responding* connotes the depth, the intensity, and the giving, illuminating, enhancing qualities of a Rogerian psychotherapeutic response better than the phrase *reflective listening*.

A key element of the third set of skills is to know when and how to move from one of these basic modes to the other in order to enhance mutual understanding, satisfaction, problem solving, and conflict resolution. Hence this third set of skills is termed *mode switching*.

The fourth basic set of skills is termed the *facilitator* mode. The purpose of teaching this mode is to enable participants to help others to master RE skills and to use them effectively in their key interpersonal relationships.

In the remainder of the chapter we will describe these sets of behavioral skills. We will explain them in the manner that they are explained to participants in an RE program during the intake interview and in the early sessions. Hopefully, this means of presentation will be helpful to potential groups leaders in conducting intake and early group sessions as well as elucidating the nature of the skills themselves.

## The Empathic Responder Mode

This mode might be explained to clients as follows.

Eliminating fear and creating an atmosphere of respectful acceptance is the function of the empathic responder. Even when you totally disagree, it is still possible to show respect, appreciation, and understanding of another person. In effect, the empathic responder says to the expresser: "I will respect and value you as a person, regardless of what your feelings and wishes may be, and whether I disagree with them or not. I appreciate the opportunity

to assist you in your efforts to understand your wishes and feelings because I want you to communicate them to me more and more openly, honestly, directly, and specifically. Such communication affords me the opportunity to understand you better and work more realistically toward enhancing our relationship." The more you can convey such an attitude to your partner, the more your partner will be able to do likewise in response to *your* communication of your own needs and feelings.

In the empathic responder mode, the *attitude* that you adopt is the most important thing. You must strive to put yourself in a receptive frame of mind. Your attitude must be: "Nobody can *help* seeing things the way they see them, and nobody can *help* feeling the way they feel." You must say to yourself:

"If my partner's perceptions are wrong, or if I think that these faulty perceptions have given rise to feelings that need not be there, or that should be different than they are, I will soon have my turn to say so. I can very shortly be the expresser and express *my* perceptions and the feelings I *wish* that my partner would be able to experience if only my partner perceived the situation as I do. But while my partner is expressing his own outlook, I can best help my partner, myself, and our relationship by completely understanding how my partner *does* perceive the situation and how he *does* feel. It is on this basis that we can best proceed to enhance our relationship in an enduring way. I can do this best by temporarily setting aside my own perceptions, and my own reactions, and my own feelings. If I do have strong feelings, I will not have to put them aside for more than a moment. In a moment I can take the role of expresser myself.

"I must strive to put myself in my partner's shoes and to try with all the energy and heart I can muster to see the world through my partner's eyes at this moment in time. I must try to understand exactly how my partner is perceiving the situation and exactly what my partner's feelings are about the situation.

"Because I can never be sure that I have fully grasped another's views or feelings, I must check out my understanding with my partner. Moreover, my feedback to my partner must do much more than establish the *accuracy* of my understanding. In the tone and in the manner of my feedback, I must also try to convey my sincere interest in my partner's viewpoint. I must try by the tone and manner of my statement to convey that I accept unconditionally my partner's right to express honestly his or her own unique feelings and view of the world."

The word *empathy* epitomizes what you are trying to do. By *empathy* we mean *putting yourself inside the skin of another person and being able to share the world that he sees and feels.* The highest level of empathic understanding is reached when you have put together *what* has been said and the *manner* in which it has been said in a way that goes beyond the words used. You can then articulate your partner's views and feelings in a way that expresses

them even more accurately and fully than he has been able to do himself. You must then communicate this deep level of under-standing to your partner in a warm and accepting manner. We *don't* mean that you will have detected something that will come as a *surprise* to your partner, but rather that you've focused his feelings in a clearer way than he has been able to do as he struggled to understand and express them himself.

When you are responding only with empathy, as we wish you to do, there are many things that you will not be doing:

1. You cannot be asking your partner *questions*. For example, you cannot be asking: "What makes you think that? How do you feel about that? How long have you felt this way? Do you always feel this way? and What do I do to make you feel that way?" Questions have the effect of diverting your partner's attention from his or her own stream of communication by seeking information that your partner has not freely chosen to give. To ask such questions would violate the expresser's right to maintain complete direction over the flow of the communication, to explore what he wants to ex-plore, and to say what he thinks needs to be said in the way, and in the order, he prefers. Often your attempt to clarify your partner's views and feelings should be stated in a questioning tone of voice. It *is* appropriate to be *tentative* in your empathic reflections of your partner's views; but *not* appropriate, as the empathic re-sponder, to seek *new information*. If you feel the need for such information in order to later express your *own* needs and views, then when *you* become the expresser you should tell your partner the information you wish to have.

2. You cannot present your own *opinion, perception,* and *view-point* about what your partner is saying. We will make it easy for you to switch from being a responder to being an expresser when-ever you have a strong urge to present your own viewpoint or feel-ings, but while you are the responder you do not express your own feelings.

3. You must not *interpret* things for the speaker. That is, you must not add your own reasoning as to causality, make connec-tions between different events, or between events and feelings, in a way that presents things in a different perspective from that in which your partner seems to be viewing the situation.

4. You must not make *suggestions* about how your partner might alter the situation in a favorable way or solve a problem.

5. Above all, you must avoid making *judgments* about what your partner has said. Your own evaluation of the validity of your part-ner's viewpoint, or the correctness, effectiveness, or morality of your partner's statements must not enter into your empathic state-ments.

When your partner takes the risk of an honest expression of needs and feelings and meets with your acceptance, there is an

increase in his expectation that he can *afford* to be open and honest with you about his needs and feelings. Each time you provide accepting understanding, you will have increased the probability that your partner will communicate more openly, directly, and honestly with you in future communications. Conversely, each time you fail to be empathic, and instead say something that denies the importance or relevance of any of the speaker's communications, you raise your partner's expectation of future rejections and diminish the probability that your partner will communicate with you in an open and constructive manner. Even a rejecting tone or manner will have this undesirable effect. It is the accumulated weight of thousands of such exchanges—some, of course, having much more impact than others—that will determine whether communication proceeds to become better and better, remains stagnant, or deteriorates.

It is almost impossible to train a person to speak openly, honestly, and constructively of his innermost interpersonal wishes, needs, and feelings, unless he has acquired faith that such expressions will meet with acceptance rather than with coolness or rejection. Until he has a measure of such faith, he will hardly be aware *himself* of what these needs and wishes are, in the midst of a dialog, let alone be capable of communicating them. Therefore, in the early phases of your training we will put more emphasis on helping each of you to acquire good empathic responding skills and later on we will put more emphasis on helping you acquire good expressive skills. However, both skills will be taught from the start of the program.

## The Expresser Mode

The following explanation of the expresser mode to clients would be spread out over the intake and a number of later sessions rather than presented all at once in such detail. Also, in the following presentation, four examples are used throughout so as to provide the variety needed for various kinds of participants. Generally just two examples—chosen to appeal to the different perspectives of the participants—would suffice as an introduction to the skills. Except for detail and length, however, the explanation would be as follows.

Let me outline the things that you are to try to do as an expresser. The expresser mode gives you your chance to let your perceptions, ideas and feelings be known to your partner.

In the expresser mode, we want you first of all to be the world's leading authority on everything you say. We want what

you say to be virtually argument-proof. When you talk about important issues in a way that doesn't tie you and your partner up into argumentative knots, you'll be able to achieve a more satisfying relationship much more quickly. Now, how do you make incontrovertible statements? You can always be the world's leading authority on a subject, so supreme in your knowledge that anyone would be a fool to argue with you, by stating things strictly in terms of your own perceptions of events, your own feelings about those events, and your own value judgments about events. Never attempt to state or claim the *objective* nature of a situation. Never attempt to state what the other person's character or motivations really are or what is really good and what is really bad. Never state what most people would or would not do, or should or should not do.

Be aware that in issues between intimates the things that really count are the perceptions, value judgments, and feelings of you and your partner: subjective things. If the objective reality of the situation is important, it can enter into the picture first by a comparison of the admittedly subjective statements of both parties. It is conceivable that later you might decide to go to some outside authority or check your perceptions with an objective, knowledgeable outsider if your perceptions disagree. But, when good communication is used, that almost never becomes necessary. What you each need to grasp first is your own and your partner's perceptions, feelings, and value judgments. This sharing of views should be done openly, honestly, and with a maximum of respect for the right of the other person to have perceptions and values that differ from your own. The discussion should be in a subjective mode—the way least open to argument and least likely to generate defensiveness. When that is done, it is usually quite sufficient to resolve issues and to move the relationship to a more satisfying level for both parties.

Therefore, the *first* rule is to state things in a way that acknowledges the subjectivity of your perceptions and judgments. Not, "Our son Johnny feels neglected by you," but, "*I believe* that Johnny feels neglected by you." Not, "The house is disorganized," but, "By my standards, the house is disorganized." Not, "We don't have an active enough social life," but, "Our social life isn't active enough for me." Not, to your teenager, "You don't work hard enough at your schoolwork," but, "I believe you're not working as hard as you should at your schoolwork."

These may seem like small differences in phrasing. In a way, I agree they are. None of the second, the preferred, ways of saying things I just mentioned are nearly as good as they should be, and I'll be going on to say how else they can be improved in a few minutes. But often this shift from the objective way of stating things to the subjective way is the best you can manage at your first entry into a given topic.

Making just that shift alone, however, does at least increase

the probability of a change in the focus of attention of your partner. If you phrase things subjectively, the other person is more likely, for instance, to wonder *why* you believe as you do, or to wonder what *your* standards are. If you had stated things as simple fact, often your partner would instead almost be forced to argue about the facts and not deal at all with your perceptions, reasons, or standards. Stating things in subjective terms makes the other person feel a shade less challenged, a shade less threatened too, because he is somewhat more free to look at this communication as an idiosyncrasy or interesting phenomenon stemming from *your* uniqueness and not *necessarily* representing a truth about him, or about his role in the issue under discussion. If, for example, your partner is very secure in his own evaluation that he does pay enough attention to Johnny or that he does work hard on his schoolwork, then he may become curious about your perceptions rather than feel compelled to correct your perception of reality to make it conform to his own. That is the first shift you can make in the way you think, and the way you should communicate. As with all the other shifts I'll be mentioning, it will have the effect of making it somewhat easier for your partner to respond to you empathically rather than argumentatively or defensively.

The *second* guideline for the expresser mode takes the issue to a deeper level, makes an argumentative response much less likely and makes it much easier for your partner to be empathic with you. The idea here is to associate the issue with the specific *feelings* you have about it. If you are discussing an issue that is really important to the relationship, then almost by definition you do have feelings about it, and probably strong feelings. So, it is important, as an expresser, to try to bring your feelings about the issue into your own awareness, and then to communicate them to your partner.

Improved versions of some of the earlier statements then would be: "I'm distressed and I'm angry with you because I believe that Johnny feels neglected by you"; and, "I'm upset, and I'm annoyed at you because by my standards the house is disorganized"; and, "I feel bored and I feel lonely because our social life isn't active enough for me"; and "I'm worried because I believe you're not working as hard as you should at your schoolwork."

This represents a much bigger shift both in your way of viewing the issue and in the way your partner is likely to view it and respond to it. The issue has been broadened to include your feelings. The equation of the problem now includes more of the elements that make it an important issue. The partner now needs to contend with your feelings, and not simply your perceptions of him or of a situation. Also, an awareness of how something makes you feel may entirely change the feelings your statement generates in him. Often the feelings generated will include some concern and sympathy. Although your partner might still be defensive and angry, it's very unlikely that he will be more so than he would have

been if your feelings remained unstated. Also, by making your feelings a prominent part of the problem equation, you become an even more credible authority on the validity of the problem as you have been experiencing it.

The *third* guideline brings in an element that is perhaps the most difficult one for you to bring to your own awareness in relation to problem issues. Even when you are aware of it, it is often the element most difficult to state out loud. It is the positive aspect of the situation, of the attitude, or of the feeling toward the person that lies on the other side of the problem coin.

Somerset Maugham and others have talked of the razor's edge separating hate on one side from love on the other. A pop song says, "You always hurt the one you love." Generally speaking, the pain and anger you feel when you are let down by someone is in proportion to the potential they have in your eyes for giving you something positive. If you expect nothing, you're not disappointed or hurt or angry when you don't get it. Certainly, that's the way it is with people who are coming here to take a program like this. They are close enough to one another to want to improve their relationship. That means that if you dig down beneath the surface level, you are almost certainly going to find the positive feature in the issue that makes the negative aspect of it hurt the way it does.

The positive side of the issue with Johnny would be something like this if it was searched for and then expressed: "Johnny likes you, he looks up to you, and I think it's very good for him when you pay attention to him. I'm distressed and angry with you because instead of seeing that happen, I believe Johnny feels neglected by you." The positive side of the disorganized house issue might be stated in the following way, "I believe that you share my desire to have a house that is organized, and also that you're interested in meeting my needs for having things organized. I also believe that generally you're capable of keeping things organized around the house. But, by my standards, the house is disorganized, and I'm upset and annoyed about it." Including the positive side of the issue about the inactive social life might lead to something along these lines: "I feel bored and I feel lonely because our social life isn't active enough for me. When we go out together with other people, it brings something out in the way that we interact with them and with each other that is very good for me, and I've been missing it lately." In the schoolwork issue, the positive side of the issue might lead to a statement such as: "One of the things that's most important to me in the whole world, is to see you grow up to be a happy adult, someone in a position to enjoy life. My experience tells me that you're not likely to succeed in life unless you are well educated. Having you succeed in school is very important to me because I believe you're not going to succeed in life if you don't succeed in school. So, it worries me that you're not working as hard as I believe you should to succeed at your schoolwork."

Making your partner aware of the positive feelings, judgments, and thoughts about him that underlie your concern or anger helps to reduce the defensiveness and hostility that your partner is likely to feel about the negative side of the issue. If your partner can see more in your statement than an attack on him or his ways, it makes it easier for your partner to listen to your concerns. We're not talking about a soft-soap job, however. If it's not a real part of the picture, we don't want any part of it, and neither should your partner. We only want you to include a positive statement if it's valid and true. If it is, it will not only make it easier for your partner to listen, but it will also help in resolving the issue, because it is a more complete and accurate statement of the true issue. You may not be able to think about positive feelings when you first raise an issue, or even if you can, you may not want to speak about your positive feelings because they are so out of tune with your predominant feelings at that moment. If so, then we won't demand it of you. But just remember that positive perceptions and feelings are very likely a part of the picture, and the sooner you can bring them into your own awareness and your partner's, the sooner the issue is likely to be resolved to your satisfaction and your partner's.

The *fourth* guideline to remember in composing a good expresser statement is to make it just as specific as you can. Specificity has a number of facets in this context. The first one to remember is to try to describe situations in *behavioral* terms: "I like it when you smile at me and put your arm around me," rather than "I like it when you are cheerful and affectionate toward me." The second is to be specific about time or occasion and place: "I like it when you come into the kitchen in the morning before breakfast, and smile and put your arm around me." Time and place are the most frequently useful specifics. In certain other situations, specifying other dimensions of an issue—such as frequency—can become extremely important.

Let's add this dimension now to the examples we started out with. I'll add emphasis to the portions that provide specificity. The first one would become something like, *"Early this evening when you came home from work, Johnny rushed over to you to show you his drawings,* and it seemed to me you hardly paid any attention to him and that you made it pretty clear *by not responding to the drawings and by telling him that you were tired and wanted to read the newspaper,* that you didn't want to interact with him. It made me think that you've been doing that kind of thing very frequently lately—I *don't think you've given him as much as ten minutes of your undivided attention in this past week.* Johnny likes you, he looks up to you, and I think it's very good for him when you pay attention to him. I'm distressed and angry with you because instead of seeing that happen, I believe Johnny feels neglected by you. *He looked so downcast tonight after that interchange, and I've noticed that look after he tried to get your attention several times in the past week."*

The second example might be stated as follows: "I believe that you share my desire to have a house that is organized, and that you're interested in meeting my needs for having things organized. I also believe that generally you are capable of keeping things organized around the house. *For the last few days when I come home from work, I find toys scattered around the living room and papers and toys scattered around the kitchen.* By my standards that means the house is disorganized, and I'm upset and annoyed about it."

The third example might become: "*We haven't seen any of our friends socially, or for that matter, done anything but watch TV for the last three weeks.* When we go out together with other people, it brings something out in the way that we interact with them and with each other—*the joking, and the things you and I talk about when the evening is over*—that is very good for me, and I've been missing it lately."

With respect to the schoolwork issue, the statement might become: "One of the things that's most important to me in the whole world, is to see you grow up to be a happy adult, someone in a position to enjoy life. *I know from my experience and from observing others, that a big part of having a happy life is to be able to have a job that you feel is useful, that you enjoy, and that pays you well enough so that you and your future family don't have to worry about living in the kind of place you want, and being able to eat and dress the way you want.* My experience tells me that you're not likely to find that kind of life unless you are well educated. Having you succeed in school is very important to me, because I believe you're not going to have the kind of life I'd like you to have if you don't succeed in school. *In the past week I haven't seen you study but once, and that was only for about 15 minutes. You received two C's and a D on your last grade card.* So, it worries me that you're not working as hard as I believe you should to succeed in your schoolwork at a level that will enable you to get into college."

What does being specific do for you? First of all, it helps you avoid one of the worst kinds of errors you can make in communication with someone who might not look at things in the same way you do: *overgeneralizing.* When you overgeneralize you make it extremely difficult for your partner to be empathic with you and extremely difficult for him not to get angry and to argue with you. When you overgeneralize, you destroy your credibility at a time when what you want most is to be believed. By stating observable, concrete behaviors that give rise to your conclusions or your feelings, by pinpointing time, place, and circumstances you will naturally tend to avoid overgeneralization. If you say, "This morning you did such and such," or, "Two times in the last week you failed to do such and such," you are going to be much more likely to avoid thinking and saying the phrases, "you always," and "you never." Those overgeneralizations have probably been a

greater cause of marital disharmony than all the four-letter words put together. Picture a shotgun in your mind now, and picture a white paper label with red letters pasted on the left barrel saying, "you always" and a similar label pasted on the right barrel saying, "you never." Remember that gun, and don't fire it unless you're ready and willing to see blood, including your own. And there are generalizations that are even worse: generalizations about the other person's motives or about his character. Examples are: "You don't really care about Johnny," or "about me," or "you're lazy," or "you're inconsiderate." Such overgeneralizations are out of the shotgun class—they are pure TNT.

Helping you to avoid those mistakes is only part of the advantage that specificity gives you. It not only helps you avoid a mistake, it actually helps build your credibility in a positive sense. It presents the evidence in a much more precise and accurate way, enabling the other person to see how you arrived at the position you are taking. As a result, your partner is likely to give your views more serious thought. First of all, it increases your partner's attention to what you are saying because, in a sense, he's being invited to compare your observations with his own. Secondly, it gives you a common base from which to start your dialog. It makes your partner less likely to issue blanket denials, and blanket counter-accusations, and it helps both of you to keep the true issue in mind.

The *fifth* prescription for being a good expresser is to become aware of the interpersonal message that you wish to convey— the behavior you wish the other person would display—and make that explicit. The same guidelines that we spelled out earlier for the message in general, apply also to this subcomponent of your communication. That is, it should be subjectively stated, linked to the feelings that such behavior would arouse in you, and be as specific as is feasible with respect to behavior, time, place, circumstance, frequency, and so on.

Generally, the interpersonal message would come at the end of your expressive statement. However, this part of the statement is the most important. In many cases, the best kind of communication would leave out all the rest, which is essentially negative, and concentrate exclusively on this part of the message, which is essentially constructive and positive.

The same four issues will serve again to clarify this guideline. However, I won't repeat the other components of the message, I'll just present the interpersonal message itself.

"I'm convinced that just five or ten minutes of your undivided attention when you come home would make a world of difference to Johnny; that it would put him in a much better mood for the rest of the evening, make him feel more important and more loved. I believe he'd admire you and look up to you and want to be like you even more than he does now. And I would like that very, very much. I'd like you to be a model for him. I'd like him to

grow up like you. And seeing him get that from you, would make me admire you more as a father and feel even more loving to you than I already do."

The interpersonal message component of the issue concerning the state of the house might be something like this: "I would feel ever so much better, so much more delighted to be home, so much more relaxed and affectionate, if when I came home I found the house organized without things scattered on the floor. I guess I look forward to the contrast between the hectic and disorganized kind of existence I'm forced to lead at work and what I'd like to find when I get home. I'm sure I'd feel more relaxed and comfortable, and my mood and attitude toward you and my desire to interact pleasantly would be much increased if you could manage to see that the toys were picked up before I came through the door, instead of some other time. You see that it gets done somewhere along the line, and this seems to be an instance where the timing would make a great difference. I don't care that much about weekends, somehow, but on workdays, it just seems to have a big effect on my mood."

An interpersonal message dealing with the social activity issue might be: "It would give me a really great boost, make me feel much happier about life, about myself, and about us, if you would go along with the idea of inviting Bill and Mary to go out to the movies and come over here, or maybe go to their home, for a drink Friday or Saturday night. That would please me a great deal, especially if I felt we could establish a pattern of doing that kind of thing at least a couple of times a month."

An interpersonal message to the teenager with respect to his schoolwork might be: "I'd like to see you working regularly on your schoolwork, an hour or two a day several days a week, at least until you got a report card without any grades of C or worse on it. You've worked at home regularly in the past and got good grades, and I'm confident you could still do it. If you did, I'd feel so much better. It would make me feel more confident and more relaxed about your future—about your being able to get a college education, which I believe would make your adult life so much happier. It would really give me a very big boost."

What does the interpersonal message do for you? First of all, it goes beyond merely focusing on the specific issues in a negative way. It suggests the specific solutions that would resolve the problem as far as you are concerned. It's a good starting point for the process of problem solving and relationship enhancement. Specifying the positive result that the desired behaviors would have for you (and therefore for the relationship as far as you are concerned) is somewhat analogous to the carrot that might invite your partner to change, whereas citing your negative feelings is more analogous to the stick that might drive him to change. There is abundant evidence from studies of behavior change that providing incentives to change is much more productive, reliable, and dur-

able, and much less troublesome and dangerous than using negative means.

If that is true, and if, as we said, it might be best in many instances to eliminate everything but the interpersonal message, then why do we spend so much time and effort in teaching you to deal with the more negative feelings as well? The answer lies in practical and emotional realities. I'm not sure just why, but it seems clear that our culture has taught just about all of us not to ask others for things on the basis that it would make us feel good or happy. It has taught many of us not even to tell *ourselves* that we are asking for something in order to make ourselves happy or more content, but rather that we are asking for something only because it is fair, or just or right. Yet in relationships such as we are dealing with here, where there may be conflict and where there is important depth to the relationship, progress is *less* likely to be made in most cases if the issue is approached on the basis of what is right or what is fair. Success is more likely to be obtained if the issue is approached on the basis of how we feel about various kinds of behaviors, and particularly how positively we would feel if we saw the kinds of behaviors we desire.

A second reason that people tend to avoid stating issues in terms of their own wants, wishes, and feelings is that to have such a bid rejected is psychologically more devastating than to have a plea for justice, fairness, common sense, the welfare of the neighborhood, or whatever, rejected. The psychological risk you take is much greater. When you say, in effect, "I want you to do this because it would make me feel better or good," and you find that your wish is not granted, the rejection is experienced as a rejection of yourself. You tend to interpret it to mean that the other person doesn't think highly of you and to think you have overestimated your importance to the other person. If, on the other hand someone rejects a plea that you've based on some supposedly objective or moral issue, you don't have to wonder so much about your own worth. Instead, the rejection only means that the *other* person is unfair, a nincompoop, socially inconsiderate, or whatever. Thus *your* armor remains intact. The battle is fought in such a way that you can't lose as much *self*-respect. If you get what you want, you've won. If you don't, it's just as you thought—the other person is inadequate in some way.

But, first of all, as we view it, you don't really win nearly as many of the things you want that way. Secondly, one of the things you really want most is precisely the feeling that you *are* important to the other person. If you avoid facing issues on personal terms, you may get into battle after battle because you never get one of the things you are looking for: evidence that the other person cares about pleasing you. Desires fulfilled because of principle, fairness, efficiency, and so on can be rather hollow compared to those satisfied because somebody really cares about *you*. But most of all, the reason for facing up to the risk is that the true issue (to the extent

that you and your partner, rather than scientists or philosophers can resolve it) *must* be in terms of your own values, needs, and feelings. Those are the only realities you can be reasonably certain of and ultimately the ones that count for you.

Another factor, also related to the culturally induced discomfort we feel about asking for something simply because it would make us feel better or good, is that we seldom *think* about troublesome issues in those terms. Thus, many of the things you will want to discuss as serious issues with your partner will first enter your mind via an unpleasant feeling—dissatisfaction, frustration, depression, and so on. If you can get beyond those and immediately onto a positive track, excellent. That would be just great. But we're trying to be realistic in this program, and we realize that you may not always be able to do that. From both an intellectual and an emotional point of view, it may be necessary for you first to develop a full awareness of how negative you feel about something before you could honestly and fully explore the positive conditions and the positive feelings that might replace the negative ones.

Therefore, we make no requirement that you must omit or cover up your negative feelings. Quite the contrary, explore them or express them if you feel the need to do so. We only ask that you convey them in a minimally destructive way and then, as soon as you feel that you can do so constructively, honestly, and productively, that you clearly set forth the behaviors and feelings that would please you—the interpersonal message.

The *sixth* and last guideline for the expressive mode is also a difficult one to follow if one is emotionally upset. It is, however, an effective way of increasing the probability that one will be listened to empathically. This guideline is: Convey empathy to your partner at the same time that you are expressing your own feelings and/or interpersonal message.

In the course of using the skills taught in the program, if your partner has just spoken, we always want you to respond empathically to what your partner has said before you express yourself. When you do that in the context of practicing your skills here, you would be exercising the empathic responder mode, then mode switching, and then taking the expresser mode. In the instance we are talking about here, however, we are assuming that you are the initiator of the conversation and that your partner as yet has said nothing to which you could respond.

Nevertheless, you should assume, as psychologists would, that if a person is behaving in a certain way—whether he is doing something that you wish he wouldn't do or failing to do something that you wish he would do—there is a reason for it; there is a motive for his behavior. It may be, for example, that he enjoys the activity that you don't like. Or, in the case where he is not doing something you'd like him to do, it may be that the behavior you prefer competes with something else he'd rather be doing.

If you are cool enough emotionally to manage it, take a

moment to try to put yourself in the other person's place before you begin to express yourself. Put yourself in your partner's shoes and picture the price your partner will be paying to do as you ask. Picture how your partner is likely to look on the statement you are about to make. Then try to include something in your statement that shows empathy for your partner's viewpoint. If you do, your partner will look on you as being a more reasonable sort of person. It will then be much easier for your partner to exert the reciprocal effort of trying to appreciate your needs and your viewpoint. Research has shown that a friendly, cooperative, interpersonal statement tends to beget its kind, and a demanding, competitive, or hostile statement tends to beget its kind. If you want to be understood, then show understanding. That fact, of course, underlies all that we are doing here. What we are now saying is that when you become truly convinced of that and very skilled in conveying empathy, you can show empathy even when the other person has not yet spoken. It is a very productive and helpful thing to do when you broach a sensitive topic.

We will turn to the examples once again to make this concept easier to grasp. In the instance concerning Johnny and his father the expresser might begin the statement with: "I know that you're extremely tired when you get home, and that you're looking for a chance to relax a while and to put the pressures of the day behind you. I know that you're under a lot of pressure at work and that you need to unwind to put yourself in a better frame of mind. Yet, at the same time . . . ."

In the instance concerning the disorganized condition of the household, the empathic portion of the statement might be: "I know you have a very rough time of it here with the kids, especially toward the end of the day, when you have to get dinner ready and all. But . . . ."

The empathic statement about wanting more social activity could be: "I know that you enjoy staying home, and that socializing with friends is not as important to you as it is to me, and I also know that you're concerned about our financial situation and the costs of spending a night out. Yet . . . ."

With respect to the teenager and his work habits, the empathic portion of the statement could be: "I know you're into a lot of exciting things now with your friends—that having an active social life is extremely important to you now and that it would be very hard for you to cut down on that. Nevertheless . . . ."

An empathic statement should *never* be used unless you are absolutely sure: (1) that based on concrete previous conversations, you do in fact understand the other person's needs and motivations in that situation, (2) that your manner of expression as well as your words will convey empathy and acceptance, and will be received as such. Otherwise, you will be in the position of analyzing another's motives for him, and increasing the risk that you will be inducing defensiveness and anger instead of reducing that risk.

It is not likely that you will think of making an empathic

statement if you are angry, and even if you think of it, it would be difficult to convey properly if you are overwrought.

Therefore, one of the keys to success with this element of the expresser mode (and some of the other elements as well) is to express your feelings, wishes, and expectations *early*, before you have experienced a great deal of frustration or anger. Unfortunately, a great many people don't feel free to talk about where they hurt or what they want, until they feel driven to the wall—until they are desperate or angry. Then the dam breaks, and they can then forgive themselves for having expressed their needs because they can tell themselves that the outburst was beyond their conscious control. It's our position that there is no good reason not to let your desires be known as soon as you are aware of them. In fact, we hope the techniques we are teaching you will help you *become* aware of them earlier than you now are.

Knowing how to express your needs in accord with all of the above guidelines—and having a partner who knows skills that will help him respond well to your efforts—should make it easier for you to express your needs *before* they become tangled up in emotions, before your emotions make it difficult for you to express them in a constructive manner.

Delayed expression of your needs and feelings, coupled with anger and accusations, or phrasing your personal wishes only in terms of what is supposedly fair, right, or necessary, increases the probability that your partner will respond poorly to your needs. The more he responds poorly, the more you will tend to delay the expression of your needs. The more you delay, the more likely it is that when they are expressed, they will be expressed in a negative manner. The more they are expressed in a negative manner, the more likely they will be responded to negatively. And so on. That is a *vicious* communication cycle.

In contrast, the skills we are teaching should make it easier for you to express your needs early. The earlier you express them, the more likely it is that they can be received well by your partner. The more they are well received by your partner, the easier it is to express them early the next time. The earlier they are expressed, the easier it is to use expresser skills. The more the expresser skills are used, the greater the chance that your communications will be well received and your needs met. When this starts to happen with some regularity, we will have accomplished what we are after in this program: the establishment of an *auspicious* communication cycle.

Obviously, the empathic and expressive modes are interrelated and interlinked. If the expresser did everything perfectly, the responder would only have to paraphrase what the expresser said, and then proceed to switch roles and become the expresser. In reality, the expresser needs a great deal of help to achieve awareness of his needs and feelings, needs help in expressing them appropriately, and needs to feel that it is safe and rewarding to express

himself. That is what the responder mode is designed to do. Conversely, unless the expresser can do a reasonably good job of executing his mode properly, the responder will have trouble in being constructive and helpful. We want each to help the other instead of making it more difficult for the other. The objective of the skill training is to eliminate vicious communication cycles and replace them with auspicious communication cycles.

## Mode Switching

The third of the primary communication and problem-solving skills is mode switching. The following explanation of mode switching is offered to clients after they have seen a demonstration of the leaders using expresser and responder skills in a dialog.

> You observed when we were demonstrating the expresser and empathic modes earlier, that each of us was able to switch back and forth easily from one mode to the other. This is a third skill that we will be teaching you after you begin to master the two primary modes. We will be teaching you to be alert to thoughts and feelings of your own that should signal you to seek a change in your communication mode from expresser to empathic responder or vice versa. We will also teach you to look for certain types of behavior in your partner that serve as signals that a mode switch would be desirable. It's too soon to go into those details now, because you don't yet have enough experience with these modes to make those cues meaningful. They will be explained further during the sessions as you become ready.
>
> The important thing I want to tell you now is that mode switching will help you to use these skills whenever you need to, or want to, in the course of your lives at home together. We believe that the expresser and responder skills are extremely useful not only at points of crisis or conflict, or when you absolutely must reach an understanding about an important issue, but also day in and day out in the course of your ordinary communication. To use the skills in your discussions together smoothly and effectively at home, we want you to become: (1) knowledgeable about which mode you should seek to employ at a given point in a discussion; that is, knowledgeable about *when* to switch modes; and (2) knowledgeable about *how* to switch properly from one to the other.
>
> The only thing I will mention now is that we will ask you always to do one thing before you switch over from being empathic toward your partner to expressing your own needs, thoughts, or feelings. That one thing is to make sure, by checking it

out with your partner, that you have provided an empathic response to the last statement your partner made. As soon as you
have done that, your partner immediately lets you become the
expresser while he in turn responds empathically to you. The
process then can go into reverse again, with the one who is now the
responder able to become the expresser again, providing he, in
turn, has shown that he has fully appreciated the thoughts and feelings that you have just expressed. In that way, when the situation
is one that calls for it, the application of the skills becomes very
much like any discussion. The crucial difference is that you both
continuously benefit from experiencing the assurance that your
partner fully understands and accepts your viewpoint and feelings
even if he may not agree with them.

Because you are able to enter into the expresser mode
whenever you wish, you are never in the position of having to
suffer in silence or hold back your own feelings for any significant
length of time. Your ability to fully express your own perceptions,
needs, and feelings is never more than a sentence or two away. You
only need first to demonstrate that you truly appreciate your partner's perceptions and feelings. And, of course, your partner must
do the same for you. That is one of the major ways you can avoid
vicious cycles created by feeling that you are not listened to, respected, or understood. Following these procedures promotes the
kind of exchange of views that allows problem solving to proceed
effectively. These procedures help to prevent possible solutions
from being washed away in a flood of misunderstandings and negative emotions.

The above explanation is appropriate to the intake interview. Then, in the course of the first six to eight hours of the
program, the participants are instructed—via explanation,
modeling, structuring, and so on—in mode-switching skills. The
explanation given in the course of this instruction would be
along the following lines.

As we have indicated, it is appropriate to initiate a mode
switch either as an expresser or as a responder. Let's first consider
the occasions when you should initiate a mode switch as an expresser. If your partner is simply trying to help you work out your
thoughts and feelings or solve a problem that does not involve your
partner's self-interest, you probably won't need to initiate a mode
switch very often. However, if your partner is involved in the issue,
then there will be numerous occasions when you will wish to initiate a mode switch. There are two major circumstances of that
nature. The first is simply when you desire to know how your partner perceives or feels about an issue, or how he would suggest resolving a problem or conflict. The second occasion on which you

may wish to initiate a mode switch as an expresser is when you have finished expressing your *major* thoughts or feelings, made your major suggestions for resolving a problem or conflict, and find yourself dealing only with elaborations or with fine points. Elaboration and analysis of fine points is appropriate when the issue is one that concerns only you. But when the responder also has a significant stake in the issue, it is a good idea to change modes at that point to find out what perceptions, feelings, or suggestions your partner has about the issue. This will save a great deal of time in focusing on the particular issues that are most important in reaching a mutually satisfying resolution. Whenever you find yourself making two consecutive statements which cover essentially the same ground with respect to *all* aspects of your response—the perceptions, feelings, and the interpersonal messages—then it is time to suggest that your partner become the expresser, and you become the responder, for at least one exchange.

There are three major occasions when you should initiate a mode switch from the responder to the expresser mode, and the first two are complements of the circumstances described above. The first is when your partner has thrice reiterated the same communication without essential change in *any* of the components of the communication, and has included all the components of a good expressive response in the communication. Before using this occasion to switch out of the responder mode, you should first be satisfied that both your own previous *two* empathic responses have: (1) captured the very *deepest, most significant* feeling implied in the expresser's communication, and (2) that you have made *explicit* any interpersonal message implied by that statement.

The second occasion to initiate a switch from the responder to the expresser mode is when you believe that you have something to say that: (1) might favorably influence the other's perceptions, or (2) needs to be considered by your partner immediately in order to keep a problem-solving or conflict-resolution topic on the correct track as far as you are concerned.

The third occasion has to do with your own ability to continue being empathic toward your partner. If it is no longer possible for you to suspend your feelings, and they are beginning to disrupt your ability to be empathic with your partner, then you should seek the expresser mode in order to unburden yourself to the point where you can again manage to be empathic with your partner. In addition to your own direct awareness of the disruptive feelings, there is another sign that can serve as a clue that you are losing your ability to be empathic. It is happening whenever you find yourself trying to sneak into your otherwise empathic response a word, a phrase, or an aside that you are hoping may serve to *change* the way your partner views the situation.

A final comment on mode switching. It is particularly important to engage in frequent mode switching when you have reached the point of working out concrete steps and plans of

action designed to solve a problem, resolve a conflict, or achieve a higher level of satisfaction in your relationship. Whenever a dialog reaches the point of deciding who will do what, when it will be done, how often it will be done, and under what circumstances it will be done, it is especially important that each party know immediately what the other person's reactions are; otherwise much time can be wasted traveling into dead-end alleys.

### The Facilitator Mode

Often among mental health professionals the term *facilitator* is used to designate the person in charge of the group. We do not use the term this way. We refer to the people in charge of the program or groups as the *leader* (or *teacher, instructor, professional,* or, if appropriate and difficult to avoid, as *therapist*). The term *facilitator* is used to designate group members when they are using the fourth basic set of skills: those involved in teaching others to use empathic, expressive, and mode switching skills. This facilitator mode is as carefully defined behaviorally as are the others in the program.

The facilitator mode has two purposes: to help the clients teach each other RE skills when they are in a group session, and to teach and encourage their family members to use the skills at home. The teaching skills that are taught to the participants as facilitators are essentially the same as those that the group leader must learn. These teaching skills will be explicated in later chapters. We will discuss the facilitator mode as it is used in group sessions, and then discuss its use in the home.

### *Facilitator Skills in the Group*

The facilitator mode as employed by clients with members of the group other than their partner is very different from the one that clients and professionals alike are apt to think of when they consider members of a group being helpful to one another. For example, the group members are specifically taught *not* to offer sympathy or understanding. They are taught *not* to offer praise or criticism of the ideas or feelings that others express. They are asked *not* to offer advice or share their

own experiences in an effort to be helpful to other group members, and *not* to indicate how they worked out a problem which some other group members may be experiencing. They are taught *not* to speculate on the possible causes of problems, on the motivations, needs, or personality of others. They are taught *not* to direct their self-disclosures to other group members.

Instead they are systematically taught to do, and not to do, exactly what the group leader does and what he refrains from doing. The facilitator mode, therefore, is one of facilitating the skill-learning process. At first, group members function as auxiliary or assistant teachers. Later (in long-running groups) as the group members become more and more skilled in using the primary behavioral modes and skilled in the facilitator (teaching) mode, the leader becomes less active, and the primary supervision comes from other group members rather than from the leader.

Instruction of those facilitator skills that are used in group sessions is accomplished by (1) briefly explaining the instructional methods used by the leader; (2) asking the members to observe the leader's instructional methods; (3) asking participants to provide positive reinforcement for the practicing pair when they do well; (4) asking participants covertly to practice formulating expressive and empathic responses that improve on the responses of the "center-stage" couples; and (5) calling on the participants, at a gradually increasing rate, to suggest better responses to the center-stage participants. By thus defining the facilitator's role very carefully, the group leader is able to eliminate nonfacilitator responses; of course, he provides positive reinforcement for facilitators who do their job well, and continues to model facilitator statements where necessary.

There are a number of programatic benefits that derive from teaching group facilitator skills to the participants. It speeds client learning directly by adding additional teachers; also, when facilitators assume the responsibility of teaching others, their own learning is increased. Providing participants with the opportunity to use the facilitator mode also makes it easy for them to avoid making unproductive or counterproduc-

tive responses to other group members. By giving facilitators an active, constructive role to play, their interest is kept high when the other members of the group are on center stage. Instruction and practice in the facilitator mode in the group is, of course, also good preparation for using facilitator skills at home.

### Facilitator Skills at Home

Facilitator skills can be used at home to encourage and instruct nonparticipating family members to use RE skills. However, we will limit our discussion to the use of facilitator skills with a participating partner. The objectives of training for use of the facilitator mode at home are to enable the participants to help each other perfect RE skills and use them whenever they can be helpful. Participants are taught and encouraged to use facilitator skills at home both in the routine course of *daily interactions* and during times that have been set aside for serious and relatively *lengthy discussions*.

*Daily-life situations.* Instructing the participants in ways to use RE skills in the course of their daily lives involves sensitizing them to a number of things. One is to help them recognize those situations, other than the relationship, in which one's partner is emotionally involved. At such times, an empathic response can be a very helpful thing to offer one's partner (and also has beneficial effects for the relationship). Of course, it is not always the most appropriate thing to do. Partners must be encouraged to explore various situations and find out the kinds of occasions on which they do or do not appreciate an empathic response.

A second kind of situation arising in everyday living in which RE skills can be useful is one that does involve the relationship. These are occasions that involve any sort of potential disagreement, including any desire to induce the partner to do something that he may not wish to do. Clearly, this covers a great many interactions in the course of the day. It is our belief that the relationship will be significantly enhanced if RE skills are used in all of them. Helping participants to recognize these situations as ones in which RE skills should be used is one of

the key jobs of the leader in training clients to use RE skills at home. The use of facilitator skills enables the participants to help each other do this, to recognize such occasions and to use RE skills when those occasions arise. There are three major guidelines, presented below, that help participants to determine when to use facilitator skills in ordinary, daily interactions.

First, *any time a person is annoyed or makes a demand, expressive skills are in order.* Thus, a daughter should not say to her mother "Hurry up, we're going to be late!" But rather, "I'm getting very nervous and upset because it's important to me that we be on time and I'm afraid we're going to be late. If there's anything you can do to help us get out faster I'd appreciate it very much."

Second, *reinforce every skilled statement of your partner by giving appropriate type of skilled response yourself.* Once expressive skills have been used, they should always be responded to empathically. Then, a mode switch to expressive skills is generally in order immediately after the empathic response. For example, the mother might reply to the daughter's skillful expressive statement, "You're upset with me because I'm not ready yet and you'd like to leave now. I'm sorry that I'm not ready. I wanted to finish the dishes before we left. I can't stand to come back home with dirty dishes in the sink. I'll hurry as much as I can. I'll be ready to leave in five minutes. I don't think your friends will be too upset with our being five minutes late."

Instead of responding as above, it is easy to imagine the mother saying something like, "Don't be such a worry-wart— we're not going to be late, and even if we are, nobody is going to care." Compared to the defensive or counterattacking things one is likely to say when criticized, or when demands are being made, the empathic response of the mother was *reinforcing* to the daughter. Thus in an exchange such as was given here and many times in the course of an ordinary day, all RE skills and modes should be brought into play.

Third, *whenever you are upset after the other person has said something, ask yourself whether the other person has completely followed RE guidelines. If he has not, then facilitator*

*skills are in order.* Usually, what is called for is an expressive statement coupled with what we will describe more fully in future chapters as a "structuring" response. For example, let's suppose the daughter did say, "Hurry up. We're going to be late," the mother might reply, "I know you are upset and annoyed with me right now; but I would feel much better, and possibly feel much more like being cooperative as well, if you would state your predictions in a subjective manner, and rephrase your whole statement in terms of your own feelings and desires."

If the daughter seemed unable to come up with a better statement, the mother might then use another facilitator skill we will also describe later ("modeling") to help her daughter rephrase her statement as a good expressive statement.

*Lengthy discussions.* One type of extended discussion involves one person's need to work through an emotionally disturbing or a perplexing issue that involves the other person only indirectly. For example, a wife who is upset about a situation in her place of work may be helped by her husband to resolve the problem on emotional and decision-making levels; or an adolescent daughter perplexed about a troubled relationship with a friend might be helped by her mother to resolve the difficulty on emotional and decision-making levels. A second type of extended discussion involves an attempt to work out a solution to an issue faced jointly by both parties. Examples of such an issue would include making a decision about the kind of apartment to rent; which house to purchase; whether a better job is worth a move to a different city; planning a vacation; and deciding how to help a child overcome difficulties he is having in school. Still another type of extended discussion is one in which a relationship issue between the participants is central. This conversation might be on a very positive issue, such as sharing positive perceptions and feelings; it might be a discussion of ways in which one or both believe the relationship can be enriched or made more enjoyable; or it might be a discussion of a serious disagreement, or a strong desire to have a partner change a disturbing pattern of behavior.

The distinction between "daily life" and "lengthy discussions" is a matter of instructional convenience to highlight the

two different difficulties that the clients must overcome in helping each other to generalize RE skills to the home via use of facilitator skills. In routine, daily life situations the difficulty to be overcome is to remember to *initiate* the use of RE skills. That is the main function of facilitation in everyday situations —to remind oneself and one's partner to bring RE skills into play. The key difficulty to overcome via facilitator skill in lengthy discussions, because clients are already conscious of the appropriateness of RE skills and have agreed to use them, is the tendency to deviate from their use because of emotional pressures.

In an extended discussion, the complexity and depth of exploration and the strong feelings generated often make it difficult to stay with RE behavioral skills, even though the participants committed themselves to doing so in embarking on the discussion. In his eagerness to express his own point of view, one person may forget to respond empathically to his partner's expressive statement before launching into his own. An arguable proposition may be stated as fact. Value judgments may be made that are not identified as one's own. Broad generalizations may be made instead of behaviorally oriented observations. And so forth.

Thus, in lengthy discussions, each person must serve as a facilitator for the other in keeping the conversation within the RE skill guidelines. The participants must do the same thing for each other as the group leader would do if he were there in the room with them. Obviously, this is a very difficult task. The more complex and emotional the discussion the more likely it is that errors will be made by party A, and when errors are made, the less likely it is that partner B will then be sufficiently self-possessed to spot the errors and to correct them with appropriate facilitator skills.

Thus, it is important that participants be given direct supervision by their instructor in their use of facilitator skills with each other. Before they are asked to use facilitator skills at home they should practice them under the leader's supervision. This practice should take place in two ways, one to prepare them for facilitation in daily interactions and the other designed

to help them be effective facilitators in lengthy discussions. The former is done via role playing daily interactions under instructions to facilitate. Practice for facilitation in lengthy discussions takes place when participants are carrying on their regular supervised exchanges in the group meetings. (They are not asked to practice facilitator skills in either of these ways until they have a good mastery of empathic, expressive, and mode-switching skills.)

After such practice, they are encouraged to begin using facilitator skills at home. Then, when difficulties arise in using facilitator skills in daily situations, the situations would be re-enacted in the meeting with the leader so that he can provide appropriate instruction. For difficulties encountered in keeping to RE skills in lengthy discussions, actual recordings of such discussions should, if feasible, be used to provide instruction and supervision in the use of facilitator skills. (In our own facility, we lend inexpensive cassette recorders and tapes to clients.) When tape recordings are not available, the exchanges that did not run smoothly in lengthy discussions at home can be re-enacted for instructional and supervisory purposes.

The guidelines provided the clients for using facilitator skills in a lengthy discussion are as follows. As soon as an error is detected the party who wishes to facilitate should hold his hand up in a "stop" motion toward his partner. Often, especially with skilled participants, this gesture alone will be sufficient to bring about the necessary change in the partner's behavior. If it is not, the facilitator may interrupt to give an expressive-structuring statement. For example, if A forgets to respond empathically to B's statement, B might say, "I'd appreciate it if you would respond empathically to me, before you express your point of view." If A states an arguable proposition as fact, B might say, "I know that must seem a simple statement of fact to you, but it will be much easier for me to respond empathically to you if you would put it in terms of your own perceptions." If A presents a value judgment without recognizing it as such, B might say "I'm sure it seems to you that everyone would agree that I was wrong, but I see a value judgment in your statement that I might or might not agree with, and it

would be much easier for me to deal with what you are saying if you restated that subjectively—that *you* see that behavior as wrong." If A makes a broad generalization about B, B might say, "Instead of saying that you perceive me as '*never* considering your mother's feelings,' I would appreciate it if you could qualify it, or deal with the problem in a more specific way."

As in the daily interactions, various combinations of expressive skills with "structuring," "modeling," and "reinforcement" (techniques that will be more fully explained later) are used in the facilitator mode during lengthy discussions.

The initial explanation of the facilitator mode that is given to participants is presented in the next chapter, "The Intake Interview," because this explanation serves a major purpose of the intake interview: to reassure group members that they need not fear criticism or intrusion into their lives by other group members.

### Summary of Four Basic Skills

The major components of the four basic skills as these are summarized in a two-page mimeographed handout for participants are shown below. The participants are encouraged to keep this summary in hand during the first few sessions.

### Partial Summary of Three Behavior Modes and Mode Switching

#### *Expressive Mode*

1. State your views in a subjective manner.
2. State your feelings.
3. Be specific and behavioral; avoid generalization, motivational analyses, and characterizations of others.
4. If there are any implied criticisms in your statement, try also to include the basic positive underlying feelings or expectations.
5. If appropriate, add an interpersonal message (your desires) that also incorporates points 1, 2, 3, and 4 above.

(This may take the form of a concrete suggestion to help bring about resolution of the issue or problem.)

### Empathic Responder Mode

1. Put yourself in the other's place to determine how the other (a) thinks, and (b) feels about the issue.
2. Convey understanding and acceptance by: (a) tone, posture, and facial expression, (b) stating the other's most important thoughts, conflicts, desires, and feelings.

### Facilitator Mode

1. Praise the expresser or responder whenever a mode-appropriate statement: (a) shows improvement over their general performance level, or (b) deals with emotionally difficult material.
2. Suggest specific phrases or feelings that would help the expresser or responder to improve on their statement.
3. Remind the expresser or responder of specific limitations imposed by the modes whenever the statement does not stay within those limits.
4. Suggest a mode switch to the expresser or responder whenever it seems appropriate.

### Mode Switching

#### Conditions for Mode Switching

1. Expresser requests it and responder agrees to it.
2. Responder requests it, and provides a response to expresser's last statement that expresser judges to be understanding and accepting.

#### When to Mode Switch

1. As expresser:
    a. When you have already expressed your major thoughts, feelings, or suggestions for resolving an issue, and only fine points or elaborations remain.

b. When you want to know the other person's views, feelings, or suggestions for problem resolution.

2. As responder:

a. When you are satisfied that you have already clarified twice over the other's deepest feelings on an issue, and the same ground is being gone over again.

b. When your own thoughts or feelings are beginning to impair your desire or ability to be empathic.

c. When you have something to say that might favorably influence the other's perceptions, or help resolve an issue.

3. As facilitator, when you think any of the above things are happening and the expresser or responder has not requested a mode switch.

*Expresser's Behavior After Responder's Request for Mode Switch*

1. Refrain from stating any new ideas or feelings.

2. Indicate that the responder has understood and accepted your last communication well enough to allow the mode switch to occur; or clarify and instruct the responder until he does convey such understanding and acceptance.

*Responder's Behavior After Expresser's Request for Mode Switch*

1. Convey understanding and acceptance of the thoughts and feelings just communicated by the expresser (including the desire to know your views if that was stated or implied.)

2. Consider carefully any request made for your views, but remember the expresser determines the topic. As the new expresser, you are not obligated to discuss a topic suggested by the former expresser.

# Chapter 3

# Intake
# Interviews

~~~~~~~~~~~~~~~~~~~~~~~~~~~~~

The first contact with potential participants is extremely important because it creates impressions that give people an idea of what to expect from the program. Intake leaders need to be particularly sensitive to the needs and problems of the clients. In addition to explaining the importance of empathy in interpersonal relationships, they must demonstrate their ability to be empathic and understanding. Thus the initial interview is intended both to help potential clients understand what RE programs are all about and how the learning of skills can help with their particular relationship issues and problems, as well as to show that the program leaders are open and accepting in their attitudes toward the clients.

## The Interviewers

Whenever feasible, we believe it is advantageous to have the enrollment (intake) interview conducted by the same person or persons who will lead the particular group that the participants will join. The feelings of acceptance, understanding, and confidence that are generated by a properly conducted enrollment interview are associated in the minds of the clients as much, or more, with the particular person conducting the interview as they are with the nature of the program being described.

With a future group leader conducting the initial interviews, rapport between the group members and the leader can be established before the first group meeting. Thus, groups led by the same person who did the initial interview get off to a somewhat faster start than groups led by people new to the participants. We also believe that people are more likely to decide to enter a program when they have had an opportunity to acquire trust and confidence in the particular professional with whom they later will be working.

There are also advantages in having the enrollment interviews led by two people instead of one. The use of two leaders makes it easier to demonstrate the behavioral skills that will later be used by the participants. The use of the male and female leadership duo has an additional advantage when the pair being interviewed are not of the same sex. In circumstances such as this, people often feel they will be better understood and accepted, and hence more at ease in expressing themselves, with someone of their own sex. In a program for parents and adolescents, in order to promote trust, identification, and modeling, it is desirable to pair as young a leader as possible with an older leader. We recognize that the use of sex-mixed and/or age-mixed teams is far easier to arrange in some settings than in others. We do not consider the use of single leaders (of any age or sex) rather than the use of teams to be a severe handicap: It only makes things a bit more cumbersome. The net economy in savings of professional time probably makes single-leader groups the most desirable kind of group in nontraining settings where resources are limited.

## Group versus One-Couple Interviews

Enrollment interviews for RE programs may be conducted with several pairs or with only one pair of participants. There are some advantages in conducting enrollment interviews with several dyads at a time. One is the economy of professional manpower. If the various couples then enter the program together, that is another advantage. It is then possible to use the intake interview to build some rapport among the group mem-

bers, thereby reducing the threat inherent in the idea of joining strangers in a situation where deeply personal aspirations and/or problems will be discussed.

However, we believe that the dangers and disadvantages of conducting an intake with more than one couple outweigh the advantages. Many clients are highly resistant to the idea of working in a group context. It is not feasible to adequately allay these fears via the phone or mail contacts that precede the initial interview. Moreover, the intake interview itself is probably the one that elicits the most fears and doubts about group participation, since it is the time that clients are most eager to make known their major concerns in order to determine the most appropriate course of action. Once it is clear that the interviewer understands and appreciates their concerns and the appropriate course of action can be determined, it is easier to assure the clients that disclosures of personal matters in the group context will occur only at a pace comfortable to themselves.

Thus, an important function of the enrollment interview is to encourage clients to air their concerns about undergoing the program together with other couples. Once such doubts are expressed, the interviewer usually can allay them by indicating that generally such concerns subside fairly quickly and by enumerating the advantages of participating in a group. Sometimes the leader may want to suggest that the pair join a group on a trial basis for several weeks with the option of then dropping out in favor of private dyadic sessions. This option is, in fact, seldom chosen once the pair has begun their participation in a group.

## Individual Interviewing

In certain instances, it may be desirable to reserve a portion of the interview for private conversation with each of the participants. When people are experiencing a great deal of difficulty in their relationship, it is often easier to talk about problems when the partner is not present. It is not a goal of the

interviewer to diagnose the specific causes of difficulty in the relationship, but it is important that each of the participants is confident that the intake worker's recommendations are made on the basis of his complete understanding of the situation. If a participant had been reticent about his concerns, he might believe that the interviewer did not fully understand the depth, scope, or nature of the problem. Separate interviews are therefore desirable whenever there is reason to believe that one or both of the participants might otherwise feel incompletely understood. It is always desirable, however, to spend most of the time during the intake interview with both partners together and especially to conclude the interview with both present.

In other instances, separate interviews may be considered useful to determine whether one of the participants should be referred elsewhere in addition to, or instead of, the RE program. Such a situation might exist, for example, in a parent-adolescent interview when information or observation suggests that the teenager or the parent is disturbed by problems that lie outside of the parent-adolescent relationship. The interviewer would probably wish to follow up this possibility in a separate private interview.

Another example of a situation calling for separate interviews for a portion of the intake time would be one in which an adolescent has not voiced much doubt about the value of the program in the presence of a parent, but displays nonverbal cues suggesting uncertainty or resistance. The teenager might talk more freely in a situation where no parent was present, thereby offering the interviewer a chance to allay the teenager's concerns. It is often difficult for teenagers to believe that they will have equal rights and participation in the program and that the burden of making changes in habitual patterns will rest as much on the parent as themselves. A separate interview will often serve to surface such doubts and make it possible to deal with them constructively.

Since we have had much more experience introducing individual pairs to our programs than we have had with group intake, the former type of interview will be used to illustrate

the intake procedure in the remainder of the chapter. A group intake would follow procedures not greatly different from the one-couple interview in general outline and methodology.

## Building Rapport and Trust

The intake interviewer attends first to establishing rapport with the potential participants. Next, he discusses the circumstances that led them to enroll in the program. If they are coming for help with problems in their relationship rather than simply for enrichment purposes, he responds empathically to each party's complaints about their relationship. He makes sure that each person expresses his own perception of the problem. This interview affords the first major opportunity for clients to sense the understanding and acceptance that is induced by someone showing the empathic acceptance that is the essence of the empathic responder skills they later will be learning themselves. It is essential that they do experience such understanding and acceptance. It is also very important that they do not get any feeling that the interviewer is "diagnosing" or otherwise weighing their strengths and weaknesses. The interviewer must also take care to avoid the appearance of taking sides or being more attentive to one person than the other. If a pair has no special problems, but views the RE program as an opportunity to further enhance an already satisfying relationship, then the interviewer focuses empathic acceptance on their hopes, wishes, and expectations.

The time devoted to discussing reasons for coming and the relationship between the participants, varies greatly. When the interviewees do not perceive themselves to have relationship problems worth discussing, this phase of the interview may last only a few minutes. In instances where serious problems exist, the leader might respond empathically to statements of these problems for an hour. When a relationship crisis exists, this phase might last several hours, either in one long interview or in a series of meetings. Generally, this first phase should be no shorter than the time it takes to acquire a general understanding of the relationship needs and wishes of the candidates as they

perceive them, and no longer than it takes the interviewer to convey to each person that his problems and needs are fully appreciated. If the participants are in crisis, intake interviewers should continue until the participants can listen civilly to one another. The belief of the participants that their personal needs and aspirations have been fully understood and respected is the foundation on which the remainder of the intake interview rests. The remainder of the procedures will be diminished in effectiveness to the extent that this foundation is incomplete.

There are other essential elements in building such a foundation. The participants must emerge from the interview feeling that (1) they truly understood the nature of the program and the skills; (2) they faced all major doubts and misgivings about the methods, technique, and skills in general and about the applicability of these methods to their own case; and (3) they received appropriate answers about such doubts from the interviewer.

The interviewer must assume that the interviewees will *not* directly raise all the questions they have. The interviewer should constantly be watchful for blank stares or fleeting puzzled expressions that indicate a need for further examples or explanations. In such circumstances, the leader could provide such further explanation without hesitation. Even when the interviewer *doesn't* get such signs, frequent inquiries should nevertheless be made as to whether the participants have any questions.

Similarly, the interviewer must be continuously looking for nonverbal cues indicating doubts or misgivings about the methods or their appropriateness for the participant's individual circumstances. Whenever such cues appear, the leader should try to elicit their expression by means of an empathic response to the unspoken doubts. Once doubts are voiced, the interviewer should not rush to provide an answer to them, but instead should continue to respond empathically until the client has fully expressed and clarified them on both intellectual and emotional levels. Only at that point should the interviewer offer his own viewpoint and reasoning on the issue. Then the leader should revert to an empathic mode of responding with respect

to the client's reactions to this reasoning. The pattern of alternating empathic responses with the interviewer's viewpoint should continue until the doubt is resolved.

In the interest of clarity of exposition, such leader behaviors are not included in the examples of leader explanations of the program presented earlier and in this chapter. Nevertheless, this type of sensitivity to, and the eliciting of, unspoken questions and doubts are regarded as key ingredients to a successful intake procedure.

There are occasions when client doubts or misgivings with respect to a certain procedure or to the RE approach may continue to exist after the client's feelings have been clarified and the leader's explanations have been given and fully understood. In these instances, it is very effective to propose an experimental orientation to the client. The client's viewpoint is fully respected. But the leader urges the client to put his doubts aside long enough to try the method or technique for a designated length of time and then reassess the issue with the leader. Clients are almost always willing to adopt such a trial period. Almost universally, in our experience, the kinds of doubts clients express are dispelled after several sessions.

### Explaining the Desirability of Communication Training

The next task of the interviewer is to explain each of the following concepts with as much elaboration and exemplification as seems desirable.

1. The more each person in a relationship can help the other to meet important needs and goals, the closer and more satisfying the relationship is likely to be.

2. A good pattern of communication, one that helps people share their likes, dislikes, and aspirations with each other, provides an understanding through which they can better meet each other's needs and goals.

3. Our culture has not provided us with good training in communicating our own needs and feelings in ways that

are honest and, at the same time, likely to encourage others to treat us with acceptance and respect.

4. It is the purpose of the RE program to provide training, practice and supervision, to help participants develop skills that will encourage mutual understanding, warmth, respect, and need fulfillment.

5. The skills that participants in RE programs are taught help them to communicate any type of need to each other: those that are psychological and emotional, such as the need for respect, understanding, and acceptance; and those that are physiological or material in nature, such as sexual and financial needs. Needs and goals can be met much more frequently and satisfactorily if they are openly and honestly communicated. Because tastes and desires change from time to time, we are dependent on continuous communication to enable each of us to meet the other's needs and to accomplish mutual goals.

6. The objective of the program—which naturally will take longer for those who begin the program with serious problems than for those who don't—is to build a relationship far more satisfying to each partner than either may ever have experienced before. The purpose of applying these skills in the course of everyday living is to create a growth-inducing atmosphere: an interpersonal climate in the home that will make each party feel deeply understood and deeply respected; an environment that promotes not only a richer understanding of the other, but of one's self; an environment in which each person can usually behave in accord with his own inner needs and nature and knows just how far he can go in satisfying his own needs without running afoul of his partner's needs; and an environment in which each person wants to, and knows how to, maximize the other's emotional satisfactions without endangering his own.

These concepts are explained at a level commensurate with the *least educated and sophisticated person present.* For

example, if a parent and a twelve-year-old child are participating, the explanation would be geared at a level the child would understand.

Examples provided by the interviewer should vary in accord with the type of program being considered. Thus, to make the same point about how communication can improve fulfillment of physiologically based needs as well as psychological needs, one might use sexual relations as an example for a married or premarital couple, and choose financial arrangements with a parent and adolescent.

It is almost always possible to *draw on the expressed problems or aspirations of the participants themselves to provide examples* of ways in which an improved pattern of communication could enhance each person's satisfaction with the relationship. Personalizing the meaning of the program in this manner is perhaps the most effective means of stimulating motivation to participate in the program.

### Introducing the Behavioral Modes

The next phase of the intake procedure provides a general introduction to the modes of communication that will be taught to the participants. The interviewer explains that:

1. In order to facilitate their learning of these communication skills, participants will be asked to take turns being an expresser and an empathic responder. In each case they will be taught to follow certain communication rules.

2. While the rules may sound simple enough, they are in reality quite difficult to follow, especially when emotionally important topics are discussed.

3. Nevertheless, research and experience have demonstrated that almost everyone who has committed himself to twelve hours or so of diligent instruction or practice has been able to learn the skills at a basic level, and with further practice can achieve a high level of skill.

The rationale underlying the use of expresser and empathic responder modes of behavior is explained to the partici-

pants with changes in examples and vocabulary depending on the leader's style, the type of program being discussed, and the educational level of the participants. An example of such an explanation follows.

> The basic purpose of the skills is to create an environment within the home in which each person feels free to explore with the other the needs and desires he has insofar as they affect, or are affected by, his relationship to the other. The orientation and skills provided by the program encourage each participant to be helpful to the other, so that the other can (1) understand his wants, his feelings, and his expectations better, and (2) be able to better express them. The attitudes and behaviors toward your partner that encourage him freely to express himself to you go under the label of the *empathic responding mode*. These are the same kinds of behaviors that research in psychotherapy has shown to be the key method by which therapists help their clients to understand and express themselves better.
>
> In addition to teaching each participant to provide such encouragement to the other, each participant is taught to express his own perceptions, feelings, and needs to the other in a way that maximizes the chances that the other person will be able to understand him, to accept him as a person, to appreciate his needs and feelings, and to be open to the possibility of change. The attitudes and behaviors that enable you to express yourself in this manner are labeled the *expresser mode*.
>
> By using these skills at home when you want to, or when you need to, you eventually can establish an environment in which each person understands both his own and the other's needs, potential reactions, and aspirations extremely well. This makes it possible for each person to develop more fully his own personality and potential. It also allows each person to know just how his needs and aspirations intermesh, or fail to intermesh, with the other's. It is then possible mutually to work out behavioral equations wherein each can maximize his own and the other's satisfactions, and minimize frustrations, anger, and resentment.
>
> Living together requires continuous mutual adjustments as individuals grow and change and as circumstances change. What we are teaching is a *process* for making such adjustments smoothly and in a way that maximizes chances for achieving mutual satisfaction with and from one another.

## Explaining the Behavioral Modes and Mode Switching

At this point in the intake interview, the interviewer would explain the rationale for the empathic responder mode, the expresser mode, and for mode switching, and explain them in the manner described in Chapter Two.

In explaining the facilitator mode, it is not necessary to go into much detail at the time of the intake interview, but it is important to emphasize that participants need not fear being judged, analyzed, or criticized by the other members of the prospective group. Rather, they can realistically expect only mutual encouragement, support, and help from others in the learning and practicing of the skills. Thus, an explanation to the client at intake might be:

> Working in groups provides you with the help of the other group members in learning the skills in addition to the help that you get from the leader. We just want to make it clear that you can *count* on getting help in learning, and you can count on getting *only* help in learning, from the other group members. Neither you nor your relationship will be subject to analysis. The members of the group will not be taking sides, or saying what they believe was right or wrong in your past behavior, or recommending actions you should take in the future. They will not be telling you how they think you should be relating to one another, or how you should resolve any problems that you might wish to discuss in the sessions. They will not criticize anything you say or do. They are taught not to do so from the very beginning, and we don't have any difficulty in getting our participants to avoid doing those things.
>
> What they *will* be doing is helping you in the manner that the leader does, to acquire skills. They will be helping you to express yourself and empathize with your partner better in accord with the expresser and responder modes. By having the participants always thinking of the best way to say something, even when it is the thoughts or feelings that *others* are trying to express, everybody learns the skills faster, and each member can help everyone else perfect their skills.

## Demonstrating the Advantage of Using the Behavioral Modes

After establishing the desirability of acquiring communication skills and explicating the skills, the next step is to show how these skills can be applied in life situations like those encountered by the interviewees. The most effective way to demonstrate the utility of the method is to show the *contrast* between dialog involving a disagreement as it might typically unfold within the home, and a discussion of the same topic as it would probably unfold if relationship enhancement skills were used. The disagreement without the use of skills is shown typi-

cally to escalate, and to become further and further removed from getting at the basic issues involved, whereas the use of skills tends to focus its discussion more precisely on the important issues, and tends to lead toward a solution. The subject chosen for demonstration should be one with which the participants are likely to identify. Both the nonskilled and skilled discussions are presented in a manner that is as realistic as possible. The aptness and realism help the participants to appreciate the value of the skills.

It is helpful in this part of the intake if there are two leaders, since they together can role play a husband and wife, a dating couple, or a parent and adolescent corresponding to the pair being interviewed. An interviewer working alone could use an audiotape, videotape, or film of a demonstration of skilled and unskilled dialogs. If no tape or film is available, the leader can give examples of typical statements and responses that people would use in conflict situations in contrast to more effective responses that result from using RE skills.

We also found it desirable to choose an area of *moderate* disagreement or conflict for this demonstration. (It is helpful for the pair to see the skills used to begin to bring about a constructive resolution of a conflict, even if they have come for enrichment purposes rather than to resolve problems.) The reason for not choosing a mild conflict for the demonstration is to minimize the probability that the participants will say to themselves, "Well, that's all very well if the conflicts are easy ones, but it won't work on the kinds of problems that we have." The reason for not choosing a severe problem or conflict is that it is extremely important that the role playing be very realistic in terms of how skilled pairs would really behave. In the role playing, the leaders, to retain the realism of the exchange, can afford to hasten the progress toward problem resolution only slightly. Therefore, choosing a severe problem or conflict would extend the role-playing time well beyond the ten minutes or so ordinarily devoted to this phase of the interview.

There are occasions, however, when the leader should choose a more serious problem, very likely one suggested by the couple, and devote more time to the demonstration. For

example, a problem of a serious nature could be demonstrated when the leader suspects that one or both of the partners being interviewed thinks, "This is too mild an approach for the kind of problems we have."

In any case, the role playing need not bring the problem to a complete resolution. Ordinarily, it is sufficient to demonstrate that each party generally appreciates the other's perspective and point of view more than before; that initial resentment, anger, and feelings of estrangement have been reduced; and that participants in the role play are clearly ready and willing to *work together*, constructively and realistically, toward a solution. The demonstration can be discontinued at such a stage, and the high probability of reaching a resolution with continued use of the skills can be pointed out to the clients. If they seem not to fully appreciate the progress made, the role playing can be resumed and continued until a further stage of problem resolution is reached.

We have found it helpful with some clients to reverse the order given here and to demonstrate the modes first *before* we explain them in detail. Once the clients have seen the demonstration, they can participate in the explanation by discussing their observations of how this conversation was different from traditional communication patterns. In this way the clients play a more active role in the intake. In either case it is important that the clients realize that the behavioral modes are very highly structured and carefully defined, and that they see how they are used and can be potentially helpful to them.

## Emphasizing Difficulty, Support, and Eventual Success

The behavioral modes appear deceptively simple to some of the people who see the leaders using the modes smoothly. It is therefore important, first, that these people be psychologically prepared for the difficulty they will probably experience, so that they do not feel disappointed and frustrated. Secondly, the leaders will be taking an active role in the early sessions by frequently modeling responses and making suggestions for improvements. If the participants are warned in advance that the

leaders will be intervening very actively, it minimizes the chances that they will misperceive the comments of the leaders as an indication that they are regarded as slow learners or as inept.

It is also important to assure the participants that they will get a great deal of help and make them feel confident that they will be successful in learning the skills. Such reassurance is entirely justifiable in terms of clinical and empirical evidence. Therefore, the interviewer says something along the following lines:

> These are initially very difficult ways to think and to behave. The new modes run counter to some strongly ingrained habits. We do not expect you to be able to avoid old ways of behaving with 100 percent success quickly. Also, for a while you may feel awkward, and you may wish you could be more free and spontaneous. Such difficulties and uncomfortable feelings accompany the learning of any difficult skill. When you learn to skate, you wobble and must laboriously learn how to put one foot in front of the other, and you need a helping hand. Later your movements become free and you can express yourself with more variety. While you still operate within the same limits imposed on you by the skates and the ice, you can use the medium to accomplish what you want to do. The sequence is the same with these skills. After you've mastered the necessary skills and practiced them sufficiently, you can use them spontaneously and without self-consciousness.
>
> In the program we will work with you very closely to remind you of what to do, and not to do, and to help you improve your skill. If you are willing to work at it, we have every reason to believe, based on a great deal of experience and research, that we can teach you to become very skillful.
>
> Our real goal, of course, is to help you learn these skills so well that you can use them anywhere or anytime they would be helpful to you. We will spend most of the time in our group meetings practicing these new skills. We also will ask you to set aside about an hour between sessions to practice at home. You will be learning to use these skills more and more in the course of your daily lives. When you have difficulties in using the skills at home we will discuss those difficulties, so that you will find it easier to use the skills in those situations the next time they arise. As in learning any new skill, the real key to success is practice.

## Specifying the Underlying Moral Values

The moral values underlying the program might be explained in the following manner:

Most people readily accept the moral value judgment underlying this program. But we feel a professional obligation to make
them very specific, since it is at least conceivable that they may
raise some questions you would want answered. In essence, the
value judgments that underlie the program are that honesty and
compassion are good; dishonesty and manipulation, or lack of
understanding of another person, are bad. Honesty and compassion
are the qualities that the program aims to strengthen and enhance
in relationships.

Of course, there is no intention on our part to ever *push*
you into being more honest and compassionate than you want to
be at any given moment in time. In this program you are never
coaxed into anything, and you are never put down for not being
honest or for not being compassionate. That would not be done by
us, nor the other group members, nor your partner. You always
hold the reins in your own hands. The point is that we believe that
in teaching you and your partner skills that are based on these
values, your own *desire* to be more honest, trusting, and compassionate with your partner will tend to gradually increase. Does this
raise any questions that you would like to discuss?

## Explaining the Group Process and Confidentiality

If a group format is being recommended to the clients, it
is explained along the following lines:

One of the reasons we conduct the training in groups is
economy: It enables us to teach more people in the same amount
of the leader's time, and makes more economical use of our physical facilities. For these reasons the cost is lower for you. The disadvantages of a group are that many participants feel more self-
conscious, awkward, and embarrassed in a group setting, particularly if they are contemplating discussing serious issues or conflicts
in their relationships at some point in the training program. These
are clearly disadvantages, which cause some people to hesitate
about entering the program in a group format.

However, there are also some significant advantages to the
group format, aside from economy. Many participants have told us
that they feel better about their own relationship when they see
that other people have similar problems and concerns. Then too,
seeing others express themselves in these areas of concern often
helps you to clarify your own thinking and to express yourself better. Also, as you and the others gain in skill, we teach you how to
help each other in further refining your skills, so that each of you
then gets help in learning and in applying the skills from the other
members of the group as well as from the leaders.

Although the group may seem threatening at first, after a

while the opposite feeling usually emerges. You come to gain a feeling of support and encouragement from the presence of the others and from the assistance they provide you in applying the skills you are learning.

Naturally, the leaders of the group keep everything that goes on in the sessions in the strictest confidence. All group members likewise must agree to maintain complete confidentiality. Is a pledge of maintaining confidentiality agreeable to you?

Another thing to consider when you think about group participation is that you use the skills at home as well as in the group. Therefore, it's possible to reserve exceptionally sensitive topics for discussion at home if you wish.

So, unless you have very strong feelings about it, we'd like you to try a group format. If after a trial period you prefer to work as an individual pair, that can be arranged. Even with people who had doubts before beginning, that choice is seldom made later on. What are your feelings about this?

## Dealing with Doubts About Making a Commitment

At this late phase in the interview, the clients most likely still to be reluctant to commit themselves to the program would be those with severe relationship problems, who believe that the program will not be strong enough medicine, so to speak, to be helpful to them. Some clients, for example, might doubt that they have the capacity to understand or work through their own problems; others may believe that they already "know" what their problem is and that it won't diminish as a result of greater understanding. In either case, they may believe that they need an expert who will tell them what to do or exactly how to solve their problem. (Sometimes, of course, they mean that they need someone who will tell their partner to straighten out.) We have discussed the circumstances in which other or additional programs might be recommended to clients. We will concern ourselves here only with those instances in which the interviewer does believe that an RE program would be very helpful to the clients, and the problem is that the clients lack an appreciation of how the method can work in terms of the specific kinds of problems they face or the extreme nature of their problems. In such cases the interviewer might pursue the following lines of inquiry with the clients.

Have each of the clients considered the positive feelings

that must lie buried from view under the negative feelings and relationship rubble? Generally, in an intimate relationship only feelings that were originally very *positive* have the power to later generate intense disappointment and animosity. The couple would not be present together in the interview were there not definite positive feelings and aspirations *somewhere* in the picture. When were positive perceptions and feelings concerning the other person last spoken about openly to one another? In the RE program, the participants will be trained and encouraged to look at *all* aspects of their feelings and problems. The complete picture includes the positive perceptions, wishes, and dreams from which the frustration and pain eventually were generated. Clients may be asked to consider whether sharing some of their positive views and hopes has been neglected in the recent past, and whether the RE program might not contribute something by bringing them back into the picture.

Is it possible that there are also other personal feelings, needs, or aspirations on the part of one or both parties that seem not to have been fully appreciated by the partner, and that, if fully understood and appreciated, might make problem solution more likely? For example, if there is an extramarital affair, has there ever been a sincere, thoughtful dialog in which each party really made an effort to fully explore what this affair was doing to and for the other? Have they been able to really examine what needs were being met by it (and/or what needs were being frustrated and mangled by it); what void it filled (and/or created)? Using the skills that the program can provide, they would be far more able to succeed in such exploration and in deciding what must be done. To take another example, one of a parent with a teenager who repeatedly gets into trouble with the authorities, lies, and runs away from home: Has each person ever really listened to the other at length and in depth about the needs, the frustrations, the anger, the anxieties that give rise to (or result from) such behaviors? Could not each of them gain something from knowing more about *himself* along these lines? Might not more mutually satisfying solutions be worked out if each one better understood the *other* along such dimensions? The skills involved in RE programs are designed to

create an interpersonal atmosphere that makes it possible to achieve such *self*-discovery and discovery of the *other* person and to promote the resolution of conflicts between them.

## Specifying Time Commitments and Options

We know that it will take about eight hours of concentrated practice before most clients begin to feel comfortable using the skills they are learning and, for some of them, it will be even longer before they can see positive effects. Therefore, we ask that they be willing to commit themselves to at least eight or ten hours of the program or not to enter it.

Another question is, "How long should the program continue?" Research in psychotherapy suggests that time-limited therapy offers advantages as well as disadvantages. The chief reason for the advantage, as we see it, is that a time limit makes everyone work harder and more efficiently and thus leads to quicker results. Also a time-limited program prevents people from staying in a program beyond the point of maximum impact for reasons that are only marginally justifiable: comradeship, sociability, good fellowship, a night out, something different to do, fear or guilt about terminating, and so on. On the other hand, it seems unnecessarily cruel, and even ethically questionable, to cut people off from a program that still seems to be helping the clients work toward relationship enrichment or problem solving with significantly more success than they could yet achieve on their own.

These observations have led to the following procedure, which is explained to the clients at this point in the interview. The basic skills training lasts for either twenty or thirty hours, depending on the type of program. Students are then free to *reenroll* either as a group, or as an individual couple, or to join another attenuated group for more training and supervision. People who seek only enrichment, or who have had long-standing and very deep-seated relationship problems, may well wish to terminate at the end of this first period. Those who wish to further perfect their skills, or who feel they could profit from further skill supervision as they work through serious problems,

or who wish to acquire skill in helping others, may reenroll for advanced programs: "Course II," "Course III," or more if they wish.

There are settings in which other arrangements would be preferable. If the clientele is such that groups could be set up knowing in advance the probabilities of short- versus long-term client needs, then couples experiencing severe relationship problems might best be encouraged to enroll for an initial course to last forty-eight hours, with the option of reenrolling for additional twenty-hour sequences thereafter.

In any case, it is our view that such a flexible yet timed approach offers the best of both worlds to the client. We call this a "time-designated" instead of "time-limited" program. Naturally, all this reasoning need not be explained to the client. The most important consideration in the initial interview is that the pair should understand: (1) that it will take a while before they can be expected to master the skills, and longer before they will benefit from them; (2) that, therefore, they should undertake the program only if they are prepared to stay with it for a minimum of $x$ hours; and (3) that they will be able to get assistance in using their skills to improve their relationship for as long as they wish.

### RE Intake Checklist

    I. Introductions and get-acquainted period

    II. Building rapport and trust—listen empathically to the problems, needs, and concerns of the clients

    III. Explaining the program

        A. Importance of communication
           (Questions or comments?)

        B. Importance of feelings
           (Questions or comments?)

        C. Importance of acceptance
           (Questions or comments?)

        D. Skill training as a therapeutic method
           (Questions or comments?)

IV. Introducing the behavioral modes

    A. Expresser

        1. Chooses subject area

        2. Speaks in regard to *own* feelings and perceptions

        3. Avoids talking about motives of partner, but focuses instead on behavior and resultant feelings

        4. Describes behaviors valued in partner and resultant feelings

        (Questions or comments?)

    B. Empathic responder

        1. No judgment of other's feelings; rather, a desire to learn and understand those feelings

        2. Empathy—try to see the situation from the other person's point of view

        3. Communication of acceptance and understanding

        4. Does not "lead" or divert with questions, advice, and so on

        (Questions or comments?)

    C. Mode switching

        1. Enables each participant to express his or her own feelings and perceptions, without having to "sit" on them long

        2. Allows each partner to share equally, frequently, and appropriately in the dialog

        3. Facilitates problem solving

        (Questions or comments?)

    D. Facilitator

        1. Active role while others practice

        2. Provides encouragement, support, and help

        3. Provides training for using behavioral modes at home

V. Demonstration of the program

    A. Role play an example of a moderate conflict that escalates under typical communication patterns

    B. Role play the same example using the skills to be taught in this program

    C. Discussion and comments regarding these demonstrations

VI. Homework for additional practice and generalization

VII. Specifying the underlying moral values

    A. Honesty

    B. Compassion

(Questions and comments?)

VIII. The group process and confidentiality

    A. Advantages of group meetings

        1. Efficient and economical use of time

        2. People learn from each other

    B. Confidentiality—a responsibility for leaders and participants alike

(Questions or comments?)

    C. The concentration is on the communication between partners, not on other group relationships. Other people's comments are limited to role facilitation only—no analysis or suggestions

(Questions or comments?)

    D. Everyone in the group starts at the same time

IX. Specifying time commitments and options

    A. Scheduling

        1. Frequency of meetings

        2. Length of meetings

        3. Number of meetings in the program—opportunity to reenroll

(Questions or comments?)

    B. Write down phone number, schedule of times available for meetings, and other relevant information

# Chapter 4

# Orientation and Objectives for Conducting Relationship Enhancement Sessions

⚬⚬⚬⚬⚬⚬⚬⚬⚬⚬⚬⚬⚬⚬⚬⚬⚬⚬⚬⚬⚬

The RE program leader is guided by educational goals. He wants to teach his students skills which will be useful in their daily lives. He wants to use the best methods possible to teach these skills. He is eager to help his students reach a level of knowledge and proficiency in which they can function without him.

### Teaching of Skills versus Direct Help

The RE program leader, since he follows an educational model, regards himself as someone who is teaching the participants skills that they will find useful in solving their problems. Because he does not follow a medical model, he does not perceive himself as being someone who helps them to solve their problems in any way *other* than through teaching these skills and supervising the participant's use of them. Accordingly, he *refrains* from utilizing any superior knowledge, skill, or expertise he may have that, rightly or wrongly, he believes might permit him to speed up problem resolution by means other than

75

teaching the clients. His major objective is to give skills to the clients that they can use to solve present conflicts and problems, to resolve future conflicts and problems, and to enhance their relationship. If the participants were to regard him as instrumental in problem solving, then to the degree that he is effective in this role, the clients would become dependent on him to solve their problems, and that would work in opposition to his goal of making them self-sufficient in such skills.

This philosophy is the opposite of the one subscribed to by most traditional psychotherapists and many behaviorists. Their orientation: (1) denies the viability of training their clients in the general principles and skills necessary to solve the widest possible range of problems; and (2) places responsibility for problem resolution by itself directly on the therapist or counselor. The behavior modifier David Knox, who subscribes to the traditional viewpoint, states it very clearly: "There is no behavioral recipe for marriage counseling. Each problem must be analyzed and treated individually. The innovative therapist will construct a specific treatment plan for his clients, as responsibility for appropriate modification lies with the counselor" (Knox, 1971, p. 34).

Like Knox, most practitioners of behavior modification have abandoned the *disease* model in dealing with clients' problems. They regard themselves as conditioners of behavior, and thus as teachers of a sort. They reject the notion that their primary task is to root out and neutralize the genesis (germ) or psychic shock (trauma) that underlies a specific difficulty (symptom). Nevertheless, like Knox, most behavior modification practitioners suffer from cultural lag and do adhere quite closely to the *medical* model in the manner in which they deliver services to clients: Although their adherence to learning theory makes it easy for them to abandon the typical one-to-one, diagnosis-prescription orientation toward clients that is modeled after the typical private practitioner of medicine, the great majority have not yet done so. Like the duckling who will follow a dog, if it was the only "mother" present at a critical stage of early development, they continue to follow the medical practitioner who was the *apparent* mother to the psychologist

when the psychologist emerged from the universities into the outside world. It is time that they recognize their true mother— the teacher.

In client-centered psychotherapy, the diagnosis-prescription aspect of the medical model has generally been abandoned. But there is no attempt by the therapist to *teach* his skills to clients in order to enable them to solve present and future problems on their own. In RE programs, it is the *participants* who are responsible for learning to do the same kind of thing that therapists have traditionally done. The leader does not act as therapist but as a teacher of therapeutic techniques, the exercise of which is the sole responsibility of the clients. Except for establishing rapport, generally, his use of therapeutic methodology is limited to the direct and so-labeled *demonstration* of these methods in order that the participants may consciously model themselves after him in the use of these techniques.

It seems that old models never die, or even fade away, unless new ones are seen as viable replacements. Most behavior modification practitioners and most client-centered therapists have not yet grasped the potential their theories afford them for modeling their service delivery system after the public educator instead of the private medical practitioner.

## Encouraging Independent Functioning

Within the educational model, the leader's goal is to work himself out of his job as quickly as he possibly can, leaving the participants to carry on relationship enhancement and personal growth processes of their own. In order to implement this purpose, he plays an extremely active role while the skills are being learned. In programs that last no longer than it takes to acquire the skills at an elementary level (twelve to sixteen hours of training), the leader would be extremely active throughout the entire program. In longer lasting programs (sixteen to fifty hours), wherein participants actually employ the skills to work on deep or chronic problems, the leader's role diminishes to that of a supervisor. In very long-running programs where group

members have achieved great expertise, the leader's role further diminishes to one of acting as a consultant and attending to administrative details. When that phase is approached, he should begin training others to take over the few remaining aspects of his functions that he has not already taught them. After that, if the group is to continue further, it can operate with a professional leader acting only as an occasional consultant. (We have not yet developed our programs to the point where we have acquired experience in this final, professionally leaderless group situation. However, it is a logical extension of the teaching philosophy involved, and we expect to develop some of our programs into this final stage in the future.)

The ultimate goal of RE programs is to make the participants capable of continuously resolving inevitable conflicts and problems in their relationships, and continually enriching the satisfactions they derive from them, independent of help not only from the professional leader, but also from other group members. The leader's orientation should be one that will enhance the growth of independence not just at some final stage, but one that envisages the necessity of such independence from the very beginning and that encourages its practice in a systematic and progressive manner.

## The Educational Attitude

We find that the adoption of attitudes consonant with the mentioned goals is difficult for students who have entered training with the traditional image of the mental health professional in mind, more difficult for professionals who have already been practicing in traditional modes, and still more difficult for professionals who have been practicing within a psychodynamic or diagnostically oriented framework.

Such trainees tend to regard people with problems not so much as people very much like themselves but as being emotionally crippled in some way. (We are excluding from this discussion people who are mentally ill as we would define them, that is, those whose major problems seem to stem essentially from a biochemical deficiency or imbalance of some kind.)

They do not look on clients simply as people whose pattern of life experiences has made them unhappy with themselves or made others dissatisfied with them. Rather, they tend to look on them as sick or as immature. With such a viewpoint, RE program trainees tend to find it difficult to think of their job as one of teaching the client new skills with which to change his own behavior (thereby changing the responses of others to him) or as one of restructuring the individual's interpersonal environment by providing ego-building, growth-enhancing behavioral skills to the people with whom he spends most of his time.

## Leader's Needs and Reinforcements

Instead of the urge to instruct and to engineer, many student and professional helpers seem to feel an almost overwhelming need to provide the direction, the nurturance, the succorance, the solution to the conflict or the problem. They want to be seen as providing immediate help and gratification to the participants.

To make things more insidious, from our point of view, the social conditioning that shapes helper-helpee roles makes it virtually impossible for the helper to realize just how ineffective he generally is in providing "help" via traditional methods. The practitioner using the traditional mental health model receives a vast amount of face-to-face reinforcement from his clients because of social desirability factors (not to mention the client's wishful thinking). Seldom is he aware of what happens after the helping relationship terminates, except in the successful cases— the only ones likely to maintain contact. It would be more than can be expected of humans for the helper to take into full account these social and selectivity factors when he assesses his own usefulness. It would be equally superhuman if he were often to think that the improvement he saw in his clients stemmed from natural restoration factors or to other events unrelated to his own endeavors. That is why therapists find it so hard to believe that the overwhelming lack of evidence that traditional helping methods generally do much good applies to *him* and to *his* clients, as well as to the *other* fellow and the *other*

fellow's clients. His own personal experience is, in fact, very much to the contrary and, being human, he cannot give full weight to the superficial, selective, and transitory nature of the feedback he personally has received.

Thus, in reality, the traditional mental health professional is socially reinforced (immediately, strongly, and frequently) for the approach he has taken with his clients—*whatever* that approach may have been. No wonder it is difficult for the traditional helping professional to abandon such immediate social rewards for the long-range ones that can be expected through skill teaching—especially since the educational approach has likewise not yet been convincingly validated, and certainly remains to be validated in his own personal experience.

The new student does not have this history of personal satisfaction and reward as an obstacle to adopting an educational orientation, but, as is fitting and proper, the typical aspiring mental health professional shares with his older colleagues strong personal needs to see himself as personally effective, influential, and helpful. These needs are met in the educator role. However, although they eventually may be much more substantial, they are not satisfied as immediately, as directly and as obviously in the role of educator as they are in the traditional roles of healer, supporter, and problem solver.

Perhaps it would be helpful to the prospective RE leader to consider that the most successful parents seem to be those who are able to gain satisfaction from providing skills to their children and then encouraging them to become progressively free of the need for parental nurturance, approval, and help—progressively more independent in their functioning. That is the kind of satisfaction for which the follower of an educational model must settle. He must be able to *avoid* patting himself on the back and feeling good when he has helped his client directly, and reserve his hearty self-congratulations for the time when he sees that he has taught somebody to help himself (or a loved one) independently.

We believe that another major reason underlying the lack of emotional appeal of this orientation, for those who do find it difficult to accept, is similar to the reason to be found in many

parents who are overprotective or overindulgent. They simply don't *trust* the capacity of those whom they wish to help to learn the same skills that the helper possesses or to apply these skills to their own lives. Once they acquire the necessary faith, based on factual information and data and, more importantly, personal experience, we believe that the great majority of mental health workers can make the necessary shift toward congratulating and reinforcing themselves for promoting independent functioning and skill in their clients in place of the older kinds of satisfactions.

We have presented our rationale and later will present experimental evidence that represents a first step toward providing a scientific basis for belief in client's capacities to learn, use, and benefit from the type of training we are talking about. We recognize that reasons and data can appeal only to the intellect. To assess our claim that powerful personal reinforcement *can* also be found by leading RE programs, we ask the experienced professional who is skeptical to learn the method well and give it a practical trial.

## Avoiding Unnecessary Diagnostic and Analytic Speculation

An RE leader should be able to identify a client who might be helped by medical (biochemical) intervention. If there is any question at all in the leader's mind about this and if the program leader is not an M.D., a referral should be made to a psychiatrist or internist. Also, we do not wish to discourage the leader from asking himself the question of whether a client's statement about his problems, or other observed behaviors, suggests that he may be in need of intensive individual psychotherapy in addition to his participation in an RE program. On occasion, diagnostic and psychodynamic speculation stemming from the need to make an immediate specific decision is entirely appropriate for an RE program leader.

The diagnostic attitude we *do* consider detrimental to efficient and maximally effective leadership of an RE group is one that is not clearly linked to a need to make an immediate specific decision. We recognize that it is difficult for leaders or

observers of RE groups to avoid considering irrelevant questions
when they are reviewing group processes. We are all tempted to
speculate about traditionally oriented diagnostic matters: Is he
manipulating her (him, me, us, them)? What's her mother like?
Is he being honest? Do you think she's having an affair? Does he
*really* want to leave his job? Is she a passive-aggressive person
(obsessive-compulsive, hysterical, frigid, or so on)? Entertaining
such questions usually is not appropriate in an educational program; they indicate the failure of a leader or supervisor to be
goal oriented and businesslike in pursuing his goals. It is up to
the client himself to use the skills provided to judge whether he
wants to speculate about what his own psychodynamics are and
to reach his own conclusions if he does. If a leader or supervisor
engages in such idle speculation, he is out of the educational
model. Engaging in such speculation is at best a waste of the
leader's precious time. Worse, it may well interfere with his or
her capacity to analyze his own leadership behaviors fully and
honestly, or with his ability to be fully empathic with certain
clients, thereby hindering his ability to teach them to be empathic with one another.

## The Educational Environment

All kinds of interpersonal environments have been used in
education: They each seem to have areas of strength and weak-
ness and perhaps work differently for different types of pupils.
We don't take the position that any one educational style or
setting will work best for all purposes or groups. We can only
point to what has worked for us and what we believe represents
a good compromise among the many, often conflicting, needs
one experiences in running an educational program. The orientation proposed here also has the advantage of being one that is
consistent with the principles being taught to the participants.

### *Acceptance and Respect*

Complete acceptance and respect for the participants is
absolutely essential in our approach. Equally essential is a belief

in the clients' abilities to reach decisions that are correct for them and for their relationship, once they have openly and honestly considered each others' ideas and feelings. In addition to showing acceptance in what he says, the leader employs all the nonverbal behaviors associated with interest, respect, acceptance, and trust—appropriate eye contact, body posture, frequent smiling, and so on.

### Friendliness, Warmth, and Informality

The leader attempts to create an atmosphere of friendliness and informality. He indicates his preference for putting everybody, including himself, on a first-name basis from the beginning. Groups sometimes meet around a table, but often simply sit in a circle of chairs. Coffee and cokes are generally available. We generally prefer not to take formal breaks in the sessions as this is often disruptive of the intensive emotional mood that has been established in the group. Rather, we encourage any member or leader to leave his seat or to leave the room for a few moments whenever he wishes to do so.

### The Leader's Appearance

We attach a fair amount of importance to the leader's attire in the early sessions. This is not because we have the slightest belief that clothes make, or even reflect, the man in a significant way. However, we regard dress as extremely loud nonverbal communication. In the early minutes or even hours of interpersonal contact between people, it may speak more loudly than any other form of nonverbal communication. Despite rapidly changing standards and norms in this area, we believe that what is communicated through dress exerts a very powerful interpersonal impact. This influence is all the more powerful and insidious because, generally, neither the sender nor the receiver of the messages is aware that attire is shaping interpersonal impressions. If the interactors were asked to account for their reactions to each other, the role of dress would be downplayed because it is socially undesirable in Amer-

ican culture to judge books—and people—by their covers. But consciously or not, until we have more to go on, we all probably do make initial judgments based on such superficialities.

Among other things, we believe that another's appearance and clothing influence the attitudes of all of us in terms of: how much faith we have in the competence of other people; how much we can trust them to understand us; how much we can trust them to treat us seriously and maturely; how much we can expect them not to behave in psychologically threatening ways; how much trust we can place on the value of their potential influence on our husband, our wife, or our child.

Are we saying that the leader should always dress "professionally," in the early stages of contact with clients? No. We're saying that the leader should try to assess as best he can what his dress will communicate to the particular people with whom he will be meeting. Sometimes the leader will know something about the life-styles of his clients that will help him to assess the potential impact his attire and grooming will have. At other times, he must base his judgment on generalities—on what would be the most likely reaction of people in a certain age group or socioeconomic class.

The important consideration is not how people of a certain age or social category themselves dress and groom. The important considerations are how they expect a professional helper or teacher to dress and whether deviations from such expectations will be viewed positively or negatively. Thus, while working-class clients may dress less formally themselves, in all probability they will regard deviations from traditional professional attire even more negatively than better dressed and groomed, more highly educated or affluent people would. At the present time, we believe that most clients over thirty-five are likely to react adversely to a leader's informal or unusual attire. Dating couples in college coming for a premarital program, on the other hand, are likely to react to a leader's informal attire with increased ease and trust. Dating couples from the same age group but from a conservative church setting, might well be as turned off by informal attire as would older couples. In a parent-adolescent program, the leader very often

needs to contend with probable conflicting reactions. More formal attire will tend to build quicker rapport and trust with the parents, and less formal or more modern attire might build better identification and trust with the teenagers. Some compromise is in order in such circumstances, but decisions should be weighed in favor of the members of the group with whom rapport is more tenuous—usually, but not always, the teenager. (Even in such circumstances, however, the most immediate and strongest danger of "turn off" may be with the parent, who often exerts greater *control* over whether or not the pair will decide to enter or remain in the program.)

In considering such equations, one should also keep in mind the fact that the age of the leader is very important in determining the expectations, and therefore the positive or negative reactions, of clients. Young leaders would not be expected, nowadays, to dress or groom themselves in the same manner as older ones; hence, the same attire would lead to different client reactions depending on the leader's age.

All of these observations about attire are, of course, simply hypotheses that we believe could be confirmed if appropriate measures and procedures could be devised to test them. Also, we do not wish to leave the impression that we consider the leader's appearance of *long-range* importance in running RE groups. They represent subtle and short-term concerns. Once clients become involved in the major procedures and objectives of the program, we believe gradual changes in the leader's appearance make no difference.

### Structure and Goal Orientation

A therapy or enrichment program that does not specify and operationally define the principles and overt behaviors that the participants are expected to learn, or that does not teach them in a systematic and orderly manner, does not fall within our definition of the educational model. To exemplify: sensitivity "training" and encounter programs do not, as we see it, fit this definition, while transcendental meditation and biofeedback programs do fit the educational model. The distinction is

not based on the degree of benefit we associate with any of these programs. Rather, it has to do with the clarity of goal definition for the client, the use of systematic, orderly methods to bring the participants closer to these goals, and reasonably clear-cut criteria by which the client can judge his progress.

As we said earlier, the range of educational methods is very wide and there is room for disagreement in such matters. Sensitivity training and encounter groups have made a tremendous contribution in increasing the public's receptivity to the idea that psychological services are appropriate for people without pathology. But if sensitivity training and encounter groups are intended to impart interpersonal skills and a capacity to consistently handle emotions in a constructive manner, and if the techniques and exercises that commonly are associated with them are to be viewed as belonging within the educational realm at all, then, from our point of view, they are best viewed as the equivalent of kindergarten experiences when contrasted with the kinds of systematic educational approaches now being developed in various parts of the country. Like kindergarten, such an experience could be considered as a sort of introduction to schooling-in-the-emotions, wherein participants indulge in emotionally and interpersonally stimulating games: emotional finger painting, you might say. And, like kindergarten, depending on the teacher, such an experience may lead the participants to feel positively toward further interpersonal, emotional education of a kind that is more rigorous, systematic, and more useful in everyday functioning.

Obviously, our own preference is for the more rigorous type of program. Thus, while the educational atmosphere we seek is one that is relaxed, friendly, and informal, it is also one that makes definite demands in terms of effort and requires systematic practice on progressively more difficult tasks, each of which builds on a previously developed level of proficiency. Participants are required to work at perfecting their skills outside as well as inside the classroom walls. The learning of skills, *not the content to which they are applied*, is always first and foremost in the mind and actions of the instructor.

In summary, the approach we favor is one that is highly

structured, systematic, task oriented, and designed to provide a capacity for continued use of the skills in daily life. We might add that the instructional methodology is one that systematically follows principles derived from three of the most widely respected theorists in psychology: Carl Rogers, B. F. Skinner, and Albert Bandura. As we understand them, the particular principles we have chosen from each are not contradictory. Rather, as some others have also found, they blend quite beautifully in practice. The Rogerian principles we follow have already been described: complete acceptance and respect for the participants and constant sensitivity to, and empathic acceptance of, their negative as well as positive feelings and thoughts. The debt our instructional program owes to Skinner and Bandura will become clear in future chapters as we go into greater detail about our specific instructional methods.

## The Relationship as Primary Client

As we have stated, the primary goal of dyadic RE programs is to enhance the relationship between the participating pair. Enhancing relationships in this context has been defined in terms of increasing honesty and compassion, which in turn increase trust and harmony. Achieving these goals does not always imply that the relationship will result in greater physical or even emotional proximity. For example, in the case of parents and teenagers, increasing empathic understanding, trust, and harmony might very well lead to an increased degree of independence and perhaps increase the chances of physical separation and psychological differentiation between the participants. As other examples: An honest, compassionate, mutual understanding and a more trusting relationship between a dating couple might sometimes result in a decision not to enter into a marriage, or an enhanced relationship between a married couple might lead to a decision to get divorced.

If such decisions truly were the result of a better relationship, it would mean that the decision was reached on the basis of a valid and sympathetic mutual understanding, rather than on the basis of misunderstandings, conflicts, animosities, and

vicious cycles of attack and counterattack or withdrawal. Also, a decision to increase legal, physical, and emotional distance sometimes augurs well, rather than poorly, for the *future* of the relationship. Given certain combinations of basic personal needs, values, and aspirations of the parties involved, increased distance may be the choice that will maximize the satisfactions that the parties can obtain from the relationship. (Of course, given the initial attractions and other bonding factors that usually develop within a dating or marital relationship, we would expect an RE program generally to lead to a strengthening of formal and proximital bonds, as well as relationship bonds, in the great majority of instances.) Whatever the eventual outcome may be in terms of the continuity of physical and emotional proximity, the leader's goal will always have been to enhance the quality of the relationship: to make the relationship more satisfying to the participants than it would have been without his intervention as a teacher.

In effect, the leader deals with three "clients" when he works with a dyad: the two clients and the relationship between them. The appropriate orientation for the leader is one that gives clear and constant priority to the third—to the relationship. The leader's goal is to serve the individual clients through, and *only* through, the relationship.

Helping the individual participants to resolve their own intrapsychic, emotional, and personal difficulties is not the primary purpose of most present RE programs. Clearly, programs for adults and adolescents based on RE methods could be developed with the intrapsychic improvement of one individual as the primary goal, just as filial therapy does for young children. In our view, the development of such programs would be a very worthwhile area for future development in the mental health field. We have elsewhere (Guerney, 1969) argued that such programs might be psychotherapeutically more effective than professional therapy. Moreover, on those occasions when one member of the pair *does* apply the skills he has learned to help the other with intrapersonal or interpersonal problems that lie outside of their relationship, this has an extremely favorable effect on the quality of the relationship. Clearly, there is an

interaction between the intrapsychic, intrapersonal, and non-relationship problems of each member of the pair on the one hand and relationship factors between the pair on the other hand. The quality of the individual's intrapsychic life affects the relationship, and the quality of the relationship affects the individual's intrapsychic well-being. Even when the primary goal is to help an individual, as in filial therapy or in prospective programs with older populations, the leader's resource for accomplishing this still lies in the interactions between the pair; that is, he strives to help the individual via the helping forces that can be harnessed within the relationship.

Despite the potential benefits of such programs, the primary purpose of the programs described in the present book is *not* to train the couples to act as psychotherapeutic agents for one another in areas beyond the relationship. Their capacity to do so, though it is a very definite and advantageous capacity, is a fringe benefit, not the major emphasis of the programs.

The orientation of focusing intensely on the relationship as the major "client" influences not only the content of RE programs, but also their structure. In the RE programs to be described here, we regard it as extremely important that the person-to-person interaction that is systematically reinforced be the interaction between the members of the natural pair. Thus, in the Conjugal Relationship Enhancement (CRE) program, we wish to reinforce husbands speaking and listening well to their spouse rather than to the leader or to other group members. Similarly, in the Premarital Relationship Improvement by Maximizing Empathy and Self-Disclosure (PRIMES) program, the flow of empathic understanding is channeled between the dating couples.

Except in emergency situations, the structure of the program activity diverts the direct flow of empathy away from group members (including the leader) who are not the natural partners. Not to redirect empathy so that it flows mainly between the natural partners would strengthen bonds other than the natural ones and result in lost opportunities to strengthen the empathic bonds between the primary couple. It is the natural dyad that is of maximum importance *outside* the group, and

this is the relationship that we wish to enhance. To have the members of a pair feel that they are understood and responded to as positively, or more positively, by members of the group *other* than their partner would work against one of the central goals of the programs. Also, in some instances, to encourage empathic responsiveness across pairs, or to encourage empathic responses directly from the leader rather than from a member of the natural dyad, can lead an individual to become convinced that many others are better sources of understanding and acceptance than is the natural partner. This may increase disillusionment and feelings of hopelessness in regard to the natural partner. Such problems can be avoided by emphasizing good communication between the members of the pair themselves rather than between members of different pairs.

We believe that the leader's adherence to procedures reflecting such an emphasis on the relationship represents an important difference between RE programs and more traditional therapeutic and/or educational group programs and provides one of its distinct advantages.

# Chapter 5

# General Methods
# for Conducting
# Relationship Enhancement
# Sessions

To be effective in conducting RE programs, the leader must be trained and skilled in a variety of techniques. His repertoire should allow him always to be sensitive to the needs, reservations, problems, and joys of each of the participants, so that he can guide them into a greater understanding of themselves and of others with whom they seek improved relationships. In this chapter we discuss those leadership skills that are an essential part of the understanding and behavior of the person who leads an RE program.

### Influencing Client Attitudes

By the phrase, *influencing client attitudes*, we mean the kinds of things a leader says and does to present the RE program and its various procedures in a maximally convincing, yet completely fair and open, way, so as to permit the client to make the best decision in light of his own needs, judgment, and experience. The purpose of such elucidation may be to motivate

a client to try something new or different or to help him to
resolve doubts of one kind or another.

Although an RE program demands a drastic change in
habitual patterns of verbal interaction and one might therefore
infer that it demands a similar drastic change in underlying attitudes, we find that this is not the case. The attitude that perceptions and feelings should be shared honestly, openly, and with
compassion is easily accepted by almost all participants.

Although many people might fear the open expression of
negative feelings, this fear is not often aroused in introducing
RE programs to clients. There are a number of reasons for this.
One reason is the absence of any emphasis on the need to "tell
your partner everything." Participants are assured that they will
not be urged to discuss anything that would make them feel
uncomfortable or embarrassed. Also, those couples who seek
the program to enhance an already satisfactory relationship are
not much worried about negative feelings, while those that have
a troubled relationship generally are already expressing negative
feelings in obviously destructive ways. It is not too difficult for
the latter type of client to see that the *manner* of expressing
negative feelings could be much improved by the skills encom-
passed in the expresser mode.

Doubt about the desirability of expressing negative feelings sometimes occurs when a member of the pair tends to use
withdrawal as a means of dealing with his hostile feelings. Even
here, however, it is not difficult to make both members of the
pair see that the mutual negative consequences of such withdrawal are greater than the negative consequences of expressing
negative perceptions and feelings, provided this expression is
done in a constructive way: a way, as we like to put it, that is
designed to *"maximize the message and minimize the malice."*
It is only necessary in such an instance to highlight for the
couple things of which generally they are already aware: that
suppressed needs and feelings have a way of coming out indirectly anyway, and that the indirect penalties to the relationship are therefore eventually greater than would arise from conveying specific concerns in a constructive manner. Often, when
the true nature of the difficulty is not faced, the problem will

exert negative effects over a longer period of time, and perhaps even begin a vicious cycle that draws the couple further and further apart.

It may very well be that there are couples who have a stable and satisfying relationship based on taciturnity and emotional distance with which they would be loath to tamper. We would not be surprised, for example, if many parent-adolescent relationships were of this nature, or if this were also true of the relationships between some married couples who grew up in less affluent times or in more restrictive subcultures. But we have not encountered serious resistance based on a desire to preserve distance and to limit communication. Thus the leader's influence is mainly a matter of making explicit and reinforcing attitudes the clients already hold.

The leader's task is, first, to help the participants see that a *failure* to communicate needs, wishes, and feelings, or *distorted* or malicious communication, will reduce chances of resolving disagreements and conflicts and will lead to more frustration and greater hostility, conflict, and estrangement. Second, the interviewer should spell out the *advantages* of communicating hopes, expectations, perceptions, needs, and feelings in such a way as to maximize the chances that they will be given full and fair consideration by the partner. The advantages are a greatly increased probability: that hopes will be more nearly realized; that there will be greater satisfaction of needs and a greater feeling of being understood, considered, respected, and loved; and that, as a result, it is possible to obtain not only a more enjoyable relationship, but a relationship that will foster each person's growth as an individual.

## Methods of Influencing Attitudes

There are several methods that the leader can use to try to clarify these points and thus increase clients' willingness to put forth the effort necessary to participate and to succeed in the program.

The first is to provide as much of the *rationale* as seems necessary. How much elaboration or exemplification is neces-

sary should be judged by the verbal and nonverbal cues provided by the participant who understands least or is the most
doubtful.

The second, and probably the much more important,
method is *role playing* by the leaders of one or more examples
of family conflict situations meaningful to the pair.[1] The role
playing should demonstrate as realistically as possible the way
that communication patterns can lead to the types of difficulties mentioned earlier, and how the use of the communication and problem-solving skills taught in the program can lead
to a more satisfying and hopeful outcome.

A third method used to encourage clients to undertake or
continue a RE program or a specific technique that is part of
the program is simply to present *factual data*. Such data may be
based on the leader's own experience with other participants. It
is easy for us to draw on such data because the reports of clients
have been so favorable, regardless of the level of doubt they
originally expressed about the method in general or any of the
specific techniques used.

For those who do not yet have a backlog of such experience to draw on, the empirical data presented later in this book
represents appropriate source material to share with clients. It
seems appropriate to share the fact with clients that there is research evidence, as well as clinical evidence, that indicates that
they are likely to find the program useful and rewarding, and
that to date such evidence is at least on a par with, and generally exceeds, scientific evidence as to the efficacy of any other
approach to enhancing intimate relationships.

The fourth approach we use to influence attitudes is to
suggest that the doubtful client try it out and judge for himself

---

[1] If there is only one leader present, appropriately selected audio- or
videotapes may be played for the participants. One way for an agency to
establish an appropriate collection of tapes is to tape all sessions in which
two leaders have participated. Role-playing segments can then be re-
recorded on separate cassettes and indexed according to the type of RE
program and the type of situation role played. Alternatively, a leader
may wish to use a set of tapes of this nature that has been prepared
by the author.

on the basis of actual experience. Of course, we prefer to enlist people's effort on the basis of winning over their minds through providing rationale, demonstration, and evidence as outlined above. However, in our view, there comes a time in some discussions about a program or technique when any one of a number of things may happen that is best handled by an appeal to try things out first and reserve judgment until later. You may find, for example, that a stalemate has been reached; that you and the client are repeating yourselves over and over; that much time is being wasted because you and/or the client are discussing things on an abstract plane. Or, not infrequently, you might believe that the client is reluctant to face the risk of a poor performance of a new skill in public; and so, instead of performing, the client engages at length in formulating intellectually interesting and/or challenging questions to whet your didactic appetite. In such instances, action and experience, or a concrete trial to serve as a basis for discussion, might break the intellectual logjam and open a new pathway for exploration. These are times for the leader to say, in effect, "Try it. You'll like it."

Adherents of some schools of psychotherapy argue that therapists should concentrate on changing a client's *attitudes* and beliefs (for example, about himself), believing that this is the best route to enduring and satisfying changes in client behavior. Others believe that therapists should concentrate on inducing the client to try out new *behaviors* with the idea that this is the best route to bringing about enduring and satisfying changes in the person's attitudes and beliefs (for example, about himself). We believe that attitudes and behaviors deserve about an equal measure of attention, and that the most effective programs for bringing about change consciously work at both attitudinal *and* behavioral levels, using one level to assist in changing the other in an alternating, complementary fashion. At any rate, the approach, "Let's try it, and then let's talk later," often seems to be very useful in saving time and eventually in influencing attitudes.

We again wish to stress the fact that these attitude-influencing methods should be used in conjunction with full sensitivity to nonverbal as well as verbal cues that reflect client

doubts and the conveyance to the client of empathic understanding and respect for those doubts. The methods that fall under the attitude-influencing category are very important during the intake session, and then on a progressively diminishing basis in the early training sessions. After six to eight hours of practice, most clients have sufficiently experienced the benefit, or can anticipate the benefits, of using the skills so that these leadership methods are no longer required.

## Demonstration and Modeling

In RE programs, the group leader never asks a participant to attempt any behavioral skill until the group leader has demonstrated the behavior. Conversely, the leader strives to avoid modeling any behaviors that he wishes the participants to avoid. Thus, ideally, the group leader models freely and frequently the kinds of behaviors he wishes the participants to follow and, as much as he possibly can, he avoids modeling those behaviors that he wishes to discourage among the participants.

We believe that the best and most efficient way to help a person understand himself and honestly share his innermost thoughts with others is to create the kind of understanding and accepting environment that will make him *feel safe* to do so. We believe that making value judgments, making broad generalizations about a client's character, analyzing his motives, or telling him how to solve his problems are procedures that are generally counterproductive in terms of encouraging honest and open communication. We believe that behaviors, such as those just cited, tend to work against the creation of a subjectively safe and secure interpersonal climate. Thus, we do not believe that such behaviors by the leader generally are desirable even aside from other considerations.

However, even if we believed such behaviors were helpful coming from the leader, we would want to discourage the leader from engaging in such behaviors because we would not wish him to model such behaviors for the clients. They certainly would not be able to engage in them with the same degree of objectivity, caution, and expertise as the leader. If the leader engaged

in these behaviors, he would have to say to the clients, in effect, "It's OK for me to do this, but not for you." Given the natural tendency and inclination for students to follow the example of their teachers, we believe that this would create confusing and conflicting tendencies within the group members, and that it is best for the leader to avoid such behavior entirely.

Generally speaking, the procedure of providing a participant with a more suitable (that is, mode appropriate) response than he himself has been able to give, and suggesting that he try it out, is what we mean by "modeling" in RE programs. Such modeling is used extensively, especially in the early training. For example, in the early hours of training, the leader will very often model entire sentences for the responder to make to the expresser *before the responder even attempts to provide his own response.* (The rationale for this will be discussed later.) Later, the leader more often will suggest only certain key words or phrases to the client. These key words or phrases provide the client with phrases to replace or supplement his own inadequate response. Both the more complete and the more limited kinds of modeling responses are used by the leader throughout the program as major instructional and supervisory techniques. Modeling responses diminish only to the extent that the general activity of the leader diminishes as the participants attain a consistently high level of performance.

### Structuring

Structuring is a statement or question that reminds the clients of the characteristics of the skills or of other procedures, such as those related to homework, handing in certain forms, and so on. In setting forth such principles and requirements, it is extremely helpful to be as specific as possible and to anticipate and head off ("structure out") all conceivable potential misunderstandings and difficulties. Take, for example, the area of homework. We often have found it ineffective simply to say to clients, "We'd like you to set an hour aside this week to work together on such-and-such a homework assignment." Although it pains most leaders to spend the time doing it with each par-

ticipant, we have found a much higher rate of compliance if, at the time of making the assignment, the leader structures the task to the extent of working out a specific day, hour, and sometimes even a specific place for doing the assignment. To provide variation and to provide participants a sense of mastery, occasionally it is desirable to use questioning techniques to draw more skillful responses from the participants. The questioning may be general (for example, "What is her feeling?") or specific (for example, "Is she annoyed?"). Questioning techniques should be limited to situations where the leader is completely confident that the client will be able to come up with the desired answer immediately. If the client is not able to answer the question immediately and correctly, his confidence and motivation will be shaken rather than enhanced. If a client does not answer with ease, the leader will know that he should have modeled, not queried.

We find it a particularly poor didactic technique to have the leader *repeatedly* trying to draw a certain response from a client: The client tends to feel frustrated and embarrassed or even belittled. Thus: *Don't ask unless you think you'll get a good answer*; model instead. And, *if you ask and don't succeed, DON'T* try again; model instead.

## Graded Expectations

The skills that the clients are learning are almost always entirely new behaviors for them and, moreover, actually antithetical to behavioral patterns they have used for a lifetime. The leader should make it clear that he appreciates this fact and should show his understanding of the difficulties involved in learning these skills. It is important to do so in order to avoid having participants feel discouraged and inadequate. To maintain high levels of client motivation, it is important that the participants meet or exceed the expectations of the group leader, and of each other, so that they can feel they are succeeding. The feeling of success keeps motivation high and enhances actual achievement.

To keep his own expectation at appropriate levels, the

group leader must be fully cognizant of individual differences in learning speed. It is important that *each individual*, not just the group on the average, *meet or exceed the leader's expectations* and thus obtain a sense of success. For each individual, the leader should expect a performance at, or only slightly above, the level of that particular participant's last performance on a task of comparable difficulty.

In the earliest phases, the group leader should feel quite satisfied if an individual in the responder mode simply can concentrate on what the expresser is saying and avoid expressing his own point of view or reactions. Once an individual has consistently managed to avoid being judgmental, expressing his own judgment or opinions, or asking questions, the leader can raise his expectations one more notch. He then would hope merely to see the participant accurately restate the content of his partner's statement in an accepting way. Once a participant has been able to perform at this level, the group leader should begin to expect the responder to attend to *any* of the feelings being expressed directly by the expresser and to show acceptance of those feelings. After the responder has been able to perform at this level, the group leader can raise his expectations again and begin to expect the responder to clarify even those feelings that are *implicit* in the speaker's remarks or that are expressed nonverbally.

The leader demonstrates the same sort of patience and gradual raising of expectations with respect to all other behaviors being taught and, in fact, has even more modest expectations with respect to expresser and facilitator performance than for responder performance in the first twenty hours of training.

It is important to note that in the RE training procedures, it is only the *leader's expectations* that begin at low levels, not the *learner's behavioral task*. There is *not* a sequential chain wherein, for example, the client first is asked to provide only nonverbal attentiveness and warmth cues for the expresser, and then for another period of time only to provide restatement of content, then only to restate obvious feelings, and finally to provide responses that clarify the most significant underlying feeling of the expresser. The learner's behavioral task is set forth

*as a whole at the highest level* from the very beginning. And the responses that are demonstrated and modeled by the leader are always at the highest, most understanding, most empathic level the leader can provide.

Experience in training many hundreds of students in professional training and clients from the community has demonstrated to our satisfaction that for the average client it is more comprehensible, more motivating, more satisfying, and more efficient to demonstrate skills at the highest level at the outset and to set the client's task as one of providing the most empathic response possible, right from the very beginning. Doing so creates problems only when the leader's expectations of performance are too high, resulting in insufficient praise, or the use of feedback methods that the client perceives as criticism.

The attempt to master the whole thing at once seems to reduce the inevitable feeling of artificiality and to generate a greater feeling of accomplishment. It is more efficient, because it eliminates the problem of first deliberately teaching a skill (for example, simple restatement of content) that is something one wishes the client to regard as a rather poor response at a later stage of training. Secondly, we find that for many people the concentrated effort to provide a fully empathic response automatically engenders most of the desirable nonverbal responses. Also, excessive conscious concentration on body posture and facial expression by the responder often acts to interfere with the effort to be fully empathic in terms of understanding and accepting content and feeling. We find that nonverbal cues of acceptance can be made to fall into place at a level we deem entirely satisfactory through vicarious reward procedures, occasional modeling, and structuring. Much instructional time is saved by not teaching nonverbal acceptance cues to clients as a skill unto itself, unless it proves necessary to do so. (More about this later.)

With the global task set for them, a surprising number of individuals can master high levels of empathic skill in the first twelve hours or so of training. It would be a great waste of time and a source of frustration to chain such individuals to a slower rate of progress. Also, without permitting these faster learners

to progress, the slower group members would lose the modeling and incentive the rapid learners can provide.

We feel sure, however, that asking the clients to perform at the highest levels from the beginning would not work well if the leader did not offer liberal praise first on the basis of simple *avoidance* by clients of certain typical response patterns and then increase his standards for praise very gradually. For each individual in the group, anything that is a shade better than what occurred in the last response, or that must have been a difficult one for him to make, must be a source of satisfaction to the leader so that he then can communicate this satisfaction to the learner. Otherwise, the sense of frustration and failure expressed by even one or two members might well lead to resistance that will effect the whole group. If the leader sets his sights too high, he will be an impatient teacher; he will fail to be generous with empathy, encouragement, and praise; and he surely will be a failure as an RE leader.

Thus, the attitudinal keys to good RE group leadership include graded expectations and accepting the responsibility *oneself* for the progress that each member achieves or fails to achieve—rather than blaming or being irritated with any client's lack of progress. These attitudes should be cultivated as prerequisites to the use of social reinforcement methods.

## A Defense of Reinforcement

Verbal and nonverbal praise of a student for good performance is part of a teacher's natural response repertoire. Very seldom is it challenged as an appropriate teaching and feedback response within a scholastic context.

Why is it, then, that we here feel the need to defend the application of this operant method as one of the important teaching methods used in RE programs? It is because we sense that a great many of our readers who are most enthusiastic about the objectives we wish to accomplish for our clients are precisely those whose teeth may be set on edge by the deliberate and conscious use of operant methodology as part of the guidelines we provide for group leadership. Why should adher-

ents to our own central goals object to this particular method of helping clients to reach them? Because the central goals include the open, honest, relatively spontaneous sharing of feelings, they include a refusal to treat the other as object, and a desire, instead, to treat the other as a person whose perceptions, needs, and feelings deserve consideration on a par with one's own. The conscious application of operant principles strikes many as involving precisely the opposite qualities: inner goals known to one party and hidden from the other; a lack of honesty and spontaneity in responding to the other; focusing on the other person's overt actions only, not on his perceptions, needs, and feelings; in short, treating the other as an object to be manipulated.

We have said that we believe that the teaching methods should be made as consonant as possible with the objectives of the program. Hence we feel the need to address this issue. As an answer to the objections just stated, we find little merit in the reply that "The ends justify the means, and operant techniques are the most efficient means." We would feel uncomfortable using this rationale because we have observed that people who use it very often are ultimately revealed to have given insufficient thought to the nature of the ends they are seeking and no thought at all to possible side effects. Further, if the means are unclean, we are not sure we would want to dirty ourselves in order to help somebody else reach good goals. Finally, we believe that the means really cannot be separated from the ends: In some measure, the means always shape the nature of the ends achieved.

We find somewhat more merit in the argument that "People are bound to use many spontaneous punishing and rewarding responses in their interactions with others anyway, so why not make conscious deliberate, organized, and more goal-directed use of such responses?" It is certainly true that we are always trying consciously and unconsciously to influence one another to behave, think, and feel more in accord with our wishes. The question, "Why not do it well, instead of poorly?" therefore, is not completely unreasonable as a counterargument to the criticism about manipulating people and treating them as objects. But it does seem to miss the heart of the objection.

The heart of the objection to the planned use of operant technology, so far as the charge of manipulativeness is concerned, seems to lie with the following argument: "You are setting yourself above the person, as someone who knows what is best for him, and you are using covert, hidden methods to influence his behavior. That is manipulative." This charge would be a legitimate one if it were not for our adherence to the educational model from the very beginning to the very end of an RE program. We will attempt to answer the challenge issue by issue.

First, it is true that we are setting ourselves "above" the client; but only in the sense of having knowledge of certain skills not known to him. We do not suggest to him that he is sick, immature, maladjusted, or otherwise inferior in any way, nor are any of the procedures based on such an assumption. The leader does not attempt in any way to put himself above the client, to encourage the client to view him as an authority figure, or to make the client more prone to the effects of suggestion.

Second, we do not believe that we have put ourselves in the position of "knowing what is best for the client." At the earliest possible time, we have specified and explained to the client the goals of the program, the underlying values on which they are based, and the probable interpersonal consequences of the program. The client has chosen to participate in the program with such understanding. *There are no goals of the leader that have not been shared with, and accepted by, the client.*

The third point has to do with using covert methods (hidden contingencies) to manipulate the client's behavior. We do not see RE methods as manipulative. It is implicit in the unwritten educational contract that we establish with the client that we will use whatever effective methods we can use to teach them certain skills. Since the limited application of the operant methods are used *only* to further the teaching of the goals understood and sought by the client, they are not being used manipulatively. Further, the operant techniques employed in RE are not covert; the group leader offers a brief explanation of the operant principles he will be using in the training, just as he explains his use of demonstration, modeling, and other instructional dynamics. We do not believe such an explanation hinders

the effectiveness of the reinforcement procedures or the general effectiveness of the program in any way. (We might also add that we heartily approve of programs to teach operant principles to intimate pairs. We do believe, however, that such clients also should be taught the dangers to the relationship in attempting to use such skills in a manipulative manner, as opposed to using them to implement mutually developed and agreed-on goals based on an understanding of the needs and feeling of both parties. We see reinforcement training as being most useful when it follows a program designed to facilitate good communication.)

There is one other underlying objection that we think many potential RE group leaders may have about consciously using operant principles. It has to do with a reluctance to exert as much conscious control over their *own* responses as seems to be required by the consistent use of operant principles. Insofar as it does not impede progress, they want to be as spontaneous and as genuine as possible and to avoid artificiality in the way they relate to clients. We do not disagree with such goals. What we try to do in our leadership training is to change the way the leader will *want* to react to RE clients. We try to convince the potential RE program leader of the appropriateness of operant principles to the teaching role. We want him to become *uninhibited* in his use of praise; we want him to incorporate into his own teaching style the frequent, *spontaneous* use of reinforcing remarks and gestures. This is the reason that so much attention was devoted earlier to the leader's own expectations.

Our goals for our clients are *not* to have them apply a thin veneer of empathic compassionate responses to their partner, but to *become* genuinely more empathic in their attitude and outlook as a result of understanding how rewarding and satisfying this can be in their relationship. The goal with the trainees is similar. We do not want them to *force* themselves to reinforce clients more frequently, we want them to *feel* like it. If they learn how to do it and *try* it, we are confident that this will be a rewarding experience, which will become progressively more a part of their spontaneous teaching behavior.

As we view it, some of the major obstacles trainees must

face on their way toward more frequent and spontaneous use of praise and reinforcement are: holding expectations that others can modify their behavior more quickly and easily than they really can; judging people according to final product standards instead of their previous level of performance; and personal inhibitions about praising others. Such obstacles make a leader less effective in helping others learn new skills. Our major goal for our leader-trainees is not to make them reinforcing machines, but to have them become more sensitive to and more *genuinely* appreciative of small steps that clients make toward their goals and more *spontaneous* in expressing such genuine appreciation through positive feedback to clients about such progress.

## Social Reinforcement

As we have been saying, social reinforcement is a basic educational method in RE programs. However, the leaders do not keep behavioral data nor ask the clients to do so. We consider it not only unnecessary, but generally detrimental to the successful running of RE groups. The cultural backgrounds of most people who have not studied psychology often leads them to be turned off by empirical and mechanistic methods of that kind. It is not too long into the sessions before the process of working through relatively heavy emotional issues by using RE techniques reaches a position of emotional importance to the participants that equals the importance of perfecting their skills by itself. At such times, the obtrusiveness of empirical and mechanistic learning aids would be aversive. Consequently, we do not use rating scales and counting techniques as a routine method of skill instruction.

In this section and in later sections we will cover the principles pertinent to social reinforcement used in the program in sufficient detail to meet the needs of aspiring RE program leaders. For those to whom this school of thought is completely new, however, it would be advantageous to acquire a deeper and wider understanding of operant principles as set forth by B. F. Skinner and the behavior modification theorists. Such under-

standing can be acquired through any of the numerous training manuals that are now readily available. We should say, however, that our view of what is occurring when one uses social reinforcement does not necessarily jibe in all respects with the view of Skinner or the behavior modifiers.

We make a sharp distinction on a theoretical level between learning and performance. We view reinforcement as the major influence underlying *performance*, while we view it as a relatively weak instructional technique for human beings. Learning, as we use it, refers to the *capacity* to perform an act at will. In a sense, our definition says that all learning is best viewed as *latent* learning and is best measured by methods developed to test for latent learning; frequency of performance in our view is largely irrelevant as a measure of what, in fact, an individual *knows* how to do. For example, by watching James Bond movies we have learned pretty well how to garrot somebody, even though we have never done it, and never will. From our point of view *most* of the client learning that takes place in the RE program takes place via the educational methods described in the sections on influencing attitudes, modeling, and didactics—*not* via reinforcement. Granted, providing the clients with social reinforcement—a remark or gesture that indicates that you are pleased with his performance and that therefore presumably is satisfying to the learner—does, in our view, make some contributions to learning by itself. That is, it makes a contribution to the person's intellectual *capacity* to perform in a certain way. It does so because the satisfying experience: causes the person to focus more *attention* on what he has done to merit the reward; causes him to try to capture the *principle* behind the performance that has earned the reward; and by giving it greater emotional significance than it otherwise would have, the reward increases the likelihood that he will *remember* the behavior and the principle. In these respects, social reinforcement makes *some* contribution to the person's capacity to reproduce at will behavior that has earned him social reinforcement, and therefore it makes some contribution to his learning of skills. However, in terms of making a contribution to the learning process by itself, as we have defined it, the significance

of social reinforcement is pale in comparison to explanations and demonstrations.

The way in which methods of operant instruction *does* make a major contribution to the instructional program is by increasing the *positive feeling* the clients have about themselves as learners and as performers of the skills in question. It makes them look more favorably on the leader and on the program. It keeps up their spirit in the face of performing a difficult task. It motivates them to try harder in order to win more approval. It enhances their desire both to improve and to *use* the skills they learn. It is mainly in keeping clients' motivation to learn, to improve, and to perform that social reinforcement makes its contribution. Until such time as the skills are thoroughly incorporated into the client's behavior and he has had ample opportunity within and outside of the formal training sessions to see how well the skills serve (reinforce) him in enhancing his relationships, such reinforcement by the leader is an essential ingredient of a successful RE program. What are the social reinforcement skills and principles that the RE leader will find most important?

### A Repertoire of Socially Reinforcing Responses

The leader should have a large repertoire of reinforcing phrases, ranging from mild to very strong. He should always be ready to use the strongest ones he feels comfortable using for a given client act. The leader, furthermore, should express his sincere appreciation of the clients' effort, self-discipline, perseverance, and so on, in longer and more detailed statements. The leader also needs to develop an ease in expressing approval nonverbally through head nodding, hand and finger gestures, facial expression, knee and shoulder patting, and so forth. We will go into this in greater detail in the technique section.

Theoretically, the leader does not know what is or is not reinforcing for a given client unless and until he sees what does or does not increase the desired behaviors. In practice with RE groups, this has proved nothing to worry about. The leader should not be thrown off the reinforcement track even with respect to the rare person who actually *says* he is uncomfortable

with the praise and does not want praise, but only critiques of his performance. Although the leader should change the form of his praise, or slow down a bit, a leader who takes such statements at face value does so at his own peril. In our experience, the unusual person who protests that what he really wants is criticism responds even more poorly to negative feedback than do most other people.

### Frequency

The leader needs to know that frequency of praise is important, and the more often he legitimately can provide praise, the better. While every bit of slight improvement is to be reinforced, the leader should bear in mind that it is not *only* improvement that is to be reinforced. As long as the leader is using other teaching techniques such as modeling, he can also afford to reinforce liberally those acceptable behavioral acts that already have attained reasonable stability in a client's repertoire. He simply needs to reinforce the newer, "best" responses even more enthusiastically than the reasonably good ones. In other words, unless a leader has been trained and is highly practiced in the art of social reinforcement, he should not worry about such things as intermittent reinforcement, partial reinforcement, ratio reinforcement, fading-out reinforcement, and other operant techniques that call for *withholding* reinforcement. Experience has taught us that leaders without extensive practice in the use of verbal reinforcement who worry about these refinements in RE programs invariably fail to provide sufficient reinforcement to their clients.

In long-term groups, when the participants have their skills well perfected, the content of the dialogs is generally so absorbing to the leader as well as to the client, that a fading-out process eventually occurs naturally as leaders sense that participants are clearly deriving the necessary rewards from the resolution of problems or the enhancement of the relationship through the use of the skills and that it is not necessary to help them to master and remember the principles, or to motivate them by reinforcement.

We believe, although we have not run across a discussion of this in the behavioral literature, that—partial reinforcement considerations aside—it is possible for a reinforcer to inflate his social reinforcement currency. That is, by making it too frequent and too easy to come by, social reinforcement from him eventually will not have the same amount of emotional impact and thus not "buy" the same degree of habit strengthening as would praise from a less liberal reinforcer. As we say, we do believe this can and does happen to some degree. However, in our experience in training hundreds of students and professionals, many of whom were familiar with behavior modification techniques, and a few of whom were skilled behavior modifiers, when a problem has existed, it has *always* been one of getting new group leaders to reinforce sufficiently, and *never* one of a needing to strengthen an inflated, social reinforcement currency by slowing down the rate of production of the leader's praise.

### *Proximity*

Another important reinforcement principle for the leader to bear in mind is that of proximity. The closer in time the reinforcement to the behavior to be reinforced, the more effective it is likely to be. Nonverbal reinforcement, and brief reinforcing phrases, can be inserted even in the middle of a client's sentence while the client continues to speak. Such reinforcements are of special importance and effectiveness by virtue of the time proximity principle. More lengthy statements to clients of encouragement and praise for effort, for discipline, self-restraint and/ or for skilled performance can be made when a couple is mode switching, or when the focus of attention is about to shift to a different couple. These more lengthy statements are extremely useful in providing the gratification that fuels a continuing high level of motivation. They also allow the leader to specify at greater length precisely what he finds praiseworthy. However, they cannot serve as a *substitute* for frequent, brief, high-proximity social reinforcement for specific verbal and nonverbal acts by clients.

*Reinforcing Generalization*

The need for social reinforcement extends beyond the clients' actions within the sessions themselves. Systematic reinforcement for completion of assignments also is a vital ingredient in leading RE programs. It is not enough simply to assign homework or practice tasks and to suggest that generalization of skills to home situations will be useful. Until the habitual use of skills is established firmly enough to provide their own rewards consistently, the skills will be practiced only in proportion to the systematic attention and reinforcement the leader provides.

It has been our observation that many clinicians, sensitivity trainers, and so on are far too optimistic about the spontaneous occurrence of generalization in their work. It certainly happens in some cases: Some clients put the bit in their mouths and run. But in most cases, a client does only what the leader assiduously encourages him to do and reinforces him for doing; in the case of RE programs, this initially includes homework and the generalization of skills to everyday life in the home.

Thus, at the beginning of each session, valuable time is devoted to a report by each pair about the performance of their home assignments and the use of the skills outside of the group session. In the beginning, it is one of the least pleasant aspects of the program for leaders and clients alike. It is too schoollike and teacherlike for most people's taste. Another reason it is unpleasant is that some clients will not have done their homework and will have to report the fact that they have not, an event that is aversive to both the students and the teacher. That is as it must be under the circumstances. But this sort of aversive conditioning is not what the leader relies on to increase home practice and performance.

The leadership methods that are relied on to increase home performance are: (1) careful help in structuring the task and the manner and setting for its completion, which has been mentioned earlier; (2) reinforcement; and (3) vicarious reinforcement. The same methods that applied to session behavior—

praising continued efforts, and praising improvements—applies also to the straightforward reinforcement of home assignments. Thus, there is only one principle that requires some elaboration at this time—the principle of vicarious reinforcement.

### Vicarious Reinforcement

In our setting, the results of vicarious reinforcement are that individual A, on seeing individual B's behavior of a certain act reinforced (that is, praised), becomes more likely to perform that act himself (to win similar praise). The reinforcement of individual B thus not only serves to increase the desired behavior in B, but also in A. That is one of the great, and often overlooked, advantages of working with more than one individual at a time. In our view, vicarious reinforcement is a powerful motivational tool that can be explained from a variety of perspectives. First of all, it acts to increase learning for A as well as B by focusing *attention* on the act, thereby increasing the participant's understanding of the nature of the behaviors being taught. Secondly, it enhances the emotional importance of the desired behavior, making it more likely to be *remembered.* And, more importantly, it increases A's *motivation* to perform the act because in effect it demonstrates to him that he can satisfy some of his own emotional needs for approval by doing as B did.

Perhaps the primary reason for being aware of the applicability of vicarious reinforcement to this situation is that it allows the leader to know and to feel that he is indeed instructing and influencing A by how he reacts to B. This reduces the pressure the leader might otherwise feel to deal with poor performance from A by behaving aversively toward A, which is something leaders should try very hard to avoid.

Being conscious of the potency of vicarious reinforcement serves the same function in another vital area. Leaders in training are often tempted to point out to a responder his weak or nonaccepting nonverbal performance. This is necessary only in rare instances. While the client is struggling to master the

responder mode, a direct demand from the leader for high performance in the nonverbal realm as well as in the verbal realm generally would create too much of a burden for the client. It is more than enough to have to worry about consciously formulating his verbal response. The behavior modifiers use an extremely important motivational phrase: "Catch the person being good." In vicarious reinforcement, this can be extended to "catch another person being good." In other words, a reinforcement is instructive for every client who is observing, as well as for the client who was caught being good. This often means that the leader *does not have to catch some other client who is deficient.* No attention whatever need be focused on a client's deficiency, yet the leader can indirectly influence a deficient client by pointing out the good qualities of another client's behavior at a different time. In effect, every client has the opportunity to learn to correct his own behavior and to become motivated to do so simply on the basis of observing someone else's *pleasant* experience. Such vicarious instruction and reinforcement (along with initial modeling) is in fact a major technique used to encourage accepting *nonverbal* behavior on the part of those who do not display it as a matter of course in their efforts to master the verbal display of empathy. Generally, a good instructional rule for the RE program leader to follow is: *When you are disappointed in a behavioral deficiency of A and demonstration or modeling is not desirable or feasible, remember to reinforce B, C, D, E, or F for displaying that behavior.*

### Maintaining Equality of Reinforcement

The leader has to be aware of the possibility of increasing group *rivalry and jealousy* in using reinforcement and, especially, vicarious reinforcement techniques. This is inherent in making overt judgments about people's behavior in a group. It is extremely important that everyone in the group should be receiving about the same (very high) total *amount* of reinforcement. The only variation between individuals should be in the specific acts being reinforced, which is determined by their own level of present and past performance. When the leader is care-

ful to equalize reinforcement in this manner, the rivalry and jealousy problem among participants is no greater than it is in any other therapeutic group and far less than in most academically oriented instructional groups. We would add just one further pair of precautions: (1) if B is A's partner, it would be better to use C, D, E, or F when one is consciously using vicarious reinforcement procedures; and (2) it is important to be especially careful to keep general reinforcement balanced between the two members of each pair. Maintaining balance between members of each dyad, and among the different dyads, is important in other respects as well, as we shall discuss in the following section.

## Equal Opportunity in the Group

It is important to the smooth functioning of RE groups that the leader keep a mental account of the *time* spent (1) by each dyad in relation to other dyads, and (2) by one member of a dyad in relation to the other member. The potential imbalance between dyads is somewhat different in nature than the potential imbalance within a pair. The imbalance *between dyads* occurs when a dyad consumes more than an equal share of the time available in the role of the *center-stage pair*. By *center-stage pair* we mean the pair that is practicing the use of skills overtly and receiving the benefits of feedback directly from the leader and the other group members.

No exact and strict method of time keeping is used in the groups. Strict adherence to a clocked time limit is likely to be perceived as being unsympathetic, mechanistic, and inefficient by leaders and group members alike. A mechanistic type of equality would be experienced by many participants as excessively rigid and psychologically unfair. (We do not rule out the possibility that in the case of extreme difficulties unresolvable in any other way, such a mechanistic approach might be warranted, but we have never found it necessary.)

Variation is permitted in the time consumed by couples within a given session so that the use of skills during the sessions can provide a more satisfying experience for the participants. It

would be extremely frustrating to the dyad, to the leader, and even to the members of the other dyads (who are acting as facilitators for the pair in question) to interrupt a pair who are in the midst of a highly emotional interchange and seem a few moments away from the resolution of a significant problem. It would seem equally unwise to have a couple stretch out their skill practice in order to fill the allotted time when the topic they have chosen to discuss has come to a logical and emotional end, and not enough time remains to make significant headway on another topic. After the first few sessions, the *content* being discussed by a couple must be given this type of consideration if the use and practice of the skills is to be a positive and meaningful experience. Recognizing such factors, the couples experience little discomfort about imbalances arising from such situations within a single session. But the leader must always remain alert to the dangers involved.

The danger inherent in such flexible use of session time, obviously, is that if any dyad feels it is not getting its fair share of session time, one or both members of the pair may become dissatisfied. A pair may feel shortchanged simply on a mechanical basis or, even worse, may feel that another pair (or pairs) is more in favor with the leader. This would give rise to rivalry and jealousy toward other members of the group and possibly feelings of resentment toward the program in general and/or the leader in particular. Worse still, there is every reason to believe that the group member suffering such feelings will not promptly bring them into the open. He may not consciously focus his attention on them; or if he does, he may feel too uncomfortable about it to bring the matter up. In either case, it is likely that long before they surface—if indeed they ever would—such feelings would create various kinds of resistance and slow the progress of the program.

It is easy for the leader not to pay attention to something as abstract as time since the content being discussed in RE sessions is so often emotion-laden and suspenseful. And, as we said, clients will seldom bring this matter to the leader's attention. However, whenever there is a *pattern* under which any couple is receiving less time than they are "entitled" to, it

would be a grave mistake for the leader to think—because of the lack of apparent dissatisfaction, or even because of clients' *verbal protestations to the contrary*—that it is not creating a problem in his group. If he succumbs to such equanimity, he may very well find certain clients failing to work at home, resisting instruction in the sessions, failing to show up for sessions, or even dropping out because of the pressure of "other commitments."

Obviously then, the leader should do everything possible to maintain the feeling on the part of all members that they are being treated fairly in all respects, including the time allocated them at center stage. He can help prevent such problems from arising by maintaining equal time opportunity for each pair in the way he administers the rotations of the couples who take center stage within each session. When, for the kinds of pressing reasons noted above, this has not been feasible, he should let the group know: that he was aware of the disparity; the reason he permitted it to happen; and the way in which he intends to administer the next session in order to equalize matters.

Furthermore, *within dyads* there is sometimes a tendency for one member of the dyad to fall more naturally into the expresser mode and the other into the responder mode. This is not necessarily a bad thing. The natural needs of the pair and of their relationship might be well served by such an arrangement. However, sometimes this pattern will occur because of a disequilibrium in the relationship not truly desired by both members of the dyad.

It is part of the leader's role to assure that each partner has the *opportunity* to spend an equal amount of time in each mode. Within each session he should try to structure for mode switching in such a way as to bring about the parity that is intended to be a natural part of the procedures.

Not infrequently, the nature of the topic will be such that this would be unnatural and undesirable, with the leader and the participants alike sensing that one or the other member of the pair more naturally belongs in one or the other of the behavioral modes for most of the time devoted to that couple. In such instances, the leader should make the suggestion that

during the next session the couple reverse the emphasis if feasible, or at least that the member of the pair who did not initiate the discussion this time be the topic initiator the next time.

Usually, there is no problem in maintaining a rough parity over the sessions. By rough parity we mean anything within the boundaries of a 60 to 40 percent split between members of the pair across sessions. If this degree of parity cannot be maintained on an average taken across a unit of about three sessions, the leader should pause to consider whether or not he has a methodological problem between himself and the couple. On such consideration, the reason for a larger disparity may be perfectly obvious in terms of the content being discussed and clearly acceptable to both members of the pair. If so, the leader can wait to see what another few sessions will bring and reconsider the problem then.

If the reason for the disparity does not seem caused by the topics under discussion, the leader must conclude that he does have a methodological problem on his hands. He has been structuring for one thing to happen, and the pair has been doing something else. For some reason the pair is unable or unwilling to follow the procedures the leader is trying to maintain. At that point, the leader should use the method we call *troubleshooting* to deal with the problem.

### Troubleshooting

Ordinarily, it is not in accord with RE methods for the leader to express his own concerns or feelings to the group. It is our view that the leader ordinarily should be in enough control of his own feelings so that they do not compete with the kinds of helping responses that are part of his professional role. As far as RE programs are concerned, except for illustrative, didactic purposes, it is generally not appropriate for a group leader to consider it as part of his role to be self-disclosing to his clients or to share the personal moods, feelings, or reactions that arise within him as he leads a group. Generally speaking, this seems no more appropriate to us than it would be for a defense lawyer

summing up his case before a jury, simply because he feels that way, to tell a jury, "Well, right now, my own faith in my client is shaken. I think he probably is guilty."

Genuineness is not an issue. If one is to act profession-ally, one's behavioral inclinations must be trained such that one *feels* like doing—*genuinely,* because one's professionalism should be part of one—what is in the best interests of the client. We believe it is only because psychological helping techniques and principles are in such a state of flux that confusion has arisen on this point. The idea that expression of a leader's per-sonal feelings somehow coincides with being helpful is wishful thinking. The whole point of professional training is to weed out those people who are outside the reach of a reasonable amount of training, and to see that those who complete training have been trained so as to respond—*with* heart and soul—in a manner designed to be helpful to the client. A therapist or edu-cator whose professional behaviors are determined mainly by personal momentary impulses is about as useful as a drunken brain surgeon.

Knowing what to do on these occasions—which should be *very rare* for the professional—when his personal feelings do *not* permit him to perform his role effectively is part of the training a group leader should receive. We will not discuss at any length temporary personal incapacities or emotions of the leader that put him in the position of needing help rather than being able to provide help effectively. A group of clients—whether trou-bled or not—is not a group of friends and certainly not a group of helpers. A professional contract, not a friendship pact, should chart the course that is appropriate, helpful, and ethical. When temporarily incapacitated, a leader should simply cancel. But what about gray areas? What about the situation where the personal feelings of the leader arise not from his personal life but rather from seemingly unavoidable difficulties arising *from his interaction with one or more members of the group*?

Of course, progress in any program represents a series of difficulties met and overcome. Some participants will be slow, others balky, some forgetful, others resistant, and yet others so distressed that they can function only with difficulty or

sporadically. The leader should be steeped in teaching methods to apply in the face of such difficulties and should regard them as a routine part of the job. But once in a great while a leader will run into a client for whom every ordinary method applied individually, sequentially, and in combination just does not seem to work. If this is happening to a leader more than rarely, he should question his own methods or seek supervision to try to find out what he may be doing wrong or failing to do. But we do believe that there will be one or two individuals in a hundred who do not cooperate or do not seem to be moving ahead despite the use of all the usual teaching methods. It is in this kind of situation in which we believe that self-disclosure does become appropriate; and in the RE program, we then would rely on the following troubleshooting procedure.

First of all, the leader should say to himself that *he* now has a problem. This problem is that he has been unable to bring the client to perform the expected skills and procedures up to his expectations. He must make a temporary but sharp perceptual shift. His major concern must cease to be the relationship between the individual in question and that individual's partner; instead, the major problem is to be perceived in terms of the relationship between that client and the RE program and its methods. Because the leader represents the program and its methods, he must focus his attention on the relationship between the client and himself. Because all routine teaching and structuring attempts have failed, he now must seek to resolve the difficulty by a joint problem-solving endeavor with the individual in question.

In the kind of troubleshooting presently under discussion, such a shift of focus should not be made on the spot, but only after the leader has had the time to think about it carefully between sessions and, if possible, has consulted with observers or colleagues about more routine principles or procedures that the leader may be overlooking. When he has thus satisfied himself that special troubleshooting procedures are in order, he structures a portion of the next session to make the client and himself the center-stage couple. As further preparation he carefully examines his own perceptions and feelings about these problems.

At the next meeting, he would indicate to the group and to the individual in question that he has a problem concerning his own reactions and feelings as a leader with respect to the behavior of X, which he would like to discuss with X, with both using the usual expresser, responder and mode-switching skills and with the remaining participants in their usual roles as facilitators. With X as the responder, the leader now states, in accord with all expresser principles, the specific client behaviors that have disturbed him; and he states his particular feelings: concern, helplessness, ineptness, frustration, irritation, or whatever. (The leader should be conducting the troubleshooting early enough, and considered the problem carefully enough, so that the feelings he has to report to the client have not reached the level of extreme hostility.)

Client X is initially the responder. But, as quickly as it is feasible, the leader should ask for a mode switch to allow X every opportunity to express fully his own perceptions and feelings with the leader acting as responder. The usual methods being taught in the program, including as many mode switches as may be necessary, continue to be used by both parties until a resolution is achieved via changes in feelings and/or in the expectations of changes in the behavior of one or both parties.

If a whole *group* is floundering, it seems very likely that the trouble would indeed lie with the way the leader has been handling his role, and consultation with colleagues should be undertaken. Conceivably, however, to remedy the situation the leader might wish to try a similar discussion open to all group members, taking expresser and responder roles in relation to all who chose to participate.

There is one other circumstance wherein the leader would consider the usual operating procedures to be inadequate to the job at hand and requiring troubleshooting. That would be in the event of an emotional breakdown of a participant in the face of which the client, the other member of the dyad, and the other members of the group as facilitators are not likely to be able to carry on as usual. To a large extent, this would depend not only on the extent of the loss of emotional control of the individual, but also on the skill level of the participants. Except in the early hours of the program, we would not consider heavy crying to

necessitate a shift in orientation by the leader. Uncontrolled sobbing or hysteria, on the other hand, might require trouble-shooting by the leader with all but the most advanced groups. In such instances, the leader might encourage the other member of the dyad to do specific appropriate things. If that does not seem feasible, the leader again should consider that the routine procedures are not appropriate and that he temporarily must become the empathic responder for the client. He himself would then take whatever steps may be required to bring the person and the group back to equilibrium.

## Administrative Guidance

Naturally, it is one of the leader's functions to provide whatever procedural guidance and structuring the participants require to make their roles and assignments as clear as possible and generally to coordinate and facilitate matters. One major aspect of such duties has already been covered in detail in discussing the need to maintain fair and balanced participation within and between dyads. Another major portion of this task, which has already been discussed in a preceding section, is the necessity to devote the first part of every session to providing appropriate social reinforcement for whatever work has been done at home and to assist the participants in making plans for completing home assignments.

For example, the leader needs to provide guidance to the participants in filling out the Relationship Questionnaire (see Chapter Seven), in which clients set forth the relationship issues that they feel are most important to them—a task that largely predetermines the initial content of client dialog in the sessions. As always, it is important that the nature of this assignment be very clear to the participants. This means providing some concrete examples of the way in which to formulate an issue specifically enough to provide a basis for discussion. (For example, the stated example, "improving our relationships," would be too broad, while "not trusting me," although a very broad topic, is a good enough starting point.) Although the Relationship Questionnaire is subject to later revision by clients, the

leader's goal is to have the client complete each assignment successfully the first time around. Thus, ample time must be allowed for questioning.

The Relationship Questionnaire also provides the foundation for a good deal of further administrative guidance by the leader throughout the sessions. At each session, the first expresser in a dyad is obligated to choose his topic on the basis of this questionnaire, or to justify his deviation from it. These questionnaires are kept close at hand during the sessions and the leader provides the structure necessary to implement discussion based on them.

Similar care needs to be devoted to promoting generalization of the use of skills into the home environment by means of guidance in advance and by a helpful and reinforcing review during the group session of what the participants have been able to accomplish in this regard during the preceding week.

# Chapter 6

# Specific Responses Used in Conducting Relationship Enhancement Sessions

~~~~~~~~~~~~~~~~~~~~~~~~~~~~~

The purpose of presenting this taxonomy of specific leadership responses is fourfold: (1) to provide instruction in RE leadership with more specificity than heretofore; (2) to facilitate research aimed at evaluation and refinement of RE methods; (3) to provide a systematic basis for supervision and self-supervision of RE leadership; and (4) to clarify how the activities of the RE leader change as an RE program progresses. This chapter is therefore highly relevant to the needs of the practitioner as well as of the researcher.

RE methods are not considered fixed, but open to continuous refinement. At the same time, it is highly desirable that a method designed to educate and help large numbers of people be described clearly in behavioral terms and be suited to quantitative analysis. The degree to which a method lends itself to specificity and quantification determines the ease with which it can be taught to others and replicated accurately. When a method lacks these qualities, research designed to evaluate and improve it tends to be haphazard.

To permit others to do accurate research, the originator of a method should present the means by which others can replicate it accurately and, for any given research project, *demonstrate* that they have done so. In the absence of clear specification of those leadership responses that are appropriate to a given method and those that are not, it is quite possible for other researchers to employ quite different leadership techniques while giving the same name to what they are doing or, conversely, to say that they are using different methods when, in fact, the methods are very similar.

This capacity to achieve and demonstrate replicability is a basic requirement of scientific research. Yet few methods of developmental or therapeutic intervention, educational in nature or otherwise, have provided the behavioral categorizations necessary to permit this. Often this is because the methods themselves simply are not clear-cut enough to determine those leadership responses that are or are not appropriate to the method. In this regard RE programs have a clear advantage. All responses not specified as appropriate may be considered inappropriate—that is, involving some kind of non-RE approach. The capacity to code a leader's responses, plus a systematic approach to leadership within a program, makes it relatively easy to set quantitative criteria to determine whether or not the method is or is not being used. This greatly facilitates replicable, and therefore scientific research.

The coding system had not been developed at the time the research reported in this volume was conducted and we wish to establish the reliability of the coding system and gather a good deal of data before we even attempt to set definite criteria. But even at the present time we would not be too uncomfortable in saying that if random sampling of a program yields more than 15 percent of the leaders' responses in inappropriate categories we would not wish to call that program an RE program. Conversely, with less than 15 percent of the leaders' responses falling outside of the appropriate categories, we would feel reasonably comfortable that such a program: (1) was an RE program, and (2) was distinguishable from all non-RE programs.

Being specific about leader responses also enables one to improve a method by studying the kinds of results different types of leader responses generate in clients. For example, it would be possible to study the question of whether clients show more rapid progress in learning skills when leaders make more use of modeling responses as compared to reinforcement responses, or whether the reverse held true.

The taxonomy of leader and client responses to be presented in this chapter also is very useful in the training process. Coding can be used in self-supervision: A group leader can listen to tape recordings of his own sessions and, by coding his responses, may more readily see the relationship between his leadership techniques and client progress or difficulties. Coding leader responses is also useful as an aid to teaching and supervising others. In our own training program, the coding system has been used most frequently by student observers to code leadership behavior in groups led by their peers. The coding process itself is instructive to the observers and, in addition, by going over the record with the leaders immediately after the session, the observers can be highly specific in discussing group processes and leadership skills with the group leaders, pinpointing the leader's most helpful and least helpful responses. The coding categories also are useful for tabulating the percentages of different kinds of responses being used by a leader in order to assess their appropriateness to the stage of the training program. For example, at all stages of the program there should be a high rate of reinforcing responses; by the sixth hour of training, there should be some degree of systematic encouragement of group members to serve as facilitators; and by the tenth hour, ample reinforcement of facilitator behavior should be present. An examination of the proportion of leader responses falling in these categories can determine whether these expectations are being met. If they are not, the leaders can make the necessary adjustments in the next session.

## Coding

The unit usually to be recommended for this coding system is a meaningful leader statement made between state-

ments of others. It is recognized that the qualifier *meaningful* is not unambiguous. Its inclusion is simply an attempt to eliminate those instances where the leader may say a few words and then be interrupted by someone else. In practice, this definition of a unit has not proved a serious problem.

The coding categories are not mutually exclusive, and a single leader statement may be classified into more than one category. However, to simplify the procedure, and to improve reliability, we do not use the same category more than once for any given leader statement.

An alternate unit for coding, which is useful when one wishes to establish response-by-response reliability between coders, is a time unit of fifteen seconds. Here again, we would recommend multiple categorizations within a time unit, if appropriate, but not the use of the same category twice in a given interval.

Coding is not begun until five minutes after the last scheduled group member arrives or until the leader indicates that the group should begin. Nor is coding conducted during the last five minutes before a session is scheduled to end, nor for three minutes after any interruption extraneous to the program, such as a client leaving the group for reasons unrelated to what has happened in the group.

## Designating the Response Recipient

In certain instances it is useful to know the *role* of the person to whom the leader had addressed his remark. This is accomplished by adding a hyphen after the basic code designation and following it with $G$ (group), $L$ (coleader), $E$ (expresser), $R$ (responder), or $F$ (facilitator, that is, a group member not practicing E or R responses).

For certain kinds of research projects or to analyze what kinds of leadership responses have been directed to a particularly difficult client, it is sometimes also useful to designate the particular recipients of leadership responses by their initials. Such an analysis would help to determine, for example, whether a slow learner is receiving, as one would hope, as much reinforcement as the other group members and more modeling

responses. This can be done by adding the initials of group members to the basic code designation.

### Breadth and Detail

The taxonomy can be used on a broad level with as few as two categories (*A* for appropriate responses and *I* for inappropriate responses) or with all of the various categories to be presented below. The A versus I system would be used simply to determine the extent to which RE methodology is being followed. The full list might be used for other research purposes—for example, to determine the contribution of different types of leader responses to client performance—and for supervision. Intermediate breadth of coverage can be achieved by dropping categories already known to be rare for the leaders under study and/or by dropping subdesignations of the role of the person being addressed (expresser, responder, facilitator).

A complete list of categories and their abbreviations is presented in Table 6-1.

## Appropriate Leader Responses

There is a wide range of responses available to the RE leader. In this section we label and define those responses considered appropriate, discuss the circumstances under which they should be used, and give examples for clarification. The responses presented here are for skill training conducted in a group; if only one pair or an individual is being trained, the responses directed to the facilitators would not be relevant.

### Administrative Responses (A)

Administrative responses are necessary to the smooth running of the group. They are necessary for collecting and giving out of research measures or homework, determining which couple will take center stage, suggesting that a couple relinquish the center-stage position, suggesting coffee-break times in marathon sessions, getting things started again after

Table 6-1. Leadership Responses

---

*Appropriate Responses*

| | |
|---|---|
| A | Administrative Responses |
| SR | Social Reinforcement |
| SRN | Social Reinforcement, Nonverbal |
| S | Structuring |
| ME | Modeling an Empathic Response |
| MEX | Modeling an Expressive Statement |
| EMS | Encouraging a Mode Switch |
| EP | Encouraging and Prompting |
| EPCR | Encouraging Problem Solving or Conflict Resolution |
| DAT | Direct Acceptance in Troubleshooting |

*Inappropriate Responses*

| | |
|---|---|
| I,DL | Directive Lead |
| I,I | Interpretation |
| I,SEA | Suggestion, Explanation, Advice |
| I,EAR | Encouragement, Approval, Reassurance |
| I,C | Personal Criticism |
| I,OD | Other Diversions |
| I,ID | Inappropriately Directed Responses |
| I,FC | Failure to Correct |

*Neutral Responses*

| | |
|---|---|
| O | Other Responses |

---

breaks, asking questions about the physical comfort of the group, helping clients set up the specific times they will do their homework, making sure that the group knows about the next meeting time, and so forth. As shown in some of the examples in previous sections, they also are used to establish readiness for other procedures such as a mode switch or EPCR response. Illustrations of administrative responses (A) are:

1. Are you both pretty well satisfied that you've explored that issue fully?

2. George and Ellen didn't have much time last week; I'd like to begin with them tonight.

3. Okay, I think it's time for us to stop now and switch to another couple [A]. [To finishing couple]: That was excellent; you both did a great job [SR-E;SR-R]. Who would like to go next?

4. Bill and Mary, what day and time are you going to meet to do your homework this week?

5. I think we better get started now rather than wait any longer for Harvey and Betty.

6. I'm sorry to have to stop you at this point, but we've run out of time.

### Social Reinforcement (SR)

The term *social reinforcement* (SR) refers to statements such as *fine, good, right, very good, excellent, great, terrific, wonderful, beautiful, You're doing very well,* and *That was excellent for a first attempt.* SR responses, including nonverbal cues, which will be discussed shortly, comprise a very large percentage of leader responses. SR responses should be used with all participants in all modes at all phases of training.

Such responses are appropriate whenever a group member: (1) responds well; (2) responds at a level better than his general level has been; (3) corrects or improves his own response; or (4) follows an appropriate suggestion made by the leader or a facilitator. SR responses are made as frequently as possible during the initial, didactic phases of training. Once roles have been perfected and clients are performing at a consistently high level, they are no longer necessary on such a frequent basis but should still be employed whenever a participant has come up with a well-formed response. Reinforcement is always appropriate when a responder does not respond defensively, but probably would have been defensive were it not for his use of empathic skills; or when an expresser has managed to formulate a fair expressive response whereas, without benefit of training, he probably would have said something accusative to his partner.

*Examples of SR responses to an expresser (SR-E).* In addition to all the brief reinforcing remarks mentioned in the first paragraph of this section, examples of SR-E responses are:

1. That was a rough thing to state subjectively; you corrected yourself beautifully.

2. Changing your statement to eliminate the accusation was excellent.

3. You rephrased it very well to eliminate the generalization.

4. You managed to state that without telling him what his motives were. That was very good and, I'm sure, very difficult for you to do. Beautiful.

*Examples of SR responses to the responder (SR-R).* Examples of the SR-R responses that are more extensive and specific than those provided in the first paragraph are:

1. You picked up a feeling there just by imagining how he must have felt. That was excellent empathy.

2. You hit the feeling just right.

3. You caught his ambivalence very well—a really fine response.

4. He didn't state it, but you picked up the implicit message about how he wishes you would behave. That was great.

5. You showed interest and acceptance not just by what you said, but also by your tone and manner, that's terrific.

6. That's much better—and your tone was much more accepting.

*Examples of SR responses to facilitators (SR-F).* Examples of SR-F responses that are more extensive and specific than words or short phrases are:

1. Bill, that was very helpful. You were rehearsing responses mentally that might lead to better responses than those the center-stage couple were making and you were able to come up with a good feeling for the responder to use.

2. Bill, that's a very good translation into subjective terms of what Harvey was saying; I can see you were working mentally while he was talking. Very good.

3. Paul, I'm glad you shared your appreciation of Mary's performance with her. I agree. I thought it was an excellent response.

4. I agree. You noticed the nonacceptance in Sue's tone that was really interfering with the expresser's ability to reveal himself.

### Social Reinforcement, Nonverbal (SRN)

Nonverbal reinforcement includes head nodding and other gestures that commonly are used to indicate approval. Nonverbal reinforcement is particularly useful because it can be used very frequently without interfering with the flow of conversation; where interference is not a problem, it is best to include verbal reinforcement as well.

In order to permit use of nonverbal cues, it is desirable for a leader to sit so that he can be seen in the peripheral vision of the participants who are at stage center. With two leaders present in a group, we recommend, as shown in Figure 6-1, that

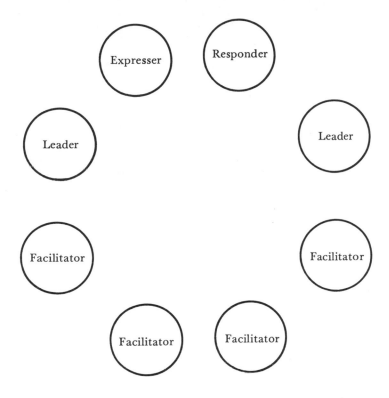

Figure 6-1. Seating Arrangement With Two Group Leaders

one leader sit beside and a bit behind the expresser, facing the responder, and that the other sit in the converse position. This arrangement permits the leaders to see and be seen by the entire group as well as by the center-stage couple. It also permits each leader to provide touch cues (for example, a pat on the back) for the closest member of the center-stage pair and to provide facial and hand gestures for the member seated opposite. If there is only one leader in the group, he should sit facing the group between, and a bit back from, the center-stage couple, as shown in Figure 6-2.

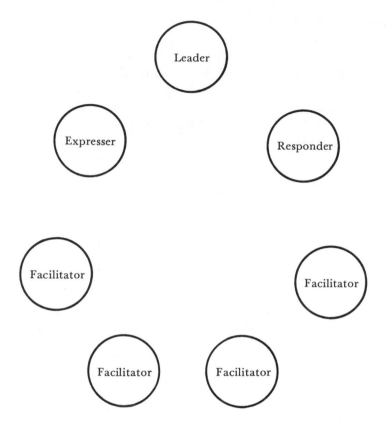

Figure 6-2. Seating Arrangement With One Group Leader

We believe it is better for a leader to change seats with other group members rather than ask the people who are about to become expresser and responder to change their seats. This reduces the "hot-seat" feelings for the central couple.

*Structuring (S)*

Structuring responses are used to remind the participants of the guidelines for the expresser, responder, and facilitator roles and to provide a rationale for the behaviors they are being asked to learn.

*Structuring for the expresser (S-E).* Initially, one of the

greatest difficulties for the expresser is to restrict his statements to his own feelings and perceptions. It is difficult for the expresser to refrain from making accusations, labeling his partner, or attributing motives or feelings to his partner as if they were fact and not the subjective speculations of the expresser. When the expresser does make such inappropriate statements, the leader reminds him of the guidelines and either, (1) models an appropriate response for the expresser to use as a substitute for the one he has made, or (2) asks the expresser himself to rephrase his remarks in such a way as to arouse the least amount of defensiveness in his partner. The following are examples of such leader guidance:

> 1. Mary, instead of saying that Jim is lazy, I would like you to mention one or two of the behaviors you have in mind and tell him how you feel about them. That will make it much easier for him to listen to you and understand your point of view.
>
> 2. Remember, as the expresser, not to try to offer your analysis of your partner's motives, or what you think are the reasons behind his behavior. Try to rephrase your statement in terms of your own feelings and desires.
>
> 3. I'd like to ask you, Nancy, to try to rephrase that before your mother responds. You're telling her what *she* thinks. That's something you can't do if you want to communicate effectively. You and she could argue about what she thinks forever and, in the last analysis, she's the only valid authority on what she thinks. It must be that something she *does* makes *you* believe she thinks a certain way. Can you tell her what that *behavior* is and how *you* feel when she behaves that way?
>
> 4. Wait. You're telling *him* why *he* behaves in certain ways. Remember that in order to keep the communication constructive, it's much better not to do that. Instead, can you just tell him how that behavior makes you feel. Or, if it's his motive rather than the behavior that is important to you, tell him what leads *you* to *think*, or to *infer*, that he's motivated by jealousy; then tell him how *thinking* he's jealous makes *you* feel.

Expressers also often find it difficult to remember the *positive* feelings that often are associated with the negative feelings that they are expressing. For example, if a wife is distressed that her husband is spending too little time with her she will seldom think to include the basic positive feeling that underlies that complaint: the fact that she enjoys her husband's com-

pany. If a husband complains about the wife's attention to other men, he seldom will remember to include the basic feelings of intense love underlying his jealousy when he discusses this aspect of their relationship. It is part of the requirements of the expressive mode to try to include *all* the important feelings and interpersonal messages associated with a particular behavior. Since the participants do not directly express the implicit positive messages, leaders should be constantly alert for these underlying feelings and provide structure for their inclusion.

Timing is very important when reminding the expresser to tell his partner about the positive feelings implicit in the negatively worded statements. The leader should judge that the expresser would not perceive such structuring as an attempt to cut him off, deny his feelings, or protect the partner, but rather as something that truly complements his communication. For this reason, this type of structuring usually is not used in the earliest exchanges dealing with negative feelings, but only after some of the negative feelings have been expressed and accepted. Examples of structuring for inclusion of *underlying positive aspects* of a communication are:

> 1. Mary, you've expressed the feelings of frustration and anger you have about Cindy not applying herself and neglecting her schoolwork. I sense a concern for her as well, a strong desire that she have a happy life as an adult and a fear that she's heading for a situation that will make her unhappy because of the failure to qualify for a good education. As I say, I sense that, but you haven't really said it in so many words. Is it a part of your feelings, and if it is, could you include it in your communication as the positive aspect that underlies the negative?

> 2. Karen, you've indicated very well how neglected you feel, and how it makes you so angry when Paul isn't willing to spend time with you. That was very open, and you expressed your feelings subjectively and very well. What you said also *implies* how much you *want* his company, how much you care about his companionship, and that you have good feelings when you are together. As we've said in the past, it's better, if it's not inconsistent with your mood, to include the positive thoughts and feelings that underlie the negative. Is that something that you would feel comfortable adding at this point?

The leader's goal is to enhance the communication and

relationship bonds between participants rather than between the participants and the leader. It is therefore necessary for the leader to direct all of the expresser's statements to the responder. Examples of structuring responses of this kind are:

1. I want you to tell that to your husband, not to me.

2. Mary, when you're the expresser, I want you to talk to your mother. Look at her while you're talking, and instead of saying "She makes me mad when she . . . ," say, "I get mad when you . . . ."

It is also helpful for the expresser to be as specific as possible about his own feelings and the behaviors of the partner that produce those feelings. The leader should help the participants pinpoint specific behaviors and feelings. Examples of such structuring responses are:

1. John, you said you believe that your father plays favorites, and he's more lenient with Carl than he is with you, and that this leads you to feel rejected. That was an excellent statement of your feelings. In the expresser mode we try to remember to be as specific and behavioral as possible. Could you be more specific about which of your father's behaviors leads you to that feeling? Could you give him as many examples as you can, so that he will have a better idea of exactly what he does that leads you to feel that way?

2. It seems as though you wish Ann would do certain things that she's not doing now. Could you make the interpersonal message explicit; could you tell her what it is you wish she would do?

*Structuring for the responder (S-R).* We pointed out earlier that it is difficult for the expresser to avoid accusations and to avoid speaking as if he knew for sure the motives or feelings of his partner; and it is also difficult for him to speak only in terms of his own feelings and perceptions. Likewise, it is hard for the responder to avoid expressing his own feelings, to avoid making interpretations of the expresser's statements, or to avoid asking questions that steer the expresser in directions the responder wants the conversation to take. It is, therefore, sometimes necessary for the leader to remind the responder that he is not permitted to ask questions, give advice, suggest solutions to problems, or make interpretations. Examples of this type of structuring are:

1. Wait. I want to remind you that you should not be asking the expresser to give you more information. Try again.

2. I think you're trying to tell the speaker *why* he believed as he did even though no such reason was implied in his statement. It was not a clarification of his feelings or his motives as he is experiencing them; that's what we call an *interpretation*. Try again.

3. I know you would like to reassure him and make him feel better at this point, but remember that is something that we don't do in the empathic responder mode. If you just stick to what he is feeling here, what would you say to him?

4. Wait. You're giving him what you think is the solution to the problem. You can do that as an expresser; but as a responder, you can't give solutions. Just concentrate on showing your understanding of the feeling and the interpersonal message that he's expressing here. If you want, as soon as you do that, you can take the role of expresser and suggest the solution.

The leader also wants to make sure that the responder picks up the explicit or implicit positive feelings in the expresser's statement. Examples are:

1. Remember, Bill, to keep in mind that there is often a positive feeling that underlies a negative one. Try not to lose sight of these in your empathic responses. Your father said that he gets very angry when you drive after drinking, and you reflected that beautifully. But underlying that, although he didn't say it in so many words, was the feeling that he's worried about what might happen to you. He cares very, very much about you, and is frightened that if you do drive after drinking you will get hurt. Could you also reflect that caring and that worry?

2. Mark, you did a good job of picking up your mother's feelings of disappointment. Now what are her positive feelings behind all of that? Let her know that you understand those too.

3. Jim, Betty said she wants you to stay home more because she loves you. Can you make your response again and this time give the love part of the message the same degree of emphasis that she did?

The leader also wants to help the responder strengthen the bond between the participating pair, so he structures to avoid being put in the position of an intermediary. Illustrations of this type of structuring are:

1. Don't tell me, tell her.

2. I know you're not sure if you're getting his feelings correctly, but direct your remarks to him anyway.

3. Jim, you can convey a lot more acceptance to Grace if you look at her, not me, when you're the responder.

*Structuring for facilitators (S-F).* We have been surprised at how quickly facilitators have learned to avoid giving advice, making suggestions based on their own experience, offering interpretations, and so on. Reminders of such prohibitions seldom are needed even in the first several hours of the group existence. Examples of structuring responses to facilitators on those rare occasions when they are needed are:

1. Harvey, I know you are trying to be helpful in suggesting a possible compromise solution to the problem that John and his father are discussing, but remember what we've said about our assumption that the people most involved are the ones in the best position to work out solutions; and we want to give *them* the skills to do that and to help them practice and perfect those skills.

2. Nancy, I know that in some circumstances it's helpful to let others know how you have worked out a particular kind of problem. But remember that we have limited time in the session and we want to concentrate exclusively on skill training. Is there anything you want to say to Anne that would improve on her expressive statement?

In addition to avoiding inappropriate responses, the leader also wants to encourage the facilitators to be involved actively in helping the other participants learn expresser and responder skills. Examples of such structuring are:

1. I'd like to suggest that during the early part of this session you all pay close attention to the way I offer suggestions to the central couple to help them improve their expressive and empathic statements. Then in the latter half of the session, I'd like you to share with the couple who are at center stage any better way you've thought of during your mental practice to phrase the feelings or ideas in accord with the expresser or responder modes. That is, if you think you can improve on any particular statement, make your suggestion to the person who has just made that statement. Also, when you think they've handled a difficult situation particularly well—that is, when they've made a particularly impressive empathic or expressive statement—I'd like you to let them know that too, just the way I do. Just tell them it was good, or gesture to them so they'll know that you think they did a good job.

2. While Karen and Paul are in the expressive modes, I want to remind the rest of you to be rehearsing mentally each of these skills as they are talking. If you can suggest something more in accord with the requirements of the mode, I'd like your help in coaching them.

Finally, the leader wants to make sure that any facilitator statements strengthen the bond between the expresser and responder. For example:

Joan, that's a good reflection of Bill's feelings you made to Bill. I think it added something very worthwhile to the response that Mary gave to him. But remember, as facilitator, you must direct your remarks only to the person whose *performance* you are helping to improve. Would you repeat your statement to Mary now so that she can add it to what she's said to Bill.

### Modeling an Empathic Response (ME)

Providing good examples of empathic responses is a major method of teaching clients the empathic responding mode, and ME responses are used frequently in the early stages of training. The leader always addresses the responder, never the expresser, in modeling an empathic response. The modeled response then is either repeated or paraphrased by the responder to the expresser, and the leader reinforces the responder for his use of the statement.

If the leader makes it clear from the outset that he will frequently model responses, then later, when the leader improves or corrects a response, the participant's sense of failure is reduced. Nevertheless, when the leader improves on a responder's statement, the latter is likely to feel a bit inadequate. Therefore, it is often desirable for the leader to model an empathic response *before* the responder has tried to make one. In this way the sense of being corrected is avoided. The leader always strives to maximize the number of straightforward reinforcements and minimize the number of corrective responses he must make. Therefore, the more the leader expects the responder to make an inadequate empathic response, the less the leader can

afford to wait until the responder makes a statement before he models a response. The less adequate the skill of the responder, the more persistent his difficulty in learning, and the more difficult the task presented to the responder by the nature of the expresser's statement, the more likely it is that the responder's statement will be inadequate and require correction. Whenever an inadequate response seems likely to occur, the leader should try to model an empathic response before the responder speaks. Conversely, the greater the responder's skill, and the more adept and cooperative the responder, the easier it is for the responder to detect and accept the feelings underlying the expresser's statements and the greater the likelihood that the responder will make an adequate response. Under such circumstances, the leader can afford to take the chance that the responder will provide a successful response without modeling and can wait to see if modeling will be necessary.

As they gain experience and skill, facilitators are gradually encouraged to model empathic responder statements for other group members whenever they feel they can improve on a responder's statement. Examples of ME responses are:

> 1. I think irritation is a bit weak for the feeling that he's expressing. I think he's saying he's really quite annoyed. Try that.
>
> 2. I think saying *furious* is a bit stronger than what he implied. Try saying, "You're annoyed with me."
>
> 3. What you said is very good, but I think it doesn't quite capture the whole picture. I think he's saying that he really feels a strong pull both ways. He wants very much to succeed in his job, and he feels he's never going to succeed unless he puts out that much effort; on the other hand he very much wants to see you happy, and it's really very difficult for him to know which way to go at this particular time.
>
> 4. What about the wish, the desire? What seems to be the interpersonal message there? It seems to me that what she's really saying is, "I wish you would act as concerned as that more often, so that I won't feel like I have to do the worrying for both of us so much of the time." See if that does catch what she's trying to say.

## Modeling an Expressive Statement (MEX)

The leader may choose to model any aspect of the expressive role by: stating things in subjective terms; labeling feel-

ings; being as specific and as behavioral as possible in describing significant interpersonal interactions; or making interpersonal expectations or wishes overt. Although instruction in the empathic mode is emphasized more than the expresser mode in the early stages of training, the expresser mode does receive attention right from the beginning and at no time is the expresser permitted to violate the role requirements. All objectified statements, all generalizations about the character of the other, all interpretations of the motives or thoughts of the other that are not specifically identified as the expresser's personal speculations and linked to some reaction or feeling of the expresser are corrected immediately. The mode of correction is usually a combination of structuring (that is, reminding the participant of the pertinent rule) and modeling a statement that carries the pertinent ideas and feelings, but does so in accord with the prescribed behaviors of the expresser mode.

Another way in which MEX responses are used even in the early phases of training is to add a statement of the feelings or the interpersonal message that were present, but covert, in the expresser's statement. If the leader thinks that the responder is going to have difficulty providing a good empathic response for the expresser, the leader has the choice of feeding a response to the responder, or he can feed essentially the same information to the expresser and ask him to rephrase his statement accordingly. In addition to helping the expresser learn the expressive mode, this procedure makes it easier for the responder to perform his role because the feelings and/or the interpersonal message is now evident and therefore easier to reflect and accept. (The possibility of modeling a good response *prior* to an expresser's statement—as is possible with the responder—is not possible since one cannot know what the expresser wishes to say until he has spoken.) Some examples of MEX responses follow.

> 1. *Expresser:* Tonight I worked hard and long getting a good dinner ready and then you arrived a half hour later than I expected you, and everything was cold.
>
> *Leader:* Would it be accurate if you were to say, "I worked very hard preparing a good dinner tonight and when you came later than I expected you it annoyed me very much?

*Expresser:* Yes.

*Leader:* Trying saying it like that—including that personal feeling in it.

2. *Expresser:* It bothers me that you never want to spend any time with our son Ricky. I know you work very hard, but you do take time out for some things. Yet you never play with him.

*Leader:* You stated your feelings there very well [SR-E], but you included a very broad generalization ("never") and you stated things in terms that didn't acknowledge them as your perceptions [S-E]. Try this: "It seems to me that you take out some time for things beside work, but you don't spend as much time with Ricky as I would like you to spend. I would feel much better if I saw you spending more of your time with him" [MEX].

3. *Expresser:* I used to think that things would improve, and that as we made more money, you would be willing to buy some of the things that I am interested in that go beyond the basic necessities. But I realize now that what I was afraid of is really true: You're very insecure about the future, and you are just not going to feel like you can ever afford to spend money on the things you consider luxuries. And I don't want to live that way any more.

*Leader:* Try it this way: "Now that I think we have more money than we used to, I would like to buy some things that I think you consider luxuries, and I'm afraid that you won't agree to do it. It distresses me and makes me angry whenever I think that you are going to object to buying some of the things I would like very much to have."

4. *Expresser:* You treat me like a baby, Mom. You're always trying to protect me or watch out for me. I'm old enough now to do things without your checking up on me all the time. You always seem to think I'm going to do something I shouldn't be doing.

*Leader:* Nancy, try to bring your own feelings into it, and try to be specific about what your mother does that makes you think that she doesn't trust you, instead of telling her what her motives are [S-E]. See if this would also get at what you're saying: "When you quiz me about exactly where I'm going and who is going to be there, I think it's because you think I'm going to do something I shouldn't be doing. [In using these examples, the leader is drawing on previous conversation not provided here.] I feel that I'm not trusted. That bothers me. I wish you would not ask me so many questions when I'm going out for the evening" [MEX].

## Encouraging a Mode Switch (EMS)

One of the leader's major instructive responsibilities is to teach the participants when and how to switch from the expresser to the responder mode or vice versa. It is important that

participants always know which mode they are in, especially when they switch back and forth rapidly. The leader must be sensitive to the needs of the participants to switch, and must teach them how to switch without either violating the rule that each expresser statement be followed by an empathic response or using the mode switch in a manipulative way.

*To the expresser (EMS-E).* One of the leader's major instructive responsibilities is to teach the participants when and how to switch from the expresser to the responder mode or vice versa. The expresser should suggest a mode switch to his partner whenever he wants to know what his partner is thinking or feeling about an issue under discussion, or whenever he wants to know his partner's reaction to a suggestion he has made to resolve a conflict or solve a problem. Sometimes simple inertia tends to keep the expresser in his role. If that seems to be the case, the leader should remind the expresser of the circumstances under which it is desirable to switch modes and should suggest to the expresser that he tell his partner that he would like to hear the partner express an opinion or feeling on the topic. (Naturally, the partner, who would then become the expresser, need not discuss this topic, since the expresser always is free to determine his own topic. But in practice a specific invitation of this kind is very seldom turned down.) Examples of dialogs in which the leader encourages the expresser to suggest a mode switch are:

1. *Leader* [to expresser]: In what you're saying now, and in what you've said in your last comment as well, you're implying that you wonder whether your husband really cares whether or not you really succeed in your job. Is that something that you would like him to reply to now, or would you rather develop your own feelings about this further [A-E]?

*Expresser:* I'm a bit afraid to hear what he has to say, but yes, I guess I would like to know.

*Leader:* Remember, you're free to ask for a reply whenever you want one [S-E]. Ask him if he'd be willing to take the expresser mode now [EMS-E].

2. *Leader:* It sounds like you're wondering whether or not she really resents the amount of time you spend in the garage. Would you like to request that she take the expresser mode to let you know whether that is the case, or would you rather continue in the expresser mode yourself?

3. *Leader:* You say you think you are repeating yourself. Would you like to initiate a request for a change in modes?

A second circumstance in which the leader should consider suggesting that the expresser ask for a mode switch is when the expresser seems to be repeating substantially the same thing several times in a row. When this occurs, the leader first should satisfy himself that the deepest and most important feelings and interpersonal messages inherent in the repeated message have indeed been recognized. If not, his help is needed to model appropriate responses for the expresser or responder in order to bring them to the surface. If all the relevant elements and feelings in the expresser's conversation already have been recognized by both parties, then the time has come to suggest a problem-solving set or a mode switch. An illustrative exchange is:

> *Leader* [to expresser] : You sound a little bit like you're beginning to run dry on this point. Have you [A-E] ?
>
> *Expresser:* Yes.
>
> *Leader:* Do you feel as though your partner has understood and accepted your feelings about it [A-E] ?
>
> *Expresser:* Yes.
>
> *Leader:* Then this would be an appropriate time to suggest a mode switch [EMS-E].

*To the responder (EMS-R).* The leader should remind the responder about mode switching whenever the leader senses that the responder is having difficulty being empathic because his own feelings are beginning to be aroused; is beginning to feel defensive; or feels a strong urge to present his own point of view for whatever reason. (Often, the pertinent cue to the leader is that the quality of the responder's statement is deficient in a way that suggests that the responder is trying to get his own point of view across while maintaining the formal aspects of an empathic response.) At that point, the leader should remind the responder that it is important that he not try to stay in the empathic mode when he begins to feel strong needs or feelings of his own that make it difficult for him to remain empathic, and

that he should switch modes as soon as he has responded accurately to the last statement of the expresser. Illustrations of the leader's role in such a situation are:

> 1. Bill, perhaps your desire to have her see the situation in the same way that you do has crept into your response. If so, this would be a good time for you to ask for the expressive role yourself, so that you can express your own point of view fully. You could try this response [leader models an appropriate response], ask for the expresser mode, and express your own feelings if she agrees that that is an accurate empathic statement.
>
> 2. That was a very empathic statement [SR-R], but I think his remarks are getting to you. You seem to be tightening up. Would you like to request a change in mode [EMS-R]?

### Encouragement and Prompting (EP)

Encouragement and prompting statements differ from structuring statements in that their purpose is not to correct an outright error or to review the requirements of a role, but rather (1) to encourage someone to try to give a response or (2) to add to or refine a response. They differ from modeling responses in that they are open ended: They do not suggest a particular response to the participant.

*To the expresser (EP-E).* Examples of EP responses to an expresser are:

> 1. How does that make you feel?
>
> 2. I can *imagine* how that made you feel. But it would be helpful to your mother if you would *say* just how that made you feel.
>
> 3. Would you rephrase that so as to make it *completely* subjective. It sounded a bit like you were stating what *he's* thinking instead of what *you think* he's thinking, or rather what you fear he's thinking.
>
> 4. I think there's an implicit interpersonal message there; it sounds as if you want him to do something. Could you state directly what it is that you wish he would do?
>
> 5. Good. You stated your feelings very clearly [SR-E]. Would you also try to be specific—before he responds to that—about exactly what it is she did that made you feel that way [EP-E]?
>
> 6. That was fine [SR-E]. You're letting him know how you would like to see him change, but it's very general. Could you be more specific? Just how do you wish he would behave in that situa-

tion? What is it exactly that you wish he would do differently
[EP-E]?

*To the responder (EP-R).* Examples of EP responses to a
responder are:

1. How is she feeling right now?
2. How do you think that made him feel [EP-R]?
3. That's good for part of what he said [SR-R], but he's ambivalent—what's the other side of his feelings [EP-R]?
4. That's very good [SR-R], but I think his feeling is deeper. Try a
stronger feeling word [EP-R].

*To the facilitator (EP-F).* Examples of EP responses to a
facilitator are:

1. Can anyone help her be more explicit in stating her feelings?
2. Can anyone help him label how he felt in that situation?
3. That was fine [SR to Bill, the responder], but [to facilitators]
can anyone help Bill to get at what John [the expresser] was *feeling* there?
4. Harry [a facilitator], I can see you thought Ellen gave a fine
empathic response. Tell Ellen what you thought.
5. [To facilitators:] That was an excellent response, wasn't it?
6. What Jane is saying is very difficult for her to phrase in terms of
her personal, subjective viewpoint. Could one of you state it in
terms of *her* personal perceptions, feelings, and behavior?
7. George [a group member with a level of skill equal to the task],
what's the interpersonal message that Joe [the responder] could
infer from what Shirley [the expresser] said? What interpersonal
message could she add to the response she just made?

*Encouraging Problem/Conflict Resolution (EPCR)*

We believe that the RE method is a procedure for prob-
lem/conflict resolution that is very sophisticated, realistic, practical and likely to lead to durable solutions. We say this because
RE methodology does not assume that the *initial* formulation
by clients of a problem or conflict is the one that best defines
the problem, or is the formulation most likely to lead to the
most satisfying and durable resolution. A conflict resolution

method that takes an initial statement of a problem and builds elaborate procedures on that initial formulation often is likely to be inefficient or inadequate to the task of solving complex problems or conflicts between intimates. Rather, room must be allowed for a constant interplay between the behavioral decisions at issue and the complex personal and interpersonal needs that they represent or may affect. Any systematic procedure for managing interpersonal conflict between intimates should allow, as an integral part of the system, ample, easy, and prompt opportunity for the problem or conflict to be redefined. Often, the most difficult part of conflict resolution between intimates is to define what the problem is. That is, the final conflict resolution often is based on resolution of a whole series of subconflicts about whether a problem exists, and/or the true nature of the problem. In our view, RE methodology is unique as a problem-solving procedure in two ways. Although it is a structured approach, and one that can be focused on resolving conflict, it (1) allows fully for the complex interplay between behavioral decisions on the one hand and interpersonal feelings on the other, and (2) permits continuous redefinition of the conflicts as part of the initial procedure rather than only as a follow-up procedure after a period of trial. (Of course, it also permits the latter.)

Once RE clients have worked their way down to their basic personal and interpersonal needs and feelings and shared these in a mutually accepting and empathic way, practical solutions to problems or conflicts usually follow, easily and quickly, as a matter of course. Here, we are discussing those exceptions to this rule wherein clients have achieved full expression and mutual understanding, but still disagree on a specific course of action, or fail to make concrete suggestions because of the kind of inertia effect we have noted earlier with respect to initiating a mode switch. It is in these instances that an EPCS response is appropriate. In such circumstances the leader has two tasks to perform.

The first is to structure for problem/conflict resolution. The groundwork for this will have been established the first time an occasion of the sort mentioned above arose within the

group. On that occasion the leader will have provided instructions as in the following example:

> First, before you enter into an attempt to settle the specifics of an issue, make sure: (1) that you have fully expressed your own pertinent ideas and feelings; (2) that the other party has shown empathic acceptance of all of them; (3) that the other party has fully expressed his pertinent ideas and feelings; and (4) that you have shown empathic acceptance toward all of them.
>
> Second, take a few moments to try to think of solutions that seem best to meet the needs of *both* parties, and that offer the least frustration or hardship to both parties. Strive to come up with *new* ways of looking at the problem that might bring about this type of mutually satisfying solution. Use empathic understanding of the other person's expressed wants and feelings plus your awareness of your own needs and feelings to generate such ideas.
>
> Third, after making this attempt, decide whether you and your partner would benefit most by continuing the problem resolution at this time, or whether you feel you could come up with better solutions if you had a longer period of time to think. If so, stop the discussion and make a definite appointment for continuing the discussion at a later time. If, on the other hand, you think you already have some good ideas, or if you think more time would probably not help much anyway, then proceed. If you decide to proceed, you should present your view of how the problem might best be resolved, regardless of how well you feel it satisfies mutual needs, or whether or not it represents a new idea.
>
> Fourth, remember that the modes are well suited for making suggestions, for negotiating and compromising, and for making behavioral commitments to one another. Frequent mode switches will facilitate the process. Also, bear in mind that the components of the expresser mode that are of most value in reaching concrete agreements on problems or conflicts are those that call for: (1) a statement conveying empathic understanding of the other's needs along with one's own; (2) the interpersonal message that states one's own wishes in the situation; and (3) an emphasis on behavioral description and on specificity of time, place, frequency, and so on.
>
> Fifth, if new feelings or issues that seem more important arise in the course of your problem-solving efforts, don't hesitate to explore those.

Having thus laid the groundwork at an earlier time, the leader uses the type of occasion we are discussing here to recapitulate briefly the instructional material just described. He then may prompt the clients to consider whether they wish to use the behavioral modes to arrive at a concrete solution, or

whether they would rather tie up these loose ends at home and use the supervised session time for more complex or problematic issues. As with all structuring, the leader's goal is not to influence the final decisions or even to be privy to them, but to make sure that the clients understand the rationale and usages of the pertinent skills. The EPCS response is therefore a special kind of structuring response.

As an alternative to allowing a few moments of time out for the clients to come up with their suggestions, the leader after an EPCS response may simply suggest an improvement on the expresser's previous statement to encourage a more concrete approach to the issue under discussion. An illustration of EPCR responses in their appropriate context follows.

A father and son (John and Harold, respectively) have had a discussion about whether the son should be allowed to drive the car to a party. The following feelings and issues have already been clarified. The son believed that the father was being concerned about what might happen to the car, and that this concern made socializing very difficult for him because they lived quite a distance from his friends. The father was not concerned about damage to the car, but was worried about the safety of the son; he was afraid that Harold might get into an accident if he drove the car to the party. Harold believed this concern was unjustified because he had never been involved in an accident or traffic violation, and he found the limitation very frustrating, and his father's attitude irritated him. The father believed this situation to be different than the son's ordinary car usage in that he believed his son might drink at the party and this would affect his driving. The son felt untrusted and was angry at the lack of trust in his judgment about drinking and driving. The father expressed the desire to help his son out and gratify his wish; he also expressed a basic confidence in the son's judgment and self-control. However, he feared that his son lacked enough experience to determine how much he could drink without having it affect his driving. He also feared that under the social pressures of the party his son would not draw an appropriate line. This last exchange was repeated essentially unchanged a couple of times, with adequate empathic and ex-

pressive statements on both sides. At this point, after a response by the father as expresser, the following response to the father is appropriate:

> *Leader:* John, you've expressed your feelings very well [SR-E]. Do you think you've pretty well covered your views and feelings on the subject and that Harold has responded to them empathically [A-E]?
>
> *Father:* Yes.
>
> *Leader:* Harold, do you feel that your dad has responded empathically to your views and feelings on this [A-R]?
>
> *Son:* Yeah, I guess so.
>
> *Leader:* Is there some idea or feeling he hasn't responded to empathically that you want to express [A-R]?
>
> *Son:* Hm, No.
>
> *Leader:* Then I'd like to suggest that we may be at the point we've talked about in the problem-solving and conflict resolution process where it's especially appropriate to emphasize the interpersonal message part of your expresser statements, and to make suggestions for solutions in terms that are as behavioral and specific as possible, trying to maximize satisfaction of both of your needs, and minimize both of your difficulties and concerns. Is that something you would like to do now [EPCR-E,R]?

(Both answer that they would, and the leader opts for modeling an appropriate expresser response, rather than suggesting that the clients take a few moments to think of possible mutually satisfying solutions.)

> *Leader:* John, tell me if this is an appropriate paraphrase of your last statement, including now the interpersonal message that I'm adding: "I am very concerned about the possibility of your drinking and getting injured in an accident, and for that reason I'm very reluctant to let you have the car. But I do trust you personally, and I do want to help you out of this. I would let you have the car if somehow I could feel confident that you wouldn't get yourself hurt. I wish you would promise me that you would not drink at the party. If you were to make that promise, I would feel much more secure about your driving [MEX]."
>
> *Father:* That's right.
>
> *Leader:* OK. Would you say that to Harold [A-E]?

The father then proceeds to do so. Harold responds empathically. In numerous following exchanges, with the father in

the responder mode and Harold in the expresser mode, Harold indicates that he believes such a prohibition seems unfair to him and seems to him to reflect a lack of trust. Harold also expresses the view that not being allowed to drink at the party would be embarrassing to him. He believes that he can be trusted not to be under the influence of alcohol when the time comes to drive home. The leader then structures again. He reminds Harold that it would be appropriate to include in his expresser statement (1) an empathic recapitulation of his father's views; (2) an interpersonal message reflecting his own wishes; and (3) a specific suggestion which takes both points of view into account. Harold does so as follows.

> *Harold:* I know you would like to feel very confident that I would not be driving under the influence of alcohol. It would make me feel more trusted, and satisfied that my needs are being met, if you would let me have the car. I am willing to promise you that I won't drive the car under the influence of alcohol.

Further dialog establishes that the father does not feel confident that the son can make such a judgment. After several more mode switches, a mutually satisfying agreement is reached that Harold can have the car, that he will limit himself to drinking two bottles of beer during the evening, and will drink no alcohol the last two hours of the party.

### Troubleshooting (T)

Troubleshooting responses are not frequent, but when the need for this type of response does arise, it is of critical importance that the leader recognize that need and perform well in his role as troubleshooter. In fact, it is a cardinal principle of RE leadership that *when issues that significantly affect the ability of the group to function smoothly do arise, they take priority over all else.* One circumstance in which troubleshooting is required arises when the primary issue under consideration is not the relationship between members of the family, but the relationship between client and (1) the RE method, or (2) the leader.

*The relationship between the client and the RE method.* This relationship frequently becomes an issue in the first ses-

sions when clients may show doubts about the desirability or utility of the RE goals or procedures. In this situation, the leader's first task—accomplished exclusively by responding empathically to the cues or statements that have indicated doubt—is to draw out and show acceptance of all doubts and disagreements. Although such leader statements are empathic responses directed from the leader directly to the client (later to be described as an *inappropriate leader response—I,ID*), they are not inappropriate in this context. Because in this context the issue is not one between the family members but between the client and the leader, it is appropriate for the leader to respond empathically directly to the client rather than through a family member. In effect, the leader is in the empathic responder mode and the client is the expresser. Such empathic responses are therefore coded *T* rather than *I,ID*.

After doubts and the feelings underlying them have been fully drawn out, the leader uses structuring responses—the underlying rationale, empirical evidence, experience, and so on—to try to allay the doubts and concerns. The leader then returns to empathic responses (that is, T responses) to make certain that the doubts have in fact been laid to rest. If so, he continues with the business at hand. If not, the cycle may be repeated until the doubts are allayed, or, alternatively, until the leader decides to ask the client to suspend questions until some later point in the program when they may again be considered on the basis of greater actual experience with the technique in question and the client agrees with this suggestion.

*The relationship between a client and leader.* This relationship requires troubleshooting if (1) the leader is criticized as a person or (2) the leader experiences such strong feelings about a client or the group as a whole that it interferes with his ability to function well, and he feels he must clear the air. Such leader-client relationship difficulties have occurred only a few times in many thousands of hours of RE group time. However, in discussions of RE programs, the question often arises of how such situations would be handled, and it is certainly important that the leaders be prepared in advance to deal with such situations if they should arise. The appropriate way to deal with either of

these two problem situations is for the leader to enter into a dialog with the other party or parties. In this dialog, parties not deeply involved at any given time in the exchange act as facilitators, while the leader and the party or parties concerned limit their behaviors exclusively to role prescription and procedures of expresser, empathic responder, and mode switching until the problem is resolved and the attention can be returned to the primary purposes of the program. With respect to coding of leader responses, so long as the leader stays within the boundaries of the basic behavioral modes, his responses are appropriate and are labeled *T*, rather than *I,ID*. Naturally, if he deviates from them, the deviations are coded, under a suitable category, as *inappropriate response*. An illustration of how a leader would initiate this type of exchange follows. The leader is expressing himself to a couple, Iris and Bill, in a Conjugal Relationship Enhancement group who have not completed their homework assignments in three consecutive previous sessions, and have just indicated in this session as well that they have not completed their homework assignments.

> *Leader* [to group]: We're going to do something different now [A]. I have a problem—some feelings that are disturbing me [T]. I think it's important to the continued smooth functioning of the group that I air these feelings and discuss my problem because it's affecting my ability to function at my best as a leader. The problem involves feelings that I have about Iris and Bill not doing their homework assignments. As I've said before, the skills we are teaching you can be applied not just between family members, but in most kinds of interpersonal situations, and should be applied especially in those situations where there is a high potential for the development of misunderstanding, conflict, negative feelings, or counterproductive attitudes [S]. That is the kind of situation I see developing because of my feelings toward Iris and Bill. So, I am asking the rest of you if you would act as facilitators while I engage in a dialog with Iris and Bill using the same skills and procedures that you have been using as couples. Bill, Iris, is that alright with you? [Iris and Bill indicate their assent.]
>
> *Leader:* Would the rest of you act as facilitators [A]? [They state their assent.]
>
> *Leader:* Bill and Iris, either of you, or both in turn, may act as responders or expressers to me after each statement I make. If you both choose to say something in a given exchange, I will respond empathically to each of you before I react as expresser. Conversely,

before you make an expressive statement to me, I would like each of you to respond empathically to me even if the other has already done so [S]. Do you understand the procedure I'm suggesting, and is it agreeable to you [A]? [Iris and Bill indicate their understanding and assent.]

*Leader:* OK, I will begin as expresser [A]. I understand from what you've told me that it is very difficult for you to stick to the arrangements we work out here each week as to when and where you will complete your homework assignments because of the demands that your work places on you, Bill, and also because of the unexpected visits of your friends and the various demands that the children's difficulties have placed on you, Iris [T]. I appreciate the fact that things are very hectic for you both right now, and I do feel sympathetic toward you because of the various strains I know you are under and, in fact, I am pleased that you come to these sessions regularly despite your problems. At the same time, though, I've experienced a growing sense of annoyance toward you, and a growing sense of inadequacy and frustration within myself, because each week we seem to take these things into account in setting up the circumstances under which you can practice together, and nothing seems to work. The annoyance comes about because I feel let down and because I think you've broken something like a contract between us. Even though I can see why the particular times set aside became inappropriate, it does seem to me that other times might have been found. The frustrations and inadequacy arises from the fact that I feel I've used every type of encouragement and planning device with you that I can think of, and I feel a hopelessness about where to go from here. I believe these skills, if you would practice them enough, could be of great help to your relationship, and could do a great deal to help you resolve your difficulties [S]. I like you both a great deal, and I want very much to be effective in helping you in this way; so it's very frustrating to me when I view myself as failing to be effective.

*When client emotions prevent smooth mode functioning.* Whenever emotions completely overwhelm a client to the point where he and/or his partner is obviously unable to carry through prescribed mode behaviors successfully, the leader troubleshoots. Troubleshooting in this situation may include administrative or other types of appropriate responses, but it consists mainly of making empathic responses directly to the overwhelmed person. Overwhelming emotion in and of itself is *not* sufficient cause for troubleshooting. The leader should intervene with troubleshooting only if the clients are unable to deal with it themselves through the use of RE skills.

A troubleshooting situation wherein the leader would respond empathically to a *responder* occurs when the expresser said something that caused the responder to choke up or perhaps to break down in tears, unable to continue in the assigned mode. At this time it would be appropriate for the leader to respond empathically to the feelings he perceives the responder to be experiencing and to continue to do so until such time as the responder regains composure. At that point, the leader should either suggest a mode switch to the couple, or suggest that the couple return to the same behavioral modes they were using before troubleshooting commenced. An illustration of the use of T responses in this type of situation with a married couple follows.

*Leader* [to responder, who is crying]: You're terribly hurt by the disappointment Bob [the husband] has expressed in you as a mother [T-R].

*Responder* [sobbing]: Yes.

*Leader:* You want very much to be a good mother, and it's very painful to be told that you're not in some ways [T-R].

*Responder* [recovering somewhat, but still sobbing occasionally]: It's really not fair of him to think that. He comes home and doesn't know what's been going on. He sees me at a time when I've been putting up with all kinds of pressures all day from the two babies as well as Billy, when I'm exhausted and at my wit's end—when I've lost all the patience I have. Bob has no idea what it's like cooped up there all day with the three of them.

*Leader:* You feel hurt; you're hurt not only by what Bob said about you as a mother, but also because it seems so unfair of him to judge you that way, not knowing what your life is like at home all day [T-R].

*Responder:* Yeah! He knows I'm not like that most of the time—if I have some help or get some relief—if he's around to help out. It's an awful thing for him to say.

*Leader:* It seems *very* unfair to you. You're very hurt and disappointed in him and angry that he would think that and say that [T-R].

*Responder* [no longer sobbing]: Yeah!

*Leader:* I think it would be good if you would share those feelings with Bob now [A]. Do you think you could clarify the last statement he made now, and take the expressive mode and tell him these feelings directly [EMS-R]?

If the *expresser's* control over his emotions completely breaks down and the responder's skills are not equal to the task, the leader should use T responses in the same manner as has just been described until the expresser regains equilibrium.

## Inappropriate Leader Responses

By *inappropriate* responses, we simply mean deviations from the type of behaviors recommended for *RE programs.* Some practitioners may wish to use some RE methods in combination with methods derived from other sources—which, in this context, we're calling *inappropriate.* In some cases, this may mean the methods are operating at cross-purposes with one another. In other instances, non-RE methods may work additively with RE techniques. Thus, we do not mean to imply that the behaviors considered inappropriate here are necessarily unproductive in all contexts, but only that they lie outside the realm of RE methodology. Being able to identify responses that are inappropriate as far as RE methodology is concerned facilitates research by making it easier to differentiate this method from others. The major and most immediate reason for labeling certain responses *inappropriate* for RE programs, however, is to facilitate peer- and self-supervision in training RE leaders.

Naturally, it would be impossible to categorize all the particular ways in which the quality of RE leadership could be diminished. There are all kinds of things a leader might say and do that would represent poor leadership with respect to this and/or any other mental health program. Also, he might do or say the "right" things insofar as a typescript could reveal but deliver his responses in such a manner—condescending, overbearing, cold, mechanical, unenthusiastic, unconvincing, and so on—as to undercut the effectiveness of what he does. Thus, we cannot hope to present a system of classification that would reflect all the dimensions of inappropriate RE leadership responses.

The only leader actions we are categorizing as *inappropriate* are the kinds of behaviors that students and professionals are likely to use either (1) because they "come naturally," when

one tries to be instructive or psychologically helpful, or (2) because they have been developed by professionals to apply to
other strategies of intervention. They represent deviations that
would occur *as a matter of course* were the leader not systematically trying to avoid them. In addition to responses the leader
*makes*, it is also sometimes obviously inappropriate within the
RE model to make a *passive* error. These inappropriate responses are failures to correct extremely inappropriate participant behaviors.

For some supervisory and research purposes, the code
designation *I*, without subcategories, will be sufficient. However, if a supervisor wishes to have a reminder of the specific
type of inappropriate response made by a supervisee, or if a
researcher wishes to have data on specific types of deviations,
subdesignations are useful. The abbreviations for such subcategories therefore are provided in the following sections. Many of
the subcategories are drawn from a system for coding therapist
responses developed by Ashby, Ford, Guerney, and Guerney
(1957).

### Directive Lead (I,DL)

Directive leads usually arise out of the leader's desire to
steer a conversation in a more fruitful direction with non-RE
responses. When the leader responds to the content of what is
being said rather than the skills or process, his response is an
inappropriate one (except in those situations defined under the
category of troubleshooting). If he tries to help a client toward
insight, or steer a couple toward a solution to the problem they
are discussing, rather than helping them to apply the RE skills
more effectively so that they themselves can reach the insight or
solve the problem, then he is using an I,DL response. If the
intent of the leader seems to be to lead a participant to discover
contradictory ideas or behavior within himself, see obscured
motivations, or discover new cause-and-effect relationships by
directing the participant to a certain area of thought or discussion, he is using an I,DL response. An I,DL response differs
from an *interpretive response*, to be discussed below, in that it

is a general invitation or steering: No specific insight on the leader's part can be inferred from his statement. A nonexhaustive group of examples would be: (1) *questions* such as "Do you feel like this in other kinds of situations?" "Do you often have some kind of argument before you make love?" "What effect do you suppose this kind of behavior has on your son?" or "How long has this been going on?" (2) *incredulity*—for example, "Absolutely never?" or "Are you sure you really mean that?" or (3) *confrontation*—"I wonder if you are being honest with yourself"; "I find it hard to believe you've never had such feeling"; or "That's not what you said a few minutes ago."

### Interpretation (I,I)

An interpretation is defined here as a fairly specific item of knowledge about a participant—an insight, perhaps—that the leader obtains through his observations and then makes available to a group member. An interpretation usually includes an implication of causality or points out contradictions or relationships. These are of course not usually offered as fact, but as a possibility for the client to weigh, and accept or reject. Examples are:

> 1. It seems that when your husband does something that is distressing to you, you end up feeling guilty; somehow it never seems to make you mad at *him*.
>
> 2. You've talked the same way earlier about how your mother made you feel when she constantly made suggestions to you. It sounds very much like the feelings you have when your wife asks you to do things. Do you think there's a relationship between your feelings toward your mother and toward your wife?
>
> 3. A little while ago you said you didn't care what your mother thought about your friends; now you're saying you feel uncomfortable when your mother is around and Shirley is visiting you. Do you think that perhaps you care a little more than you like to admit?
>
> 4. It seems as though it's easier for you to make passionate love after you've had an argument.

### Suggestion, Explanation, Advice (I,SEA)

Other common ways of trying to be helpful are to make suggestions about how to look at things, to give advice about

how to behave, or to describe standards for clients to use. Responses that offer a participant a suggestion, advice, standards, or explanations about psychological or interpersonal phenomena (beyond those pertinent to the concepts and skills employed in the program) are designated *I,SEA*.

Examples of such responses are:

1. Try going out together more. Find something you both like to do, and do it together.

2. Have you thought about a more positive approach to the problem—offering your son some kind of incentive, some form of reward when he does do a good job with his homework?

3. Very often, when children misbehave, it's because they want to get back at someone, and that becomes more important to them than the negative consequences they suffer themselves.

4. Sometimes behavior like that is really a cry for help.

5. At fifteen, children are in a stage of development where what their peers think of them can be more important than anything else.

6. Perhaps a good compromise in this situation would be to allow him half an hour to himself to relax or do what he wants when he first gets home. After that he might feel much more like doing some of the things you'd like.

### *Encouragement, Approval, and Reassurance (I,EAR)*

Other kinds of responses that virtually all lay persons, and most professionals, frequently wish to provide for clients are encouragement, approval, and reassurance. Such responses are designated *I,EAR*. As generally used, they share in common the intent of making the recipient feel good or, more frequently, less bad. They are usually elicited from a leader by a client's complaint, expression of anxiety, or a self-belittling statement. Again, it is necessary to distinguish using such responses in the context of reinforcing or encouraging the client with respect to the RE program and skills, and the use of these responses as reactions to the *content* of the problems the clients are dealing with in their personal or interpersonal lives. Of course, only the latter types of responses are designated *I,EAR*, the former type being classified as described earlier in this chapter.

Examples of I,EAR responses, some mixed with I,SEA responses, as is often the case, are:

1. Sometimes it takes a while for a new pattern of behavior to really sink in with people [I,SEA]. I'm very confident, really, that if you keep it up you'll start to get the recognition you deserve [I,EAR].

2. You know that kind of feeling you're describing of being lost at sea, not knowing what you want to do with your life, a kind of hopelessness about finding the right direction for yourself and the way in which it's affecting your relationship with your husband? That's not an uncommon feeling for mothers when the youngest child goes off to school [I,SEA]. It takes a while to work it through, but I feel you're approaching it very constructively and that you *will* work out a direction that will be satisfying for you [I,EAR].

3. I think it's just great that you've made the decision to go away, just the two of you, for a weekend. That kind of thing can really turn out to be a revitalizing experience [I,EAR].

4. You know, Bill, feeling that you've given in by agreeing to wash the dishes and cook many of the meals is a very understandable thing. As you say, your father never would have done those chores. But work assignment according to sex is rapidly becoming a thing of the past. In circumstances such as yours, it's probably a minority of the men who aren't pitching in like that [I,SEA]. I think you're doing the right thing, and that you'll feel very differently about it in the long run [I,EAR]. At least, that's what I've observed with many of the men that I've worked with.

5. I think you've reached an excellent compromise there [I,EAR].

### Personal Criticism (I,C)

When we refer to *personal criticism* (I,C), of course, we are not referring to corrections of responses for instructional purposes, but rather to statements that tend to belittle the hearer. I,C responses include anything that is a put-down, such as sarcasm or ascribing socially undesirable characteristics of any kind to another member of the group. This is probably the worst type of inappropriate response that can be made in an RE program, because it models behavior that the leader is seeking to eliminate from the behavioral repertoires of the participants in their communication with one another. Such statements tend to make a participant anxious and defensive, alienate him, and diminish his chances of learning, all reactions that increase the probability that he will terminate the program. Our experience is that there are better ways to accomplish improved perform-

ance than personal criticism. If the leader has negative feelings toward a client that are seriously impeding the relationship, he should use troubleshooting methods rather than resort to direct criticism of the person as an individual, sarcasm, or put-downs.

Examples of I,C responses are:

1. You're not really trying very hard.

2. If you're not willing to put that much effort into your assignments, you couldn't really care as much about improving things as you say you do.

3. You always seem to want to have the last word in the discussion.

4. That was a nasty crack.

## Other Diversions (I,OD)

Unfortunately, not only neophytes, but experienced professionals, who may be charging $50 an hour or more for their time, are not immune to straying from the task at hand. The I,OD category is a catchall category for responses that divert the participants from the educational purpose of the group that have not been included in the previously described inappropriate types of leadership responses. Included here are sharing of thoughts, judgments, opinions, experiences, anecdotes, and so on. Self-disclosures are also coded *I,OD*. Despite their modeling properties, we regard leader self-disclosures as relatively inefficient instructionally, and too often simply diversionary. The major purpose of this I,OD category is to pinpoint downtime—time the leader is spending in ways other than in administration, instruction, supervision, and troubleshooting. What we are interested in tagging here are leader responses that take away a significant amount of time from pursuit of the group's goals. It must be acknowledged that a certain amount of humor, social conversation, sharing of experiences, good spirit, and friendliness are lubricants that are necessary to the smooth running of groups. Such behaviors by the leader are conducive to good morale and, what is most important, contribute to a good atmosphere for learning. A certain amount of such behavior is therefore to be encouraged rather than discouraged. To

allow for enough, but not too much, play as opposed to work time, we use both the circumstances and the number of consecutive nonproductive responses in defining I,OD responses.

Some social conversation is almost mandatory in beginning and ending groups sessions and when participants are entering or leaving the group in midseason. As indicated earlier, no coding at all is conducted at these times. At other times, only the *third* and each consecutively following diversionary responses of a leader should be coded *I,OD*. (*O* stands for *Other* responses, which will be described in a later section.) In practice, all diversionary responses are coded *I,OD* as they occur. This is simply a clerical device to keep track of consecutive *OD* responses. The *I* and the *D* are later crossed out for all but the third consecutive diversionary response and consecutive diversionary responses thereafter. Responses with the *I* and the *D* crossed out become *O* responses.

For purposes of coding these diversionary responses, both leaders are counted as one, so that if the leaders team up in a sequence of diversionary responses, each consecutive diversionary response after the second, no matter which leader said it, is coded *I,OD*. (Intervening client responses, whatever their nature, do not affect this coding.)

Examples of I,OD leader responses (ignoring time and frequency) are:

> 1. I had some rough experiences myself with my parents when I was a teenager. It wasn't until I graduated from high school that things began to look a little better to me in terms of our relationship [If this seemed to be an attempt to reassure a participant, it would instead be classified *I,EAR*].
>
> 2. I like to watch _____ on TV too; it's one of my favorites.
>
> 3. Did your car make it through inspection?
>
> 4. I was very impressed with what you said about your food budget. How do you manage to get by on so little with five in the family?

### Inappropriately Directed Responses (I,ID)

An inappropriately directed response differs from the previously discussed responses in that it is not determined on the basis of *what* is said, but rather *to whom* it is said. The two types of responses that comprise this category are: (1) an em-

pathic response to the expresser (I,ID-E), and (2) reformulation of an expressive response to the responder (I,ID-R).

*An empathic response to the expresser (I,ID-E).* An I,ID-E statement may be an accepting empathic response of the very best kind. The error resides not in the content, but in the fact that the leader has addressed the expresser rather than directing his statement to the responder so that the responder can deliver the statement to his partner. As indicated earlier, an empathic response delivered directly to a client is appropriate only when the leader is troubleshooting. The leader most often is tempted to use I,ID-E responses when he is impressed with the importance and depth of the client's statement (especially when it expresses a negative, or "down" feeling), believes that the client deserves or needs the best possible response quickly, and does not believe that the partner will be able to provide it. Hence, instead of modeling the response for the partner, the leader finds himself doing what the partner should be doing. Examples of inappropriately directed responses to the expresser are:

> 1. *Expresser* [to husband] : I don't see us changing, so what hope is there? I can't take it much longer the way it is.
>
> *Leader* [to wife] : You're feeling very discouraged about the relationship right now; you're almost ready to give up on it.
>
> 2. *Expresser* [daughter, to leader] : She [mother] gives me orders like I'm some kind of slave or something, and if I say anything about it, I just get in worse trouble.
>
> *Leader* [to daughter] : It makes you very angry when she talks to you that way, and it's very frustrating too, because you don't have any workable way to deal with it.
>
> 3. *Expresser* [son to father] : I did everything you said, I tried as hard as I knew how, and the only thing you said was: "Next time work harder; I know you can do better."
>
> *Leader* [to son] : It's very, very distressing to you that no matter how hard you try, you can't seem to please your father.

*An expressive statement to the responder I,ID-R.* A reformulation of an expressive statement directed to the respondent is a far less frequent type of misdirected response. The leader usually is tempted into this type of response because of the desire to facilitate the task of the responder by making the ex-

presser's statement a better one; one that the responder will be able to handle more readily than the original. Instead of helping the expresser to reformulate his statement or modeling a better one for him, the leader attempts to save time and trouble by addressing his reformulation to the responder. The reformulation, as in the examples below, may be excellent; the problem lies in the fact that it is directed to the responder rather than used to instruct the expresser. Examples of this type of the response are:

1. *Expresser* [wife to husband]: You're very inconsiderate of me at parties. You pay so little attention to me that I might as well not be there.

*Leader* [to responder]: She's saying that she feels neglected and hurt at parties at those times when you seem to her to be ignoring her.

2. *Expresser* [husband to wife]: The house is like a pigpen most of the time—you just don't give a damn where things are thrown.

*Leader* [to responder]: Let me rephrase that before you respond: "The house often looks more messy than I like to see it. When it does, that upsets me and makes me mad at you. I wish you would take more time and care and keep things more orderly."

3. *Expresser* [wife to husband]: It upsets me greatly that you never want to spend time with the children.

*Leader* [to responder]: She's saying that she wants you to spend more time with the children, and that she gets very upset when she thinks that you don't want to be with them.

### Failure to Correct (I,FC)

Obviously it would be impossible to develop a reliable coding system designating all failures to provide responses that would be useful to clients. To make the task merely difficult, rather than impossible, we shall limit our concern to failures of this nature that are peculiar to RE methodology. Secondly, we will not deal with omissions that represent merely lost opportunities to move the group forward toward its educational goals, but rather will consider only failure to provide a response that allows a serious misstep by a client to go uncorrected. Thirdly, we will limit our concern to those responses that are most likely

to be useful in training group leaders or in differentiating RE from other types of approaches.

It should be noted that in many instances the leader may not need to make a corrective response because a facilitator may make it for him, or he may invite a facilitator to make a corrective response rather than make it himself. In either case, an *I,FC* coding would not be appropriate. As with other codings, the role of the participant—expresser, responder, or facilitator—who should have been corrected and was not, can be designated by adding *E, R,* or *F.* Within each of these subcategories, there are two types of failures to correct the participant's responses. These are failure to correct responses that are: (1) inappropriate because of what has been said (content) and (2) inappropriate because they are directed to the wrong person.

*Failure to correct expresser (I,FC-E).* The use of the *I,FC-E* designation to record a failure to correct *content* will be considered first. The expresser is allowed considerable leeway in his responses, and *early* in an RE program the leader is not expected to correct the expresser for content errors except for serious deviations. Thus, only failure to correct serious deviations from the expresser mode are coded *I,FC.* Serious deviations are those in which content that is psychologically threatening to the other person is stated: (1) in objective rather than subjective terms; (2) in general, blanket terms rather than in terms of specific behaviors, or (3) in terms of the *other* person's motivations, thoughts, or feelings rather than in terms of the expresser's *own reactions* to specified behaviors of the other.

The need for the leader to correct such statements is twofold: (1) to increase accuracy and validity in order to advance problem solving and conflict resolution, and (2) to increase the probability that the responder will be able to respond empathically, rather than be psychologically forced to pit his perceptions against the expresser's, or become too upset or too angry to fulfill the requirements of the empathic responder mode. The effect of corrective responses is to prohibit accusation, character assassination and mind reading by the expresser, and instead to encourage the expresser to get at the specific perceptual and situational roots of the issue and thus to increase chances for

constructive dialog. It is when the leader fails to make such corrective responses in these circumstances that the code *I,FC-E* is used.

Now let us turn to expresser responses that require a corrective response by the leader because they have been *directed to the wrong person*. Except when seeking help with the formulation of his response, the expresser should always be addressing the responder, and deviations from this rule are considered serious enough to warrant a corrective response. However, this does not apply to nonverbal behavior. We would consider it damaging to the communication process if the expresser were not permitted to look downward or into space when discussing difficult issues. We also would consider it damaging rather than helpful if the expresser were not permitted occasionally to look at someone in the room other than his partner. The kind of response that consistently demands correction by the leader is a *verbally* misdirected response: The client uses the responder's name (unaccompanied by *you*) or uses a third-person pronoun to refer to his partner. The *I,FC-E* coding is used only when the leader fails to correct these verbally misdirected responses.

*Failure to correct responder (I-FC-R)*. Obviously, there are innumerable instances other than those we will discuss here in which a failure of the leader to restructure or otherwise assist the responder would be most regrettable. But again, it does not seem possible to build a reliable coding system without concentrating on extreme circumstances and a limited number of leadership failures.

Those content deviations from the responder role that are considered extreme enough to warrant an *I,FC-R* coding whenever they go uncorrected are ones in which the responder: (1) makes no effort even to restate what has been said to him by the expresser, or (2) enters into a clear statement of his own point of view without going through mode-switching procedures.

Certain noncontent cues may be used in coding live or from recordings. However, once again the cues that merit an I,FC-R coding are limited to extreme circumstances, because the leader should proceed with caution in correcting all but the most blatant noncontent deficiencies. The extreme circum-

stances are those in which there is a clear-cut rejection of the expresser's view by the responder. Such rejection may be shown by the manner in which the response is made even if the content is appropriate—for example, by an incredulous or sarcastic intonation—or by obvious gestures—for example, shaking the head in disbelief.

*Failure to correct facilitator (I,FC-R).* As we've indicated earlier, we believe that the systematic training of group members to avoid potentially intrusive, threatening, or just plain time-wasting behaviors and instead to become supportive, positively oriented instructors in the manner of the leader represents a major advantage of the RE program over traditional group therapy. All group members are in effect coleaders in training. Hence any statement that is inappropriate for a leader is also inappropriate for a facilitator. Group members should not be permitted any more leeway than the leader for expressing personal viewpoints, experiences, suggestions, value judgments, insights or social conversation. When the leader fails to correct such behavior by a facilitator, the leader's inaction merits an *I,FC-F* coding.

### Other Leader Statements

Any leader statements that do not fit into any of the preceding categories are designated *Other* (O). *Other* responses are not considered inappropriate until they have continued for a while. Thus as indicated earlier, the first two I,OD responses are converted simply to O responses whenever a third I,OD leader response is made.

### Response Distribution Over Time

The proportion of responses of different types the leader should use over the course of an RE program should change as the program progresses toward completion. During the first twenty-four hours of a program, social reinforcement would remain very high. After that, as self-reinforcement becomes more consistently evident, social reinforcement would decline

somewhat. It would always, however, represent a very high *pro-portion* of leader responses. Structuring responses would, of course, represent a moderately high proportion of responses in the first six hours or so, and would gradually diminish in frequency thereafter. Modeling responses would represent a very high proportion of responses in the first twelve hours or so of training, after which such responses would tend to be less frequent, generally coming into play with slow-learning participants or when extremely difficult topics were being discussed. Encouraging and prompting responses should be moderately high throughout the first twenty-four hours or so of training, diminishing after that as the skills become more habitual. Like most other responses, administrative responses are highest during the first twelve hours or so of training. Administrative responses never represent a very high proportion of responses, but they are always needed to some extent. Troubleshooting is sometimes required, though low in proportion to other responses, during the first twelve hours. It is rarely required after that.

Eventually the participants should be able to use RE skills without the help of any leader. The leader's goal is to work himself out of a job by teaching his clients how to interact more constructively with each other. The leader responses discussed in this chapter will enable him to meet this goal most efficiently and effectively.

# Chapter 7

# Relationship Enhancement Administration and Formats

▲▲▲▲▲▲▲▲▲▲▲▲▲▲▲▲▲▲▲▲▲▲▲▲▲▲▲▲▲▲

*Bernard G. Guerney, Jr.*
*Edward Vogelsong*

Relationship Enhancement programs are flexible and can be used with different formats and in various settings. In this chapter we discuss some of the variables related to setting up and running RE programs. The leader should be thoroughly familiar with all the considerations presented here in order to make the best possible use of these programs with his clients.

### Informing the Public

One of the advantages of programs based on the educational model is that they can avoid the stigma associated with "mental illness." If one wishes to preserve this advantage, it is important to avoid offering such programs to the public only as a way of alleviating problems. Instead, RE programs should be presented for what they are: programs designed to enhance life's satisfaction through establishing better relationships with

other people, and applicable whether one is highly troubled or very happy, and whether the relationship in question is highly precarious or extremely stable. The major consideration is simply whether or not a potential client wants to add these behavioral skills to his interpersonal repertoire.

Referrals from other psychotherapists and from psychologists, social workers, human development and interpersonal relationship specialists, and from physicians, clergymen, teachers, and so on, should be encouraged, just as they would be for any other mental health service. However, because educational programs are also potentially beneficial to the public at large, additional ways of seeking participants become appropriate.

The programs can be explained to a wide variety of social, fraternal, religious, and public service groups. As a way of providing a stimulating and thorough understanding of each type of program to such groups, films and videotapes that demonstrate the principles and the methods can be used.[1]

Unlike methods that offer to "cure" people, it is accepted practice to advertise educational programs via mass media when the programs are offered by genuinely nonprofit institutes or community service organizations. Such advertisements should be phrased carefully to avoid exaggerated claims and benefits. They should avoid gaudiness and gimmickry, but they need not be so dull as to fail to catch the public's attention or arouse curiosity and interest.

### Facilities

No special facilities or types of equipment are necessary for conducting an RE program. The only requirement is a room large enough to seat the people involved. If there is no such room available within a mental health facility, or—if it seems desirable to do so in order to avoid the stigma that may be associated with such a setting, to gain a sense of informality and

---

[1] Such a film or videotape may be rented from The Individual and Family Consultation Center, The Pennsylvania State University, University Park, PA 16802.

comfort, or for a variety of practical reasons—space often can be provided by a church, a synagogue, a fraternal association, or some other public-spirited organization. In some instances, it is practical to hold meetings in the homes of the participants.

In settings where professionals are being trained to use RE methods, it is desirable to have rooms equipped with one-way mirrors so that the trainees can learn by observing skilled leaders. Such mirrors also permit inconspicuous use of videotaping for supervising trainees or providing clients with video feedback of their own performance on those occasions where this seems desirable for some special instructional reason. (Although we have facilities readily available to permit this, we seldom have found it desirable to take the time away from the regular training methods to employ this special training technique.)

## Group Training versus Individual Training

Group training provides participants with the opportunity to learn by observing each other. It is often of great benefit for one pair to see how another pair uses RE skills to come to a fuller understanding of each other and to work out solutions to their problems. Clients also benefit in a group by actively practicing facilitator skills. By making constructive suggestions to each other regarding the use of RE skills, facilitators improve their own skill level as well as that of the practicing dyad. They are thus better prepared to be successful in their skill practice at home. The group format also allows each of the participants to see that other people also have conflicts in their relationship, often similar to their own. This feeling of sharing something in common often brings the group closer together and increases the trust level, while making each of the participants feel less pessimistic about his or her own relationship problems.

In other instances, there are advantages in working with only one dyad at a time. People who are reluctant to discuss problems or intimate issues in a group are often more comfortable in an individual setting. The length of each meeting is usually shorter when a leader is working with only one pair,

since he is able to focus his entire attention on the dyad for the whole session. There also can be more time for skill practice and for going over homework and generalization skills. The leader does not have to be concerned with equalizing time among couples. When additional sessions may be required, or when it is necessary to change the meeting time, the schedule of one couple is much more flexible than that of a group. Of course, it is always possible to supplement group sessions with individual sessions.

The choice between training several pairs in a group or training one pair individually must be made by the leader and the participants. Generally, we have not found it extremely difficult to convince our clients to enter groups. When clients are reluctant to join a group, the intake workers can try to persuade them to undergo a trial period of three or four weeks in a group. After this, if they still wish to do so, they can continue as a single pair. Usually, the clients decide to stay with the group after the trial period. Whenever there is strong resistance, however, we certainly would not hesitate to work with a single dyad.

The discussions and materials we are presenting in this chapter are designed for group training. Of course, the same principles apply in training individual couples. It is more difficult and complex to work with groups. Thus, it will be very easy for the leader to adopt the group methods for use with only one dyad. In a later chapter we will discuss alternatives to the dyadic model, including the use of RE with an individual as well as multilateral training for families and other relationships that are larger than two people.

## Size of Groups and Length of Meetings

The optimal size of groups and length of meetings are interrelated factors. The smaller the group, the more time each client has to practice RE skills under supervision. Groups of six to eight clients (three or four dyads), with meetings lasting about two and one half hours, generally has been the most suitable arrangement in our own setting.

The duration of the program over time is a third factor in the format equation. A program can be concentrated into longer meetings and compressed over a small number of weeks or months. Such a program can accomplish a great deal if it is carefully planned. Weekend training programs and other marathon formats are suitable for many types of groups and settings.

In other circumstances, the participants' needs are served best by meetings lasting anywhere from fifty minutes to three hours, depending on how many couples are included. How many weeks this type of group should run depends also on the type of client for which the group was established—that is, whether or not their relationships are troubled ones and, if so, how severely troubled.

If, for example, a weekly two-and-one-half hour group is set up for couples known to have severely troubled marriages, everyone should have the expectation that it will run for a minimum of six months. At that time, the clients and the leader weigh the probable benefits to each couple of their continuing and set another date for termination or review. A premarital group on the other hand, set up for weekly two-hour meetings, initially might be scheduled for only ten weeks, after which time *some* of the couples might wish to reenroll for an additional specified time. Groups composed of some pairs with highly disturbed relationships and other pairs with few if any problems could be scheduled to meet for an intermediate number of sessions, again with options for reenrollment.

Still another variable to be considered in enrolling people and scheduling groups is whether or not a pair is confronted with a *relationship crisis*; for example, with a threat of immediate separation for a married couple or of an adolescent running away from home. There are a number of special procedures that might be appropriate in such instances. First of all, such cases would logically involve *extended enrollment or intake sessions*, totaling three to five hours of contact. The extended intake (or early stage of therapy, if you prefer) allows the participants to ventilate their feelings as fully as possible, which hopefully will then permit them to take a calmer look at the recommendation to undergo RE training. It also allows them to

feel that they have presented—and that the interviewer has fully understood—the intensity of their feelings and the depth and scope of their problems. Thirdly, the extended intake also permits brief preliminary training to get the parties to the point where they listen to one another without frequent emotional breakdown and without interrupting each other. Sometimes it is best to hold some of these interviews with the participants separately—the wife alone and the husband alone, for example, or just the children and then the parents—before they are brought together again. Finally, in instances of severe discord and crisis, two or three marathon training sessions, each lasting half a day or an evening, also might be desirable. After the crisis has passed, the participants could enter a more routine format. The marathon format is described below.

## The Marathon Format

The marathon format, or Intensive Relationship Enhancement program (IREP), is particularly useful at both ends of the spectrum of relationship satisfaction. On one hand, it is an excellent format for people who already have good relationships and desire enrichment training that can be obtained quickly and conveniently. On the other hand, it is an excellent way to provide quick help to people with severely disturbed relationships who are experiencing a relationship crisis. In the former instance, the format may be used in a "retreat" type of weekend program for marital, parent-adolescent, or family enrichment. In the case of disturbed families in a crisis, the participants may be seen in a series of extensive sessions to help them over the crisis and to set the stage for longer-range participation if that proves necessary. One particular marathon format has been developed by Rappaport. It employs a sequence of alternating four- and eight-hour sessions. If desired, these sessions could be regrouped into different time blocks (for example, a series of only four-hour sessions or only eight-hour sessions) with little difficulty. It was developed originally for marital couples, but could easily be adapted to use to enhance other intimate relationships. The following summary of the four sessions of the

IREP paraphrases the description provided by Rappaport (1976).

*Session One.* This eight-hour session emphasizes the rationale and philosophy behind the intensive RE program and concentrates on learning the expresser and responder modes. Leaders use didactic teaching methods, as well as modeling techniques, to familiarize spouses with the expresser and empathic responder modes, mode switching, and facilitation. Couples rotate in the expresser and empathic responder modes, while other group members and the leaders serve as facilitators. To make the task easier and increase group cohesiveness, participants first practice their skills with group members other than their spouse. Facilitation and discussion of positive areas in the relationship (Clarke, 1970) are integral parts of this first session. At the close of the session, the following homework is assigned: (1) complete four sessions in the *Improving Communication in Marriage* booklet (Human Development Institute, 1970); (2) practice expresser and empathic responder modes at home on nonthreatening areas for half an hour every other day and bring the *seven* completed homework forms to the next session; and (3) make a tape recording of one of the half-hour home sessions and bring it to the next meeting. (Homework sheets, audiotapes, and *Improving Communication in Marriage* booklets are distributed to all couples.)

*Session Two.* This four-hour session emphasizes learning to use the modes in more threatening areas. A few home tapes are reviewed during the early part of the session. Later, the couples separate to practice the roles independently, while group leaders circulate among the couples making comments on their progress. The final part of the session is spent answering client questions and assigning homework. Couples are instructed to: (1) complete the final four sessions in *Improving Communication in Marriage*; (2) practice the skills at home at least five times over the next two weeks and bring the completed homework sheets to the next session; (3) make a recording of one of the half-hour home sessions and bring it to the next session; and (4) *independently* prepare a list of the *two* most serious problem or conflict areas in the marital relation-

ship and bring it to the next session. Group members are instructed not to show their lists to their spouses before the next meeting. Furthermore, all clients are informed that they will be asked to communicate on these problem areas at the next session.

*Session Three.* This eight-hour session is devoted to communication between dyads on specific areas of conflict. During the first three hours, each couple communicates on the second problem on their lists in front of the group. After a break, each couple independently spends one hour communicating on their primary problems while the group leaders circulate among the couples, facilitating whenever necessary. Later in the day, couples meet in the group to communicate on positive areas of their relationships. For the final half-hour, the group remains together for discussion of the day's activities.

For homework assigned at the end of the third session, participants are asked to: (1) practice skills at home with respect to positive or negative relationship areas at least five times over the next two weeks and bring the completed homework sheets to the final session; (2) make a tape recording of one of the half-hour home sessions and bring it to the next session; and (3) *independently* prepare a list of possible solutions for the two problems discussed at this session; include possible ways in which the couple could change or modify behaviors for the well-being of their relationship (that is, compromise, bargaining, and alternative behaviors); spend some time thinking about these issues before preparing their lists; and bring the list to the final session.

*Session Four.* This four-hour session focuses on conflict resolution within the marital relationship. Each spouse, while *consistently continuing to use all RE skills, and only RE skills*, applies such techniques as compromise, bargaining, and alternative behaviors to their specific difficulties. Other group members facilitate the dyadic discussions. At the close of this session, there is an informal gathering at which participants relax and discuss their experiences in the program.

## Number and Type of Group Leaders

If resources permit, in groups with three or more pairs it is desirable to have two leaders and ideal to have a male and

female as coleaders. Not only are two heads usually better than one, but some clients establish rapport more quickly and prefer to model themselves after or learn from a male rather than a female (or vice versa). A dual leader situation is also ideal for training purposes: A less-experienced group leader can serve as a coleader, learning from a more experienced person as he works. However, we do not consider it a serious handicap for an experienced leader to run a group alone. We also would not hesitate to use two males or two females to colead a group when it is difficult to arrange for a mixed pair.

RE programs are highly specific and systematized, requiring leaders who are very well trained. However, because the principles and techniques and the methods of teaching them are so clearly defined, this training can be accomplished in a reasonable period of time. We train graduate students without previous practicum experience of any kind to function very well as junior coleaders in about eighty hours. In addition to appropriate reading, such training includes observation of live or videotaped groups-in-progress and supervised role playing, with the student role playing first a client and then a leader. After receiving brief postgroup session supervision from the senior coleader for ten sessions, such a junior leader is generally ready to be a senior coleader and a cotrainer.

We train experienced professional persons in three to five days of intensive workshop training, often in their own agency setting. It is our hope, in fact, that a professional trained in Rogerian psychotherapy and in the principles of reinforcement would be able to attempt running a group after a very careful reading of this book, although he might well have questions to ask a supervisor or want some feedback before or after he gets underway.

On-site training and/or continuing supervision is now available anywhere in the country through a nonprofit institute organized to disseminate mental health programs based on an educational model: the Institute for the Development of Emotional And Life-Skills (IDEALS).[2]

[2] For further information, contact IDEALS, P.O. Box 391, State College, PA 16801.

## Guiding Topic Selection

When participants begin to learn RE skills, it is important that they be able to give their full attention to the skills themselves. Leaders should thus require that participants avoid discussing relationship issues during the first several hours of training and only gradually work up to discussing those areas of their relationships that involve strong emotions. Although many clients are eager to work out their most troublesome problems almost immediately, it is important that they postpone these topics until they have sufficient skills to deal with them. This delay may be frustrating, but in the long run it is much more efficient. It is easier for the clients during the early phases of training to practice using RE skills with relatively neutral subject matter. Leaders do clients no favor when they permit them to perform tasks that have little chance of success. In order to assure that the participants will have the greatest opportunity for being successful in their use of RE skills, it is important that they progress in order through four levels of practice.

### *Level One*

Before the participants are asked to begin practicing expresser and responder skills, they are given an explanation and a demonstration of the skills. It is desirable to demonstrate RE skills during both the intake interview when the program is explained and at the beginning of the first training session. If there are two leaders they can demonstrate together the communication skills that will be taught, by taking turns being the expresser and responder and then switching roles. This demonstration need not be extensive, but should give the participants a good understanding of what they will be asked to learn and should help them to see how this program can be beneficial to them. If there is only one leader, a video- or audiotape recording or a short film demonstrating expresser and responder skills may be shown and discussed.[3]

---

[3] For information on audiotapes demonstrating the contrast between unskilled and skilled dialog in resolving various types of family

On the first level, participants practice with someone in the group other than their partners. It is easier to practice and learn new ways of speaking and responding with a stranger than with someone with whom there are already well-established patterns of communication. This is the only time in the whole program when participants do not practice with their own partners. In a group of married or dating couples, the men are asked to practice with other men and the women with other women. In a parent-adolescent group, the adolescents practice with other adolescents and the parents with other parents.

Participants are asked to talk about subjects that have nothing to do with their partners. If, as sometimes happens, the topic changes course and begins to include mention of the partner, the leader intervenes to prevent it from continuing. By thus avoiding areas in which there may be conflict between partners, the participants are able to concentrate their attention on learning the skills. While one pair practices, the other group members observe. The leader does not encourage an extended conversation or mode switching at this time, since his goal is to involve everyone by moving quickly from one pair to another. The conversations are usually three to seven minutes long, so that clients do not feel great demands are being made on them and in order to give everyone an opportunity to practice as soon as possible.

The leader makes certain that all the group members practice both expresser and responder skills before going to the next level. If the practice times have been short (less than four or five minutes), and/or if it seems advisable to provide more practice before advancing to the next level of training, the leader can suggest that everyone take another turn. This stage of training usually lasts about ninety minutes.

### Level Two

Beginning with the second level of the training procedure and continuing throughout the rest of the program, each group

---

problems, contact B. Guerney at The College of Human Development, University Park, PA 16802.

member practices his skills only with his partner. During the second level, the topic of the conversations again is restricted to areas that do not involve partners, so that the participants can better concentrate on learning and using their skills.

It is usually more difficult for the participants to use their skills when practicing with their partners than it is when they practice with another group member. It is necessary for them to suspend the patterns of communication that have become a part of their usual way of relating to each other in order to practice and learn new sets of communication skills. This task is not an easy one. Leaders must demonstrate patience and understanding as they coach the participants. The leader uses a great deal of modeling, and adjusts his expectations to the participants' abilities. With such extensive modeling, reinforcement can be used for 80 to 90 percent of the participants' statements.

Everyone is given a chance to practice both expresser and responder skills. Before proceeding to the third stage of training, it is essential that all participants demonstrate an ability and a willingness both to express their own feelings and perceptions about an issue, and to respond to their partners by communicating understanding and acceptance of each other's feelings.

### Level Three

At the third level, the topic itself for the first time becomes an important part of the training as participants learn to use their skills while discussing a topic of interpersonal relevance. Each participant practices skills by discussing with his partner positive aspects of their relationship. Discussions in this level of practice are restricted to the expression of *positive* feelings in order to prevent undue strain on the new skills, and to keep the success level high. Participants who begin to talk about negative feelings are stopped immediately by the leader and asked to hold that discussion until a later time.

There also are other benefits to setting this rule. When partners discuss with each other the positive aspects of their

relationships, they become more conscious of the actual and potential strengths in their relationship. Far too often the problems of a relationship are the sole focus of attention, and the strengths and positive aspects ignored. By being asked to discuss the things he or she finds positive in the relationship, each person becomes more aware of his own and his partner's commitments to the relationship. Later discussions of problem areas can then be seen in a different context: The problems are being discussed so that they can be resolved because the relationship is important. Participants are then in a better position to structure their behavior in a way that will have a positive effect on the relationship.

Partners are encouraged to switch modes before another pair takes its turn. In this way, the responder has an opportunity to react to what has just been said as well as to express his own positive feelings toward his partner. The leader does not advance to the fourth level of practice until everyone has practiced both expresser and responder skills on a positive aspect of the relationship with his or her partner.

### Level Four

At the fourth level, participants are permitted to discuss aspects of their relationships that they would like to enhance or change, including problem or conflict issues. These topics are, of course, the most difficult ones to discuss skillfully. The use of the Relationship Questionnaire helps the clients proceed from topics that are easier to deal with to those that are more difficult as their skill level increases.

### The Relationship Questionnaire

Participants are asked to select topics for discussion by filling out a Relationship Questionnaire (RQ). A copy of this form appears in Appendix L of this book. This instrument helps participants think about important aspects of their relationship with their partner to use as topics for their skill practice. The RQ is distributed to all participants after the first stage of train-

ing, that is, after they have practiced the skills with someone in the group other than their partner. At this time, the participants are informed of the purpose of the RQ and are told to begin to fill it out *without discussing it with each other.* The RQ is read aloud and explained by the leader. Group members are provided with appropriate and inappropriate examples (mainly in terms of level of specificity) and encouraged to ask questions about how to complete it. In asking clients to give careful thought to their Relationship Questionnaires, leaders stress the importance of using group time as constructively as possible. The topics people discuss should be ones that are meaningful to their relationships.

When they have completed the RQ's, the leader discusses them with the participants, reinforcing them for any efforts made to fill them out and helping them with any difficulties. The participants are told that during the next phase of training they will be asked to choose from their RQ's one of the positive things they have listed and discuss this area with their partners, using expressive and empathic skills. At the end of every subsequent group session the participants are told to come to the next session prepared to discuss with their partners a topic they have listed on their RQ's.

During the course of training many of the participants will want to make changes in their RQ's by deleting certain topics and adding others. They should be encouraged to make these modifications. This process can be facilitated by the leader if he distributes blank RQ's every three or four weeks and encourages participants to continue to revise them as part of their homework assignment. Participants indicate for each topic how comfortable they feel about discussing it in the group. The leader explains that the RQ should always list at least one topic that the participant is willing to discuss in the group.

The leader stresses the importance of the RQ's and structures each session so that the topics come from them. Of course, the nature of a discussion may change direction once it is underway, but participants are not permitted to initiate topics that they have not listed in the RQ unless they can jus-

tify them as being of more critical importance to the relationship than those listed, or unless the unlisted topic requires an urgent decision on a matter very important to the relationship.

### Homework, Generalization, and Maintenance

The goal of RE programs is to teach participants certain skills that they can apply to their daily situations and continue to use beyond the termination of training. The success of these programs lies not only in the acquisition of the requisite skills by the participants, but also in the participants' ability to incorporate these skills in their repertoire of responses in order to use them for relationship enhancement and problem resolution. It is, therefore, extremely important that clients use and practice their skills outside the group meetings, especially in their homes. Homework assignments are designed to review the principles taught in the group meetings, to encourage clients to set aside specific times for additional skill practice, and to help participants use expressive and responsive skills in their daily lives.

Optionally, a programed course of instruction, the *Relationship Improvement Program* (Human Development Institute, 1964), can be assigned as a prelude or supplement to the group meetings. This book is published in two forms: the *General Relationship Improvement Program* (ten parts) and *Improving Communication in Marriage* (eight parts). If participants indicate at the time of the intake interview that they want to participate in an RE program, and it is anticipated there will be a waiting period of several weeks or more before they can actually begin, they can be given one of the books to take home and asked to complete two or three lessons a week as preparation for the program. In instances where this is not done in advance, a book can be distributed at the first session. Participants can be asked to complete two sessions between each group meeting.

A series of exercises has been developed for mother-daughter and family participants (Vogelsong, 1975a) to structure home practice sessions. Similar materials are now being prepared for other client populations. These exercises review

RE principles, provide participants with examples from daily life situations, suggest topics for skill practice at home, and include logs that stress the generalization of RE skills to the home setting. Participants are asked to keep logs on a weekly and a daily basis indicating those times when they used RE skills as well as the times they might have used the skills but did not. Clients are asked to bring their completed logs to each group session. The leader uses them as a measure for determining how frequently the participants are using their skills at home and as a basis for discussing the importance of generalization. He reinforces clients who employ their skills regularly, and discusses with the group suggestions for increasing their expressive statements and empathic responses on a daily basis.

Participants in all RE programs are asked to set aside a period of time between each group session to practice their skills at home. This assignment is usually made for the first time after participants have had four to six hours of group training, but never until the leader is certain that the participants will be able to use the skills on their own. All homework assignments are made in accord with the participant's needs and abilities; the leader wants to provide them with structure for improving their skills and to be sure that they can complete *successfully* the tasks he assigns to them.

When the leader thinks that partners can begin to work on their own, he asks them to set aside thirty to sixty minutes before the next group meeting to practice their skills together at home. The leader takes a few minutes to make sure that each pair agrees on a firm time when it will practice at home before the next group session. The leader carefully structures this first home practice session to maximize the chances of success and satisfaction. The participants are instructed to talk only about an area that is easy for them to discuss (such as something outside their relationship); they are told that if they run into difficulty they should stop immediately. Participants are given copies of the Practice Home Session form (see Appendix M) and are asked to fill them out and bring them to the next group session.

After participants have begun to practice their skills at

home, the leader begins each group session with a discussion of the home practice. The Practice Home Session form can be used as a basis for this discussion. Indications of satisfaction and success are pointed out and areas of difficulty discussed. If participants express difficulty, they should be encouraged to use the same topic with which they had difficulty at home as the basis of their skill practice in the group. In this way, the leaders can identify the problems and correct them.

If cassette tape recorders are available, they can be lent to participants who do not have one of their own. By recording their home practice sessions and giving the tapes to the leader, group members can receive help and supervision on specific areas of difficulty in their home practice. The leaders may want to set aside a period of time at the beginning of each group meeting to listen to a portion of a tape for supervisory purposes.

Home practice assignments should always take into account the reports the participants give about their last effort. People who have a lot of difficulty should be told to wait until they have had more practice in the group session before continuing to practice at home; those who do well should be encouraged to continue with topics that are appropriate to their skill level. They should be instructed that, generally, they should not discuss a topic at home that is emotionally more difficult to discuss than one they have already discussed in the group. A major goal of the program is to help participants have success at home practicing their skills with topics that are increasingly difficult for them to discuss, so that they can eventually communicate effectively with each other about any area of their relationship.

In addition to the regularly scheduled home practice session each week and the spontaneous use of RE skills in daily situations during the week, participants also are encouraged to set up additional extended discussions using the skills whenever relationship problems arise or a crisis occurs. The leader helps participants to recognize times in their daily lives when it would be helpful to set aside time to use RE skills to resolve a conflict, gain greater understanding of each other, and thus reduce inter-

personal stress. These opportunities for skill use should be scheduled as soon as feasible whenever a problem situation arises. By discussing instances when RE skills could be helpful and encouraging their use and by asking participants at each meeting whether they did in fact use their skills in such situations, the leader can be very helpful to the participants in enabling them to make the most effective use of the skills they have learned.

Toward the end of the program, the leader's role becomes more and more that of a supervisor and consultant, helping and encouraging participants with their practice at home and with their use of RE skills in their daily lives. Group time is used more and more frequently to work out problems clients had with their home practice and to discuss the generalization of skills to everyday situations.

During the final phase of the program, the sessions with the leader are held less frequently and are viewed primarily as supervisory sessions. Participants continue to return report forms from their regular home practice sessions. Eventually clients meet with the leader only occasionally, perhaps every few months, for "booster" sessions and then just once or twice a year. The leader should remain available as a consultant or supervisor who can be contacted if the participants need him.

### RE Session Outlines

The following checklists are used to guide the leader through the format of RE programs. It is assumed that an intake interview has preceded the first training session. The explanation of the program in the first session is brief and serves as a review and introduction for the demonstration and practice of RE skills. The general session checklist can be used for all subsequent meetings.

### First Session Outline/Checklist

I. Introductions and explanation of program

    A. Names and informal conversation

B. Confidentiality
  1. Respected by leaders and participants alike
  2. Make sure all participants verbally agree to adhere to confidentiality
     (Questions or Comments?)
  3. If research is conducted, explain research forms, observers, one-way mirrors, tape recordings, and so on
     (Questions or Comments?)
C. Explanation of program
  1. Meaning and importance of "acceptance"
     a. Give behavioral examples
        (Questions or Comments?)
     b. Verbal and nonverbal acceptance
        (Questions or Comments?)
  2. Expressive and responsive modes
     a. Explain rules of each mode and give examples
        (Questions or Comments?)
     b. Mode switching
        (Questions or Comments?)
     c. Demonstration—group leaders role play a conversation using both modes and switching modes
        (Questions or Comments?)
  3. Group leaders' role
     a. Educator, not analyst or problem solver; teaches and supervises skills that clients use to enhance relationships and/or solve problems
     b. Very active in early sessions
  4. Facilitators' role
     a. Limited to helping others learn expressive and responsive modes and mode-switching skill

      b. Therefore, does not ask questions, analyze problems or motives, try to provide solutions or suggestions, or express own opinion or ideas (Questions or Comments?)

II. Skill practice

    A. In the first stage *only* of skill training, participants practice with someone other than their own partner

    B. Members of same sex (or same age group, if a parent-adolescent group) are asked to volunteer for expressive and responsive modes

    C. Topic—an area outside of their relationship with their partner

    D. All participants practice both modes at least once; with six to eight participants in a group, minimum total group practice time for this topic would be ninety minutes before going on to the next training stage

III. Homework and scheduling

    A. Distribute Relationship Questionnaires to each participant to fill out at home and bring along to next session

      1. Explain the use of the Relationship Questionnaires

      2. Give examples
      (Questions or Comments?)

    B. Prepare for next session

      1. Explain the progression of the subject area of discussions for skill practice for next session, and tell participants to come prepared to talk with their partners about a topic outside their relationship
      (Questions or Comments?)

      2. Confirm date and time of next session

      3. Stress importance of regular attendance

## General Session Outline/Checklist

I. Review homework

    A. Collect any written work and reinforce

    B. Discuss any difficulties and questions

II. Discuss generalization

    A. Importance of using skills in everyday situations

    B. Ask participants for specific examples of when they could or did use skills since last session, apart from home assignments

    C. Encourage use of skills between now and next session

III. Skill practice

    A. Participants practice with their partners only

    B. Subject area of discussions progresses in order through the categories listed below (Points 1 and 2, following, are required topics only in the early hours of training)

        1. At about the third and fourth hours of training, partners talk with each other about an area outside their relationship

        2. At about the fifth and sixth hours of training, partners talk with each other about an area of their relationship that engenders positive feelings (should be an area listed under Category I on Relationship Questionnaire)

        3. At about the seventh hour of training, partners talk with each other about either (a) an area previously discussed if they think it is still a high-priority item, or (b) other areas from the Relationship Questionnaire (Categories I, II, or III)

IV. Homework

    A. Give assignments and have each dyad agree on the time they will do them before the next session

B. Ask participants to review the Relationship Questionnaire and make changes, if desired; periodically distribute extra, blank Relationship Questionnaires

C. Come to next session prepared to discuss issue from Relationship Questionnaire

### Contraindications to RE Programs

Experience to date suggests that there are very few people who cannot benefit from participation in an RE program. Obviously, some people will gain more than others, and some people should undertake different programs or treatment either before participation in an RE program, concurrently or afterward. It is the leader's responsibility to be sensitive to the needs of people and to recommend to them appropriate courses of action, preferably during the intake interview, but also later on, if such advice seems to be in order. No single method or program is appropriate for all types of people or for all problems.

We have found, however, that the skills taught in RE programs can be helpful to a wide variety of people in many different kinds of situations. The participants are always free to decide whether or not to use the skills they have learned. They are at liberty to pursue other courses of action and are often encouraged to do so by their leader.

### Demographic Factors

Some people might argue that educational programs are not suitable for clients of low socioeconomic status. It can be expected that those who value education and are more highly educated might benefit more from the methods used in RE programs. However, even if this is true, there is no evidence to suggest that people with less education would benefit less from an RE program than from any other program designed to have a lasting effect on interpersonal relationships. Research on RE programs that has included participants from low socioeducational strata clearly indicates a positive effect on relationships.

We therefore believe that it is appropriate and desirable to offer RE programs to people of all levels of education and social class. We are aware of no harm that could be done thereby, and we have every reason to believe that the programs can be as helpful, or more so, as other types of enrichment or therapeutic experience.

## Value Conflicts

Some people may decide for themselves that they do not want to participate in an RE program. They may be afraid of the results of open and honest communication on their relationship with their partner. Others may find the values underlying the program to be in conflict with their own values. It is our view that value decisions related to entering the program should be left to clients: The professional should not make the *prejudgment* that a client's values will prevent the client from benefiting from the program. The degree and depth of change in values that can take place in clients undergoing RE programs suggests that it would be a mistake to assume that *initial* values determine how much a client will benefit. The possibility that the program will change the initial values seems at least as strong as the possibility that initial conflicting values will prevent clients from benefiting from the program if they are willing to undertake it despite some initial doubts or conflicts.

## Inability to Learn

It is justifiable to screen out a client who expresses a desire to participate in an RE program but who is *certainly* going to have a great deal of difficulty learning the cognitive and behavioral skills taught in RE programs. Persons with a mental age below ten years, psychotics, incipient psychotics, and the severely depressed generally would belong in this category. The other instance in which it seems appropriate to screen out a client who wants to participate in an RE program is one in which *probable* incapacity to learn RE skills is coupled with the likelihood that such failure would result in the client suffering a

serious loss of self-confidence or hope. In these circumstances, the following questions should be considered: (1) Are there alternate programs that would entail a lower risk of failure? (2) If not, and if failure were to occur, is it likely to be more debilitating than failure through following an alternate course of action or taking no action?

## Other Considerations

Hopefully, the days are over when thinking that any one method is a cure-all for all sorts of problems and all types of people. Obviously, more research is needed to permit better individual fit of programs to particular people and special needs. Unfortunately, research indicates that, at the present time, neither clinical judgment nor psychological testing offers a highly dependable means of predicting an individual's chances of success in any type of psychotherapeutic endeavor.[4]

In light of this limited ability to predict, it is always desirable to avoid an either/or frame of mind in making recommendations to clients. When in doubt about which type of program is most appropriate, another program could be recommended that would run prior to, concurrently with, or after an RE program. In some instances, the other program might be the primary one and the RE program auxiliary; in other instances, the reverse might be true. If limited time or resources prevent a diverse approach, an RE program would deserve very careful consideration as the treatment of choice. We believe the potential benefits to be very high, and the risk factor very low, for all cases in which an exceptionally understanding, empathic relationship might prevent or alleviate serious emotional or interpersonal problems.

[4]We expect that the use of remedial programs based on an educational model, and the development of new predictive measures geared specifically to them, eventually will lead to significant improvements in making such predictions (B. Guerney, L. Guerney, and Stollak, 1971/1972).

## RE and Other Programs and Therapies

Clients may find it helpful to participate in other skill-training programs simultaneously or consecutively with their training in RE. For example, a therapist might suggest that a couple would profit from a program of instruction in certain sexual techniques, in value clarification, in goal setting, in behavioral contracting, or in reciprocal reinforcement. We encourage clients who are working on relationship issues to receive RE training first, because it will usually provide the mechanism for couples to explore every aspect of their relationship. Honest and open communication and sensitivity to each other's feelings and desires are the essence of good contracting, problem solving, and a fulfilling sexual relationship. Where additional therapy and techniques seem useful, RE provides a base for facilitating the couple's ability to make the most effective use of such training.

We hope that many therapists will find RE programs beneficial for their clients and that they will use them in conjunction with or as a supplement to their own preferred methods of therapy. The compatability of RE and traditional therapies is related to several factors. First, RE assumes that the clients, not the therapist, must make the crucial insights and decisions affecting their relationship. Second, RE gives the clients responsibility for working on their relationship at home, not just in the therapist's office. Third, in RE programs, problems are resolved by compassionate understanding and consideration of each partner's subjective attitudes, values, and perceptions, not by "objective," "healthy," or normative standards. To the extent that the therapist's own goals and preferred methods of treatment are in harmony with these principles, he will find the programs to be compatible and complementary.

# Chapter 8

# Experimental Evaluation of a Six-Month Conjugal Therapy and Relationship Enhancement Program

*Jerry D. Collins*

In contrast to many approaches to marital counseling, the Conjugal Relationship Enhancement (CRE) or Conjugal Therapy program attempts to have not only the therapist, but also the client incorporate and utilize the variables shown by research to be involved in a positive therapeutic change. The variables referred to are genuineness, nonpossessive warmth, and accurate empathy. These variables, central to Client-Centered Therapy (Rogers, 1951), have been found to be characteristics shared by effective relationship-oriented therapists (Carkhuff and Berenson, 1967). Therapists offering high levels of these variables had patients (hospitalized schizophrenics) showing dramatic personality and behavior change on a number of measures. Patients offered low levels of these variables exhibited deterioration (Truax and Mitchell, 1968). In two studies, a 75 percent improvement in schizophrenics was reported when their psychi-

atrist possessed these characteristics, 27 percent when he did not (Betz, 1963a, 1963b). In other studies (Truax, 1963; Truax and Carkhuff, 1965), where one group of patients received high levels of empathy, warmth, and genuineness, while a second group received low levels, and the control group no treatment, the high-level group showed significantly more positive change and spent significantly more time out of the hospital than either the low or control groups. There was no difference in change between the low-level group and the control group.

It has been found that more effective counselors tend to perceive people as more able, dependable, and friendly than do less effective counselors (Combs and Soper, 1963). Questionnaires indicate substantial correlations between some psychoanalytically oriented therapists' ratings of outcome and how well the therapists liked the patients (Strupp, Wallach, and Wogan, 1964). These authors concluded, from their survey of therapists and clients, that the "warmth" factor contributed to the patient's conviction that he has the therapist's respect. They considered this conviction to be the capstone of the therapeutic relationship.

Clients offered high levels of combined empathy, nonpossessive warmth, and genuineness show greater improvement than clients who receive low levels (Truax, Carkhuff, and Kodman, 1965) whether they are hospitalized patients, institutionalized juvenile delinquents (Truax and Wargo, 1967), noninstitutionalized juvenile delinquents (Truax, Wargo, Frank, Imber, Battle, Hoeh-Saric, and Stone, 1966) or underachievers (Dickenson and Truax, 1966).

In sum, it can be concluded that higher levels of nonpossessive warmth, genuineness, and accurate empathy can make a therapist more effective with many types of clients in various contexts. It is presumed that it also would be an important asset in marital therapy to have husbands and wives behave in this manner toward each other. The research reported in this chapter provides evidence that it is not unreasonable to expect husbands and wives, as nonprofessionals, to learn to provide higher levels of warmth, genuineness, and empathy to each other and to become effective psychotherapeutic agents for their own marital relationship.

## Use of Paraprofessionals

In earlier times, high levels of warmth, genuineness, and empathy were thought of primarily as the given personality characteristics of a therapist. However, it was found that the trainees of one supervisor who explicitly attempted to teach specific empathic behaviors were substantially higher on these variables than other trainees (Bergin and Solomon, 1963). Then it was reported that graduate students in clinical psychology and paraprofessionals could be taught to show empathy and nonpossessive warmth to the degree that they

> could not be differentiated significantly from levels of these variables offered by a group of relatively effective and highly skilled therapists [and] the level of patient depth of self-exploration achieved in therapy did not differ significantly among the three groups. [Carkhuff and Truax, 1965a, p. 335]

Similar results were reported with graduate student trainees (Truax and Mitchell, 1968) and undergraduate dormitory counselor trainees (Berenson, Carkhuff, and Myrus, 1966).

Pierce, Carkhuff, and Berenson (1967) report training two groups of volunteers for a lay mental health program. One group was trained by a trainer who had a high level of empathy, genuineness, concreteness, respect, and self-disclosure. The other group was trained by a trainer who scored low on these variables. They found the group trained by the former leader to be higher on these variables than was the group trained by the latter and concluded that trainees tend to move toward the level of functioning of their trainer. Stover and Guerney (1967) trained mothers in the use of reflective and other nondirective play therapy techniques for use with their own emotionally disturbed children. The experimental group was found to be significantly higher in responses displaying empathic understanding than the control group. Carkhuff and Truax (1965b) also provided evidence of the feasibility of empathy training. Truax and Mitchell (1968, p. 72) provided evidence that

> even nonprofessional persons lacking expert knowledge of psychopathology and personality dynamics can, under supervision, pro-

duce positive changes in chronic hospitalized patient populations after specific training in the communication of accurate empathy, nonpossessive warmth, and therapist genuineness.

Strupp (1960) found that of 126 psychiatrists, only 4.6 percent of their 2,474 responses could be classified as communicating any degree of warmth and acceptance, and that 51 psychiatrists were rated as having clearly negative, cold, or rejecting attitudes. Considering all the mentioned findings, the case can be made that using nonprofessionals trained in empathy might be even more effective than traditional psychotherapy by professionals (B. Guerney, 1969).

## Communication in Marriage

The importance of communication in marriage is clearly supported by the literature (Bernard, 1964; Burgess and Wallin, 1953; Cutler and Dyer, 1965; Hobart and Klausner, 1959; Karlsson, 1963; Locke, 1951; Locke, Sabagh, and Thomas, 1956; Shipman, 1960; and Terman, 1938). Most of these studies support the commonly held notion that good communication is highly correlated with good marital adjustment, while poor communication is generally found in marriages with poor marital adjustment.

One of the chief complaints of dissatisfied wives was that their husbands did not talk things over with them frequently enough (Terman, 1938). Happily married couples report talking things over more frequently than couples who ultimately divorce (Locke, 1951). Locke, Sabagh, and Thomas (1956) found correlations ranging from .36 (for randomly selected couples) to .72 (for group-affiliated couples) between communication and marital adjustment, all beyond the .01 level of significance. And Hobart and Klausner (1959) concluded from their study that communication and marital adjustment are significantly related for both husbands and wives. This conclusion was supported by additional research (Ely, Guerney, and Stover, 1973; Karlsson, 1963; and Navran, 1967). Thus, there seems to be a body of evidence that both quantity (for example, Terman, 1938; Locke, 1951) and quality (for exam-

ple, Hobart and Klausner, 1959; Navran, 1967) of communication are positively related to marital adjustment.

Udry (1966) has cautioned that the relationship is a very tenuous one, suggesting that the communication process should sometimes be inhibited as a safeguard against hearing what is hurtful to the listener. This suggestion received some support from Cutler and Dyer (1965) who found that open communication about violations of expectations between spouses can lead to nonadjustive responses. However, it has also been found that full disclosure of feelings tended to be positively correlated with marital satisfaction and even more so with good feelings about the spouse (Levinger and Senn, 1967). In summary, the available evidence indicates a positive relationship between good communication and a good marital adjustment, although "good" communication may mean being careful about voicing complaints or disappointments.

Recently, there has been an increased emphasis on improvement of marital communication based on the view that an improvement in communication can lead to improvement in marital adjustment. Books have been published elaborating on the importance of communication in a successful marriage (Lederer and Jackson, 1968), offering instruction in expressing constructive aggression (Bach and Wyden, 1969), and on *Improving Communication in Marriage* (Human Development Institute, 1970). Hickman and Baldwin (1971) found that although counseling alone was more effective than the last-mentioned programed text alone, the text was more effective than no help at all and was an extremely useful supplement to the traditional counseling process.

Many therapists stress communication in therapy (Haley, 1963; Watson, 1963). Employing many of the constructs suggested earlier by Don Jackson (1959, 1965), Virginia Satir (1964, 1965, 1967) looks for cognitive and affective change in a client's perception of self and others, in thought and feeling manifestations, and in reactions to stimulus and feedback from others during family therapy. Communication is analyzed into such components as who speaks to whom; who blames or praises; message clarity; and verbal and nonverbal message con-

gruency. Satir teaches communicative techniques and serves as a model of good communication for her clients. Brammer and Shostrom (1960) have suggested a specific model for improvement of dyadic communications, but did not develop a training program for married couples that emphasized these communicative skills.

Broderick (1969) compiled an excellent review of communication theory as applied to the marital dyad while suggesting a model closely related to the one advocated by Brammer and Shostrom (1960). These models, and the relationship enrichment program for married and engaged couples developed by Hinkle and Moore (1971), Nunnally (1971), and G. Miller (1971), have goals similar to those of the CRE model.

Although the literature points to a positive correlation between effective communication and marital adjustment, and marriage and family therapists are concerned with improving communication among their clients in therapy, questions remain concerning this relationship. For example, can marital adjustment be improved by improving the quantity and/or quality of a couple's communicative techniques? If so, how much time is needed: Would six months be enough to show a change in a positive direction? Would both husbands and wives perceive an improvement in their relationship?

Such questions led to the study to be reported here.[1] We sought to investigate the possible effects of engaging in a six-month Conjugal Relationship Enhancement (or therapy) program on married couples' perceptions of their marital adjustment and communication.

## Hypotheses

There were two major hypotheses that guided the evaluation. The first was that there would be improvement in communication by the couples trained in the Conjugal Relationship

---

[1]This chapter reports the results of a doctoral dissertation conducted by the author under the chairmanship of Bernard Guerney, Jr., at The Pennsylvania State University (Collins, 1971).

Enhancement program (experimental group) relative to the untrained (control group) couples. The Primary Communication Inventory (PCI) and the Marital Communication Inventory (MCI) were used to measure such communication.[2]

The second hypothesis was that there would be improvement in marital adjustment by the experimental group relative to the control group. The instruments used to measure this variable were the Locke Marital Adjustment Test (MAT) and the Conjugal Life Questionnaire (CLQ).

## Method

A form letter was sent to all the married students, staff, and faculty of The Pennsylvania State University informing them of a new service research program for married couples and inviting them to participate whether or not they presently had significant marital problems. It indicated that the program consisted of teaching husbands and wives skills designed to improve their communication, help them attain mutual understanding, and facilitate conflict resolution. The letter indicated that the program was appropriate for a wide range of married couples, "from those experiencing the most extreme kinds of marital problems to those wishing to still further enhance an already satisfactory marriage." Letters also were sent to the lawyers and clergy in the State College, Pennsylvania, area encouraging them to refer clients, and an article describing the program appeared in the local newspaper.

### Procedures

Couples who inquired about the program were first given an interview during which the program was explained and examples given of the communication skills and rules they would be taught. All couples were told that groups would be forming over the next six months and that they would be contacted as soon

[2] The instruments used to measure the dependent variables in this study are described in Appendices A and B.

as one was available. If a couple decided to participate in the program, they were given the test packet to fill out at that time.

These couples were then placed randomly into either the experimental (E) group or the no-treatment control (C) group. The E group couples were contacted and placed in groups, each consisting of three couples and two cotherapists. These groups were taught, and practiced, CRE techniques once a week for one and one half hours. Each couple spent about thirty minutes practicing the skills together under the supervision of the group leader-therapists. After the six-month period, all couples were retested on the same questionnaires they had filled out during the initial interview.

### Group Leaders

The group leader-therapists were graduate students who had participated in a practicum course in Modifying Conjugal Life for ten to twenty weeks at the Individual and Family Consultation Center at The Pennsylvania State University, where the study was conducted. All cotherapist combinations were male-female, except for one male-male combination. None of the graduate students had led a group before.

### Subjects

All couples who requested interviews and agreed to participate in the research program were included in the project. There were twenty-nine experimental and twenty-five control couples at the beginning of the experiment. Five experimental couples dropped out of the program, all before two months had elapsed. Four control couples did not fill out the posttest questionnaires. This left forty-five couples in the study: 48 clients in the experimental group and 42 clients in the control group.

The couples lived in or around the State College area, primarily a middle-class, university-related community of 33,000, not including some 24,000 students. The index of social position mean score was 18.5. This falls within Social Class Two in Hollingshead's index of social position. This socioeconomic

position, barely missing Class One, reflects a highly educated, professional, and semiprofessional group. The mean age of the husband was 31.1 (median = 29), and of the wife 29.7 years (median = 27). The couples had been married on an average of 7.0 years (median = 4.5), and had 1.7 children (median = 2).

The average couple in the present study probably was neither as happy as the average married couple in general, nor as troubled as the average couple seeking marital therapy, judging from a study by Navran (1967). In that study, couples testing high on a test of marital adjustment had a mean Primary Communication Inventory (PCI) score of 105.3, while couples seeking marital counseling at a psychiatric clinic had mean PCI score of 81.4. Scores on the PCI and on marital adjustment correlate fairly highly, and the mean PCI score on the pretest for the group in the present study was 91.4, about midway between Navran's two groups.

## The Training Program

As indicated, the teaching process took place in groups of three married couples. In the first session, the behavioral modes and group procedures as described earlier in the book were explained and then modeled by the cotherapists for the group. We will here only recapitulate the modes partially and briefly.

First, the expresser maintains the choice and direction of the topic. Second, it is of particular importance that the expresser "own" his perceptions and feelings. This means that he should use particular phrases that clearly acknowledge that he is dealing with his own perceptions and feelings (for example, "I am angry with you because. . . ."), rather than stating things in "objective" statements (for example, "Well, you were very inconsiderate of me."). The empathic responder must be sensitive to the interpersonal and feeling messages that underlie the content messages. For example, if a wife tells her husband that he is spending too much time with his friends and should be working around the house more, she may be feeling angry and/or hurt and not commenting only about the best way for him to spend his leisure time. The responder should be sensitive to, and

respond to, these latter components. When the responder becomes skillful at reflecting in an accurate, empathic manner, the expresser is thereby reinforced for self-explorative behavior and for revealing deeper feelings.

It is important that the empathic responder perceive and understand all of the messages being sent, positive as well as negative, for communication to be complete and fully meaningful. For example, the husband might tell his wife that she does not look good in the dress she is wearing. On one level, there is a definite negative message being communicated. But on another level a positive message is there, too, if it can be heard. The husband is communicating that he really cares about his wife's appearance and feels that she is not doing herself justice in choosing that dress. Looking for positive messages underlying negative ones is at best difficult, and for most couples initially it is nearly impossible. Help is given by the other members in the group, acting as facilitators, as well as by the leader.

The role of the facilitator is to see that the responder does not go past the limits of his role; for example, interjecting his own feelings about what the expresser has said, asking questions, or otherwise commenting on the message. Also, the facilitator should detect and reflect any messages or cues the expresser may have communicated to the responder that the responder may not have picked up, as long as these are not likely to lie outside of the phenomenological field of the expresser. The facilitator would then help the responder to include these missing components in a new, modified response to the expresser. Similar help may be offered to an expresser who has not complied as well as he might have with the requirements of the expresser mode. Thus, other group members who at that time are not participating as expresser or responder are encouraged to assist the group leader. The group members should use the behavior of the group leaders as a model for their behavior as facilitators.

In the initial phase of the training program, each couple's interaction was supervised particularly closely, virtually sentence by sentence. The cotherapists would point out to the responder possible feelings that had been missed, encourage the

expresser to state his feelings more clearly, model the type of reflection that might have been more appropriate, and reinforce with praise those behaviors that were done well. The leader thus shaped more desirable behaviors and extinguished (through lack of reinforcement) behaviors not in line with desired role performance.

In addition, each couple was instructed to read and perform exercises from *Improving Communication in Marriage* (Human Development Institute, 1970), a programed instruction course about communication. The authors stated in the introduction that "the object of the course is twofold: to increase a married couple's understanding of the factors that affect communication; and to facilitate, if possible, an actual improvement in their communication with each other." The emphasis is on genuineness of expression: "the inherent value of honest communication (not to mention its more practical benefits) far outweighs discomfort that sometimes accompanies it."

When the couples had demonstrated proficiency in performing the roles and understanding of the principles involved (after about six weeks), they were instructed to start practicing the roles at home for about thirty minutes each week.

Once the behavioral modes were learned, couples were expected to move into areas of a serious interpersonal nature. However, certain procedures that we believe are improvements were not a part of the CRE program at the time of this study. Currently, the Relationship Questionnaire is used to obtain systematic written designation, by the couples, of a hierarchy of topics that they believe are most important to their relationship. The leaders then encourage the participants to adhere to these topics in their dialogs. At the time of the study being described, topics were chosen spontaneously by the couples each week.

### Illustrative Transcripts

We have selected segments from some of the group sessions for transcription to show the way in which the leader coaches the participants in their skill practicing, to show some

of the types of issues discussed by the participants in the group sessions, and to show that clients experience the skills as meaningful and useful outside of the group sessions as well as within them.[3]

We have chosen mostly early sessions to transcribe because they best show the teaching and learning processes at work. In these particular early excerpts, the couples managed to make reasonably good use of their skills in discussing even troublesome aspects of their own marital relationships. In current practice, as indicated earlier in this book, spouses do not practice together in the first session, and troublesome issues between them are not discussed during the first three sessions, in order to ensure a higher degree of initial success in the use of the skills. The first excerpt is from a second session. The couple, Karen and Doug, are in their early thirties, and have been married for seven years.

> *Karen:* Well, you know, you fall in love and you get married and this is something, you know, very special. And then you're going to be the best housewife that there ever was. And this gives you a goal or something to work toward. Just about the time you get bored with that, along comes your first baby and then you're going to be the best mother there ever was, and you wrap yourself entirely around doing that. And then, after the two kids or the three kids, or whatever it is, get to be about two or three years old, I guess it just all, uh, maybe you don't have, uh—
>
> *Doug:* You start to wonder whether it was all worth it.
>
> *Karen:* Well, not really whether it was all worth it. It's definitely all worth it, but you're being involved in always reaching some goal, you know, high school diploma, then it's college, then it's get married, then it's having kids.
>
> *Doug:* At this point, you begin to feel you have nothing to look forward to, that it's going to be the same thing.
>
> *Leader 1:* Very good.
>
> *Karen:* Well, right! It's—you begin to think, you've always poured your life into something or somebody, and all of a sudden you're staring yourself in the face and you say to yourself, "Now what good, really, am I?" At first, when you get married, you're very

---

[3] The transcripts in this chapter have been edited to achieve brevity and clarity of the content and the instructional procedures. All names in the transcript are pseudonyms.

willingly an appendage or an extension of your husband and uh, then after, you know, all the fiery love and everything cools off a little bit, you begin—just like a parent and child relationship—you want to see if you can really make it on your own.

*Doug:* You feel like making it on your own.

*Karen:* Well, in a way. Just, uh, to be an important or special person. If a man can make a woman feel that way, then possibly she never would have to look elsewhere—if he could make her feel needed and important and special to the point that she felt like she was doing the things for him and for the family that no one else could do. And, of course, he does feel this way and she knows this but, she needs to be reassured, she needs to be told it's just—Ahh—

*Leader 2:* Talk about yourself, about what *you* want and what *you* need. You're asking yourself a question, something like, "If I didn't have my husband, if I didn't have my child, who would I be? What would I be? Would I be something special? Would there be something about *me* that would be really worthwhile and outstanding?"[4]

*Karen:* Well, in many ways I think I have a lot of self-confidence in what I can do. I feel like I could definitely be very independent. I think I could be OK on my own.

*Doug:* It gives you comfort to feel that you can, that you're independent enough, to stand alone?

*Leader 1:* Good.

*Karen:* Uh, yes, I feel like I could comfortably stand on my own, you know, get a job, have an apartment and live completely on my own. I'm not saying I'd *like* it particularly because I enjoy having a lot of people around—my family, my friends, all the people I know—uh—

*Doug:* That would be a different experience, a worthwhile experience compared to some of the things maybe you're doing now.

*Karen:* I got off the track. I feel like I could do it if I had to, but [pauses] I would rather not. I'd rather have the situation like it is with people that I love and who love me around me. I like to feel *needed*; I guess maybe that's the whole point of everything, and yet I don't really know whether that's a valid [pauses again] desire.

*Doug:* You get confused over this, whether you want to be needed, or—

*Karen:* In the first place, I can't go on strike and say I'm going to *quit*. And I can't go around and say, "Do you like this? See what I

---

[4] Both leaders mistakenly neglected also to include the component of wishing for reassurance of appreciation from her husband. They thus diverted Karen from her main theme. She was, however, able to return to it before long.

did? Tell me that I'm good and special." It's got to come, uh, from somebody *else*. And, uh, I guess this is why I get angry and I resent —I resent when you don't do it. It makes all the difference, and I don't really understand it. For instance, dinner time: When you were smoking and so unhappy in your job and everything, I would prepare dinner and I didn't ever expect you to say, "Oh, that was yummy," and all that stuff. But you didn't eat it either, and this gave me a sense of futility. You know, I say to myself, "What the hell am I going through all this work for, putting myself out, and he's not—you know, what good is it? I might as well throw a TV dinner in front of him!"

*Doug:* "What good am I?"

*Leader 2:* Very good!

*Karen:* Yeah! It's everything that I do, it's not appreciated or anything. It's a reflection on me and perhaps I'm more sensitive about this than other people are, because I think, in many respects, I'm more sensitive to other people's wants and feelings. Because when I care about somebody, I'm constantly on the alert to see what they want, what they like.

*Doug:* You feel you aren't being repaid in return for your feelings. People aren't paying you back with the same consideration.

*Leader 1:* Good.

*Karen:* Well, I guess so, and, uh, I kind of push it all back and I say, "Well, that's trivial and childish," and all that. But I guess that, uh, they are my feelings, you know. That's the way I feel!

The next transcript is from a third session. The couple, Sue and Ed, have been married thirteen years. As would be expected at this stage of the program, the husband is more attuned to the content of what the wife is saying than to the feelings underlying them, and he tends to repeat the same words she uses. However, given the early stage of the training, and the fact that he was accepting enough of her convictions to allow her to go into them more deeply, the leaders refrained from trying to improve his responses by modeling responses less repetitive and more attuned to feeling as they would do in other circumstances. The excerpt illustrates the use of skills in an early session. The first part of the excerpt serves to show how the emphasis, in the expresser role, on being specific about the emotional impact of a particular behavioral pattern (here, the voice level) can open new pathways for change in a marital relationship. This particular aspect of the husband's behavior had

been bothering the wife all of her married life, but she had never really clarified it for her husband. Notice too, that although the husband's skill is still quite primitive, he does provide acceptance, and that under the influence of this acceptance, what started out as a simple plea for mutual behavioral change by the wife turns into an exploration of the wife's own deep feelings—feelings that are of central importance for improving the relationship.

*Sue:* I don't like it when you raise your voice at me.

*Ed:* You don't like it when I raise my voice at you.

*Sue:* No, it makes me furious.

*Ed:* It makes you furious when I raise my voice.

*Sue:* Yes, I believe, I guess, that my own defense is to turn it off.

*Ed:* So your only defense when I raise my voice is to turn it off.

*Sue:* Yeah, because I feel like I'm being attacked.

*Leader 1:* Very good.

*Sue:* Ripped apart.

*Ed:* In other words, you feel whenever I raise my voice that you're personally being attacked and being ripped apart.

*Sue:* Well, yes. Yes, I really do, but I mean—first of all, I must accept the fact that usually the things you say are justified: "The floor isn't swept," "I don't have any slippers"—uhm, "How come dinner isn't ready?" I'm already in a jam, you see, and it's just like throwing lighter fluid on a fire. Because you know you're already in trouble. I'm already in a jam, it's a bad scene to begin with, and it's a terrible feeling!

*Ed:* So you know you're in trouble before anything is said.

*Sue:* Then, like I said, I just feel like I'm being attacked. You know, like I'm really worthless. I can't do anything right.

*Ed:* So when you feel that you're in trouble, you don't like to be attacked.

*Leader 1:* Good.

*Sue:* Yeah, and like I said, it makes me feel like I'm just a dumb ninny. You know, that I don't have any business just trying to be a housewife or a mother!

*Ed:* You feel as though your efforts are futile when you know you're not doing your job and someone comes in and criticizes you. Or when I come in and criticize you.

*Leader 2:* When you criticize her, she feels insulted and worthless.

*Ed:* You feel insulted and worthless when I come in and criticize

you for not doing your work when you already know you haven't done it well.

*Leader 2:* Good.

*Sue:* Right, yeah, that's good. As I've said many times, I—I feel like I'm always being compared to your mother or your sister, who are just magnificent housekeepers.

*Ed:* You always feel you are being compared to my mother and sister.

*Sue:* Yes, I do.

*Leader 1:* And how does that make you feel?

*Sue:* Well, it makes me feel like, you know, "What the heck!"—I'm *not* your mother or your sister and I don't perform like your mother and sister do, and so maybe I feel just like a drag.

*Ed:* You feel as though you don't even want to try.

*Leader 1:* Very good.

*Sue:* What I'm saying is that I'm not the kind—apparently I'm not the kind of a person your mother and sister are as far as the home is concerned and then, you know, I'm continually being measured against these people—your mother and your sister—and I feel then, well—I resent being compared to them because I don't feel it's fair.

*Ed:* You *resent* being compared to my mother and sister because you're not my mother and sister.

*Leader 1:* Very good.

*Sue:* No, I'm not, because I wasn't raised the way your mother and sister were. And I don't have the same values they do. And I'd like to be valued, for a while anyhow, because I'm me, not your mother or your sister. I'm me!

*Ed:* You resent being compared to my mother and sister because you feel as though you're *you* and not *them.*

*Sue:* And when I'm continually being measured against them, I don't have a chance.

*Ed:* You don't feel you have a chance when you're being measured against my mother and my sister.

*Sue:* I wouldn't get any points, because the things that are important to you and were important to them stand a little differently in my book.

*Ed:* You have a different set of values than my mother and sister have, or had.

*Sue:* And I would like to be appreciated for *my* values—

*Ed:* You want to be appreciated for your own values rather than being compared to someone else.

*Sue:* Yeah, that's right, and I feel like I have a couple of good things too, although they're different. They're not along the

domestic lines entirely. I don't feel that those things are important to me as an individual, as they may have been to them.

*Ed:* And you feel as though you should be judged on your own values rather than by someone else's.

*Leader 2:* That's good.

*Sue:* Yes, then I could feel appreciated as a person. I could feel I'm a worthwhile person the way I am.

*Ed:* You want to be appreciated just the way you are.

*Leader 1:* Very good.

*Sue:* It's kind of like you're always trying to take a piece of clay and mold it into something. It makes me feel—

*Leader 1:* That's the way you *see* it.

*Sue:* This is the way I see you doing this—the way I *feel* you're doing this.

*Ed:* It makes you feel uncomfortable to think that I'm always trying to mold you.

*Leader 2:* Good.

*Sue:* Or to change me. When you get married, they say, "Well, don't try to change your husband." This is what you hear. But you don't ever hear them say to the husband, "Don't change your wife." I feel like it's in reversal here; the situation is completely turned about and I would feel much better if I felt like I were accepted on my own ground, in terms of my own background and—

*Ed:* It would make you feel good if you were accepted on your own merits. You want to be accepted on your own merits for what you are, rather than being compared to someone else. It makes you feel very unconfident.

*Sue:* Yeah, and I just feel like a crumb, because I'd really like to make you happy. I'd really like to –I wish—I'd like very much to be a marvelous housekeeper and a fantastic cook. And I feel this would make you very, very happy if this were true.

*Ed:* You'd feel, you'd feel—let's see. You'd feel happy if you were a marvelous cook and a wonderful housekeeper because it would make *me* feel good.

*Sue:* Well now, I didn't say that. I said, "I know it would make you feel good if I were a marvelous cook and a wonderful housewife." I know that it would make *you* feel good if I were.

*Ed:* You know that it would make me feel good if you were these things.

*Sue:* Because I—I think that's what you thought you were *getting*.

*Ed:* You think that I didn't get really what I was expecting, and this makes you feel unhappy.

*Sue:* Oh, it doesn't make me feel unhappy, but I think it must make *you* unhappy.

*Ed:* In other words, you think I'm disappointed because I didn't get what I wanted.

*Sue:* Yeah, right.

*Ed:* And that makes you feel disappointed.

*Leader 2:* Good.

*Sue:* Yeah. Basically you know, I'd really love to please you in all respects, but I have a feeling that I have to accept my limitations.

*Ed:* You would like to please me in all respects, but you have limitations.

*Sue:* I'd like you to accept me for my strengths and also my weaknesses.

*Ed:* You'd rather be accepted for your strengths *and* weaknesses.

*Sue:* I would just say that I'd like you to accept me for just what I am instead of carrying this hope that I'll become more.

*Leader 2:* How does it make you *feel* when you see him as not accepting you?

*Sue:* Oh, I feel completely—just completely worthless. Just like I'm a complete failure.

*Leader 2:* That's it.

*Ed:* You feel very worthless when you don't meet my expectations.

*Sue:* Yeah, worthless.

*Ed:* Worthless.

*Sue:* Yeah, I believe that. I think that people have things that they enjoy doing, things that no matter what, they're going to find time to do. And then there are other things that you won't ever find time to do. And I have a feeling that we don't see eye to eye on those things.

*Ed:* You feel that we don't see eye to eye on the things that have to be done and can be done.

*Sue:* Let me use a very explicit example. For instance, let's say the weeds need to be pulled in the garden. If I enjoy pulling weeds in the garden, I'll find time to pull weeds in the garden. But if it's something I really don't like to do, well, I'll probably let the weeds grow all summer and it wouldn't matter to me. You see what I'm saying is, there are things that *are* important to me, and I want to find time to do those things. And there are other things that twenty years from now aren't going to make any difference anyway; those are the things that I have the tendency to let slip. And I have a feeling that the way we categorize these things, would be quite different.

*Ed:* It's easy for you to do things that you feel are important.

*Sue:* I find the time to do them.

*Ed:* Things that you don't feel are important will tend to slip.

*Leader 1:* "And you think we don't see eye to eye—"

*Ed:* And we don't see eye to eye on our values, priorities.

*Leader 2:* Now one more thing—"And you wish I would quit trying to make you change your priorities or your values."

*Ed:* And you wish that I would stop trying to change your priorities.

*Leader 2:* Good.

*Sue:* Yes, I wish you would let my priorities be my priorities. Perhaps this would help things be a little more pleasant.

*Ed:* So you'd feel better if your priorities were left alone.

*Leader 2:* "Respected."

*Ed:* Respected.

*Sue:* Just let me be what I am. I feel very strongly that it's wrong to try to change people.

*Ed:* You feel that it's wrong to change people; you feel strongly that it's wrong.

*Sue:* Yeah, I really do. It's sort of like they're not even worthy of being a person if their priorities are different than someone else's. But every person, I feel, should be respected for what they are.

*Ed:* People should be respected for what they are.

*Sue:* I don't feel you have to *agree* with everything they say or do. But yet *respect* them for what they believe.

*Leader 2:* Could you be more direct and own your feelings: "I see you as trying to change me and I resent that."

*Sue:* OK. I see you are trying to change me and I resent it.

*Ed:* You resent the fact that I'm trying to change your priorities— or you.

*Leader 1:* Very good.

*Sue:* Yes, I think that's it, basically. Priorities are built into a person, and what I would like is acceptance for me as a person—my own individual peculiarities and everything that goes with it.

*Ed:* You would feel better if I would accept you as you are. Not try to change you.

*Sue:* I've never really felt accepted, never really measured up to your ideals as a wife.

*Leader 2:* How did you feel about that?

*Sue:* Oh, I just feel awful [near tears].

*Ed:* It just makes you feel awful that you don't ever measure up to my expectations.

> *Sue:* It sort of feels like—like you go out the door and they shut the door [long hesitation] sort of like you walk out of the room and they shut the door and don't come back in; you start to feel—I feel—I feel rejected.

The following excerpt is from a third session in which the clients, Karen and Bob, were specifically asked to discuss something positive in their relationship. This procedure, as we have indicated earlier, has since become a regular one. In fact, the impact of these expressions of positive feelings is generally so favorable that we now ask couples to discuss positive issues periodically. In this transcript, the husband's expression of a positive feeling has such a pleasing emotional impact on the wife, that it almost overwhelms her. After nine years of marriage, she must reach back to her wedding night to find a comparable emotional peak.

> *Bob:* One thing that I especially liked and have always appreciated about you is the feeling of esteem and worth that I get when I'm with you. I get it from you and through you. Just being with you publicly or privately.
>
> *Karen:* Gee, I'd like to respond to that personally.
>
> *Leader 1:* It's harder to listen now, isn't it? [Laughter.]
>
> *Karen:* Yeah, it is. OK. You feel good when you're with me. I make you feel at ease with yourself because it gives you self-esteem. You enjoy my company.
>
> *Leader 2:* Good!
>
> *Bob:* Yeah. There's certainly a great deal more involved in it. Going back any number of years I still get that same strong feeling. When I walk down College Avenue on Saturday afternoon with you, I feel bouncy.
>
> *Karen:* You enjoy my company. You have enjoyed my company for a long time and you still do. You like to be seen with me. It makes you feel real good to be seen with me.

At this point Karen began telling the group how she felt about what her husband has just told her. The leader suggested that they switch modes, and that as expresser she tell Bob her feelings.

> *Karen:* I like the things you say to me. I like the way you always express things to me with your eyes and with your special caring

words. You have a special way of saying simple things that mean a great deal to me.

*Leader 1:* That's fine.

*Bob:* What I say to you makes you feel good inside. You feel that I'm able to express to you, sincerely, things that you feel strongly about.

*Karen:* Um hm. I feel as though there are many things about our relationship that are still on tap because we really do live in a very busy world and I think you have a desire to slow it down. I think you want to listen to me and I feel like you really want to help me. That gives me a good feeling of hope.

*Bob:* You sense my desire to help you, and you also feel my desire to want to savor the life that we enjoy together rather than to rush through.

*Leader 2:* Good, Bob.

*Karen:* In talking to you right at this moment, I feel a feeling, of almost—it's almost a new feeling because we lead such a busy life. You make me feel the way I felt the night when we took our marriage vows—like we really looked in one another's eyes and we really were thinking about those words we were saying. It's a very nice feeling, and it makes me feel good because you really are listening to me.

*Bob:* You're feeling, you're feeling good because you sense that I'm hearing what you're saying this evening. You remember the way we felt the night that we were married, when we were also sure that we were both listening.

*Karen:* I have another feeling also, but it's being overcome by the fact that you're listening the way that you are. I feel slightly frightened by this, you know, a little unwound. It's not anything that embarrasses me. Only, within myself, I feel frightened. But you make me feel very comfortable. I can say this and you make me have confidence that what I'm saying isn't silly.

*Bob:* You have a feeling that is somewhat overwhelming but you feel that I will take care of you and protect you.

*Karen:* Mm-hm [on verge of tears]. Now I'm going to shut up, 'cause that's how I feel.

Part of the rationale underlying CRE is that operational negotiations usually should not be undertaken until the wishes and feelings underlying a conflict are clearly understood. When the emotional and motivational aspects underlying a request for behavioral change are spelled out by A, and responded to with empathic acceptance and then with similar expressive skills by B, certain further developments become possible that, we be-

lieve, usually make for more reliable and enduring relationship changes. With the deeper level of understanding that the expressive and empathic skills engender, a new perception may develop of whether, or what kind of, change is needed. If the other's behavior comes to be seen as meaning something different than was originally inferred, the desire to change the other person's behavior may diminish or even disappear. Or, on the other hand, the request may be altered to one that is of a more basic nature, striking closer to the heart of the issue. Whatever the case, if the person of whom change is requested fully understands the meaning and importance his behavior has for the other person, and feels his own needs have also been fully understood and taken into account by the other person, he will almost always have a much stronger and more enduring motivation to change his behavior and for continuing to strengthen new behavioral patterns. The following excerpt from a fourth session illustrates the incentive for changing one's behavior that can arise from understanding another's emotional needs. A couple of weeks prior to this exchange, the husband, Tom, had communicated some of his emotional needs to his wife, Mary, in a skillful manner. The communication induced her to change certain behavioral patterns in her interactions with him.

> *Tom:* This evening, when you were going to get dressed, you said that, if I wanted to, I could do the dishes or clear off the table. You invited me to help if I wanted to. You didn't tell me to do it. Like you were saying, "I would appreciate if you want to do it, if you want to help."
>
> *Mary:* In other words, I gave you that freedom.
>
> *Tom:* M-hm. It wasn't that I was being expected to do something or ordered to do something. It's just as if you had said, "Well, here's something that needs to be done and I don't have time to do it now, and you would be helping me if you would do it; but if you would like to go read the paper, then you can sit down and relax and we'll do it later. But I would appreciate it if you feel like doing it." You're *allowing* me to do things.
>
> *Mary:* You have the *option* of sharing it and that gives you some sense of satisfaction.
>
> *Tom:* Yeah, because I know that I can do something useful now. And I also know that if I don't feel like doing that, you're not going to be all upset. It makes me feel good that you changed because I told you that when I was a kid, I was never *asked* to do

anything, I was *told*. That really makes a difference in the attitude with which you approach the task. I was always *told*, "Do this, go rake the leaves, cut the grass, go take out the garbage." It was never put in an optional way or a way that would make me feel like a human being while I was doing it, not just like a robot or a slave. Like, "We pay your allowance every week, go do this or you don't get an allowance." It was never, "Would you help me by doing thus and such?" or "Would you please go do it?" So, since I mentioned that, I get the impression that you're approaching these things with that type of an attitude. It seems like you picked up what I was trying to say in that conversation. You understand, and you're trying to use it continuously.

*Mary:* So, you like the feeling of being needed and useful and, better, you have the option to do it or not to do it.

*Tom:* Right.

*Leader 1:* That's very good. Would you like to switch modes?

*Mary:* I feel terrific because, well, you know I'm not very tactful, and I don't have a way of dressing things up. I just lay it on the line, and I never had a nice way of asking you to do something. This is why I never asked you to do anything, because it would come out wrong. So now I think twice before I say anything and I give you the option, and I didn't even realize it was working. Besides, it's good to know that—I'm glad that if it's not tact, at least it's thinking before I speak and I'm glad to know that it's working.

*Tom:* So you did realize what I was saying, and you're trying to apply it and comply with my wishes and treat me in the special way that you knew I wanted.

*Mary:* Right. Not only that, but now I feel that it's important. It's almost like a progress report. You told me that it was working. I didn't know that. And now that I know, I can keep on doing it; but I might have just dismissed it if I hadn't realized that it was the right way of "handling" you, so to speak.

*Tom:* So then you feel that it was important for me to tell you these things so that you knew whether you were doing what I had wanted you to do.

*Mary:* Yes.

*Tom:* That it was the correct way, and now you feel great. You feel confident that you knew what I was talking about and that you can carry out these wishes.

*Mary:* Well, I'm pleased about two things. One, that I responded to you in a way that was favorable to you and two, that I sort of corrected a personality defect by not being so blunt, being a little more tactful, as close to tactful as I can be.

*Tom:* So it wasn't just that you were able to respond to something that I had expressed to you, but that you were able to do something that you've never been able to do before—

*Mary:* Right.

*Tom:* —a new tactfulness, a new technique in talking with or dealing with people.

*Mary:* Right. Not that I haven't done it before, but very infrequently.

*Tom:* So you're pleased with this particular experience and it's showing you that you can deal tactfully with a problem.

*Mary:* Yes. Right. You know, in our fight this weekend [a little laugh] and in our discussion after the fight, it became evident to me that once you know what I want, you're very eager to please me. Finding out what I want is the hard thing but, you know, I think it's amazing that all you have to do is know what I want and you'll do it. It's just a nice feeling. I can't tack an adjective onto it.

*Tom:* You feel that I'm kind of henpecked.

*Mary:* No! You're not henpecked. Actually, by my mother's terms, you would be. By old-fashioned terms you would be, but you're not. You're just helpful. You want to be helpful, and you want to please, and there's nothing wrong with that, and it makes me feel good to know.

*Tom:* You're glad then that I want to make you happy.

*Leader 2:* Good, Tom.

*Mary:* Yes. You tell me that every time, or rather you don't tell me, you show me.

*Tom:* You feel good that I'm trying to make you happy.

*Mary:* Yes, I do. I'm amazed because every now and then I kind of forget and when I rediscover it, I'm kind of awed.

*Tom:* You're sort of amazed that I really want to make you happy.

*Mary:* Right! Although I tend to forget it, I do realize it. That's good: to think that *you* want to make *me* happy. That's a big sentence.

*Tom:* You appreciate that.

*Mary:* Yes. Special—you make me feel special.

*Tom:* That makes you feel special. You feel like someone special.

*Leader 1:* That's very good. I thought that was a really good exchange. You picked up a couple of feelings. She labeled her feelings—she did a really good job of labeling her feelings, but you didn't repeat the same ones that she used. You tried to go a little deeper. It was very good.

*Mary:* I feel much more at ease this time because it seemed natural. It seemed to just flow this time.

*Leader 2:* It was much more comfortable for you.

The next excerpt, also from a fourth session, illustrates

the fact that even in the early stages of the training, many couples begin to apply the lessons learned to their everyday life interactions. In this instance, the prescribed expressive pattern of stating things strictly in terms of one's own subjective perception and feelings, thereby eliminating direct accusations, begins to affect the behavior of John toward his wife Alice. They are a young couple who have been married two years.

> *John:* I would like to learn how to be less accusative when I've had a bad day at school or there is a problem or something. I would like to be able to use less accusative approaches. When I'm under pressure or I've had a bad day, I get accusative.
>
> *Alice:* You feel kind of sorry about this problem and you would like to change it.
>
> *Leader 1:* That's good. You got to the feelings.
>
> *John:* Yes. I sense that it makes you close up, and it really keeps us from getting at the feelings and the discussion. It really kind of sours the whole thing. I didn't really realize this. I didn't really become strongly aware of it until we talked in the class here and then I realized it and I really want to work on it now.
>
> *Alice:* You hadn't really realized that it's difficult for me to respond to you in a good conversational way when you spout off like that.
>
> *Leader 2* [to Alice]: And say, "You feel sorry about that" or something like that.
>
> *Alice:* And you feel sorry about it.
>
> *John:* Yes, because it makes it so much more difficult for us to get into something constructively.
>
> *Alice:* And you regret that.
>
> *Leader 2:* Good!
>
> *John:* Right, and I've been trying not to do that so much since we started this class. I'm really making a conscious effort and I find that it has been more successful.
>
> *Alice:* And you're trying, and it seems to work better and you're happy about that success.
>
> *John:* Right. I feel it's been a somewhat limited effort but I did see that it did happen. I can correlate that progress with what we've done through our exercises here.
>
> *Alice:* You're gratified that the effort is beginning to show some good results.
>
> *John:* Right.

The next excerpt has been chosen to illustrate the fact

that good communication can have a positive impact on virtually all aspects of a relationship. This can come about because of the direct impact of communication in changing the specific mutual behavior at issue. But it can also come about indirectly—good communication serving to enhance general positive feelings, mutual attraction, goodwill, comradeship, and the spirit of giving and sharing. In this way, many things that could have been destructive never become problems, and interactions that were previously unwelcome or dull can take on new joy. Just as a poorly handled conflict or disagreement, and lack of understanding in one area of interaction can create vicious cycles that cut destructive swaths in many areas not directly associated with that area, so, conversely, successful communication, and the understanding and effective problem solving it engenders can create a warmth and sense of closeness that permeates many other areas of interaction. In this instance, the husband talks of the impact that the general relationship improvement has had on the couple's sex life and vice versa. The couple, Phil and Joan, have been married for twenty years, and have been in a CRE program for about six months.

> *Phil:* Most of our married life, I felt there wasn't enough sex in our house and I didn't ever think I could come anywhere near to fulfilling my desires. And in the past six months it has. I really feel good about this. I really feel satisfied in this sense. Not that I don't want sex anymore! [Laughs.] Not sated, just satisfied!
>
> *Joan:* You felt this was a fulfillment not ever reached before. You realized it in the past six months. You're happy about it, the way it is, the sex life, your sex life and mine.
>
> *Phil:* Yes, I would prefer you to say *our* sex life because I feel *our* sex life is improved, not just mine. There was some response there, so that I could approach you without being rebuffed, or without your saying, "OK, but make it quick, I'm tired tonight."
>
> *Joan:* You felt I was very responsive, more so than I have ever been. This started six months ago.
>
> *Phil:* Yes.
>
> *Joan:* You are very pleased about it.
>
> *Phil:* Yes, I am. I like this. It was always *me* before, most of the time, you know, except for the rare weekends or the rare instances.
>
> *Joan:* You feel that I'm happy about it now too, and this makes you feel good.

*Phil:* Yes, this is what particularly makes me feel good. Sex has become more of a two-way street in our house in the last six months that it ever was before. And I like this! [Pause.] It's good, and this is one of the very good things about our relationship. You know, when the sexual relationship is a one-way street, I feel a little bit guilty about it. I feel like, "Well, why should I always be pushing myself up on her just because I have an animal desire." You know, I feel, "this isn't the way sex should be." And when there is response on your part, then this guilty feeling goes away.

*Joan:* You feel guilty when you are the aggressor all the time, when you're the one who wants all the time. You'll get a positive response, or a negative response, and you'll feel guilty that maybe you have gone too far, or expected too much.

*Phil:* Yes, that's right. Not so much *being* the aggressor, but being the aggressor and finding a lukewarm or negative *response*. That is the thing. Then it twists around and I feel guilty about it in the end. Sometimes with this guilty feeling I would say to myself, "Well, is this the only way we can be together? Is this the only thing we really do together, sex!" So when we can find intimacy outside of sex, then this too is very fulfilling. One doesn't take the place of the other, but one supplements the other.

*Joan:* You feel they're *both* very important.

*Phil:* I feel they're both very important and that this latter thing, this nonsexual intimacy, has really been more lacking in our relationship then the sexual intimacy has. But they have all improved together. Things in our life are much better and have been much better over the past six months. I have alluded to this in here many times. I am not sure what is the result of what. I'm not sure whether our sex relations have improved because of better communications; or whether perhaps because our sex relationship improved, our communication has also improved.

*Joan:* You feel maybe the whole combination has really helped us.

*Phil:* The combination of all these things has helped our lives.

*Joan:* It makes you feel good. You've really been feeling a lot happier in the last six months.

*Phil:* I've been much more contented in our marriage in the last six months than I ever was in the entire time that we have been married. I still feel this way. Sometimes I get down in the dumps and things don't look so good that day or that hour, but overall we're a lot better off. And this pleases me.

*Leader:* Joan, would you like to take the expresser role?

*Joan:* With many things we *have* been able to discuss, we started out feeling very badly in the early part of the evening, many times, and later on we feel great! Both of us like this feeling very much.

*Phil:* You feel that whenever we have really worked at our communications skills that we really got something out of them, and that lots of times we haven't worked at them when we should have.

*Joan:* That's right!

*Phil:* You feel that knowing that we can get this out of it, why don't we do it more often?

*Joan:* Yes. Because it's beautiful, what we do get from it. I think we're both very happy for it. At least, I am. I know I am very happy.

*Phil:* You're happy generally because of the change in our relationship.

*Joan:* Yeah, I am.

The next transcript is from a final session, at which time the usual format is not used. In the last session, a leader asks the couples for reactions to the program and suggestions for improving it. The couple, Bob and Jane, have been married for eight years. This excerpt was chosen for transcription because the couple's reaction echoes our sentiments that relationship-enhancing communication skills should be taught before marriage, in fact as early as possible.

*Jane:* I think we've both grown as a result of having had the course. I just wish we'd had it a lot sooner.

*Bob:* It ought to be a prerequisite to marriage for everybody.

*Jane:* I see so many other couples who have such little problems. Really they're big to them, but they could handle them if they only could have learned to communicate before their problems really get to the point where there's no return. Of course, there's no way you can tell them that. Nobody could have told us that either.

*Bob:* I feel satisfied with the job we've been able to do with the skills we've learned here.

*Leader:* Do you find yourself listening reflectively when you're talking these things over?

*Bob:* Yeah, I think so. I notice it on both sides. I've caught myself responding reflectively, and *thinking* that way too.

*Leader:* You're getting to feel less uncomfortable about doing that?

*Bob:* Yeah. I don't think it goes on like we do here. I don't think we go quite as long. We change back and forth a lot more often.

*Jane:* Yeah, that's right.

*Bob:* But the skills are there.

*Jane:* And another helpful thing is cutting out the accusations, because that's something that, you know, everybody just *does* that. And now you get ready to say "But you—" and then you say, "I." And I can see mistakes now in other people, you know.

*Bob:* We've become the world's greatest critics. [Jane laughs.] You know, we see other people having trouble and we think, "Well, they're not doing this right." I think a lot of people have more communication problems than they realize.

*Leader:* It is amazing the number of people who think they are communicating well, and aren't really.

*Jane:* They're talking to each other but that's not communicating at all. Because you've got to *listen* to be able to communicate. I just look around—well, like at our friends, so many of them are in so much the same trouble, you know, the seven-year itch or something. I don't know what you might call it. It's always been there but now more people are speaking up and saying, "Yes, I am unhappy; I am dissatisfied; we are having troubles." Former generations have gone through it. But most of the women have kept quiet because this was a "No-no." They felt they should never act like they were unhappy at all—they just kind of stuck with it. And I think this kind of training ought to be offered on a high school level. I think it's a very important part of learning how to deal with people.

*Bob:* As you were saying earlier, this could be a life-style. I don't know. Something like this would probably be better at any time rather than never to have it at all, but I don't know. I wonder what would happen if you had a society based on this—where parents raised their children knowing these things. You know, obviously you can't. Well, I guess you could. You could give them the right to have their feelings and try to understand. I wonder what the result would be.

*Jane:* Well, I think it would be helpful. You know, even in a health class, you know, I don't know whether they have health classes anymore but they used to tell you all about your body and all this kind of thing that half the teenagers know by that time anyway. I think it would be more helpful even then to have, say, a course in feelings—and just telling the kids that there are such things as conflicting feelings and that you shouldn't feel guilty if you get mad at somebody. That would be a start, and then there could be some kind of a program where this kind of a thing was available for anybody who wanted it. You're taught to do everything; there's a class available to teach you how to have a baby if you want to. Everything. But unless you seek somebody out—like your minister or somebody like that—and half the time they don't really tell you too much—nobody tells you about marriage. In a few years things start to get rough, you know, you have doubts and all. Nobody ever tells you anything about what it's going to be like to be married. They just expect that it's going to come naturally and here's one of the biggest times. People get married and most have rough spots along the way, and they're just expected to handle them without ever having been taught. It's just supposed to work out, you know, by instinct or something.

*Bob:* I think if this started early enough it would take care of a lot of problems before they became problems.

## Results

To determine relationships among dependent variables, Pearson Product Moment Correlations were run on the pretest data of the four questionnaires, combining experimental and control groups. The correlations range from .63 to .78 ($p <$ .001). This implies a fairly high relationship between the communication and marital adjustment variables which tends to support the close relationship between these two variables described in the literature (Locke, Sabagh, and Thomas, 1956; Hobart and Klausner, 1959; Karlsson, 1963; and Navran, 1967). The correlations also indicate, as was expected, that the results for the two hypotheses in this study cannot be considered as completely independent of one another; instead, the findings should be regarded as complementary.

### Marital Communication

The means and standard deviations on communication, along with all the dependent variables, may be seen in Table 8-1. The first hypothesis was that the experimental couples would perceive greater improvement in their communication relative to the control couples. The analysis of the Marital Communication Inventory showed a significant improvement in the experimental group relative to the control group ($F[1.85] =$ 4.820; $p = .031$). There was no significant sex difference, nor interaction between sex and treatment condition, on the MCI. Although the results were in the appropriate direction, there was no significant difference between the experimental and control groups in improvement on the Primary Communication Inventory ($F[1.84] = 1.113; p = .294$). There was no significant sex difference, nor significant interaction between sex and treatment condition on the PCI.

The reason that more than one instrument was used to test this hypothesis was an uncertainty as to the relative sensi-

Table 8-1. Pretest and Posttest Means and Standard Deviations for
Husbands and Wives in E ($N$ = 24) and C ($N$ = 21) Groups
on All Dependent Variables

|  | Pretest | | Posttest | |
|---|---|---|---|---|
|  | Mean | S.D. | Mean | S.D. |
| Control Group: Husbands |  |  |  |  |
| Marital Communication | 89.10 | 20.83 | 90.67 | 18.14 |
| Marital Adjustment | 94.76 | 14.64 | 94.00 | 16.72 |
| Conjugal Life | 73.52 | 13.02 | 73.90 | 13.63 |
| Primary Communication | 89.71 | 10.73 | 91.14 | 12.06 |
| Experimental Group: Husbands |  |  |  |  |
| Marital Communication | 85.13 | 16.70 | 93.92 | 12.08 |
| Marital Adjustment | 88.33 | 14.54 | 94.04 | 13.61 |
| Conjugal Life | 68.83 | 11.08 | 73.17 | 10.73 |
| Primary Communication | 89.43 | 12.49 | 93.22 | 10.03 |
| Control Group: Wives |  |  |  |  |
| Marital Communication | 87.80 | 27.07 | 94.60 | 20.76 |
| Marital Adjustment | 93.67 | 11.32 | 94.76 | 12.42 |
| Conjugal Life | 71.10 | 10.00 | 74.10 | 11.05 |
| Primary Communication | 94.00 | 10.30 | 95.10 | 10.72 |
| Experimental Group: Wives |  |  |  |  |
| Marital Communication | 86.96 | 15.19 | 97.50 | 16.07 |
| Marital Adjustment | 90.08 | 15.16 | 91.92 | 14.19 |
| Conjugal Life | 69.25 | 11.52 | 73.71 | 12.80 |
| Primary Communication | 91.52 | 12.52 | 94.84 | 10.72 |

tivity and appropriateness of each test for the expected kinds of changes in communication. Apparently the MCI is the more sensitive instrument for assessing the types of changes produced by the Conjugal Relationship Enhancement program. Although it cannot be concluded that the hypothesis would be confirmed on a variety of measures in communication, it does seem reasonable, on the basis of the significance achieved with one measure and the parallel movement on the other measure, to consider this hypothesis confirmed.

### Marital Adjustment

The second hypothesis was that the experimental couples would perceive a greater improvement in their marital adjustment relative to the control couples. The results on the Marital

Adjustment Test analysis showed a significant improvement in the experimental group relative to the control group ($F[1.86]$ = 4.170; $p$ = .044).[5] There were no significant sex difference or interaction effects between sex and treatment.

Although the results showed a strong trend in the appropriate direction, there was no significant difference between the experimental and the control groups on the Conjugal Life Questionnaire ($F[1.86]$ = 3.241; $p$ = .075). There were no significant sex or interaction effects. Again, although the results of treatment are not so strong as to show up on both instruments, it does seem fair to conclude that the second hypothesis was confirmed.

### Use of Skills at Home

By inspecting homework forms, the following questions were explored: Were the subjects using the techniques well in the home, and if so, were they seen to be effective in the home context as opposed to the group context?

There was quite a difference in the number of reports of home practice sessions handed in from group to group, and sometimes from couple to couple within a group: Some handed in most of the reports, while others did not hand in many. Of the 18 possible homework reports to be handed in over the six-month period, there were an average of 12.2 reports per participant, with a range from 4 to 16. This variance seemed to be related to how insistent, systematic, and reinforcing the particular group leaders were in dealing with homework reports.

There were three statements in the homework report forms that could be crudely quantified—simply for the purposes of giving an overall picture of the respondents' answers. These

---

[5]The Bartlett's test of homogeneity was significant for the MAT ($X^2$ = 10.9; $p$ = .01), and not significant on any of the other data. A Mann-Whitney U Test was performed on MAT group data in order to examine differences between the experimental and control groups without the assumption of homogeneity of variance. This test also showed that the experimental group improved significantly more than the control group ($Z$ = 2.264; $p < .025$).

were statements evaluating understanding of self and spouse. On these questions, answers of "very well" or "much more" were assigned a score of 1; answers of "pretty well" or "somewhat more" were assigned a score of 2; and answers of "rather poorly" or "no more" were assigned a score of 3. For the statement, "I feel my spouse understood me: a) very well; b) pretty well; c) rather poorly," the average answer (Mean = 1.6) fell in the "very well" category. For the item, "I feel that as a result of this week's half-hour conversation, I understand myself: a) no more; b) somewhat more; c) much more," the average answer (Mean = 2.3) was "somewhat more." For the statement, "I feel that as a result of this week's half-hour conversation, I understand my spouse: a) no more; b) somewhat more; c) much more," the average answer (Mean = 1.9) fell in the "much more" category. Most of the topics discussed in the sessions, and reported as discussed at home, were of a feeling or emotional nature. At times the discussions became very intense during the session, and they were often reported as being intense at home, too.

Often a speaker would remark in a session about how much better he or she felt having been able to express his or her feelings to their spouse at home, and subsequently know from the spouse's reflections that their message had been understood and their feelings accepted. The following transcript, describing the use of the skills at home, makes the point about how gratifying it is to someone to have their feelings accepted rather than denied.

> *Carol:* I have a very different feeling about last night. It's a very interesting thing. I was aware of being very tired. I was also aware of being so incredibly wound up—everything in the world seemed truly shitty. I couldn't say two consecutive words without crying. My safety valve is tears. Without them I would be insane. I really feel, I have felt in the past that you take them too seriously. Even now, when I'm coming to be aware, I get crazy. I have perhaps five to ten minutes of insanity where I just weep and wail and moan and groan. And what you were able to do last night, what you did not give yourself credit for, is you were able to just listen and just let me get it all out. You didn't tell me that I wasn't feeling that way. You didn't tell me that the world was really much better than what I was saying. You didn't tell me, "Go to bed." There is nothing more outrageous to a fatigued person when they're nervous than to be told to go to sleep. And I know that it puts a burden on you. I really feel that it puts an incredible burden on you. But you didn't feel that I was attacking you personally. By being able to say that, I really feel better about it.

And because you didn't rush in to tell me that I didn't feel that way, it made it really possible for it not to turn into a free-for-all.

*Ed:* You're asking me to recognize the range of your feelings. And you're also commending me for letting you go through that phase and not sitting on you.

*Carol:* Absolutely. Oh, yes. You weren't condemning me. I sense it when you don't like me. And I wasn't picking that up at all. I knew that you didn't like what I said. I bet you thought I was crazy. And in the back of my head *I* could see that part of it was insane. You weren't condemning me. I cannot see myself as being a tower of clarity all of the time. I just can't function that way. Because I'm very much an emotional person. And when things get too much, I have to release my tensions somehow. And far better for me to release them in one place and at one time and then become more rational. I really feel you helped me do that.

Thus, clients' replies on the homework forms and anecdotal evidence suggest that the skills are used in the home situation to improve mutual understanding.

### Limitations and Suggestions for Further Research

There are a number of suggestions that can be made for future research, some of which are based on the need to overcome limitations of the present study. First, the results from this project cannot be generalized to all segments of the population. Future research is needed in order to prove the model's efficacy with populations of lower social and economic status. Studies should be conducted that rule out placebo, experimenter demand, suggestion, thank you, and attention effects. Future investigation should also be conducted to attempt to isolate the most important ingredients of this multifaceted approach.

Also, further research should include variations on the methodology. For example, there might be a concentration on first learning the CRE techniques in a very short period of time, possibly as in a marathon weekend session. The CRE method might also be combined with other educationally oriented methods. For example, once the roles have been learned well the couples might also be taught to bargain on an exchange basis for what they want from each other, and/or to modify each other's behavior by giving or withholding reinforcement for the behaviors they wish to be increased or extinguished.

Using a group format, rather than working in a single-couple format, is desirable in order to make more economical use of time and manpower. There are also other advantages. For example, clients working in a group can profit from what the others say, including the mistakes they make and the corrections that occur. They can help each other by facilitating each other's role performance. And there does develop in may groups a feeling of togetherness that seems to facilitate attendance at the weekly sessions, doing the homework, and accepting the roles to be learned. However, there are couples who seem not to like the group context, seem to get bored with others' problems, and prefer to work on their problems without others present. Thus, research should be conducted to find out whether or not the group is in fact the better context in which to do marital counseling of this kind, or to determine which types of couples or problems are best suited to an individual rather than a group approach. Teaching the techniques to couples in a group setting, then separating all the couples or allowing some groups to separate if they wished to do so, would be a method worth trying.

To achieve greater emphasis on generalization during the home sessions, cassette tape recorders could be lent to each couple and tapes made of the home sessions in place of or in addition to a written homework report. Another methodological variation worth exploring would be to exert more control over the topics discussed. For example, perhaps for a given number of negative feelings or topics discussed, at least one positive pleasant topic might be discussed (Clarke, 1970). This would serve to remind the couples of the pleasant things about their relationship, and assure that the skills are used periodically in a positive context, rather than only in a problem-solving context.[6]

---

[6]Supervision of taped home sessions, and the use of the Relationship Questionnaire to systematize topic selection, have become standard features of RE programs since the present study was completed. The idea of requiring the participants to discuss positive aspects of their relationship has become more prominent through greater emphasis on this aspect of the expresser mode, as well as through periodically asking clients to select positive aspects of their relationship for discussion.

Chapter 9

# Parent-Adolescent Relationship Development Program

*Barry G. Ginsberg*

As is well known, adolescence is a very difficult period of development both for the adolescent and his family. This period of development has, therefore, probably attracted more professional attention and interest than any other. There are at least four major problems that generally need to be resolved during adolescence: (1) a shift in ways of relating to parents; (2) the need to establish a personal sexual identity; (3) the need for adopting a suitable system of values; and (4) a choice of a life work.

These changes and achievements take place within the context of the family and, in turn, have a major impact on family functioning. In fact, when major difficulties and conflicts arise, one usually can look to the family for the etiology of the crisis and/or its resolution. Even when the adolescent leaves his family, he carries within him the relationship patterns and predispositions that he developed within the family. This approach does not discount the strong influence of his peer group, but even the nature of his relationship with his peer

group is to a large extent an outgrowth or reaction to his relationship with his parents and family.

While the adolescent is experiencing these difficulties and problems of mastery, his parents may be reaching a problematic stage of life. Their physical condition and sexual drives may be beginning to wane. Also at this stage, parents often begin to see more clearly the limitations of their lives, work, and marriage. Thus, not only do the adolescent and his parents suffer difficulties arising from within themselves, but they also must deal with difficulties arising out of the internal conflicts and frustrations of the others in their family. Unless mutually satisfactory adjustments can be made, conflict escalates and the emotional growth of the individuals and the unity of the family are threatened.

Investigation into the attitudes of adolescents reveals some sense of alienation from the world they are entering. This alienation is particularly manifested in relation to parents and family. Much of this may be the result of rapid change of parent-child relations (Bettelheim, 1962; Hess, 1970; Keniston, 1962). Bettelheim (1962) makes the point that in past times carrying on of family tradition and business was shared between father and son, but that rapid industrialization and social change have led to an extended period of socialization and a longer period of dependence.

Erickson (1968) suggests that the major tasks of adolescence are emancipation from family of origin, attainment of a firm sense of identity, and the development of a greater capacity for intimacy. This is an age when adolescents can begin to take on a new interpersonal awareness. Concern about how others think and feel about them assumes particular significance. Identity, definition of "who I am" and "what I am," is also a major concern.

The importance of identification in childhood is well documented in the psychological literature (Bandura and Walters, 1963; Bronfenbrenner, 1961; Kagan, 1958). Since the program described in this chapter involved fathers and their adolescent sons, the literature reviewed here will generally be limited to that relationship. In adolescence, identification becomes a

particularly crucial issue (Erickson, 1968), and for adolescent boys, identification with the father takes on special significance. There is some empirical evidence that there is stronger adolescent identification when the father is a highly rewarding, affectionate person (Payne and Mussen, 1956). Mussen (1961) found that highly masculine adolescent boys, who were well identified with their fathers, were better adjusted than boys low in masculinity.

Offer (1969), in a comprehensive investigation of normal adolescent boys from middle-class backgrounds, found that boys tended to feel close to one of their parents, but rarely to both. Although the boys stated that they were more like their fathers, the majority felt that they were closer to their mothers. He also found that communication patterns were good in these families. In another study (Marcus, Offer, Blatt, and Gratch, 1966), families with "disturbed" adolescent boys were found to have poor communication.

Offer (1969) found that relationships between fathers and sons were very complicated. Sons were willing to accept the respectful distances they experienced with their fathers, but Offer inferred they wanted closer relationships, even though they were not aware of it. He also found that parents viewed the early adolescent years as the most difficult and that this was the period during which communication was the most difficult.

Despite the nearly universal recognition of parent-adolescent problems, there is a dearth of clearly defined and evaluated programs to help improve parent-adolescent functioning. This deficiency is particularly evident with respect to remedial methods that seek to strengthen family bonds and to use the strength of the family to promote the positive growth of both the adolescent and his parents. In fact, clinical methods of dealing with the problems of the adolescent and his family often attempt to separate the adolescent from his family and move him in the direction of his peer group. Parents are usually given help separately. These approaches may or may not be helpful and effective, but clearly they fail to use the potential capacity for mutual aid inherent in the family's emotional attachments.

## The Program

The Parent-Adolescent Relationship Development (PARD) program was established as an approach that would bring adolescents and their parents together to learn more effective ways of relating to each other. The goal is to enable a parent and child to become more open about all of their feelings and more accepting of one another. Accepting and respectful behavior acts to enhance mutual understanding. The greater the acceptance, the more readily the individuals involved in a relationship are able to express their innermost feelings—positive and negative—regarding each other and themselves. As communication becomes more open and more often meets with acceptance, individuals in a relationship are less likely to express their feelings indirectly in destructive and antisocial ways. It is possible that as the adolescent begins to form his own identity and makes efforts to separate himself from his parents, an accepting parent can help the adolescent to develop more positive feelings about himself, facilitating the transition toward greater independence. At the same time, as the parent becomes more accepting of, and accepted by, his adolescent, he can more adequately fulfill, and derive satisfaction from, his parental role in the family.

Implicit in this approach, as in client-centered therapy, is the concept that greater acceptance from others leads to a greater sense of self-acceptance. The PARD approach is designed to increase the acceptance of the parent by the adolescent and of the adolescent by the parent. Given enough time, for the adolescent this can be expected to lead to a better self-concept, better peer relationships, and increased interpersonal competence; for the parent greater acceptance by the adolescent should lead to improved functioning in his roles as parent and spouse, and eventually to an improved self-concept and better general adjustment.

The father and son dyad was chosen for the initial evaluation of the PARD program, and consequently this chapter will emphasize the father-son relationship. Since the completion of the research cited here, the author and others have used this

approach successfully with mother-daughter dyads, and a family program has been developed employing similar basic elements. In his work at a community mental health center, the author continues to be very impressed with the efficacy of the PARD model in achieving therapeutic, problem prevention, and life enrichment goals.

## Special Problems

Working with parents and adolescents is dynamic and exciting, but it also can be frustrating and difficult. Frequently, feelings are heightened and conflict strong when parents and their adolescents come together. Adolescents frequently come to clinical settings, and to the PARD program as well, feeling controlled and treated unfairly. Parents are unsure of how to deal with problems and conflicts that arise with their adolescents. In addition, parents frequently look on the difficulties they are experiencing with their adolescents as resulting from their own failures. Often, the result is for the parents to behave out of guilt or defensiveness and thereby create further problems.

The PARD program can help parents and adolescents to identify their feelings. It can help the adolescent clarify what he wants and needs, and show the parent that his child is an independent being and that the parent need not blame himself for the feelings and behavior of his adolescent. It can help all family members to identify factors underlying their difficulties and enable them to find solutions to these difficulties.

The defensiveness of both the adolescents and parents is strongest early in the program. Almost all participants reveal some signs of anxiety. Parents may be concerned with loss of role and authority as well as feelings of inadequacy and guilt. Adolescents, already feeling relatively powerless, are usually fearful that they will be still more overpowered and that their efforts toward independence will be undermined. It is this author's firm belief, based on clinical experience, that only when such defensiveness and resistance are reduced significantly can lasting change occur. The methods used in PARD are designed to minimize these obstacles to change.

## PARD Formats

The variety of time and meeting formats possible in the general RE model are, of course, also possible in the PARD program. For expository purposes we will describe a format consisting of only ten 2-hour meetings, with a group of three father-son pairs. Reasons for describing this particular format are that it is the one in which we have the most experience, was employed in an experimental study that will be described in later sections of this chapter, and was the one for which illustrative transcripts were available. This format is one useful for educational, enrichment, and problem prevention purposes. For a therapeutic program (that is, when the participants feel they have severe relationship difficulties, or when a participant has serious emotional problems), participants may enter with an understanding that the program will continue for a much longer period. During that longer time period, the participants would attempt to resolve their problems by using, with supervision by the leader, the therapeutic communication skills taught in the program.

In the program format we are using for illustrative purposes, the participants are asked to spend one half to one hour at home before the first group meeting discussing the first lesson of the *General Relationship Improvement Program* (Human Development Institute, 1964). This lesson introduces the concept of acceptance in interpersonal relationships. Making this assignment establishes some structure as to what they later will be doing in the group, and it provides an opportunity to elicit questions and anxieties as well as objections to the program.

Also prior to the first session each member of the pair is asked to complete the Relationship Questionnaire (see Appendix L) asking them to list the most important positive aspects and concerns in their relationship. This procedure provides the topics for the early sessions. In addition to these topics, in later sessions the participants also may be asked to talk with each other on the topics of love and anger in their relationship. The emphasis on structure in the group provides a task orientation that enables the participants to move quickly into feelings about their relationship and about themselves.

## Doubling

Doubling is a part of the PARD program that has not been used in the other RE programs. The procedure was inspired by, but differs from, the doubling procedure used in psychodrama (Greenberg, 1974; Moreno, 1959). In the PARD program, doubling begins in the second session of PARD groups. In this procedure, one pair follows the expresser and empathic responder modes to discuss topics of mutual concern, while a second pair acts as their doubles. For example, if the father were the expresser, he would speak, and the second father would attempt to rephrase his statement even more closely in accord with the expressive mode. The son of the first father would then respond empathically, and the son of the second father would then try to improve on that response. Members of the second pair speak in the first person singular, as if the member speaking were the original father or son.

This variation of the facilitator mode serves several purposes. It provides a more active role for the facilitators early in the program and seems to enhance and speed the learning of the skills. Also, since the different pairs often have similar feelings and problems, the second pair frequently becomes more aware of their own feelings in the process and more comfortable about later expressing them in their own right. Also, the leader may ask a son to double for a father (or vice versa) and thereby increase his ability to identify and empathize with his own father's (or son's) feelings. As the participants become more skilled, doubling phases out as a formal procedure and fades into use of the usual facilitator mode.

## The Early Sessions

Considering the defensiveness and resistance likely to be involved, the leader structures the first session very carefully. The liberal use of positive reinforcement by the leader, and his full acceptance of the views and feelings of the participants while avoiding even the implication of criticism, are even more vital in the PARD program than in the other programs because of the special sensitivity of adolescents to criticism. The leader

attempts to elicit the expression of any negative or uncomfortable feelings as early as they arise. The structure of the PARD
program, and the leader's use of empathic skills to build trust,
can help to eliminate a good deal of resistance and defensiveness.

In the beginning, however, the structured nature of the
PARD program may itself become a focal point for resistance
and defensiveness. The early elicitation of these feelings and the
leader's empathic acceptance of them will facilitate eventual
acceptance of the methods. Very often those participants who
are able to express their resistance early become the best learners and use the program most productively.

At the beginning of the first session, all participants, including the leader, introduce themselves and talk about their
reasons for coming. The expresser, the empathic responder, and
the facilitator modes, mode switching, and the underlying
rationale of each are described and questions are elicited and
answered. Next, the lesson from the General Relationship Improvement Program is discussed. After this, practice of the
behavioral modes begins.

In the study to be described later in this chapter, the first
session began with the leader taking the role of the father,
modeling the responder mode for a while, and then asking the
father to take the responder mode with his son. Also, the participants often began discussing problematic relationship issues
in their first session. In current practice, the leader models
responses for the participant instead of assuming their role, and
a father and his son first practice with nonfamily members, discussing issues not related to family problems, before they practice with each other. When a father does begin practicing with
his own son, they discuss nonrelationship issues first, and then
positive aspects of their relationship, before they discuss issues
that may be problematic. After discussing a nonrelationship
issue, the Relationship Questionnaire is used to pinpoint positive aspects of the relationship and aspects that the participants
wish to develop further, which often points to problematic
aspects of the relationship.

In the early sessions, interactions are usually kept fairly

short to assure that all participants will have a turn in both empathic responder and expresser modes. Also, the leader frequently models responses for the responder even before the responder attempts to make his own response.

The leader sometimes uses doubling in the early sessions. Doubling serves many purposes. At this stage, the major function of doubling is to involve the participants in actively practicing empathic and expressive modes while others are at center stage, and to introduce them to the idea of facilitating the performance of others. Sometimes, usually in the later stages of the program, it is useful to have a son double for somone else's father, and someone else's father double for a son, to broaden their perspectives. In the early stage, it is best to have a father double for a father and a son for a son. The following transcript of an early session illustrates the doubling procedure.[1] Bill and his son, Paul, are the center-stage pair. Another father (John) acts as Bill's double, and John's son Larry acts as Paul's double. To make the transcript easier to follow the center-stage pair will be designated simply *F* and *S*, and the doublers will be designated *FD* and *SD*.

> *Leader:* A doubler really takes the role of another person. In this case, John, you sit next to Bill and be his double. Bill will be the responder. John, *after Bill is finished* reflecting what Paul says, you try to come in with either an added feeling or to try to repeat the feeling—that will give you extra practice in the responder mode. Later, when Bill is expresser, you try to add a more open kind of expression if you can, or a feeling that's there, perhaps one that Bill hadn't *directly* expressed in so many words, but that catches his mood.
>
> *FD:* If Bill's the expresser, I'm the responder.
>
> *Leader:* No, if he's the expresser then *you're* the expresser and if he's the responder, *you're* the responder—you're kind of his second.
>
> *FD:* Oh, OK.
>
> *Leader:* OK, Larry, you sit next to Paul. Now, when Paul is expresser, Larry will come in and, if possible, give an even better expresser statement of what Paul said. Paul and Bill are the primary

---

[1] All transcripts have been edited and annotated in order to make the names fictitious and to help clarify the statements and methods.

ones. John and Larry, as seconds, you try to make a better, clearer expression of feeling or a more empathic response.

*FD:* OK. That's a good idea.

*S:* Shall I start?

*Leader:* Pick a topic that has to do with your relationship.

*S:* OK. I am bothered by the fact that you want me to be the sort of person that you think I should be, and you want me to follow in your exact plan for what kind of person I should be. I feel you won't allow me to be myself with my own kind of personality.

*Leader:* Good. [To SD]: OK—can you add something there in your role as double?

*SD:* Not right now.

*F:* In other words, you feel that through some regimentation I'm kind of directing you in a mode of conduct that you don't agree with. Or that's what I *feel* that you're saying: that I am regimenting you in a mode of conduct that you don't like. [Pause.]

*FD:* I think you feel a little bit of my standards, or at least to the point that I won't let you *be* what you want to be. [Pause.]

*Leader:* Good.

*S* [looking at FD]: Uh, yeah, *I* know what kind of person *I* want to be; and he has certain ideas—

*Leader:* Tell it to your father directly.

*S:* Yeah, you have certain ideas about what type of person *you'd like* for me to be; and I'd like to form my own personality. I'd like to have my own personality without you directing what kind of person I am. I just think that's one of a person's rights. [Long pause.]

*SD:* So I—I'd like to form my own opinions of what I want to be instead of what you'd like me to be.

*Leader:* Very good, Larry.

*F* [after a pause]: In other words, you feel that, uh, you've reached a stage of maturity where your ideas and feelings are, uh, pretty important and, uh, you feel that you're being hampered. [Long pause.]

*Leader:* Very good.

*FD:* Uh, I can't improve on that.

*S:* OK, uh, and I'm also bothered by the fact that when I *try* to be myself, and you don't agree with me, I think you take the stand that because "I am your father you have to be what I want you to be." And I don't think that's fair to me. And I think you might be ashamed of what kind of person I might turn out to be if *I* decided what kind of person I wanted to be; and I think you don't want to have a son that you're ashamed of; so you want me to follow your standards because you think that will show up good in front of everybody.

*Leader* [to S] : "And that kind of makes me feel—" [Indicating that S should finish this sentence.]

*S:* That bugs me!

*Leader:* Very good.

*SD:* It really bothers me.

*Leader:* Very good, Larry.

*F:* So you—you have the feeling then that, uh, that I have a set of standards for you; and I know exactly what kind of person I want you to be; and I'm in the process of making that kind of person out of you. And it *bothers* you a great deal that, uh, I'm doing this. [Long pause.]

*Leader:* Very good.

*FD:* Uh, I think again that you feel resentment because [pause] this goes *against* the way *you* feel and you think that this isn't right. [Pause.]

*S:* Yeah. I *don't* feel that it's right *completely.* To a point, the parents *should* have some control over the actions of the child, but when it comes to forming what kind of *person* you're going to be, and the things that determine your character, well, I think that's something an individual has to decide. [Long pause.]

*SD:* Like, uh, well, when it comes to like, wow, uh, what kind of person I *want* to be; I want to do it my way; not have anyone else, uh, interfere with me.

*Leader:* Good.

*F:* That's right. In other words, you're expressing a feeling that, uh, that, uh, I'm putting clamps on you—too much regimentation. You feel that it just hampers you from developing into the type of personality that you think you have.

*Leader:* John, do you want to add something?

*FD:* Ahhh—no.

*Leader:* OK. You want to switch modes?

*F:* Yeah. [Short pause.] I, uh, have a feeling—this is kind of hard. It's so new to me. I have a feeling that I'm not aware of, uh, of the type of personality that you'd like to be. And, uh, I'm not aware of the regimentation. And I also have a strong feeling in me that, whether you believe it or not, you've *already* been influenced by your parents and your teachers. Your personality already reflects this, and I think it'll continue to reflect it. And I feel that it *should.*

*FD:* Oh, *I* feel that in these instances where you feel that you're being regimented—that you haven't communicated this to me, and that I'm *really not aware* that you feel this way at the time. And I *think* that it would be a good idea if you really felt that the clamps were put *on* you, that you should communicate this to me. I feel that, uh, the people around you, just because of the proximity, are

*going* to influence you. And I don't think that you should try to shut all this out *just* for the sake of being your own kind of person.

*Leader:* That was very good. Now let me add another feeling: "I'm kind of surprised. It's really new to me—it kind of surprised me because I wasn't aware of, uh, these feelings that you have. It's kind of hard for me to see how you *couldn't* be affected by my thoughts and my feelings, my ideas and thoughts."

*S:* It's tricky. OK, so you feel that I haven't made you completely aware of those feelings. So you really haven't given it some thought. But, uh, despite the fact that I don't want to be directly affected by you, I won't be *able* to be myself: I *already have* been affected by other people. [Pause.]

*Leader:* Paul, try to reflect a little *more* of the feeling there—your father's feelings.

*S:* Well, really [a big sigh] I think you're *bothered* by this new issue because you haven't thought about it before.

*Leader:* Good!

*SD:* And you don't really understand what I told you, I don't think.[2]

*F* [after a pause] : Well now, this is *very* interesting because I had been concerned—in fact, if you'll read my answer to Question Number 1 that I wrote on the Relationship Questionnaire—it's pretty obvious that I *had* been aware of the issue of choosing standards and goals in life. But you see the thing is that I was *not* aware of the fact that *you* were concerned. I *have* been. I was interested in finding out what *you* thought was a desirable mode of life and that is what you're really talking about. In other words, I am concerned about what you are going to set for your standards of ethics and conduct. These are things which I think a boy of fourteen *ought* to be starting to develop on his own and be ready to stand up and *defend*.

*FD:* I'm *really aware* of this problem, but somehow I didn't think that *you* felt about it like you do—like you expressed a minute ago. And what *really* bothers me is [pause] that I'm not really sure of what your motives are or *what* your standards are *yet*—so that *I* can gain confidence in *what* you want to do or *how* you want to do it. Somehow or other this escapes me. I don't have confidence yet in you, as an individual, picking the way you want to go. I think if I *did* know, it would be more acceptable to me to let you *do* this.

*S:* OK, I have given *some* thought to you thinking about this. [Big sigh.] You're *really* in the dark as to what *my* ideas would be. That

[2] This was a poor response, but this participant has been feeling insecure in this doubling role, and the leader did not wish to discourage him in one of his earliest efforts at doubling.

may be *part* of the reason why you won't allow me to carry them out. And you would like to know what some of my thoughts are, because you're bothered by the fact that you don't know.

In the transcript just given, observe that Larry, the second son, was uncomfortable in the doubling role at first. As he began to identify with the first son's concerns, he found doubling more acceptable. The transcript also reflected the fact that the leader concentrated more of his attention on helping the father with the responder mode rather than the son with expresser mode in the early phase of the program, in order to provide a climate in which the son could evolve toward expression of his deeper feelings and experience acceptance.

### Dealing with Resistance to the Program

As mentioned earlier, it is important for the leader to elicit frank and open expression of the resistance and defensiveness that will often be present. An example can be seen in the following excerpt from an early session. Bob is the son and Mike the father.

> *Leader:* Bob, I thought maybe you'd like to start out as the expresser.
>
> *Bob:* I don't have anything to say.
>
> *Leader:* Well, I kind of sense that you feel uncomfortable in this setting.
>
> *Bob:* Well—yeah.
>
> *Leader:* It's hard to take the expresser mode.
>
> *Bob:* Well, I just don't have anything to say.

The leader reflects the feelings of discomfort elicited from Bob. The leader is helping the son feel more accepted while he is also providing a good *model* of empathic acceptance for the group. Since Bob is uncomfortable about taking the initiative, the leader, in the excerpt below, asks him to respond empathically to his father. This got them started, and the son then became motivated to take the expresser role. Bob was chosen last because he was seen as the most resistant, and this

was confirmed. Note how the structure and the practice of the behavioral roles draws Bob into relating to his father, Mike.

> *Leader:* Well, could you—could you respond empathically to some of your father's feelings?
>
> *Bob:* I don't know.
>
> *Leader:* All right, let's try.
>
> *Mike:* Yeah. You want me to be the expresser?
>
> *Leader:* Yes.
>
> *Mike:* Well, Bob, I guess we haven't had any problems, but I've been concerned that I'm not really reading *you*. I don't quite know, uh, what your feelings are, because you usually say, "I don't know," or "I don't care," and this leaves me with a kind of *lost feeling* about where to go from there. [Pause.]
>
> *Leader:* Do you want to reflect some of the feelings, Bob?
>
> *Bob:* Well—there isn't too much—there isn't anything wrong or anything like that, you know. It's just that there really isn't *that* much to talk about. Just like, you know, there's no real problem or anything.
>
> *Leader:* There was a concern that your father expressed: He'd kind of like to hear more about how you're feeling about things. It's important to him. Could you reflect that back to him?
>
> *Bob:* Uh, there isn't too many things that I feel, you know, kind of like everything's OK.
>
> *Leader:* Now you're expresser, right?[3]
>
> *Mike:* You find, uh, satisfaction, then, in our relationship, even though we don't talk, necessarily.
>
> *Bob:* Yeah, uh, we don't fight or anything at all. Everything's OK.
>
> *Mike:* Then things are fine as far as you're concerned most of the time.
>
> *Bob:* Yeah.
>
> *Mike:* OK. I'll be the expresser. Maybe I should be aware of that because I know that we can spend long times together and not need to talk. I seem to know how you feel and you seem to reflect how I feel. We don't get in each other's road, we don't seem to rub each other the wrong way too much. But it's this lack of oral communication that I've been concerned about. Maybe we're not doing a job for each *other*. And that's why I thought this program would

[3] In order to avoid increasing Bob's defensiveness, fear of failure, embarrassment, and reluctance to participate, the leader chose not to comment on a role switch that occurred in an inappropriate manner. However, in this gentle manner he made it evident to Bob and the others that Bob was in the expresser and not the responder mode.

be helpful: It would help us communicate verbally, rather than just communicating by *not* communicating.

*Bob:* Well, you see, I didn't really —

*Leader:* You have to reflect his feelings first.

*Bob:* Well, what you're saying is that we—we could get a better relationship by coming to this program and discussing what we aren't talking about, right?

From here on, both father and son continued to use expresser and responder modes to discuss a major area of their relationship.

Often, participation in a PARD program suggests to the adolescent that there is something wrong with their relationship and this may lead to a sense of vulnerability and fear of exposing oneself. The father often is concerned not only about exposing himself, but over the possible loss of role and authority. Generally, both fathers and sons learn fairly quickly that these fears are unfounded and that openness and acceptance in their relationship leads to more trust and greater respect for one another and a stronger, more satisfying relationship.

The problem created by the notion that coming to a PARD program necessarily implies serious deficit and dissatisfaction and the way such a problem is resolved in the program are illustrated in the following excerpt. Bob attended the first session, in which he brought up (prematurely, in terms of current RE methods) an issue in their relationship that had not previously been revealed to his father. He missed the next session because of illness, and his father attended without him. (It is possible that this "illness" may have been an excuse not to attend because of anxiety arousal during the first session.) Before the third session, the leader received a call from Mike, who said that Bob was upset as a result of the first session. Bob thought his father was indicating, by participating in the PARD program, that something was wrong with their relationship and this made him feel different from his peers. Mike further said that he had hoped this program would improve their relationship and now he was fearful the opposite was true.

The leader first reflected all the feelings Mike was expressing and then suggested that the type of skills learned in the

PARD program would help them work through this problem. The leader suggested that they both come to the following session and encouraged the father to discuss this topic during the meeting using the expresser and responder modes. Mike agreed. In the third session, when it was their turn to interact, he opened with this topic and the following interaction ensued.

*Bob:* It makes me feel different from other people. Uh, like [long pause] well, just different from other people. It makes me feel like [pause] uh, we have a real problem, and I didn't think that we had a real problem.

*Mike:* You feel like you're an *oddball*, and that I think you're an oddball; that all the fathers and sons that you know, with the exception of the other two in *here*, don't go to something like this, right? Everything seems to be OK, and you're really wondering why we have to do this, or why I'd even attempt to do this, right?

*Bob:* Right.

*Leader:* That's a good reflection!

*Mike:* OK, then I'll take the expresser mode. I had a *great* deal of doubt in my mind—and I still *do* have some. The *last* thing I wanted to do, by signing up for this program, was to [pause] *adversely* affect our relationship. Yes, I was happy, OK? And I'm a little bit worried that our relationship *has* been affected a little bit by it, because I can't seem to make you *understand* the real reason for me doing this.

*Leader:* OK. Now, stop and give him a chance to just reflect that part. We'll come back to you.

*Bob:* You feel that I don't understand why, uh, you took this course, and, uh, that maybe I could understand better by your explaining to me, uh, *why* we took this course—not because we have a problem, but maybe to improve our relationship.

*Leader:* Good!

*Mike:* I'm *greatly worried* that now that I have experienced [pause] this program, and that I can see how I have benefited from it, you know, I would like to continue going and try to regain everything that we might have lost and gain some more back. You see, I would like to come out of this with a real good way of expressing ourselves to each other, just between you and me. If I don't get anything else more than that, I would be extremely happy. [Long pause.]

*Leader:* It's really important to you, Mike, to let Bob know that you had reservations about this too. You were not sure of it yourself and after coming here that time when Bob wasn't here,

having kind of experienced it, you're feeling a lot differently now.[4]

*Mike:* Yeah. I *like* this program, for the reason that it has shown me where I have got—where I have problems, OK? And it's made me *aware* of the problems I didn't think—I never even thought about before. I just went day to day and I didn't even think of some of the real serious problems I *had* with different people. And, uh, *already* I've benefited from it. And I think, uh, I *feel* that, uh, if you would have a more positive attitude toward the program [pause] that *you* could benefit from it also.

*Bob:* So, so far the program has been beneficial for you; and if I'd take a better attitude toward it, I might find it beneficial also.

*Leader* [to Bob]: Want to switch modes now? I can sense that you have a lot of feelings, and it's hard for you to be a responder. [A very long pause.] I kind of sense that you're still bothered by something, that you still have some feelings about this that [pause] are still bothering you.

*Bob:* I can't help feeling different from other people by taking this course [a deep sigh]. Because, uh, I feel that not many people take this course, and that if I were to tell my friends that I was taking this course, they would probably think that I had some kind of *big* problem. And [pause], you know, difficulties with my family and people.

*Leader:* Good.

*Mike:* Well, you're [pause] *concerned* about what other people would think of you, right? May I be expresser?

*Bob:* Yeah.

*Mike:* I can appreciate that. I can understand that like I was sitting there in your place. And that's the part that—that I'm really upset about. I'm really upset about that because [pause] you think that I think that you have a real big problem; and, uh, that has affected our relationship. I didn't have a good relationship with *my* father. All my personal problems I kept to myself and I thought, you know, "Gee, I need somebody to *lean* on" and there wasn't anybody *there.* So I recognized that as a potential problem and in our case and I feel like, uh, I feel like you and I, Bob, *do* have a problem discussing personal relationships. For some reason or other, we just don't get down to the nitty gritty of discussing our true feelings about things like that. Maybe it's not a serious problem *now,* but I can foresee that it *could* be a serious problem. And this is an attempt to try to avoid that kind of a problem.

---

[4] In current practice this empathic response would not be made to Mike, but would be modeled for Bob. Bob would then make the response to his father.

*Bob:* You feel that this program we're coming to is a chance to avoid having [pause] difficult relationships in the future. And express our feelings with each other. [A long pause.]

*Leader:* Another thing that he's saying, Bob, is that it's *very* important to him to have a *really* close relationship with you.

This interaction helped resolve the issue and this pair continued in every session thereafter. At the last session, they brought in a tape of a home session in which they both indicated that the program had been very helpful in enhancing their relationship.

## Supervision of Home Sessions

Home sessions are deemed extremely important to the success of the PARD program. It is not sufficient that the participants learn to communicate well within the group sessions. The skills should also be used at home. One of the biggest difficulties in education and treatment is the generalization from the particular educational or clinic setting. The home session is a major attempt to accomplish this generalization of skill training.

The first five home sessions for the research groups were taken from the text, *General Relationship Improvement Program* (Human Development Institute, 1964). This text utilizes a programed format to help in understanding and practicing some of the concepts utilized in the PARD program. Its use permits work at home in the beginning of the program (or even during a time prior to the first meeting). In addition, it reduces significantly the possibility of frustration with the difficulty of the approach in the early stages when the skills are still too new to be practiced effectively in the absence of the leader.

After the first five lessons of the *General Relationship Improvement Program*, the participants are asked to practice the expresser and responder modes at home for half an hour discussing some topic in their relationship that is at a level of difficulty no greater than that of other topics they have already demonstrated their ability to handle in the group. Supervision of these home sessions is important and helpful for generalizing these skills to the home situation as well as for continued learn-

ing. Such supervision can be accomplished in part through the Home Session Report forms, but it is very useful for the PARD program participants to tape-record home sessions and bring them to the group for supervision. If possible, inexpensive cassette recorders can be loaned to participants who do not have their own.

Tapes are reviewed for supervisory purposes and to reinforce the participants for practicing at the beginning of every session. Participants choose which parts of the tape they wish to play in the group, or make selections at random. As always, supervision concentrates on skills and technique, not content. Some examples of the leader's supervisory responses are: "That was a good reflection"; "That was a good way to say that"; "What was the feeling there?" "That was kind of accusative— how could you rephrase that in terms of your own perception?" Supervision of the taped sessions takes half an hour to forty-five minutes in a two-hour session.

### The Importance of Structuring

The leader of a PARD group sets the style and direction of a group. Because of the difficulties in learning the roles during the early phases of the program and then at later phases because of the stress created by the discussion of problems and concerns in the relationship, there is often a temptation to get away from the structured format of the approach. To do so, however, would lead to the usual interactions between parents and adolescents, often resulting in the leader acting as an intermediary in a conflict. As a result, the group would grow to depend on the leader to solve problems, taking this role away from the parents and adolescents. In developing a dependence on an outside authority to solve problems, they are failing to develop through practice the skills that would enable them to solve their own future problems. It is a major role of the leader to hold the participants to the structure of the program in order to equip them with the attitudes and skills necessary to deal successfully with their problems and conflicts themselves and in order to foster trust and openness in their relationship.

Careful adherence to the structure of the program makes this possible.

## An Experimental Study of the Effectiveness of the PARD Program[5]

An experiment was conducted to assess the effectiveness of the PARD program on father-adolescent communication, relationship, and adjustment (Ginsberg, 1971). It was hypothesized that relative to father and son pairs who had not undergone the program (control, or C, group), father and son pairs participating in the PARD program (experimental, or E, group) would show greater improvement.

### Dependent Variables and Measures

Five dependent variables were used to assess the differences between the experimental and the control groups. Copies and descriptions of the measures designed for this study are included in the appendix. Readers requiring greater detail may consult Ginsberg (1971) and Grando (1971a).

*Specific communication skills.* It was hypothesized that fathers and sons in a PARD program would show greater improvement in communication skills in terms of: (1) empathic acceptance of one another, and (2) more open expression of attitudes and feelings. To provide a means of measuring specific communication skills, each father and son pair, while alone with each other, audiotaped four 4-minute conversations in which their task was to discuss important personal and interpersonal topics in a way that was open and helpful with respect to facilitating expression of feelings. The instructions and other procedures used in this Verbal Interaction Task (VIT) are described in Appendix I. The verbalizations of fathers and sons in this situation were rated for: (1) empathic acceptance via the

[5]The study reported here was a doctoral dissertation (Ginsberg, 1971) conducted at The Pennsylvania State University under the chairmanship of Bernard Guerney, Jr.

Acceptance of Other Scale (AOS); and (2) open expression of personal attitudes and feelings via the Self-Feeling Awareness Scale (SFAS). The AOS and SFAS are described in detail in Appendices J and K.

In the VIT, the fathers and sons in the experimental and control groups were *aware* that their conversations were to be used in the research. Positive results on this measure would indicate that the fathers and sons in the experimental group had indeed learned the skills they had been taught and could apply them appropriately.

*Unobtrusively observed specific communication skills.* It was hypothesized that fathers and sons who had participated in the PARD program also would show (1) greater empathic acceptance of each other's views, and (2) more openness in expressing feelings in their ordinary interactions when they were *unaware* that their behavior was to be evaluated in any way. The purpose of this unobtrusively obtained measure was to determine if PARD participants who had learned the skills being taught in the program would apply them not only when they knew they were being evaluated, but also when they did not believe anyone else was interested in what they were doing, in a situation that was less structured and more spontaneous.

To obtain data pertinent to this question, the AOS and SFAS scales were used to code four 2-minute taped interactions during which the subjects had just finished their assigned tasks in the VIT and believed themselves to be simply waiting for the experimenter to give them their next assignment.

*General communication patterns.* It was hypothesized that the fathers and sons who participated in the PARD program would show greater improvement not only in such behavioral skills as have been mentioned above, but also in terms of their general communication with one another in the course of everyday living. These general communication patterns were measured by a variety of self-report instruments, described as follows.

The Adolescent-Parent Communication Checklist (APCC) was devised by Clare Beaubien (1970). She conducted a factor analysis on the form for the adolescent (Form A) that indicated

that there were three factors in her test: (1) adolescent action, which measures the selection and transmission of communication; (2) parent reaction, which assesses feedback from parents; and (3) adolescent satisfaction, which measures the adolescent's perception that the parent understands and respects the communications of the adolescent. A total score is also obtained, which affords a summary of these communication patterns.

Beaubien's form for parents (Form P) measured only parent satisfaction using items paralleling the parent satisfaction subscale of Form A. The present writer devised two more parent subscales for use in this study by modifying items from the two remaining adolescent scales of Beaubien's Form A. These scales permitted the study of parent action and adolescent reaction.[6]

The Parent-Adolescent Communication Inventory (PACI) was developed by Millard Bienvenu (1969) to measure the general ability of communication between parents and their adolescent children. Because the present author modified the inventory to tailor it specifically to the father-son relationship, it is here called the Parent-Adolescent Communication Inventory, Father-Son (PACI-FS). To tailor the adolescent form of the PACI specifically to father-son communication, eight items pertaining to mothers that duplicated items for the father were dropped. Also, all items that pertained to the mother that were not duplicated for the father in the original were modified to pertain to the father. These modifications resulted in a thirty-two-item inventory. Bienvenu's inventory to assess the parent's side of adolescent-parent communication was similarly modified to thirty-two items applying specifically to the father-son relationship. Sample items for the modified form for sons are: "Do you discuss personal problems with your father? Do you feel your father trusts you?" Sample items for the modified form

---

[6] Beaubien reports that the reliability of her measures, as assessed by retesting twenty students one week after their original testing, is very good. Pearson Product Moment correlations for the three adolescent subcomponents of the test, in the order in which they were mentioned in the text, were .92, .88, and .81. Test-retest reliability for *parent satisfaction*, assessed with eighty-two parents, was .85.

for fathers are: "Does your son talk to you in a disrespectful manner? Is it easy for you to trust your son? Do you criticize your son too much?" On both forms the answers can be "Yes," "Sometimes," or "No."[7]

The Awareness Questionnaire (AQ) is a two-part, open-ended measure jointly devised by Bernard Guerney, Jr., and the author to assess change in awareness in two areas: awareness of another's feelings (AQ-F) and awareness of another's ideas (AQ-I). These can be combined into one total score (AQT). The subjects are simply asked to list (1) the feelings and (2) the ideas of the other person that they have become aware of in the past month. The score in each case is simply the sum of the items listed.[8]

*The quality of the general relationship.* It was hypothesized that, relative to the control group, the participants in the PARD group would show greater improvement in the quality of their general relationship. This was assessed via the following measures:

The Family Life Questionnaire (FLQ) was devised by Bernard Guerney, Jr. to assess the degree of harmony in family relationships. The measure is described in Appendix D.

---

[7] Bienvenu established face validity for the PACI by finding that a team consisting of a psychiatrist, a psychologist, and a social worker regarded all items as relevant to family communication (1969). Other evidences of validity presented by Bienvenu are: All items were found to discriminate between high school students ($N = 358$) in the upper percent versus the lower 25 percent of academic standings; the inventory discriminated successfully between delinquents and nondelinquents ($N = 59$ per group); and the inventory discriminated tenth-grade honor students ($N = 25$) from remedial students ($N = 20$) in the same school. The evidence of validity is of course quite indirect. Other powerful variables—for example, differences in intelligence, socioeconomic status, and social desirability standards—might also account for these results. Like the PACC, however, the inventory was attractive to the investigator because of its face validity. Grando (1971a) obtained an alpha coefficient of .85 for the parent form and an alpha of .92 for the son form, thus revealing good internal consistency.

[8] A test-retest reliability study with a ten-week interval, using the fathers and sons ($N = 30$) in the control group of the present study, yielded the Pearson Product Moment correlations: AQF, .53; AQI, .82; AQT, .72.

The Father-Son Semantic Differential is based on the form used in the Semantic Differential developed by Osgood, Tannenbaum, and Succi (1957). The Semantic Differential consists of a concept to be rated and a list of polar scales. The polar scales are generally antonyms. There are generally seven blanks between a pair of antonyms. The subject checks the space between the antonyms that most closely corresponds to the concept presented. The usual method of scoring involves assigning a number from one to seven. For the Semantic Differential in this study, a score of seven is indicative of a positive father-son relationship, and a score of one is indicative of a negative father-son relationship.

The relationship concepts measured in the present study have to do with the father's and the son's perceptions of their feelings about themselves and about the other at the times they were together during the week prior to completing the scale. Often three scales (evaluative, activity, and potency) are employed in using semantic differential measures, but in this instance we were interested only in the evaluative area: positive vs. negative feelings. There were four such scales used to assess the relationship: two completed by the son and two by the father. On the Semantic Differential, Self-Son (SDS-S), the son indicated what his own feelings were in the presence of his father. On the Semantic Differential, Other-Son (SDO-S), the son indicated what he thought his father was like during that week. On the Semantic Differential, Self-Father (SDS-F), the father indicated what his own feelings were in the presence of his son. On the Semantic Differential, Other-Father (SDO-F), the father indicated his perception of his son's behavior during the preceding week.

Three sample items from the Son's Relationship scale for his own feelings are "This week in the presence of my father I have felt: a) far (distant) _ _ _ _ _ _ _ close); b) bad _ _ _ _ _ _ _ good; c) trusted _ _ _ _ _ _ _ not trusted. Three sample items for the son's relationship scale providing his perception of what his father's behavior was toward him are: "This week with me, my father has been: a) not-caring _ _ _ _ _ _ _ caring; b) unfair _ _ _ _ _ _ _ fair; c) encouraging _ _ _ _

_ _ _ discouraging." Three sample items from the Semantic Differential completed by the Father in terms of his own feelings in the relationship are: "This week in the presence of my son, I have felt: a) proud _ _ _ _ _ _ _ ashamed; b) warm _ _ _ _ _ _ _ cold; c) reasonable _ _ _ _ _ _ _ stubborn. Three samples of items assessing the father's perception of his son in the relationship are: "This week with me, my son has been: (1) warm _ _ _ _ _ _ _ cold; (2) trusting _ _ _ _ _ _ _ not trusting; (3) unselfish _ _ _ _ _ _ _ selfish."

All scales were chosen from the 50 suggested by Osgood, Tannenbaum, and Succi (1957). Some wording was changed to fit the vocabulary level of teenagers. The changes were accomplished by consulting the *Roget's Thesaurus* for synonyms and antonyms, as was done by Osgood. The scales were based on ones used in studies by Grinker, Grinker, and Timberlake (1962) and Offer (1969). A number of changes were made on these to provide more relevance to the father-son relationship itself and to eliminate all but evaluative scale items.

The overt responses on the Semantic Differential serve as an operational index of the representational mediation process or meaning. Osgood states, "The significance of meaning as a critical variable in personality is most apparent in the process of therapy itself, where the principal changes in significance or meaning that various persons, events and situations have for the patient are changes in the interrelationships between these significances" (Osgood, Tannenbaum, and Succi, 1957, p. 273). The most important concepts seem to be the self, father, and mother concepts (Endler, 1961). Endler (1961) found in his study that changes in these concepts were significantly related to estimated improvement in therapy.[9]

---

[9]Reliability studies (test-retest) have been performed on a considerable number of Semantic Differential scales, and reliability is considered good (Osgood, Tannenbaum, and Succi, 1957). The internal consistency of the present instruments was assessed using pretest scores from the present study (Grando, 1971a). Alpha coefficients of .88 for the fathers ($N = 30$) and .90 for the sons ($N = 30$) were achieved for Semantic Differential Self measures. Alpha coefficients of .88 (fathers) and .89 (sons) were obtained for the Semantic Differential-Other measures. Test-retest reliability was

*Self-concept.* It was hypothesized that fathers and sons in the PARD program would show greater improvement in their self-concepts. The primary goal of the PARD program is to teach certain interpersonal skills and thereby improve a particular relationship. In the long run, we would also expect this to result in improved self-concepts as the individuals using these skills win more affection and respect from those around them, especially the significant person with whom they participated in the program. But we were extremely dubious that a ten-week program would prove sufficient time for changes to spread from the relationship, by itself, to changes in self-concept. Nevertheless, we decided to propose and test this hypothesis with the view that if negative results were obtained in this short-term study, it should not discourage further research into this question using a longer PARD program.

To measure self-concept, another instrument in the semantic differential format was used. The phrase to be completed was, "This week I am ___" The antonyms chosen corresponded to those presented in the examples in the descriptions

---

also assessed on control group data. Correlation coefficients of .41 ($p <$ .05) and .61 ($p < $.001), respectively, were achieved. These were considered satisfactory for group analysis, especially since the time span was long—ten weeks. The Semantic Differential is considered to be relatively free of response bias, and studies have shown good construct validity (Osgood, Tannenbaum, and Succi, 1957). A study by R. R. Grinker, Sr., and his associates (1962) sheds light on the construct validity of the Semantic Differential as it is being used here. He used a modified version of the Semantic Differential to determine the degree to which three adolescent male adjustment groups (very well adjusted, fairly well adjusted, and marginally adjusted) maintained positive feelings toward their parents. He found that very well-adjusted groups saw both parents in a significantly more positive light than the marginally adjusted group. Offer (1969) used a form similar to Grinker's, calling his a Family Interaction Scale. He used this to assess the degree of open communication in presumably normal families. He correlated this scale with the Self-Image Questionnaire that he developed and found results that verified good communication between family members. This was significant in light of a related study (Marcus, and others, 1966), in which poorer communication patterns were found in disturbed adolescents and their parents. Taken together, these results offer favorable construct validity evidence for the general type of measure used in the present study.

given earlier of semantic differential types of measures of the relationship: warm-cold, angry-affectionate, good-bad, and so on. The form Semantic Differential = I am (SD=IA) was used for both fathers and sons.[10]

## Procedures

A comprehensive effort was undertaken to interest adolescent boys and their fathers in the PARD program. School, community, civic, religious, and professional groups in Centre, Bucks, and Blair counties, Pennsylvania, were contacted in person, by mail or telephone. Initially, forty father-son pairs requested an interview. Of these, thirty-seven completed the initial questionnaire forms and the taped interactions.

After the initial data collection, eighteen pairs were randomly assigned to the E group and nineteen to the C group. Of the eighteen E pairs, two dropped out, apparently because of time and business commitments of the fathers. Another pair dropped out after four sessions, apparently because of lack of motivation of the father and resistance of the son. A fourth pair was dropped from the analysis for not meeting the criterion of attending seven sessions. Of the nineteen C pairs, four failed to complete the post-waiting-period forms and taped interactions. The final sample, therefore, consisted of fourteen E pairs and fifteen C pairs.

Demographic data were collected and analyzed, revealing a group with relatively high socioeconomic status as determined by the Hollingshead Index of Social Position (Hollingshead, 1957). The mean for socioeconomic status for the E group was

---

[10]Endler (1961) has found that changes in the "me" or self-concept are significantly related to estimated improvement in therapy, and Offer (1969) has found his similar Semantic Differential form to be significantly related to his Self-Image Questionnaire. Grando (1971a), using the pretest data of the present investigation, found the measure to have good internal consistency. The alpha coefficient was .81 for the fathers and .76 for the sons. A test-retest study on the C group in the present study after a ten-week interval, using father and son groups combined ($N$ = 30), yielded a Pearson Product Moment coefficient of .83, indicating good test-retest reliability.

1.9 and for the C group, 2.1, on a five-point scale. The mean age of the E sons was 12.6 years and of the C sons, 13.2 years. The mean age of the E fathers was 41.6 years and of the C fathers, 44.9 years. The differences among these three variables were not statistically significant. The questionnaires and taped interactions were readministered to the E group after completion of the PARD program. The C group also underwent posttesting after waiting a period equivalent to that of the PARD program (ten weeks).

*Own-control quasireplication.* An additional testing was obtained from ten C pairs that went on to complete treatment after the waiting period. This permitted a quasireplication of the experiment by means of using this group as its own control. That is, the degree of change shown by this group from the time immediately before they entered treatment to the time of termination was compared to the change shown for a comparable time span prior to entering the program. In this way, the hypotheses tested via comparison of the E group and the C group were retested on the group that previously acted as a control group.

## *Results and Discussion*

The summaries of the most important data are presented in Tables 9-1 through 9-3. Table 9-1 presents the means and standard deviations for the experimental versus the control group study. Analysis of variance of repeated measures was performed on all measures in the main analysis (E versus C) to determine whether the E group changed more positively than the C group during the time covered by the training period. The probabilities resulting from these tests are reported parenthetically where they are discussed. Table 9-2 presents the *F* values and probabilities for this E versus C study. Analysis of variance of repeated measures also was used in the own-control study to assess change from pre- to posttreatment in comparison with an equivalent time period prior to the beginning of training. Table 9-2 presents the results of Newman-Keuls *t*-tests for this data. T-tests were conducted to determine whether there were statis-

tically significant changes in the positive direction for the PARD (E) group, regardless of comparison to the C group. The statistically significant correlations among the dependent variables are shown in Table 9-3.

*Relationships among dependent variables.* If, as suggested by research and our own theoretical assumptions, acceptance of another by the responder is made easier by the expresser's feeling awareness, and conversely, the responder's acceptance facilitates the expresser's feeling awareness, then one would expect these variables to be correlated. Such was the case.

If behavioral skills like these were to carry over into relatively spontaneous interactions, one would expect a correlation between the skill level in a conspicuously observed, structured situation and skill level in situations that are relatively unstructured and unobtrusively observed. That too was found to be the case.

If such behaviorally measured communication skills were related to the general quality of communication, then one would expect a correlation between these behaviorally measured skills and questionnaire measures designed to tap the general quality of communication. This was found in some instances and not in others. The lack of uniform findings here is hardly surprising, however, in light of one important consideration: The correlations were run on pretest data. Our experience suggests people are very unskilled in these behaviors and use them, if at all, in a very unsystematic fashion. The limited range and sporadic rate of appearance of the variables would severely cut down the possibility of revealing any correlation that did exist in just a four-minute sample of behavior. Thus, the fact that some correlations supporting such a relationship were attained surprised us far more than the fact that some were not.

If the general quality of intimate relationships is dependent on the quality of communication, one would expect correlations between measures assessing these two variables. Correlations between these two groups of measures were found consistently except for the Awareness Questionnaire (which failed to correlate with other measures of general communication, as well as with the relationship measures).

Table 9-1. Means and Standard Deviations for PARD Experimental (E) (*N* = 28) and Control (C) Groups (*N* = 30) at Pre- and Posttesting

| Variable | Group | Fathers Pre-test Mean | (SD) | Fathers Post-test Mean | (SD) | Sons Pre-test Mean | (SD) | Sons Post-test Mean | (SD) | Fathers and Sons Pre-test Mean | (SD) | Fathers and Sons Post-test Mean | (SD) |
|---|---|---|---|---|---|---|---|---|---|---|---|---|---|
| **Specific Communication Skills** | | | | | | | | | | | | | |
| Acceptance of Other | E | 4.6 | .8 | 5.8 | .7 | 4.6 | .5 | 5.8 | .7 | 4.6 | .7 | 5.8 | .7 |
| | C | 4.5 | .7 | 4.2 | .7 | 4.0 | .6 | 3.9 | .5 | 4.2 | .7 | 4.1 | .6 |
| Self-Feeling Awareness | E | 4.5 | .6 | 5.6 | .5 | 4.6 | .5 | 5.3 | .4 | 4.5 | .5 | 5.5 | .4 |
| | C | 4.6 | .4 | 4.6 | .6 | 4.8 | .4 | 4.5 | .6 | 4.7 | .4 | 4.6 | .6 |
| Unobtrusively Observed Acceptance | E | 4.2 | 1.0 | 4.8 | 1.3 | 4.3 | .9 | 4.8 | 1.0 | 4.2 | 1.0 | 4.8 | 1.1 |
| | C | 4.3 | .8 | 4.3 | .8 | 3.9 | .5 | 4.0 | .7 | 4.1 | .7 | 4.1 | .8 |
| Unobtrusively Observed Feeling Awareness | E | 4.1 | .9 | 4.6 | 1.1 | 4.7 | .8 | 5.0 | .9 | 4.4 | .9 | 4.8 | 1.0 |
| | C | 4.0 | .9 | 4.4 | .6 | 4.5 | .7 | 4.7 | .8 | 4.2 | .8 | 4.5 | .7 |
| **General Communication** | | | | | | | | | | | | | |
| **APCC:** | | | | | | | | | | | | | |
| Action | E | 41.2 | 5.5 | 46.7 | 5.4 | 42.1 | 4.0 | 45.4 | 6.7 | 41.7 | 4.7 | 46.1 | 6.0 |
| | C | 41.8 | 7.0 | 44.1 | 6.9 | 42.4 | 6.6 | 40.6 | 6.4 | 42.1 | 6.7 | 42.3 | 6.8 |
| Reaction | E | 61.6 | 10.7 | 67.6 | 6.7 | 65.9 | 7.3 | 68.9 | 6.0 | 63.8 | 9.3 | 68.2 | 6.3 |
| | C | 55.5 | 7.9 | 56.3 | 6.7 | 61.6 | 7.7 | 57.8 | 9.3 | 58.5 | 8.3 | 57.1 | 8.0 |
| Satisfaction | E | 54.6 | 9.0 | 61.2 | 5.0 | 44.2 | 9.9 | 50.4 | 6.3 | 49.4 | 10.7 | 55.8 | 7.8 |
| | C | 51.1 | 8.2 | 52.9 | 6.5 | 44.3 | 6.4 | 42.5 | 7.7 | 47.7 | 8.0 | 47.7 | 8.8 |
| Total | E | 157.4 | 22.0 | 175.5 | 15.0 | 152.3 | 17.8 | 164.8 | 15.7 | 154.9 | 19.8 | 170.1 | 16.0 |
| | C | 148.4 | 21.3 | 153.3 | 17.3 | 148.3 | 19.4 | 140.9 | 21.0 | 148.4 | 20.0 | 147.1 | 20.0 |

| | | | | | | | | | | | | | |
|---|---|---|---|---|---|---|---|---|---|---|---|---|---|
| Parent-Adolescent Communication Inventory (FS) | E | 73.8 | 10.9 | 79.3 | 8.7 | 66.9 | 15.0 | 71.6 | 12.1 | 70.4 | 13.3 | 75.4 | 11.0 |
| | C | 67.5 | 17.2 | 73.3 | 9.6 | 56.2 | 23.0 | 58.8 | 14.6 | 61.8 | 20.8 | 66.0 | 14.2 |
| Awareness Questionnaire: | | | | | | | | | | | | | |
| Feeling | E | 6.0 | 3.6 | 6.9 | 2.7 | 2.9 | 2.1 | 3.1 | 2.4 | 4.5 | 3.3 | 5.0 | 3.1 |
| | C | 6.2 | 3.9 | 4.3 | 4.2 | 4.1 | 3.4 | 1.7 | 2.6 | 5.1 | 3.8 | 3.0 | 3.7 |
| Ideas | E | 2.6 | 2.6 | 4.0 | 2.6 | 1.7 | 1.8 | 1.9 | 2.8 | 2.2 | 2.2 | 2.9 | 2.9 |
| | C | 3.3 | 3.6 | 2.0 | 2.7 | 1.7 | 2.7 | 1.0 | 2.0 | 2.5 | 3.2 | 1.5 | 2.4 |
| Total | E | 8.6 | 5.8 | 10.9 | 5.0 | 4.6 | 3.3 | 5.0 | 5.0 | 6.6 | 5.1 | 7.9 | 5.8 |
| | C | 9.5 | 6.8 | 6.3 | 6.6 | 5.8 | 5.9 | 2.7 | 4.1 | 7.7 | 6.6 | 4.5 | 5.7 |
| Relationship | | | | | | | | | | | | | |
| Family Life Questionnaire | E | 67.5 | 8.1 | 75.4 | 9.2 | 71.6 | 8.5 | 73.9 | 7.3 | 69.5 | 8.4 | 74.6 | 8.2 |
| | C | 70.4 | 10.7 | 71.7 | 9.5 | 60.2 | 16.2 | 59.7 | 12.7 | 65.3 | 14.4 | 65.7 | 12.6 |
| Semantic Differential for Relationship: Self | E | 55.1 | 7.4 | 58.0 | 7.3 | 51.8 | 9.7 | 58.1 | 10.5 | 53.4 | 8.6 | 58.1 | 8.8 |
| | C | 54.0 | 9.3 | 55.1 | 7.7 | 42.8 | 13.6 | 46.9 | 7.1 | 48.4 | 12.8 | 51.0 | 8.4 |
| Semantic Differential for Relationship: Other | E | 52.1 | 4.3 | 52.1 | 7.7 | 57.0 | 9.4 | 59.0 | 8.3 | 54.5 | 8.8 | 57.5 | 8.1 |
| | C | 48.6 | 11.4 | 52.7 | 9.2 | 49.7 | 12.9 | 46.1 | 7.4 | 49.2 | 12.0 | 49.4 | 8.9 |
| Self-Concept | | | | | | | | | | | | | |
| Semantic Differential: "I am" | E | 49.7 | 9.3 | 52.2 | 8.1 | 47.5 | 9.6 | 50.8 | 9.4 | 48.6 | 9.3 | 51.5 | 8.7 |
| | C | 53.2 | 8.3 | 50.3 | 9.4 | 44.5 | 8.8 | 42.9 | 9.3 | 48.8 | 9.5 | 46.6 | 9.9 |

Table 9-2. Comparison of Prewaiting Period, Postwaiting Period,
and Posttreatment Period Means of Significant Dependent Variables
in Own-Control Design Using the Newman-Keuls Test

| Variable | | Treatment Period (in ascending order) | | |
|---|---|---|---|---|
| Acceptance of Other | | 2 | 1 | 3 |
| Self-Feeling Awareness | | 2 | 1 | 3 |
| Unobtrusively Observed Acceptance | | 1 | 2 | 3 |
| Adolescent-Parent Communication Checklist: | Reaction | 2 | 1 | 3 |
| | Total | 2 | 1 | 3 |
| Awareness Questionnaire: | Feeling | 2 | 1 | 3 |
| | Ideas | 2 | 1 | 3 |
| | Total | 2 | 1 | 3 |
| Family Life Questionnaire | | 1 | 2 | 3 |
| Semantic Differential for Relationship: Self | | 2 | 1 | 3 |
| Semantic Differential: "I am" | | 2 | 1 | 3 |

Note: $N = 20$. Treatments underlined by a common line do not differ significantly at the $< .05$ level; treatments not underlined by a common line do differ at the .05 level or better.

Finally, if good self-concept is linked to the quality of one's relationships with significant others, one would expect these two types of variables to be linked. This was found to be the case in that the relationship-self and relationship-other variables were correlated with the self-concept measure. The self-concept measure did not significantly correlate, however, with the Family Life Questionnaire, which used a questionnaire as opposed to a semantic differential format. Generally, there was, as would be expected, some tendency for the measures that used a similar format (behavioral, questionnaire, semantic differential) to correlate with each other.

In general, these results tend to provide concomitant validity evidence for the measures used, in that measures designed to measure similar kinds of variables tended to correlate with each other. Also, since the measures of different variables are not completely independent of one another, the hypotheses, and the tests of their significance, should not be regarded as completely independent of one another but as an interlocking

Table 9-3. Significant Intercorrelations Among the Major Dependent Variables ($N = 58$)

| | AOS | SFAS | U-AOS | U-SFAS | APCC-T | PACI-FS | AQT | FLQ | SDR-S | SDR-O |
|---|---|---|---|---|---|---|---|---|---|---|
| **Specific Communication Skills** | | | | | | | | | | |
| Acceptance of Other Scale | | | | | | | | | | |
| Self-Feeling Awareness Scale | .30* | | | | | | | | | |
| Unobtrusively Observed Acceptance of Other Scale | .52*** | .40** | | | | | | | | |
| Unobtrusively Observed Self-Feeling Awareness Scale | | .56*** | .32* | | | | | | | |
| **General Communication** | | | | | | | | | | |
| APCC: Total | | | | .27* | | | | | | |
| Parent-Adolescent Communication Inventory—Father-Son | .38** | | | .32* | .71*** | | | | | |
| Awareness Questionnaire: Total | | | | | | | | | | |
| **Relationship** | | | | | | | | | | |
| Family Life Questionnaire | .39** | | .26* | .30* | .62*** | .73*** | | | | |
| Semantic Differential for Relationship: Self | .29* | | | | .46*** | .38** | | .40** | | |
| Semantic Differential for Relationship: Other | .35** | | .32* | | .47*** | .29* | | .38** | .65*** | |
| **Self-Concept** | | | | | | | | | | |
| Semantic Differential: "I am" | | | | | | | | | .58*** | .29* |

Note: * = $p < .05$; ** = $p < .01$; *** = $p < .001$

set. On the other hand, none of the variables are so highly related to any other as to make separate hypotheses and separate tests of significance redundant.

*Observed specific communication patterns.* The first hypothesis, that the E group, relative to the C group, would evidence improvement in observed communication skill as measured by the AOS and SFAS, was strongly confirmed. Both the fathers and the sons successfully learned means of communicating greater empathic acceptance of one another as a result of treatment. This was demonstrated by change relative to the C group ($p < .001$) and absolute change ($p < .001$) of the E group on the AOS. Relative ($p < .001$) and absolute ($p < .001$) improvement was similarly demonstrated in expressive skill as measured by the SFAS.

*Unobtrusively observed specific communication skills.* The hypothesis that the E group, relative to the C group, would show improvement in unobtrusively observed communication skill was confirmed, but not in all respects. Relative ($p < .05$) and absolute improvement ($p < .05$) in empathic acceptance were found for both fathers and sons, who changed in approximately equal measure. Absolute improvement of the E group was found in the ability to express personally relevant attitudes and feelings ($p < .01$) as measured by the SFAS. However, improvement of the C group, though not a statistically significant change, was sufficient to offset the gain of the E group in the relative analysis. In a brief PARD program as was studied here, empathic skills are given priority over expressive skills. With a somewhat longer PARD program, it seems likely that significant changes on the SFAS also would be achieved. The AOS results demonstrate that fathers and sons not only improved in acceptance in a structured situation, but also that this improvement was translated into more spontaneous interactions.

*General communication patterns.* The pattern of changes on the APCC confirmed the hypothesis that fathers and sons of the E group would improve the overall pattern of general communication in their relationship. This was significant both relative to the C group ($p < .001$) and in absolute terms ($p < .01$). All the subtests of the APCC, as well as the total score, revealed

statistically significant improvement at the .05 level or better for relative and absolute change.

The PACI-FS showed movement in the same direction as the APCC, with the fathers and sons in the PARD program demonstrating more movement than those in the control group. However, the difference did not prove to be statistically significant. In selecting self-report measures to assess the general pattern of communication between fathers and sons in the home, inspection of the items led us to believe the PACI-FS and the APCC were tapping very similar dimensions, and we suspected that they would be highly correlated. This expectation was confirmed by correlational analysis done on the total pretest sample of our study ($N = 58$): The total scores of the two tests correlated highly (.71). The reason both tests were used was that there was no way of knowing in advance which instrument would prove to be more sensitive and powerful with respect to revealing communication changes resulting from the PARD program. Perhaps it was because of the greater number of items, and the greater range of possible responses to each item, that the APPC proved more potent than the modified PACI in revealing changes.

The third set of self-report measures used to assess change in the general pattern of communication in the home was the Awareness Questionnaire. The fathers and sons in the PARD program showed improved awareness of each other's current *ideas*, while those in the control group showed a decline in awareness, the difference being statistically significant ($p <$ .05). The same differential change held for awareness of *feelings* during the ten-week span covered by the program. The fathers and sons in the PARD program showed an increased awareness of each other's feelings, while those in the control group showed a decline in this aspect of general communication patterns, the difference being statistically significant ($p < .01$). Of course, the total awareness score also revealed the difference ($p < .01$). The decline of the control group's awareness of each other's ideas and feelings contributed more to this relative difference than did absolute improvement of the PARD-trained fathers and sons. The improvement in awareness of current

ideas, feelings, and both combined were not statistically significant for the PARD group, while there was a statistically significant decline in awareness of feelings ($p < .001$) and the total score ($p < .001$) for the control group. Possibly the decline in the control group reflected not a decline in the *usual* level of awareness, but rather an initial surge in awareness level of the applicant population, which stimulated the desire to enter a program like PARD, and was followed by a return to normal levels of awareness. If so, the PARD group, in contrast, continued to increase their awareness to levels even beyond the usually high initial level.

In summary, the hypothesis of greater improvement in general patterns of communication at home between fathers and sons as a result of participation in a PARD program was strongly supported by the results, although significant *absolute* positive change was not shown on every self-report measure.

*Quality of the general relationship.* The relationships of fathers and sons in the PARD program significantly improved in harmony and trust as measured by the Family Life Questionnaire. The fathers and sons in the PARD program achieved a net gain in harmony and trust in their relationship, as measured by the FLQ, relative to those in the control group ($p < .05$), and perceived their relationship as better after completing the program than they had before entering it ($p < .05$).

Although the direction of all the results on the Semantic Differential instruments were as expected, none reached statistical significance. (As will be discussed in more detail later, self-perception in the relationship did change positively and significantly in the own-control, quasireplication study.)

In light of the clear-cut results obtained with the FLQ and the direction of most changes in the Semantic Differential-Self, the hypothesis that participants in the PARD program would show greater general relationship improvement than would be achieved by nonparticipants may be considered confirmed.

*Self-concept.* There was improvement in self-concept (SD=IA) on the part of both fathers and sons. Considered alone, this improvement did not reach statistical significance. But in

the more important test of comparison with the control subjects, who tended to decline in self-concept, the gain almost
reached the significance level ($p = .052$). As indicated earlier,
the short program was viewed as providing only a very remote
chance of yielding an improvement that would generalize from
relationship improvement to improvement in self-concept. Thus
these results are viewed as providing some support for the idea
that improvement in the relationships between symbionts will
also lead to improvement in adjustment for the individual by
itself. (Further support for the hypothesis that participation in
the PARD program leads to improved self-concept will be presented in the report of the own-control study results.)

*Fathers' versus sons' response to the PARD program.*
Fathers and sons in the PARD program, compared to fathers
and sons outside the program, responded to PARD training in
the same way. That is, in every area studied, the fathers as a
group, and the sons as a group, did not significantly differ from
each other in the direction or degree of improvement they
showed as a result of participating in the PARD program.

## The Quasireplication Study

The results of the own-control quasireplication study,
employing clients who were originally controls and who later
entered the program, generally confirmed the results of the primary study. Those dependent variables that did not show statistically significant change in the experimental versus control
group comparisons also did not show change in the own-control
analysis. Those variables for which statistically significant
change in favor of the experimental group was found in the primary study also showed statistically significant improvement in
the quasireplication. Newman-Keuls tests showed that these
positive significant changes took place from the prewaiting
period to the end of training, and between the beginning and
completion of training, while no significant changes took place
during the comparable pretraining waiting period.

One set of exceptions to the confirmation of the original
findings was in the realm of awareness of ideas and feelings. In

the original study, significant improvement was not demonstrated for the PARD group by itself, but only improvement relative to the control group. In this replication, there was significant absolute improvement in the PARD group from the beginning to the end of the program ($p < .05$). However, even in these instances, the results did parallel the primary findings in a way: There was a statistically significant decline during the waiting period, and mutual awareness of ideas and feelings was simply restored to the higher pretreatment levels after PARD training. (This renewal was less than complete for the sons, while fathers reached or exceeded their initial levels.)

Another exception to the confirmation of the findings in the E versus C comparisons was that two subtests on the APCC showed only trends, rather than reaching significance levels (APCC Action, $p = .13$; APCC Satisfaction, $p = .14$). In light of the small number of subjects in the replication study, these probability levels do not seem to offer a serious challenge to the positive finding for these subtests in the primary study.

Another variable that was not significant in the E versus C study did reach significance ($p < .05$) in the quasireplication: There were positive changes in perception of self in the relationship (Semantic Differential-Self).

Finally, improvement in self-concept, which was marginally significant in the E versus C study, was clearly significant ($p < .01$) in the own-control study.

We conclude that both the main study and the own-control study offered evidence of the effectiveness of the PARD program. Through the PARD program, fathers and sons can learn expressive and empathic communication skills that permit them to be more accepting and trusting of one another. There was also evidence that these skills are generalized to spontaneous interactions. The improvement in empathy, acceptance, and other aspects of communication taught in the PARD program also seems to result in improvement in the general relationship and even in self-concept.

## Limitations and Suggestions

There are many possibilities for future research suggested by the present study, some of which arise from recognition of its

limitations. The improvement observed in this study was obtained in a short treatment period (ten weeks). It would seem worthwhile to study change in a longer program such as one lasting six months or a year. Follow-up studies six months after termination of a short- or long-term PARD program also would be illuminating.

Suggestion, attention, demand, and "thank you" effects were probably ruled out as accounting for some of the results obtained in this study (unobtrusively observed communication), but such effects remain possible alternate explanations for most of the findings. Therefore, in order to determine in a decisive way whether the specific methodology employed here was the key factor producing change, it will be necessary to compare this treatment approach with a placebo control group, with other treatment approaches (for example, individual or group therapy), or with a PARD method with certain components left out. Such studies would help to clarify which are, and which are not, the critical or essential elements in the PARD program.

Research should be conducted using the PARD program with populations of a different character. For example, its effectiveness should be studied with populations of lower social position, with delinquency- or drug-prone populations, and so on. It would be of interest to test the usefulness of this approach with mother-daughter, mother-son, and father-daughter pairs. It is also possible that a mixed group of fathers and sons with mothers and daughters would be appropriate groups with which to use this approach.

Anecdotal reports from the participants suggested that the treatment had an improved effect on family relationships beyond the particular pair involved. Many fathers reported that they were not shouting around the house as much. Others stated that their relationships with their spouses had improved as a result of skills learned in the program. Even extrafamilial results, such as improved relationships with colleagues and co-workers, were reported by some fathers. Several boys reported improved relations with their siblings and peers as a result of their improved communication skills, suggesting the possibility of adopting such communication training to an all adolescent group. Since peer relationships are so important to adolescents,

what would be more helpful to them than learning to improve their interpersonal communication and empathy? Edward Vogelsong has developed such a program for the elementary grades. Also, a program called the Pupil Relationship Enhancement Program (PREP) has been developed by Eric Hatch and Bernard Guerney, Jr. (1975), to make this feasible in junior and senior high schools.

*Implications of the research.* The adolescent period of development, especially in this time of rapid cultural change, is not only one of difficulty and change for the adolescent but for his family as well. The stresses of this period become even more difficult to deal with if there is little trust and/or acceptance in the parent-adolescent relationship.

A frequent theme in the literature about adolescents is that acceptance by parents, particularly the father, is vitally important for the adolescent male's acceptance of himself and his healthy emotional and social development. The present study lends significant support to the view that in a PARD program both fathers and their adolescent sons can learn communication skills that permit them to show more acceptance and understanding of one another; that this improved acceptance can be utilized in real-life situations; that such improvement results in an improved relationship and improved self-concept. Therefore, considering the fact that the PARD program has a relatively low professional time-cost ratio, it may be a practical means of helping more families meet this normal developmental need; that is, the PARD program may be viable for wide-scale use as a means for primary prevention of emotional and social problems.

There is also a great need to help families deal with problems and crises. Although the sample used in this study was not selected on the basis of either pathology or nonpathology, it is believed that a long-term PARD program would prove to be a highly effective approach for remediation of severe family-related difficulties of the adolescent. In fact, although no formal studies have been conducted with a population selected for deviancy, the PARD method, within and outside the study reported here, has been utilized successfully in families undergoing crises of delinquency, adolescent runaways, a suicidal

adolescent, school problems, and many of the general problems that bring clients to mental health clinics.

The clinical literature documents the difficulty of bringing the father into treatment (Levitt, 1957; McCandless, 1967). We have found no reports of previous experimental investigations of integrated, systematized, structured, and replicable therapeutic and preventive mental health approaches for fathers and adolescent sons. Thus, we can hope that the present study, by demonstrating that a replicable treatment approach for improving father-son relationships *is* available, may serve to facilitate recruitment of fathers into remedial and preventive mental health programs. Of the pairs who participated in the treatment groups, only three pairs failed to complete the program. Thus the PARD program offers the mental health professional a new approach for bringing many more fathers into mental health programs, for helping adolescents who have psychological and social adjustment problems, and for preventing the development of such problems by early enhancement of relationships between fathers and sons.

# Premarital Relationship Improvement by Maximizing Empathy and Self-Disclosure: The PRIMES Program

*Barry G. Ginsberg*

*Edward Vogelsong*

In this chapter we will describe the teaching of RE skills to premarital couples via the PRIMES (premarital relationship improvement by maximizing empathy and self-disclosure) program, which was initiated by Stephen Schlein. We believe this program can foster the dating-premarital relationship and the individual personal growth of the participants. RE programs are designed to help participants focus on the strengths of their relationships as well as on the areas that require remediation. Participants learn to discuss with each other the behaviors they desire and value as well as those that arouse negative emotions. The PRIMES program can benefit premarital and dating couples by giving them tools of communication that they can use to

plan the future of their relationships, to become more aware of the effects of their behaviors on their partners, to increase their intimacy, and to deal constructively with present and future problems. If a couple can learn skills to help them establish a more meaningful and rewarding relationship prior to marriage, then the possibilities for a successfully functioning marriage and family seem much more likely.

There is a great deal of insecurity and testing in premarital relationships with respect to mutual perceptions and expectations. There appears to be an effort toward self-validation in this significant relationship. The establishment of intimate interpersonal relationships may very well represent the state of transition in the development of the individual from a less mature to a more mature stage in life. When people become involved in significant relationships with others, adjustments need to be made and responsibilities developed in regard to both the self and the other person. Modifications must be made to accommodate the other, and one is confronted by previously submerged or new aspects of self. Premarital relationships are often formed during a period of increased self-awareness. It appears quite plausible that to work toward self-awareness through one's primary peer relationship (the premarital relationship) might very well meet individual growth needs. The skill of being able to identify and express personal feelings is a major aspect of self-knowledge and acceptance. There is every reason to believe that the process of having these aspects of self accepted by a significant other person can only lead to greater self-awareness and self-acceptance.

Little attention has been given to efforts to enhance and improve the premarital relationship. (In fact, there is much more literature and research directed toward divorce and divorce counseling than toward premarital relationship development and enhancement.) The bulk of the literature that is available about premarital relationships in general comes from family sociology. Moss, Apolonio, and Jensen (1971) published a review of the literature dealing with the premarital dyad during the 1960s. Their article identified many theoretical constructs and discussed factors such as residential propinquity,

love and empathy, complementary needs, validation of the self-image of one by the other, similarity in backgrounds, and stresses impinging on the pair. There is little integration among these concepts, however, and no generalized theory encompassing the premarital relationship has seemed satisfactory. Much of the literature on the premarital dyad deals with mate selection. Lewis (1972, p. 18) states that some theoreticians "have suggested that the process of mate selection in an open marriage system is more complex than any of the major theories have implied." He has suggested a developmental model and framework to encompass much of the literature on the premarital dyad. His framework is the interrelation of the following six pairing processes that mobile, middle-class American couples experience progressively from their dating and courtship experiences: "(a) the process of perceiving similarities, (b) the process of achieving pair rapport, (c) the process of including self-disclosure, (d) the process of role taking, (e) the process of achieving interpersonal role fit, and (f) the process of achieving dyadic crystallization" (p. 22). It is clear from Lewis' analysis that communication is a consistent and necessary component of the development from the premarital to the marital relationship in our society. The importance of communication continues into marriage and throughout the life span. Providing the premarital pair with skills of effective communication, therefore, would seem an important task in preparing couples for a satisfying marriage.

The importance of communication in the marital relationship also has been established by a number of researchers and clinicians. Targow and Zweber (1969), in attempting to evaluate the effects of a psychoanalytically oriented group experience for married couples, concluded that the major change stressed by the couples involved was improved communication. Ard and Ard (1969) identified a growing body of literature that attests to faulty communication as a source of marital difficulties. Burgess and Wallin (1953) studied 1,000 engaged couples and their subsequent marriages. These couples indicated that verbal communication was important to them in under-

standing the attitudes and behaviors of their spouses. Locke, Sabagh, and Thomas (1956) found a significant relationship between communication and marital adjustment as measured by the Primary Communication Inventory and the Marital Relationship Inventory. Navran (1967) compared a sample of happily married couples and poorly adjusted couples from a psychiatric clinic and a dental clinic. He found that the happily married couples showed significantly better communication in their interactions. Kind (1968) used paid volunteers and couples who applied for marriage counseling to evaluate the relationship between marital happiness and communication. He found that happily married couples reported more effective communication than unhappily married couples. His results also indicated that happily married couples were more willing to undertake threatening communication and demonstrated more openness in their relationship than unhappily married couples. Lederer and Jackson (1968) also identified good communication as essential to good marital relationships.

In addition to being a source of deep satisfaction in its own right and laying the foundation for future marital happiness, there is every reason to believe that a good premarital relationship can serve as a primary ingredient in the individual psychological well-being and personal growth of each of the partners, even including the remediation of very disturbing emotional difficulties (Guerney, 1969). In all of these ways, the PRIMES program represents a potentially significant mental health program of a preventative nature.

Recent trends in the field of mental health have suggested the desirability of making programs such as PRIMES available to the public. The educational approach to the delivery of mental health services has made possible the availability of services to greater numbers of people and has increased greatly the opportunity to provide effective preventive programs. The PRIMES program is viewed as a way of teaching complex and sophisticated interpersonal skills to premarital couples in order to facilitate the present relationship and to increase potential for future marital and family growth.

## The PRIMES Program

An introductory interview, which can be conducted with one couple, with small groups, or with a large audience in a church or school, explains the program and helps couples determine its usefulness for their relationships. It includes demonstration of good and poor communication patterns in situations of interest to the potential participants, and it provides the opportunity for asking any questions they may have about the program.

The training program itself can be conducted with one couple, but usually takes place in groups consisting of three or four couples. In addition to allowing efficient use of the leader's time, working in groups also allows the participating couples to learn from observing each other. The couples take turns practicing empathic and expressive skills, with only one couple practicing at a time. The leader strives to give each of the couples an equal share of the practice time. The groups are kept small so that each couple can have approximately thirty minutes of supervised practice during each session.

The basic training program runs for a specific period of time that is usually determined before the group begins. All participating couples are asked to make a commitment to attend each of the sessions. The program can be applied in other formats (for example, in marathon sessions), but in the typical program—which is the one to be described here—couples meet weekly for two or two and a half hours over a period of 8 to 12 weeks.

During the first group session, the couples are introduced to each other and given a brief overview of the program. The importance of confidentiality is discussed, and each of the group members is given an opportunity to practice the empathic and expressive modes. For this initial session only, members are asked to practice with another group member of the same sex rather than with their partners. These interchanges are kept short, so that everyone is able to practice both modes by the time the session is over. The expressers are asked to choose topics that have nothing to do with their relationships with

their partners. The group leader is careful to reinforce each of the participants for what they do well and to help them where they have difficulties.

Beginning with the second group session and continuing for the rest of the program, participants practice their skills only with their partners. In the second session, expressers again are asked to discuss topics that are outside their relationships, this time with their partners. In the early stages of the training, the subject matter does not involve emotional issues in the relationship, so that the participants can concentrate more effectively on learning the skills. The leader continues to budget the time so that all participants are able to practice both expresser and empathic responder skills. Participants are encouraged to ask questions, but the leader strives to give everyone as much practice time as possible.

In all of the remaining sessions, participants are encouraged to direct their conversations to topics dealing with their relationships. In the third session, they are asked to deal with positive issues in their relationship. As their skills increase, they are permitted to discuss mutual expectations, problems, and conflicts.

The couples discuss subjects that they deem to be of central importance to their relationships as listed on the Relationship Questionnaire (see Appendix L). This questionnaire is distributed to each of the participants at the end of the first group session. The leader explains that these forms will be used as the basis for topic selection beginning with the third session. All participants are asked to list on the form aspects of their relationships with their partners that they value highly and areas that they would like to see developed or enhanced in order to improve the relationships. Participants are asked to complete the forms at home and bring them to the next session. During the second session, the group leader reviews each of the Relationship Questionnaires and helps the participants specify other topics they want to discuss during the program. Participants thereafter bring their Relationship Questionnaires to each group session and, as expressers, use them to select discussion topics. The leader suggests periodic revisions of these questionnaires,

asking the participants to make sure that the topics listed reflect their current perceptions of the most fundamental issues in their relationships.

During each of the group sessions, the leader's role is to help each couple practice and learn the skills. He uses principles of learning theory, such as structuring, modeling, and social reinforcement, to help the participants in their acquisition of the skills. His goal is not to solve the problems of the participants himself, but rather to provide each couple with skills that they themselves can use both to solve and prevent future problems in their relationships, to minimize misconceptions and friction, and to achieve high levels of understanding, harmony, and intimacy.

While one couple is practicing the expresser and responder modes, the other group members are taught to be facilitators, who encourage and help the others in their skill practice. Facilitators give social reinforcement, suggest mode switches at appropriate times, and help others to stay within the limits of their roles. Facilitators are not permitted to give advice, ask questions, or make comments of an evaluative nature. Their comments, like those of the group leader, are restricted to helping the expresser and responder learn and practice the skills.

After the third session, each couple is asked to spend an hour a week practicing the skills together outside the group sessions. The purpose of this homework is to give the participants additional practice time and to encourage them to use the skills in their day-to-day relationships. Practice Home Session forms (see Appendix M) are distributed for each couple to evaluate their practice during the week. The leader begins each session by collecting and going over the reports of the homework. Areas of difficulty encountered in the homework sessions are discussed. Situations are often recreated, in order to work out any problems that occurred while using the skills outside the practice sessions, or to show how the skills might have been helpful in real life situations where they were not used by the participants but should have been. As in the group sessions, discussion of difficult topics at home is postponed until the couples have achieved a high level of skill proficiency.

## Illustrative Excerpts

The following transcript illustrating skill practice by a couple, Gloria and Earl, is from a fifth session.[1] As the discussion develops, Gloria expresses quite well the importance of distinguishing between a *person* and certain aspects or behaviors of that person. Such a distinction is essential if one wishes to help another make positive changes, to encourage communication, and to enhance an intimate relationship. This, of course, is one of the basic skills RE programs seek to develop. Gloria is discussing the problem of the lack of acceptance she sometimes feels from Earl, and in doing so she describes a situation where she could not do a certain type of math problem, came to Earl for help, and felt he was disappointed in her.

> *Gloria:* I was sort of taken aback. I thought, "Why should he be disappointed?" It was sort of like you were saying: "Boy, you're really *dumb*. Gee, I didn't *know* you were that dumb!" And it, I don't know, kind of hits you.
>
> *Leader* [after a pause] : Can you reflect what she just said?
>
> *Earl:* You were really upset that I could have a feeling of disappointment.
>
> *Leader:* Good.
>
> *Gloria* [pause] : Yes, I was [pause] angry. That was my first reaction when you said it. I just sort of went into a shock 'cause I thought, "Gee, I'm really, you know, not what he *expected*." And I just felt hurt [pause] , and then I was disappointed *in you* because then *you* weren't what *I* expected. It was—I don't know, uh, you're supposed to take me for what I am, more or less; I mean I see myself saying, "Here I am; here's my faults." And you went, "Oh, no!" like, "You're not *that* bad; I don't *believe* it!"
>
> *Leader* [after a long pause] : What's she saying, Earl?
>
> *Earl:* You're saying that you were angry and hurt and disappointed that *I* was disappointed with you.
>
> *Leader:* Good! And she's also saying, I think, that she wanted very much to be accepted by you, but accepted for *who* she *is*, and she was hurt by what she perceived as your disappointment and lack of

---

[1] Transcripts in this chapter came from groups run in Stephen Schlein's (1971) doctoral dissertation conducted under the Chairmanship of Bernard Guerney, Jr., at The Pennsylvania State University. They have been edited for brevity and clarity.

acceptance. She wants you to be accepting of *who* she *is*. Earl, can you try—I don't want you to repeat my words—but try to tell her a little bit of what I just said?

*Earl* [To Gloria]: You want me to take you [pause] for what you *are*—to accept you even though your knowledge is so basic.

*Leader:* Good.

*Gloria:* Well, yes. I guess this is a specific instance, but it can be generalized beyond my limited knowledge. It seems as if I want that acceptance because I feel that [long pause] what I want is—I want *you* to *accept* me. And to be accepted, you've got to offer something, and you rejected it. *I* was *offering* you [pause] *me*—in this case me and this one fault, but Gloria has a lot of these and [pause] she's offering herself to *you*, saying, "Accept me." Don't overlook them; understand them; instead of saying, "No, I don't believe they are there." That's rejecting them. In a sense, I felt you were rejecting me.

*Earl:* You want to be accepted [pause] as *you*, without having to change yourself. You want to be accepted as *you* [pause] *despite* your faults.

*Leader:* Good, Earl.

*Gloria:* What I want is [pause] *acceptance* and understanding [pause], not a criticism. I don't think in some cases—this specific case—I *needed* criticism. I knew what my fault was; otherwise, I wouldn't have been there. I guess it takes a while for me to say, "I have a problem," and I was doing that, more or less. So, instead of you saying, "All right, I'll help you," [pause] you were criticizing me. I was at a loss; I needed help; I couldn't *do* it—I needed help. I went to *you* [pause] 'cause I thought *you* could *accept me* with the fault and *help* me. But you didn't, so I was disappointed.

*Earl:* What you're saying is that you want to be accepted and understood even *with* the fault.

*Gloria:* Yeah! But it sounds like you're saying that I want you to forget the fault, but I *don't*. I want you to realize that *I* know *what* the fault *is*, and [pause] accept me *with it*. I *want* criticism when I've missed a fault or something. But in this specific incident, I realized my fault, and I went for help—assistance, whatever—in solving it, and becoming more the type of person I want to be. But instead of getting that acceptance and that help—you just compounded the feeling of inadequacy. I got awfully quiet [pause], but I couldn't have told you why then.

*Earl* [short pause]: So, you're saying you couldn't tell me *then*—at that time—and that you thought it was better to go into a shell.

*Gloria:* Well, yeah, it would have been only exposing myself *more*. [Pause.] If I couldn't tell you then because I would have said—I would have been exposing *my feelings*, which you'd already hurt, and I was afraid that [pause] they'd get—they'd be rejected again. I'm that way; I don't know how to explain it any better.

*Earl* [after a long pause]: You're saying that you need *me* to talk to. You need me to help you when you have a problem [pause], and somehow when I start criticizing you like I did, you don't want it; you build a shell. And then you can't talk to me about it; it's getting harder to *depend* on me [pause] with your problems.

*Leader:* Very good, Earl.

*Gloria:* Yeah. It's a reluctance [pause] to admit a problem for fear of criticism that is a rejection of *me*. It's me as a whole that has the problem.

*Earl:* So you feel that *if* you *do* open up, you tell me your problems, that you may [pause] be put down. My disappointment in you would just shut you off completely.

*Gloria:* Yeah. Because you telling me that I disappointed you would make me, [pause] I guess, well, I wouldn't feel accepted; I'd feel less than a person.

Note in the above excerpt the inadequacy Gloria feels in regard to both herself and to her relationship with Earl. The structure of the program helped Earl to be accepting and understanding. In other circumstances, he might have told Gloria that she was foolish for thinking of herself as inadequate and thus stopped her from expressing herself in an open manner. By Gloria's following the guidelines of the expresser mode and by Earl's desire to understand and respect her feelings, they were able to deal more directly with Gloria's need for greater acceptance.

The next excerpt is from a seventh session. The topic being discussed was the desire to enhance openness and trust, and John has expressed his pleasure that Mary had told him about her interactions with a previous boyfriend in her hometown and her general fear of his reactions to this and other aspects of her feelings. The excerpt illustrates generalization— the carry-over of the attitudes and trust engendered by the training to interaction outside of the group sessions and the assigned practice sessions.

*John:* This Sunday, when we came back, I was really happy that you told me about the town and what happened. You seemed really upset about it, and I think you felt I would be upset about it. But I wasn't upset about it really at all. And I was just really happy that when you came back, you told me about it right away. Like sometimes before, it would be a month later or something.

But you told me right away, and it made me really happy when you told me then.

*Mary:* You were happy when I came closer to you to tell you something like that.

*Leader:* Very good.

*John:* It seemed to me that even though you thought I might be upset for a little while, that in the long run I really wouldn't be upset. You may be finding now that I really wanted to know things like that—good or bad.

*Mary:* It's more important to you that I tell you everything, even if they weren't things that make you happy when I tell you.

*John:* Not only that, but the reason it makes me happy was because it was happening because you're only human—it's really a part of you, and I really love you.

*Mary:* I didn't lose faith, and I didn't try to hide it from you and that really pleased you.

*Leader:* Good.

*John:* Before I felt we couldn't talk about anything; it wasn't a big barrier between us, but it still kept us apart. It was something that seemed to make you unhappy and afraid. I think you were always wondering what I would do or what I would think if I ever found out! And I kept worrying about it for a long period of time; and it's made me unhappy for a long time until you did tell me. And this time you told me right away, as soon as you saw me, and that made me happy. Because we don't have all that waiting around and all that unnecessary anxiety between us—worrying what's wrong and wondering what would happen if you told me. To get to the even more important point—I think this is just about the biggest problem we have, and it's the thing that bothers me the most. I want to feel sure that if there is something that bothers you, you'll tell me about it.

*Mary:* You're happy that I can talk to you about something that is as important as that, that I need you, and that I want your help.

*Leader:* Good.

*John:* Yeah, that's what it is, and I feel good that you told me.

*Mary:* You're seeing this change in me, and it makes you feel good.

*John:* And myself, too, 'cause sharing works both ways. The more you share with me, the easier it is for me to share things with you. Because I know that you need me, and so I need you more. It's good to feel that it's both ways and that you want to share things with me as much as I want to share things with you. Because that gives me a better idea of how you feel about me, and it makes me think that you feel the same way about me as I feel about you. And that you love me just as much, and we can share things a lot.

*Mary:* It made you happy 'cause now we can turn to each other.

*Leader:* Do you get the impression, John, that Mary really understands what you're saying?

*John:* Mm-hm, she does. I think she understands better than I did.

*Leader:* How about switching modes—unless you have more to discuss?

*Mary:* I guess I should start with how I felt about telling you about it; I had mixed feelings about it. I wanted to tell you about it very much, but I wasn't sure how you would react. I guess at first I didn't have confidence; I didn't think you would understand. I wanted to tell you, so I had to take the chance anyway because I wanted to tell you about it. After I told you, I was very happy. Because, you know, you understood. And it made me feel like if anything happens like that again, anything really important, I could tell you about it.

*John:* It makes you feel much more secure that now you'll know I'll understand something, and that instead of worrying about whatever it is, I'll try to understand how you feel about it.

*Leader:* Very nice.

The importance of training in interpersonal communications in the premarital relationship is demonstrated by these transcripts. Relationships are formed in which people are unsure of themselves, vulnerable, and quick to be hurt. The need to work through these sensitivities and develop trust is an important part of being able to adjust to the changes required in an intimate relationship. Trust develops not only through the learning process of the training sessions, but is fostered throughout the relationship as these skills are used. Even if the couple does not continue their relationship, the skills learned in this program can help both members in the establishment of new relationships as well as working through the hurts of the old one.

## Experimental Evaluation

Research on the PRIMES program was conducted by Stephen Schlein (1971). The research was designed to determine whether dating or premarital couples participating in the program could learn to communicate in a more open and empathic manner and thereby improve their relationships.

*Procedures*

Conducted in a university setting, the PRIMES program was advertised through letters, posters, announcements, newspaper articles, and individual contacts. All advertisements described this program as a new service and research program for dating couples that was designed to teach interpersonal communication skills to promote a more meaningful and satisfying relationship.

All couples who requested interviews and agreed to participate in the program were included in the project. Of the forty-eight couples who agreed to participate, twenty-one were randomly assigned to the experimental treatment group and twenty-seven to a waiting-list control group. Two couples assigned to the experimental group dropped out of the program within a few weeks and four more were excluded from analysis because of poor attendance, leaving a total of eighty-four participants: thirty in the experimental group and fifty-four in the control group.

The mean age of the participants was 19.8 years. The Hollingshead Index of Social Position showed a mean rating of 2.6, reflecting a middle-class sample. One participant was black, the rest were white. All participants were full-time undergraduate college students, with the exception of one adjunct student and one college graduate.

During the initial interview, after the program had been explained, each couple received a packet that contained the pre-treatment paper-and-pencil measures. When these forms were completed, the couples were given the Verbal Interaction Task (see Appendix I), a twenty-minute tape-recorded dialog, in which each member of the pair discussed two topics in turn: (1) "something you would like to see changed in yourself," and (2) "something you would like to see changed in your partner." Partner A was asked to express his or her feelings about the first topic and partner B was told to help A express his or her feelings as much as possible. They then switched roles, with B expressing his or her feelings, and A in the helping role. They then

discussed the second topic in the same manner. These conversations served as a behavioral measure of communication for each couple and concluded the administration of pretreatment measures.

After ten weeks, participants in both the experimental and control groups returned and were administered the same measures. This testing period provided the posttreatment data.

The control couples were told they would have to wait ten weeks before they could begin the program. They received no formal training during the ten-week waiting period. This waiting control group served to control for changes that occur over time, and for the effects of enrolling in such a program and of participating in the assessment procedures.

The groups were led by graduate students who had received training in RE methods. Each group had two leaders, with the exception of two groups that were led by the experimenter alone. The group leaders met every two weeks with the experimenter to clarify issues, resolve difficulties, and receive guidance in the effective use of the PRIMES training program.

### Hypotheses and Measures

It was hypothesized that the PRIMES group would show relatively more improvement than the control group in: (1) communication and (2) in the general quality of the relationship.

*Communication.* Communication was measured in two general areas: specific communication skills and general communication patterns. Specific communication skills were assessed through ratings of the tape-recorded interactions in the Verbal Interaction Task along the dimension of (1) empathic acceptance as measured by the Acceptance of Other Scale or AOS (see Appendix J), and (2) openness and feeling-awareness as measured by the Self-Feeling Awareness Scale or SFAS (see Appendix K). General communication patterns were measured by the Premarital Communication Inventory (PMCI) and the Primary Communication Inventory—Partner (PCI-P). The PMCI

was developed by Bienvenu (1968) and parallels his Marital Communication Inventory in many respects.[2] The PCI-P is a slightly modified version of the Primary Communication Inventory (see Appendix A) developed by Locke, Sabagh, and Thomas (1956). It was modified here only by changing the word *spouse* to *partner* throughout the inventory.

*Quality of the relationship.* The variables studied here were improvement in (1) the capacity to handle relationship problems; (2) trust and intimacy; (3) empathy, warmth, and genuineness; (4) relationship satisfaction; and (5) the quality of the relationship. The capacity to handle relationship problems was measured by the Handling Problems Change Scale or HPSC (see Appendix F). Trust and intimacy were measured by the Interpersonal Relationship Scale, or IRS (see Appendix E). Empathy, warmth, and genuineness were measured by the Relationship Scale—Partner (RS-P) and the Relationship Scale—Self (RS-S).[3] Relationship satisfaction was measured by the Satisfaction Change Scale or SCS (see Appendix G). Improvement in the quality of the relationship was measured by the Relationship Change Scale or RCS (see Appendix H).

[2] Test-retest reliability of the PMCI in the present study was .59 ($p$ < .001) for the control group in the ten-week interval between pre- and posttesting. Because of the long interval, this should be considered only a minimal estimate.

[3] The RS-P and RS-S were based on a modification of the Barrett-Leonard Relationship Questionnaire. On this thirty-item questionnaire the person makes a judgment about the person being rated on a five-point scale: "strongly agree," "mildly agree," "neutral," "mildly disagree," and "strongly disagree." The resulting scale is the Relationship Scale—Partner (RS-P). In addition, a parallel scale, the Relationship Scale—Self (RS-S), was devised using the same item and scale, but allowing each person to evaluate himself. Test-retest reliabilities in the present study for the control group from pre- to posttesting for the RS-P and RS-S were .31 ($p$ < .05) and .40 ($p$ < .05), respectively. Since the interval was long (ten weeks), these correlations should be considered a minimal estimate of test-retest reliability. Shapiro, Krauss, and Truax (1969) demonstrated construct validity for Shapiro's form of the RS by demonstrating that subjects did show greater self-disclosure toward people they perceived as having higher levels of the therapeutic qualities of empathy, genuineness, and warmth.

## Preliminary Analyses

As would be expected, a correlational matrix of the dependent variables (see Schlein, 1971, p. 60) showed that there were numerous significant relationships among measures of communication, trust, intimacy, empathy, warmth, genuineness, and the quality of the general relationship. The correlations were not so high, however, as to justify eliminating any of the measures as redundant.

*Sex differences.* Analyses of variance of repeated measures showed that, with the sole exception of women in the experimental group having higher pretreatment (but not posttreatment) scores than men on the Self-Feeling Awareness measure, there were no differences between men and women on the variables studied or in changes on the variables. Therefore, the data and the results of analyses will be presented here for men and women combined.

*Equality of groups at pretreatment.* The means and standard deviations on all variables for the experimental and control groups are presented in Table 10-1. As may be seen from this table, the means on all variables at pretesting for the experimental and control groups were very close to each other. Analyses of variance showed that in no case were they significantly different: The random assignment of subjects was effective in equating the two groups at the outset of the study. The same was true with respect to each of the demographic variables measured. There were no differences between the experimental and control groups on age, socioeconomic status, length of dating, or educational level.

## Results and Conclusions

To test the hypotheses, one-tailed *t*-tests were used on the gain scores from pre- and posttesting for men and women combined. Probability levels adopted were $< .05$ for significance and $< .10$ for a strong positive trend. The *t* scores and the probability that differences between the PRIMES and

Table 10-1. Pre- and Posttreatment Means and Standard Deviations of Experimental (E) and Control (C) Groups

| | | Experimental Group | | Control Group | | t for E versus C Gain-score | p |
|---|---|---|---|---|---|---|---|
| | | Pretest Treatment | Posttest Treatment | Pretest Treatment | Posttest Treatment | | |
| Acceptance of Other Scale | Mean | 8.2 | 11.5 | 6.9 | 7.6 | 6.8 | <.001 |
| | S.D. | 1.5 | 1.5 | 1.0 | 1.1 | | |
| Self-Feeling Awareness Scale | Mean | 9.7 | 11.3 | 8.2 | 8.7 | 3.1 | <.005 |
| | S.D. | 1.2 | 1.3 | 1.2 | 1.0 | | |
| Premarital Communication Inventory | Mean | 123.1 | 125.6 | 122.2 | 121.3 | 1.1 | <.29 |
| | S.D. | 14.1 | 15.5 | 12.9 | 18.6 | | |
| Primary Communication Inventory—Partner | Mean | 100.1 | 101.0 | 99.7 | 99.0 | .8 | <.45 |
| | S.D. | 8.5 | 9.9 | 9.0 | 14.5 | | |
| Handling Problems Change Scale | Mean | .70 | .93 | .67 | .35 | 2.1 | <.05 |
| | S.D. | .74 | .78 | .89 | 1.0 | | |
| Interpersonal Relationship Scale | Mean | 225.9 | 230.2 | 227.6 | 224.7 | 1.9 | <.10 |
| | S.D. | 17.3 | 19.5 | 20.9 | 24.8 | | |
| Relationship Scale—Partner | Mean | 134.1 | 133.8 | 132.8 | 129.2 | 1.2 | <.24 |
| | S.D. | 8.1 | 10.7 | 9.0 | 14.1 | | |
| Relationship Scale—Self | Mean | 130.7 | 131.7 | 131.4 | 127.7 | 2.1 | <.05 |
| | S.D. | 8.6 | 10.1 | 9.8 | 13.3 | | |
| Satisfaction Change Scale | Mean | .53 | .27 | .70 | .13 | 1.0 | <.35 |
| | S.D. | .97 | .73 | 1.20 | 1.30 | | |
| Relationship Change Scale | Mean | 105.6 | 110.2 | 106.3 | 98.0 | 3.4 | <.01 |
| | S.D. | 9.7 | 13.6 | 12.9 | 17.2 | | |

Note: The number in the experimental group was 30 and in the control group 54 except that four control subjects who did not take these particular posttests were not included in the analysis for the AOS and the SFAS. Also, mean scores for the AOS and SFAS should be halved in comparing them to ordinary scale values because "self and other" topics were summed to provide one score in the data reported above.

control group gain were caused only by chance are presented in Table 10-1.

*Improvement in communication.* Preliminary analyses showed that the two topics discussed by the couples in the Verbal Interaction Task dialogs yielded results similar to each other and to the total score on *specific* communication skills; hence, only the total score will be reported and discussed for these variables. The subhypothesis that, relative to control couples, couples trained in the PRIMES program will show greater gains in their ability to show *empathic acceptance* (AOS) toward communication from their partner was strongly supported. Similarly, results with respect to *open expression of feelings* (SFAS) strongly supported the subhypothesis that there would be greater gains for the PRIMES-trained group.

On each of two self-report measures used to assess *general* communication patterns (PMCI and PCI-P), the control subjects moved in the direction of poorer communication patterns and the PRIMES participants moved in the direction of better communication patterns. However, the differences between the groups were not statistically significant.

*Quality of the relationship.* The Handling Problems Change Scale (HPCS) measured each person's perception of improvement in the ability of the couple to handle relationship problems at the present time in comparison with a retroactive judgment of ability to handle problems three months earlier. The subjects made this comparative judgment twice: once at pretesting and once at posttesting. Three months approximated the length of the PRIMES program. Thus, the subjects were, in effect, assessing the degree of improvement in their ability to handle problems from pre- to posttreatment with the degree of improvement over a comparable period prior to entering the program. The participants in the PRIMES program showed an increase in their perceived ability to handle relationship problems over the time span covered by the program as compared with improvement over a comparable earlier period. The control group showed a relative decrement in the second as opposed to the first three-month period. The difference between the two groups was significant, confirming the subhypothesis that

PRIMES training would increase participants' ability to resolve relationship problems effectively.

As measured by the Interpersonal Relationship Scale (IRS), the control group moved downward, while the participants in the PRIMES program increased their trust and intimacy. The difference was not statistically significant, but was sufficient to constitute a very strong trend in the expected direction for the subhypothesis that PRIMES training would increase trust and intimacy in dating/premarital relationships.

The variables of empathy, warmth, and genuineness were assessed by the Relationship Scale for partner (RS-P) and for self (RS-S). From pre- to posttesting, both the PRIMES and the control group perceived their *partners* as moving in the direction of decreased empathy, warmth, and genuineness. The PRIMES group perceived less of a decline than the control group, but the difference was not statistically significant. The control group also saw *themselves* as declining in empathy, warmth, and genuineness. The PRIMES-trained group, however, saw themselves as more empathic, warm, and genuine. The difference between the groups was significant. Thus the subhypothesis that PRIMES training would increase empathy, warmth, and genuineness was partially confirmed.

The manner in which the Satisfaction Change Scale assesses change parallels the Handling Problems Change Scale as earlier described. Both the PRIMES and the control groups reported more satisfaction at posttesting than their recalled satisfaction three months earlier; for both groups, however, the improvement at posttesting was smaller than the same relative improvement over a three-month span they had reported at pretesting. The relative decrement for the PRIMES group was smaller than that of the control group, but the differences between the two groups was not significant. An examination of only the current level of satisfaction (excluding recollections of satisfaction three months earlier) revealed the following information: At pretesting the two groups did not differ significantly in satisfaction level, whereas at posttesting the current level of satisfaction reported by the PRIMES group was significantly higher than that reported by the control group ($t = 2.37$, $p <$ .05). Thus, the hypothesis as originally formulated was not con-

firmed, but the results on the whole leave some room for believing that the PRIMES program can result in improved satisfaction with the dating or premarital relationship.

The Relationship Change Scale is another measure designed to examine relative change over three-month periods. The PRIMES group showed a greater amount of positive change in the three months between pre- and posttesting than they had reported for the three months preceding pretesting. The control group perceived less improvement in the second period than they had perceived in the three months preceding the study. The differences were statistically significant, thereby confirming the subhypothesis that PRIMES training would result in positive change in the general quality of the relationship.

*Discussion*

In summary, the results showed that, as a result of participating in the PRIMES program, dating or premarital couples learned to express their feelings more openly, to respond more empathically to each other, and to improve certain aspects of the quality of their relationship, especially their ability to handle relationship problems. Further research is required to determine the extent to which Hawthorne, demand, thank you, and other effects nonspecific to the PRIMES method may account for the positive results. Research comparing the PRIMES program to other methods, isolating the differential effectiveness of specific subcomponents of the PRIMES method, or studying the comparative effects of PRIMES programs of different durations, would shed light on this question. On the other hand, the results may be regarded as conservative estimates of the efficacy of the program for several reasons.

First, the program was conducted by graduate students who generally had little or no experience in leading groups of any kind and had not led a PRIMES group before. Presumably, more experienced leaders, particularly those more experienced in this particular method, would help participants achieve even more positive improvement.

Second, comparison of the initial scores obtained on many of the measures used in this study with the same or simi-

lar measures used with marital couples in Rappaport's study (1976) and those obtained by Ely, Guerney, and Stover (1973), reveals that on all but the behavioral communicative measures the PRIMES participants started out at extremely high levels. Possibly because they were riding high on "romantic illusion," the participants showed a very strong positive rate of improvement in their relationship in the three months just preceding entry into the program. Thus, there was relatively little room for upward movement on the questionnaire measures and a great deal of potential for downward movement and for a deceleration in rate of positive change. Sensitivity to relative changes between the experimental and control groups may be significantly reduced in the high-scoring range of the questionnaires, thereby making it difficult to reveal possible positive effects of the program.

The third factor suggesting that the results obtained are conservative estimates of the favorable impact of the program is that the "no-treatment" control group was not a no-treatment group in the strictest sense. Before the random assignment to experimental and control groups, all couples received forty-five to sixty minutes of explanation and demonstration of the communication skills involved in the program, to illustrate their usefulness. Quite a few subjects in the control group spontaneously remarked at their second testing that they had found the initial session helpful to their relationship. To the extent that the introductory interview did help the control couples, it would tend to reduce the visibility of the program's effectiveness in the results obtained.

In closing, it should be noted that the anecdotal evidence offered by the PRIMES participants indicated that they regarded the program as extremely effective and helpful. Many couples expressed a desire for further training. Comments such as, "We thought we knew how to communicate before we began this program; boy, were we mistaken," and "We thought we had a good relationship before, but now we know each other so much better and things are much more satisfying," were made very frequently. The general mood of the participants was one of excitement and of great enthusiasm for the program.

Chapter 11

# Range of Application of Relationship Enhancement Programs

⋀⋀⋀⋀⋀⋀⋀⋀⋀⋀⋀⋀⋀⋀⋀⋀⋀⋀⋀⋀⋀⋀⋀⋀⋀⋀

*Edward Vogelsong*
*Bernard G. Guerney, Jr.*

Previous chapters of this book have dealt primarily with the use of RE programs in dyadic relationships in which pairs of people learn and practice their skills together. It is also possible to teach RE skills to one person or to a small group of people. In this chapter we discuss the use of RE in nondyadic relationships and explore the potential of RE programs for use in various settings and with different populations.

### Nondyadic Relationship Enhancement Programs

We believe that the skills we have been discussing can be used to improve almost any interpersonal relationship in which people desire a greater understanding of themselves and each other. There is no reason why a family with parents and children cannot benefit from improved communication and problem solving skills, or why a staff or group of people who work

289

together should not seek to improve their relationships. Nor is there any reason why an individual cannot learn more constructive ways of expressing himself and responding to others in an effort to improve his relationships. In this section we will discuss first *unilateral* RE training with one person and then *multilateral* training with units larger than dyads.

### Unilateral RE Training

There are often circumstances that make it impossible for all significant persons in a relationship to receive training. Schedule conflicts sometimes prevent one or more people from participation. It is not unusual to find that some people refuse to participate; for example, a wife may be eager to improve her relationship with her husband, but he is unwilling to come, or a parent may want to help a delinquent adolescent who refuses to participate. A young adult might be too intellectually retarded to master RE skills, but other people may want to improve their relationships with him and therefore seek training. If a member of a family is institutionalized, it may not be possible to involve him in training, yet other members of the family may want to learn more skilled and constructive ways of dealing with him when he returns home.

It is more difficult and less immediately rewarding to use RE skills with people who have not received similar training. The skilled person often may feel that he is playing by the rules, while others are at liberty to take advantage of him. Although the trained persons cannot expect others who have not received training to respond to them in kind immediately, they can hope that their own use of RE skills will have a positive effect on the relationship and that, in time, their modeling and facilitation skills will affect the way others react to them. Of course, the absent partner should be told that the participant is undertaking a training program in an attempt to improve the relationship.

In teaching RE skills for use with people not participating in the training program, the therapist can work with a single person or with a group. A homogeneous group could be formed, for example, of several parents who have adolescent children, or

of wives whose husbands are unwilling or unable to participate. Heterogeneous groups, such as parents of absent adolescents meeting with wives of absent husbands, are less advantageous but not undesirable.

In working with individuals, the leader may be more tempted than he would be in working with dyads to discuss problems and difficulties as such, apart from skill training. Such digressions could be harmful to the relationship, however, since only one point of view is represented. In our view, the leader makes best use of his time by teaching skills, rather than by providing an empathic "third ear," attempting to provide norms, giving advice, or providing "insight."

*RE therapy with one person.* The same general principles, procedures, practices, and instructional aids as are used with dyadic RE therapy also may be used in working with an individual. In training individuals with absent partners, however, there are several differences in technique or emphasis.

First, the leader must use more extensive modeling to show how the skills can be used in the relationship with the absent person(s). Thus, the mother of an adolescent should be provided with a wide variety of examples of how to express her feelings in a way that will arouse the least amount of defensiveness and hostility and be most likely to help the adolescent listen and respond with his own feelings. It is better for mothers to say, "I'm hurt that you came home so late without telling me where you were; I was really worried about you," than to say, "You're so inconsiderate; you don't care about anyone but yourself; why didn't you tell me that you were going to be so late?" It is better for mothers to say, "I'd appreciate it if you'd clean your room," than to say, "You're such a slob." It is better for mothers to say, "You're really mad at me. I want to understand, I'd like to talk about it," than to say, "What is it now? You're always upset about something. I just don't understand you." By providing this kind of modeling, the leader gives the participants examples of how they can use their skills constructively in daily situations.

Second, the leader must provide realistic opportunities during the training for the participating person to practice using

his skills in a way that will help him to gain confidence and make it possible to use his skills in his relationship with the person who is not participating. In this regard, the leader makes extensive use of role playing, in which events in the relationship are simulated and the use of skills practiced.

Third, the leader must take a much more active role in planning the circumstances in which the skills may be used effectively in the home. With the client, he determines when the skill level is sufficient to provide good chances of success, and under what conditions the use of skills will first be practiced, and later expanded.

Fourth, the leader must be more active in helping the client deal with difficulties encountered in his actual use of the skills with the person who is absent. These problem areas become the basis for further practice and learning. For example, if a husband indicates that he started to respond empathically to his wife during the past week when she confronted him about family finances, but that he soon became defensive and began yelling at her, the leader would suggest that they role play that situation. The husband would practice his skills through role playing until he feels confident that he can be more successful the next time his wife brings up a similar issue, or one of equal emotional intensity.

Fifth, the nonparticipant should periodically be invited to join in the training program. If he continues to refuse, the leader must emphasize the facilitator mode more, so that the participant can gradually train the nonparticipant in the skills at home.

Clients begin to learn RE skills by observing a model of the empathic responder mode; the leader can demonstrate this mode either by playing a recording[1] or by responding to statements that the client makes. Clients then practice this mode by responding to the leader, who chooses topics that carry imme-

[1]Persons interested in obtaining audiotapes providing role-played examples of unskilled versus skilled interpersonal problem solving and relationship enhancement dialogs should contact Bernard Guerney, Jr., at Catharine Beecher House, University Park, PA 16802.

diate interest and feelings, but that are not deeply personal or confusing. The expresser mode is introduced in the same way, with the leader first providing a demonstration and then asking the client to practice. When the client has learned to use his skills in this nonthreatening situation, practice proceeds to role playing situations in his relationship with the nonparticipating partner, beginning with positive issues, then advancing to moderate and difficult topics.

Role playing is a major tool used by the leader in teaching RE skills to individuals with absent partners. At times, the client plays the role of the nonparticipating person while the leader models skills as the client might use them in the relationship. At other times the leader plays the role, as realistically as possible, of the person who is not participating, while the client practices his skills.

When the client has become proficient in the use of RE skills with the leader, he or she begins to employ the skills in real situations with the nonparticipating partner. At first, the skills are employed in relatively "safe" situations that involve very little emotion, and then gradually they are introduced into the more difficult areas of the relationship. Each time the leader and client meet, they discuss what effects the client has experienced in using RE skills since the last meeting. They recreate those situations in which any difficulties were experienced, in order to further refine the client's skills. They then create new practice situations to role play based on other issues vital to the relationship and commensurate with the skill level of the client.

Take as an example a mother who is trying to learn ways of improving her relationship with her daughter. In the roleplaying phase, the leader first determines the nature of the mother's views, feelings, and interpersonal wishes about the issue. He uses this knowledge as a basis to play the mother's role in a discussion of the issue using RE skills, while the mother uses her knowledge of her daughter to play the daughter's role. (Having the client play the role of the absent partner has the important fringe benefit of broadening the client's empathy with the partner.) The roles then are reversed, with the mother following the model of the leader and playing her own

role using RE skills, while the leader plays the daughter's
role.

Such dialogs are interrupted as frequently as necessary to
help the client master the use of RE skills and especially to give
frequent encouragement and to provide strong reinforcement
for skilled responses made by the client. The leader uses the
same kinds of instructional methods in training individuals as he
would in working with dyads.

The following marital case of Esther and Bill exemplifies
the use of RE methods for an individual with an absent partner.
Esther, forty-five years old, had seen a number of therapists
over the past five years, but complained that her relationship
with her husband Bill had only gotten worse. He consistently
refused therapy although he admitted that his marriage was
unsatisfactory. He had had a number of affairs with other
women and had left home twice, once for six months and once
for four months.

Esther wanted to save her marriage if possible, but felt
that she could no longer tolerate the kind of marriage she had
had for the past several years. She said that every time she and
her husband talked about their marriage they had a big fight
and things became worse. Esther systematically learned RE
skills by practicing with the therapist one hour a week. She
gradually began making empathic responses to her husband on
relatively "safe" topics, such as his feelings about his boss, his
reaction to recent news stories, and other areas that did not involve their marriage. She explained to him that she was trying
to learn new ways to understand him better than she had before. She also began to state her feelings to him on a number of
areas that did not involve their marriage.

As she gained confidence in her ability to use RE skills,
Esther decided that she wanted to employ them in a discussion
with her husband about their marriage. She practiced these
skills very carefully with the therapist who played the role of
her husband. When she felt prepared, she told Bill one evening
that she would like to know his feelings about their marriage.
He was reluctant to begin such a discussion, but when he did,
she responded empathically to what he said. For over an hour

she remained empathic until he indicated that he had nothing more to say. She then asked him to listen to her as a silent partner while she stated her views, using her best expressive skills. She said later that this conversation was the most satisfactory one she had ever had with anyone. It was the first of many discussions they had.

As a result of these discussions, both Esther and Bill began to assume more responsibility for the success of their marriage. They changed the time of their evening meal so they could enjoy it in more relaxed circumstances. Esther got a part-time job to help with family finances. As it turned out, she had always wanted to work, but had been afraid Bill would disapprove; without ever saying so, he had always resented her *not* working, yet criticizing him for not making enough money. As the result of other problem-solving discussions, they sold the house they lived in and bought another one farther away from his parents. Eventually Esther went to night school to learn additional secretarial skills and got a much better job. Although Bill never came to therapy, he freely attributed the vast improvement in their marriage to her participation in an RE program.

*Unilateral RE therapy in a group.* The same basic approach as has been described above is used when two or more clients without partners are trained together. The goal is still to improve the relationship between the individual and the person(s) not participating. The major difference in training is that after the leader has engaged in role playing several times with each participant, he begins to have the group members role play with each other. He carefully points out that effective role playing should not be "acting," but trying to *become* the person whose role is being played. Sometimes the client role plays the absent partner, while another group member takes the role of the client. At other times, another group member role plays the absent partner, while the client assumes his own role.

It is inevitable, especially in a small group with similar interests, that people will become interested in each other's problems and successes. There is always the temptation for the group to degenerate into a discussion, with people offering

advice and solutions to each other. The leader needs to be task oriented to avoid this kind of digression and to ensure that the group time is spent in the best way possible—by continual skill practice. Thus, in a group of six parents with adolescent children, one group member can be most helpful to another one by role playing situations in the relationship of that parent with his or her child. By helping each other practice the use of skills in those areas that are most difficult in the parent-child relationship, group members not only help each other relate more effectively to their children, but also gain insight into how they can deal more constructively with their own families.

The advantages and disadvantages of working in groups as compared to working with individuals are much the same as has been described earlier for dyadic groups. The one significant difference is that working with groups makes other individuals available to role play and more often frees the leader to concentrate entirely on teaching.

*The Filial Relationship Enhancement Program.* Parents with children under the age of ten have been taught to use RE skills to enhance their relationship with their children and to achieve an increased sense of emotional well-being. Developed in 1962, the Filial Therapy program was the first program designed to train lay people systematically to use psychotherapeutic skills in enhancing an intimate relationship. The experiences with Filial Therapy gave rise to the other RE methods that have been developed since. With young children, play is considered the medium initially most likely to lead to emotionally relevant expression and interaction. Therefore, the play situation is viewed as an excellent starting point for training parents. From this starting point, a variety of relationship-enhancing and child-rearing skills are taught to the parents for use in all types of situations. This method of teaching parenting skills and of working with emotionally disturbed children has been described elsewhere (Guerney, 1964; Guerney, Guerney, and Andronico, 1966; Andronico, Fidler, Guerney, and Guerney, 1967; Guerney, Stover, and Andronico, 1967; Stover and Guerney, 1967; Guerney, Guerney, and Stover, 1972).

*Relationship enhancement skills for single adults.* An RE

program has been designed for single adults who wish to improve their ability to establish and develop close relationships with others. The program is appropriate for those who do not experience any special difficulty in relating to others, but who do wish to reach an exceptionally high level of intimacy with friends, as well as for those individuals who may have severe problems in establishing or maintaining close relationships with others. The program (Guerney and Hatch, 1974) is called Singles Training in Interpersonal Relationship Skills (STIRS).

Some of the skill practice revolves around dyadic interaction between the group members themselves and the remainder focuses on homework assignments and supervision involving individuals not included in the group. The areas for skill practice in the STIRS program range from elementary ones, such as striking up a conversation, to very complicated relationship problems, such as resisting unwanted sexual advances when one nevertheless wishes to maintain and strengthen the relationship. Individuals can concentrate on areas where they feel the greatest need.

### Multilateral Relationship Enhancement Training

It is possible to teach RE skills to several people who are in a multifaceted relationship. This flexibility in the RE model expands even further the range of possibilities for applying RE skills to interpersonal relationships. It means that RE programs can be useful not only for an entire family as a unit, but also for people in business and industry, in institutions and schools, in churches and civic organizations, in order to improve communication, problem solving, and decision making. The descriptions that follow are simply several examples of many potential uses for RE programs.

*Family Relationship Enhancement.* In the Family Relationship Enhancement program the unit of focus may be larger than the dyad, but the teaching and use of RE skills still involves a high degree of structure in training, practice, and supervision. By making family members very active as facilitators for each other, by ensuring that each involved person in the family

has an opportunity to express his or her feelings fully, and by making certain that each person feels understood and accepted by every other family member, families can deal constructively with their problems by using RE skills. We do not know of any other program that provides family members with the opportunity to deal with family issues in a way that systematically seeks to ensure that each person will be understood and accepted by all the others.

Family Relationship Enhancement therapy is often combined with other RE programs. A husband and wife who are having difficulty with their marriage may be encouraged to participate in a conjugal program as well as in the family program. Families with adolescents as well as younger children may participate in both filial and family therapy, either by meeting twice a week or by alternating weeks, with filial one week and family the next. It would be possible to teach adolescents as well as parents the skills of play therapy as taught in the filial program, with the goal of improving sibling relationships.

*Staff Relationship Enhancement training.* Many organizations, businesses, agencies, and institutions could provide RE training for staff members with the goal of improving interpersonal relations, work satisfaction, efficiency, and quality. It is not at all unusual for members of organizations to complain that lack of good communication between administration and staff, between supervisors and supervisees, and between peers and colleagues is frustrating and adversely affects the way people perform their jobs. Lack of communication wastes time, makes people feel unimportant, duplicates some tasks and ignores others, and generally sets a mood that is demoralizing and nonproductive.

Relationship enhancement training for staff personnel can provide an alternative to the usual grumbling to self, to a trusted colleague at work, or to a spouse at home. It can provide an opportunity for people to deal directly with the source of their discontent in an open and constructive manner. It goes far beyond the anonymous suggestion box and encourages people at every level to express their frustrations, make suggestions for improvement, and deal with each other as people. By

demonstrating to each person on the staff that his or her feelings and ideas are welcome and valued, morale may be increased and people's potential more fully developed.

The Staff Relationship Enhancement training program uses the same principles, techniques, practices, and instructional aids as are used to teach RE skills to dyads or individuals. Meeting in small groups of no more than eight, the leader first models the skills and then asks participants to practice them, beginning with "neutral" or unemotional topics and gradually working toward the more difficult relationship issues. Sometimes the topics may be dyadic, with two people working on an issue in their relationship; at other times the subject may involve three or more members or even the entire group. In every instance, the leader's job is to maintain a high degree of structure, to teach and encourage all members to facilitate actively, and to reinforce, prompt, and model effective use of skills so that learning will be most productive. He discourages and cuts off digressions that are inappropriate by asking group members to deal with all issues within the framework of the RE program. In this way, he teaches participants to use RE skills in dealing with significant complaints, frustrations, conflicts, wishes, and desires.

An important part of any RE program, and one that can be easily overlooked in staff training, is to provide, both during and after the formal training period, regular opportunities for people to practice their skills and deal with pertinent issues. Perhaps the best way to ensure that these opportunities will be provided is to encourage people to set aside a brief period of time at regular intervals in which they can discuss issues and make plans without distractions. (It is important to emphasize that positive as well as negative topics are appropriate for discussion.) In this way, people can be assured that they need wait only several days to bring up issues that are important to them. Of course, if emergency issues arise during the middle of the week, there should always be the chance to deal with them immediately or at greater length. In all cases, it will be helpful to have a facilitator present who can help each person make the maximum use of his RE skills.

## Use of Relationship Enhancement in Special Settings

In this section we discuss the use of RE programs in various settings, such as schools, business and industry, churches and civic organizations, and anyplace where people live or work together in close relationships. We believe that the teaching of RE skills and the resultant improvement of understanding and acceptance among people can lead to greater satisfaction and a happier life for everyone. We have taught people many skills; why should we not also teach them ways of getting along better with each other?

### In a School Setting

The schools provide many opportunities at all levels for the use of RE programs. They can be the sponsoring agency for teaching parenting skills to parents of children in the lower grades and for parent-adolescent and family programs for students in the upper grades and their parents. Relationships between students and teachers can be enhanced, and problem areas dealt with constructively, as can peer relationships among students, among teachers, and relationships between administration and staff. Indeed, we believe that skills of interpersonal relationships should be a part of the curriculum of every school. Just as students are taught to read, to perform mathematical functions, to speak another language, to write research papers, to learn vocational skills, and to study social and historical issues, so we think they should be taught skills of interpersonal relationships, such as how to express themselves constructively, how to be empathic, how to initiate friendships, and so on. The program descriptions that follow are illustrations of several of the many ways that RE programs can be used in the school setting.

*Enhancing parent-child relationships.* Many schools consider it their responsibility to offer programs to enable parents to relate more effectively to their children. They thus advocate a partnership between school personnel and parents in serving the best interests of the child. RE programs can serve these

interests very well and can provide additional opportunities that go beyond what most schools are doing currently. For example, a group of mothers could meet weekly with an elementary guidance counselor to learn to use RE skills in their relationships with their children. Extensive skill practice for parents, in play sessions if feasible or by role playing if not, provides the best format for such a group, rather than a general discussion session or a didactic program that involves relatively little actual skill practice. As in other RE programs, the participants first learn their skills in the group, and then begin to apply them at home. They discuss particular areas of success and difficulty at each weekly meeting, and recreate difficult areas and role play them to work out the problems.

Schools can provide similar programs for older students and their parents. Wherever possible, it is desirable to involve both the students and their parents in a dyadic program, such as PARD, or in a Family Relationship Enhancement program as was described earlier in this chapter. Where it is not possible to involve both parents and their children, unilateral training can be offered either for the students or for the parents. In either case, the use of extensive role playing in the group sessions can give the participants skills and practice in being able to relate more effectively to their parents or their children.

*Enhancing teacher-student relationships.* Similar programs can be used to enhance relationships between students and teachers. Here again, many variations of training are possible. Skills can be taught to dyads to work out particular relationship issues between a teacher and a student. In this case the leader (probably a guidance counselor or school psychologist) can meet either with one pair, or form a group of three or four pairs to work on their relationships. The goal is to work through particular difficulties in each relationship, but there is much carry-over into other relationships. Unilateral training can also be provided, in which a group of teachers or a group of students meets regularly to learn RE skills. Again, extensive role playing is used to give the participants practice and experience in using skills to relate more effectively to other people. In cases where a teacher is having difficulty with several students, or where there

are problems between several teachers and students, multilateral training is advisable.

Apart from specific problem situations, RE skills can be helpful in the classroom setting in a very general way. If teachers can be empathic with their students, and can express themselves constructively when difficulties arise, the use of RE skills can serve a preventive as well as a remedial function. Teachers who are skilled in RE methods can make tremendous strides in increasing a child's self-concept and in creating an atmosphere in which the child is eager to learn. These skills can be acquired through in-service training, continuing education, special workshops, and/or weekly practice sessions with a qualified trainer.

In the same manner, to the extent that school students are taught RE skills, they will be that much better prepared to deal constructively with their teachers and hopefully to avoid serious classroom problems.

*Enhancing relations among students.* The capacity to form meaningful and growth-enhancing friendships is crucial to emotional and social well-being. There is no reason to believe that the capacity to form and to enjoy friendships is an area that is best left outside the realm of the classroom. There is every reason to believe that skills can be taught to individuals that will enhance their abilities to establish friendships and to gain more enjoyment and personal fulfillment from existing friendships. Vogelsong (1974) conducted a program in an elementary school in which empathic responder skills were taught to students ten years of age. We consider this to be about the youngest age at which group instruction in such skills might yield generally successful results.[2]

A similar program for junior and senior high school students, the Pupil Relationship Enhancement Program (PREP), has been designed to teach students RE skills for establishing and strengthening friendships and for working out problem areas in their relationships. This program has been described in detail elsewhere (Hatch and Guerney, 1975).

---

[2]We do not mean to imply that other program formats (for example, Bessell and Palomeris, 1969) are not beneficial in facilitating other types of relationship-enhancing skills at younger age levels.

*Enhancing staff and administration relations.* Another area in which RE programs can be useful in school is in improving communication and understanding among staff members and between administration and staff. If complaints are not channeled constructively, and if ideas for improvement are not welcomed, morale and the quality of the work can be expected to decline. If school teachers have complaints or suggestions regarding school policy, they should be communicated directly to the administration. If there are administrative dissatisfactions about the ways certain classroom procedures are being handled, these issues too should be dealt with as openly and constructively as possible.

By teaching RE skills to staff and administrative personnel and by providing frequent opportunities for constructive dialog to take place, it can be expected that more harmonious relationships will develop and an atmosphere will be created that is more conducive to good educational processes.

## RE in Business and Industry

We spoke earlier in this chapter about the many benefits of improved communication among colleagues and peers, between administrators and staff, and between supervisors and supervisees. There are, of course, many implications of improved relationships at all these levels for business and industry. Improved relationships can be expected to lead to more pleasant working conditions and increased feelings of self-worth. These in turn can be expected to increase productivity, decrease absenteeism, decrease personnel turnover, and yield better relations between the organization and its customers or community.

The knowledge and use of RE skills by administrators, supervisors, foremen, and forewomen can be very helpful in their relations with each other and with those people who work under them. The use of expresser skills can enable these people to assign tasks, correct deficiencies, and deal with problems in ways that minimize resentment and hostility. Workers can be encouraged to bring problem areas to their superior's attention if they know that they will be understood and that their communication will be welcomed.

Training can be either unilateral or multilateral. In many situations it may not be practical or even possible to provide training for all employees. Unilateral training can be conducted with administrators and others in supervisory roles. These people then have an additional set of skills that they can use in relating to the people they oversee.

Another area in which unilateral training is useful to business and industry is with people who are in public relations work and sales. In relating to the public, the use of RE skills enables business people to communicate much more effectively. The salesman who conveys understanding of his clients' point of view and feelings is much more likely to sell his product or services than one who is oblivious to the needs of others.

In both of these instances, the teaching of RE skills is accomplished most efficiently in small groups and in the same manner that has been described earlier in this chapter. Extensive role play and familiarity with RE skills precede the actual use of the skills outside the training group. Difficulties encountered on the outside are discussed with the trainer, who may provide more structure or model the use of RE skills in the role played recreation of the situation.

Multilateral training in business and industry can be very useful in helping administrators relate more effectively to each other and to staff. The increase in good communication and the establishment of an open, supportive atmosphere create a spirit of cooperation that greatly enhances creative and constructive problem solution. By training administrators and staff together in small groups of six to eight people, and by encouraging personnel to meet regularly in small groups, opportunity can be provided for each person to make input in a constructive way and to be assured that others listen and understand him. Not only can conflicts more readily be resolved in this kind of environment; they can be dealt with early, before they grow out of proportion.

### RE in Churches and Civic Organizations

Churches and civic organizations also can find many helpful uses for RE programs. Pastors, priests, and rabbis will find

RE skills invaluable in relating to the public and in dealing with people's problems. Civic and church leaders who do much work in small groups and task forces will find that they can accomplish their jobs much more efficiently and cooperatively by using RE skills in their relationships with people. The following descriptions suggest a few of the many ways churches and civic groups can find RE skills and programs to be useful.

Leaders in these organizations can be trained in the use of RE skills in board and committee meetings. By being able to convey understanding of each point of view that is expressed, by being able to avoid becoming defensive when attacked or confronted, and by being able to assert their own point of view in a way that decreases defensive and hostile reactions from others, organizational leaders can avoid being sidetracked by useless debates and can accomplish their jobs much more constructively. The appropriate use of RE skills by a group leader can keep tempers under control and maintain a more friendly, cooperative spirit and increase the efficiency of group meetings. Unilateral training for organizational leaders that involves extensive role play experience can provide these leaders with the skill and confidence they need to work most effectively in groups and committees.

At other times, multilateral training may be possible and desirable. Training all members of a governing board of a church or organization in the use of RE skills can not only prepare these people to be leaders in their work with committees and groups, but also can enable them to work most effectively with each other in making decisions and solving problems in their organization. Such training can be provided by an RE leader who introduces the skills in nonthreatening situations apart from board meetings by using role playing to deal with progressively more difficult areas. As a final step, the leader may attend several board meetings and provide modeling responses where board members have difficulty using their skills.

Many churches and civic organizations also are interested in providing enrichment programs for their members or for the public and many have already sponsored marriage enrichment groups or parenting skills programs. In such programs, church members can be taught RE skills over a weekend, a week-long

retreat, or by meeting once a week. The facilities of a retreat center, a church parlor, a community meeting hall, or a person's home all lend themselves quite readily to skill-training programs.

Premarital counseling is another service often provided by clergy. The previously described PRIMES program provides an excellent way to teach premarital couples skills that enable them to evaluate their current relationship and to encourage open communication in their later marriage.

## Use of Relationship Enhancement with Special Populations

If RE programs can be used in various settings they can also be used with special populations. We believe that the use of RE skills can help many people overcome difficult problems. In this section we discuss the use of RE with people such as psychiatric inpatients, delinquents, rehabilitation patients, addicts, and prisoners. In many of these instances RE may not be the sole modality of treatment, but it may well complement the type of therapy that is currently being used. In each of these instances, the use of RE with family members offers great potential.

### Psychiatric Inpatients

We have discussed earlier in this book that from an educational point of view we see no problems with people participating in RE programs while simultaneously undergoing another form of treatment. There are several different ways that RE programs can be used with psychiatric inpatients and their families.

First of all, with patients who are functioning at appropriate levels, RE skills can be taught in small groups on a ward of a hospital or institution. Such a program could be designed to enable patients to relate more therapeutically with each other. By being able to express themselves appropriately and to respond helpfully to each other, patients could serve as therapists for each other, as an adjunct to the therapy they receive from hospital staff.

This same type of group also could be useful in teaching patients RE skills that they could use with their families when they returned home. By having first the leader and then various members of the group role play different family members, the patients could receive practice and experience in relating more effectively with their family members. After they had practiced their skills and become thoroughly familiar and comfortable with them, the patients could be encouraged to employ their skills on a weekend visit with their families, starting first with "safe" areas and gradually building up to more difficult subjects. At this point, the group meetings at the hospital would be used for supervision of the use of the skills in the home and for role playing more difficult areas.

In a similar manner, family members could provide the most supportive environment in the home when the patient returned by using RE skills in their relationships with the patient. Small groups of members from several families could meet regularly to learn RE skills. Various members of the group could role play the patient, thus giving the family members experience in responding empathically and making constructive expressive statements to the patient. Once again, these skills would be employed gradually with the patient, either in family visits to the hospital, in patient visits to the home, and/or when the patient was discharged and returned to live at home.

In addition to this unilateral method of training, multilateral training also could be used. The patients and family members could be trained simultaneously, apart from each other. After they had learned their skills, they could meet with a leader to work on using their skills together. Or the training could be multilateral from the beginning. Possibly this approach could be implemented on a regular basis while the patient was still hospitalized, by using a portion of the time that family members spend in regular visits to the patient. The family group training or supervision also could be continued when a patient is transferred to outpatient or follow-up status. If we can provide in the home an atmosphere of greater warmth and acceptance, the chances of the patient's being able to continue to function effectively surely will have been increased.

*Delinquents*

There is increasing concern in our society about the rising rate of delinquency among adolescents. Many observers relate this increasing delinquency to a breakdown of family relationships. The earlier described Parent-Adolescent Relationship Development program has been shown to increase communication, trust, and warmth in parent-adolescent relationships. Possibly such a program would actually decrease the rate of delinquency. We are aware of one probation board that is experimenting with the Family Relationship Enhancement program to reduce the incidence of delinquency.

There are other areas in which RE programs offer hope for rehabilitating delinquents. A model similar to the one described earlier in this chapter for psychiatric inpatients is worth considering for delinquents who are institutionalized. Teaching RE skills to small groups of delinquents can provide them with alternatives to relate to each other in different ways. If the right atmosphere is created, it may be easier for these adolescents to talk with each other than with a professional counselor, a parent, or another authority figure. As they acquired and used skills with each other, they gradually could begin to role play the use of RE skills with other people, such as parents, law enforcement personnel, houseparents, and so on. And if, at the same time, these other people were also taught to relate to adolescents with empathy and warmth, there would be a still greater chance of meaningful dialog and cooperation.

*Rehabilitation Patients*

We see RE skills as an adjunct to other approaches that many rehabilitation counselors will find useful. We believe that many people in rehabilitation programs can profit immensely from RE methods. There are several models that we suggest for consideration.

People who have similar problems, such as amputees, or people who are about to be, or recently have been, discharged from institutions, may find it very useful to discuss their views

and feelings with each other. It is often easier to believe that someone who has undergone a similar experience can be empathic. By training these people in RE skills in small groups, such people can be taught to develop very therapeutic relationships with each other.

Family members can also be very helpful in the area of rehabilitation. They can be trained unilaterally to communicate effectively with the rehabilitation patient, or better still, trained dyadically or multilaterally. For example, patients who have recently undergone a mastectomy, a colostomy, an amputation, or any operation or illness that significantly effects self-concept or life-style, would find it very helpful to be able to talk about their feelings with their spouse or other family members in a way that they knew they would be understood (and vice versa) and could work through the problems created by the handicap.

Also, if people knew in advance of an impending serious operation, curtailment of functioning, or even death, members of their family could be most supportive if by using RE skills they could help the prospective patient explore his ideas and feelings in preparation for the traumatic event and its after-effects.

### Addicts

We advocate the trial of RE programs in both overcoming and preventing addiction. With respect to prevention, it has long been believed that a harmonious supportive home environment helps to prevent addiction. With respect to overcoming addiction, groups of alcoholics or drug abusers may find it very useful to be able to discuss with each other their problems and concerns in an empathic, supportive environment. They may find within such a group the strength they need to overcome their debilitating habits. Once again, it may be easier initially for adults to talk with each other and be empathic with each other than with a professional because they share a common problem.

By teaching family members to be empathic and to relate more meaningfully to the alcoholic father, mother, or adoles-

cent, we believe an environment will be created that will aid in working through the problems of the alcoholic. Once again, unilateral training can be provided for the nonalcoholic family members, the alcoholic can be trained in a dyad with a spouse or parent, or multilateral training can be offered for the entire family. The experience we have had to date in RE therapy with alcoholics and their spouses has been extremely positive, but limited.

We know that much drug therapy involves crisis intervention as well as long-term treatment. Methadone centers and other treatment facilities are involved in research to find the most effective ways of helping the addict. We urge the simultaneous use of skill-training programs and programs incorporating the family in the process, such as RE programs, to deal with many of the underlying issues in this treatment process.

### Prisoners

There are many potential uses of RE programs with prisoners. Once again, it makes sense that people with similar concerns and problems could be very helpful to each other. It may be possible to form small groups of prisoners and teach them to talk with each other using RE skills. In addition to providing this opportunity for prisoners to relate meaningfully to each other, the groups also could be used for role playing and practicing the use of RE skills with other people, such as spouses or family members. After prisoners have learned RE skills and role played their use with others, they could be encouraged gradually to use them when they have visitors. The learning of these skills may be especially helpful for prisoners who are preparing for parole in the near future and must deal with family readjustment problems.

Of course, it also would be very beneficial to train family members in RE skills, to use them either during their prison visits or when the prisoner was paroled and returned home. Once again, by providing simultaneous training (or dyadic or multilateral training, if feasible) for prisoners and their families, strains on the relationship may be decreased. If family members

can learn to respond with warmth and empathy, they can be very helpful in making the parolee feel welcome and in helping him to readjust to community living.

## Summary

We have described here only a sample of the programs that have been and could be developed for training individuals to relate more meaningfully with significant people in their lives. RE or similar programs can be useful in areas such as pregnancy and childbirth, for adoptive parents, for foster parents, in half-way houses and attention homes. The purpose of this chapter has been not only to acquaint readers with the flexibility and the wide range of application of RE programs but, we hope, to challenge them to be resourceful and creative in their use of RE methods.

# Chapter 12

# Summary and Implications for Future Mental Health Practices

‸‸‸‸‸‸‸‸‸‸‸‸‸‸‸‸‸‸‸‸‸‸‸‸‸

This chapter summarizes the major features of RE therapy and programs: objectives, basic skills (and their generalization to everyday life), leadership skills, and research. Under each of these categories we will take a perspective that will often include within its focus the implications not only of RE methods, but the use of the revolutionary educational model, which the RE approach exemplifies, as a means of promoting the mental health and emotional well-being of the general public. We will conclude with consideration of a new, specific kind of institutional framework, the "School for Living," which we believe will emerge as a logical vehicle for the expanding use of the educational model in the treatment and prevention of emotional dysfunction and in the enrichment of our lives.

## Objectives

The broad objective of this book is to add to the repertoire of mental health professionals a new means of accomplishing three goals: (1) alleviating emotional and interpersonal dysfunctioning and suffering; (2) preventing the development or

recurrence of emotional and interpersonal dysfunction and suffering; and (3) increasing emotional and interpersonal satisfaction in living. The route by which RE methods attempt to facilitate these objectives is by training people in skills that are essential to those objectives—especially such skills as have a great effect on interpersonal relationships with significant others. Except for those who are mentally ill (defined here in terms of biochemical or physiological imbalances or deficits leading to bizarre behavior), we believe that the questions of what is "dysfunction" and what is "satisfaction" in the last analysis come down to culturally determined value judgments. We believe that all those who seek to help others to change should make it clear first to themselves, and then to their clients, what values their efforts will serve to strengthen, diminish, or implement.

The values that tend to be diminished by the RE method are those that depend on a "higher order" or authority, whether the higher order be the state, or beliefs based on a religion, a philosophy, or a particular psychological theory. For individuals, the RE method may therefore mean the loss of a certain type of security and of the kind of order, clarity, and efficiency that comes about when a group of people unanimously accept such a higher order of authority as opposed to their own judgments.

The values that tend to be implemented or enhanced by the RE method are those that depend on the acceptance of a pluralistic, democratic social orientation. At a broad level of analysis, the values implemented by RE methods are those that tend to place the wants of the individual or the small subunit, such as a marital pair or family, in the dominant, determining position.

The RE method, eschewing appeals to tradition or a higher authority, concentrates on harmonizing the needs of individuals within a small group with a minimum of friction and a maximum of individual need satisfaction based on subjectively experienced desires. It assumes that each individual has a right to be heard and given full consideration in reaching group decisions. The RE approach tends to further the development and

authority of the individual or small group by making the individual or member of a small group feel respected, understood, and important. This result tends to reduce that type of anxiety that stems from personal frustrations and self-doubt, and to reduce the use of reality-distorting defense mechanisms based on such anxiety. Further, RE methodology places a premium on intrapersonal and interpersonal honesty. The RE method assumes that truth and compassion can compete successfully as primary values with any other set of values as having long-term survival potential, not only for the individual and small group, but also for the larger society in which such values thrive.

At this stage in the development of our society, and perhaps of all societies that have reached a certain stage of industrialization, it seems that valuing adaptability and fulfilling the wants of individuals and small groups comes to the forefront. Thus the values implemented by RE programs have a wide acceptance, and such acceptance will likely remain on the ascent unless and until a reversal of basic moral, political, and cultural trends takes place in our society.

### Broader Implications

Previous programs that were considered remedial in nature (therapy) were not considered appropriate for those who were not "sick" ("neurotic," "disturbed," "dysfunctional," "maladjusted," or whatever). Likewise, programs that aimed at broadening people's psychological or interpersonal horizons or skills—Sensitivity Training, Parent Effectiveness Training (Gordon, 1972), and so on—were not considered therapy. Advocates of such programs very carefully distinguish them as something different and apart from therapy.

Perhaps the advocates of these other programs built on the educational model are justified in drawing the distinction. Perhaps their programs are too inflexible in duration, too general, too unsystematic to be considered as generally having remedial impact on the lives of those who participate in them, and perhaps people in need of help with serious psychological interpersonal problems should look elsewhere. But perhaps not.

Perhaps such a distinction is drawn not on the basis of any comparative evidence, but on the basis of tradition and on the basis of distinctions among professionals as to who is allowed to do what with whom. We are not aware of any substantial body of comparative research that favors traditional approaches for any given type of problem over *skill-training* educational programs that are designed to accomplish similar objectives. (Part of the problem here, of course, is that similar objectives may be sought under different labels, hence in practice the comparisons between different approaches are not even considered.)

Without evaluating one way or another the other approaches that use an educational model, we are willing (with due trepidation) to throw down the gauntlet in behalf of RE methods. We refuse to label RE methods as being only *preventive, enriching,* or *therapeutic.* We say they are all three. Which of these functions an RE program is serving is a matter of when it is undertaken, how long it lasts, and, most of all, what perspective guides it—the perspective of the agency offering it and the person participating in it.

It is our view that in designing a program to alter radically the way in which individuals deal with their emotions and with other people, it is counterproductive to make sharp distinctions between therapy, prevention, and enrichment. For the sake of clarity, take as an example a program that is not an RE program and that is as much of a "primary prevention" program as we can think of: a program designed to change the attitudes and behaviors of impoverished, culturally deprived mothers so that they will spend more time interacting in a more constructive way with their infant children. Let us assume that for a given mother who would otherwise have related to her child in a very detrimental manner, the program is markedly successful and that she relates to her child in a very positive and constructive manner. Instead of having a dull, sullen, disobedient child who helps to drive her mother to despair and drink, the child turns out to be bright, inquisitive, well-behaved, and very affectionate toward this mother, whose response in turn is to experience a great blossoming of confidence and self-esteem and renewed ambition to make a successful life for herself and her

child. If the mother had been in "therapy," could the therapist have wished for more? Even if he had wished for more, would he have been more likely to have achieved it? Is such a program therapeutic? Or is it preventative? Or is it enriching? Of course, it is all three.

Can we call this program *therapy* if it was carried out in the home and not in a mental health center? Can we call it *therapy* if it was carried out by a neighbor of the mother who before entering a training program one year ago was as impoverished and deprived as the mother she trained, and not only lacks an M.D., a Ph.D., and an M.S.W., but also lacks a high school diploma? Perhaps the best answer to these questions is to say that the mental health establishment will call it whatever it wants to call it. However, it is our belief that mental health professionals should not deceive themselves as to what they are striving to accomplish because of this kind of labeling. Sharp distinctions between *therapy, prevention,* and *enrichment* in considering such programs are based on the inappropriate application of medical analogies to the life-styles of individuals and their social behavior.

Programs such as we are discussing are designed to be undertaken willingly by the public. They are designed to lead to accomplishment, effectiveness, enrichment, enhancement, improvement, and so on, in the lives of the participants. Hence, these labels are the most appropriate ones for *every* program designed to bring about emotional and behavioral functioning that, from the point of view of the participant, is better than it was before.

The purpose of labels, however, is to communicate the nature of something. Thus, unless and until professionals and the public come to understand and accept an educational as opposed to a medical model in viewing such matters, it is desirable not to exclude the label *therapy* from the list of labels that may be used to describe any program that seeks to bring about fundamental, general, and long-lasting improvement in the way in which a strongly dissatisfied person feels about himself and conducts his life. That is, if it takes the use of the term *therapy* attached to a program to allow certain professionals and clients

to see that program's potential for accomplishing what these people now think of as something only *therapy* can accomplish, then it seems desirable to use the term *therapy* when describing such a program to such people.

With a breakdown of the sharp distinctions that now exist among various programs designed to change people in vital ways, an increased realization of what their business really is about can be expected of those mental health practitioners (including many psychiatrists) who are not practicing medicine. When the realization becomes widespread that they are engaged in nothing more or less than education, mental health professionals will concentrate on developing methods that are more *effective* educationally. More sophisticated programs can then be expected to help people change the course of their lives and favorably influence the lives of those close to them. It can then also be expected that the term *therapy* for psychosocial change programs will no longer be part of the vocabulary of professionals or lay persons, and more and more people will feel free to take advantage of such nonstigmatized programs to resolve personal and interpersonal conflicts and misery. There is, then, the chance that, just as mass education has eliminated illiteracy, *effective* mass psychosocial education—which we think of as almost synonymous with *skill training*—can alter behaviors on a wide scale and eradicate the mass emotional and interpersonal illiteracy that presently prevails.

## Leadership Skills

In the past, most therapeutic efforts that tried to influence the intrapsychic or interpersonal functioning of an individual have relied essentially on one or the other of two approaches. The most traditional approach has attempted to use the relationship between the helper and the individual to bring about changes in client understanding, self-concept, and behavior through transference, unconditional positive regard, or interpretative confrontation of a hard or soft variety. The other major approach has been to change the client by conditioning, desensitization, or selective positive and/or negative reinforce-

ment. The same two general models were then carried over to treating people in groups and, finally, to trying to influence the relationships between intimates.

In the first type of approach, wherein the relationship between the helper and client was regarded as the primary vehicle of inducing change, lip service is paid to the fact that an educational process is at work in a general sense, but few attempts were ever made to specify the teaching methodology by which the process worked. The helper using this model seldom, if ever, really thought of himself as a teacher.

In the second model, the method of teaching—reconditioning—was given careful consideration. The importance of the relationship between helper and helpee was given short shrift. The target of change was often conceptualized in a restricted fashion—as modifying overt behavior. Underlying values were not much considered, nor were attitudes, thought processes, and emotions. The teaching technology was similarly conceptualized in a restrictive way: Reinforcement, aversive conditioning, and extinction were the primary tools. The client, although he often was asked to do certain things, essentially was viewed not as an initiator, and not as one who played an active role in incorporating new skills into his repertoire, but as one who essentially would react automatically to changes in stimuli as these were managed by the professional.

As social learning theory, with modeling and behavior rehearsal, is being incorporated in the behavior modification movement, and as cognitive functions are beginning to be recognized as important targets of reeducation, behavior modification methodology is beginning to change in many of these regards. However, the importance of the emotional life of the client, his self-concept, and the effects of his interpersonal relations on these dimensions of his inner life, are still generally given short shrift by the adherents of the second model in choosing targets for change. Likewise, the *teaching methods* used by adherents of the second model generally pay minimum heed to emotions (other than anxiety), to self-concept, and to psychodynamic defense mechanisms. (Individual practitioners of behavior modification often may act instinctively in accord

with the realities these variables impose on their practice. However, they generally do not consciously build their techniques and programs to take full advantage of the benefits that paying careful attention to such variables can bestow on any program designed to help people change.)

In developing the RE method, an attempt has been made to give full benefit to self-concept, defense mechanisms, and all varieties of emotions not only as targets of change, but as variables of great importance in the design of the teaching methodology. The therapist's manner of behavior—that is, the way in which he relates to clients—is considered the foundation on which his other didactic methods rest. At the same time, it is the didactic methods themselves that largely determine the nature of that relationship. In designing the RE program, we have consciously regarded the client-helper relationship as a student-teacher relationship. We have tried to design teaching techniques to foster a strong, positive relationship. We have tried to design the relationship so that it provides the client fast, effective, and efficient learning. The successful learning, in turn, quickly makes the client independent of the need to further rely on the relationship to fulfill his psychosocial needs.

Thus, the teaching methods provide empathy and unconditional positive regard to the client insofar as the client needs it to have confidence and respect for the leader, himself, and the program. The teacher continues to apply such relationship-oriented methods whenever the need arises, through the technique of troubleshooting. However, from the start, RE teaching methods work toward giving the client the capacity to *win empathy and respect from other people by his own behaviors*. The teaching method seeks to train the person's intimates, and to have the client himself train his intimates, to provide him with empathy and unconditional positive regard. The techniques of *modeling, covert rehearsal, behavioral rehearsal, prompting,* and *reinforcement* are systematically employed as instructional methods. To these behavior modification techniques, the time-honored instructional methods of *structuring* and *demonstration* have been added. The technique of structuring, among other things, provides the client with the reasons underlying the

request that he adapt new behavior. Structuring is, of course, a direct attempt to alter cognition and the attitudes that underlie behavior.

In RE methodology, the format of instruction is flexible. One or more leaders may be used. Groups may vary in size from one or two people to reasonably large numbers. The time format, called the *time-designated approach*, is also flexible, and is meant to combine the best features of the "time-limited" and "open-ended" approaches that have been used traditionally in psychotherapy and marital and family therapy. The programatic features are also such that they lend themselves to a wide variety of ages, types of relationships, and settings.

The teaching program is a carefully graduated one in which the participants gradually are brought to levels of greater skill in increasingly emotional and complex undertakings, and in which they steadily learn to assume more self- and mutual responsibility for using and perfecting the skills and to rely less on the instructor or fellow participants to provide encouragement and supervision.

In describing our leadership methods, we have endeavored to indicate the circumstances under which each instructional technique is to be used—specifying which techniques are appropriate to what circumstances. We also have attempted to establish a developmental framework—providing the leader with a sense of the extent to which each instructional technique is to be used in each phase of the training as it progresses from the beginning to the end. Finally, we have attempted to define the teaching techniques in a manner specific enough to permit reliable codification by observers.

### Broader Implications

Most mental health theorists and practitioners have concentrated too much on developing theories and methods limited to a single perspective, failing even to try to combine elements from different philosophical and theoretical perspectives into one program, even when such an effect might create a more realistic and powerful program than any single perspective could provide. In trying consciously to combine the more humanistic,

relationship-oriented objectives and methods with the techniques derived not only from behavior modification but from pedagogy, we believe we are adding something to what is a growing trend: the recognition that no major theoretical position and no psychological technology has a claim on the full truth, yet that all probably have something valuable to contribute to the overall struggle toward reducing intrapsychic and interpersonal conflict and increasing personal satisfaction and social harmony.

By specifying very precisely those leadership and instructional techniques that are and that are not to be used in implementing the program, and by indicating how each of the techniques are to be used, we believe we also have helped to implement two additional mental health objectives.

First, if we are about to see an explosive proliferation of effective educational programs designed to help people shape their own life-styles, it would be highly desirable to have *research* that could effectively assess the value of such courses and eventually provide empirically based guidance to the public concerning which courses will best enable each individual to accomplish his particular objectives.[1]

---

[1] Research-based psychoeducational guidance should eventually become possible to offer assistance to individuals in selecting those courses that best meet their objectives. It is important that such guidance be based on sound research, because the effects of a given program may extend beyond the client's immediate purpose. For example, a Conjugal Relationship Enhancement program, or an eating-control program might easily improve a participant's self-concept, and an assertiveness training program might well relieve many people's tension headaches. Psychosocial guidance personnel should have such knowledge available to them to help individuals select appropriate courses.

Educational guidance could also be based on research that has demonstrated how varying kinds or degrees of interests, goals, aptitudes, complaints, and so on relate to goal achievement in various psychoeducational courses. Such types of research eventually would permit a guidance system in psychosocial education comparable in nature to the empirically based educational guidance available in college based on interest and aptitude tests. Such guidance procedures have, it seems to us, demonstrated stronger validity and utility than most clinical diagnostic procedures. It is equally pertinent that, as follows naturally from the educational model, such guidance counselors act as interpreters of data and as consultants to students, rather than as decision makers.

Sound research is all but impossible if one cannot define the methods one is using with some precision and thereby hold them relatively constant from leader to leader, client to client, group to group, and setting to setting. It is no accident that more sound research has emerged from Rogerian therapy and behavior modification approaches than from approaches in which the role of the helper was much less clearly defined. Having been encouraged by these precedents to be precise in defining the leader's role behavior, we believe other program designers will in turn be still further encouraged by our precision, thereby continuing the process of establishing a firm base on which to build research that assesses educationally oriented mental health programs.

Second, such specificity about leadership behaviors helps to make the method easier to teach, to learn, and to supervise. Ease of teaching and of learning to teach is especially important if one shares the view that we are in the early stages of a great proliferation of effective courses designed to teach people various ways of shaping their own personalities and patterns of interpersonal interaction. If we are to develop a corps of people who are well trained to deliver such programs, the instructional methods on which their effectiveness rests must be easy to identify and thus easier to master. We believe we have made a contribution toward this goal because each program that does provide such specificity encourages other program designers to do likewise.

Moreover, the specificity of leadership skills in the RE method is high enough to permit not only the training of paraprofessionals, but the training of one client to help train another, one family member to train another family member, and, in nonfamily settings, peers to train each other.

Thus, the method contains within itself the means of its own proliferation. The use of paraprofessionals is one level of revolutionary change in the mental health movement. Person-to-person training is explicitly incorporated in the facilitator mode of RE programs. This may contain the seed of a revolution, even broader than the paraprofessional revolution. The "each one teach one" model has helped whole populations in certain

countries to learn to read quickly within one generation. Why not attempt to eliminate mass psychosocial illiteracy the same way?

## The Basic Skills

Four modes of behavior—sets of skills based on specified attitudes or rationales—are taught to the participants. Two of these modes involve cognition and communication skills. The other two involve using the first two not only in the training program but outside of it, in day-to-day interactions. Within and outside of the RE sessions, the skills can be used to resolve conflicts, to solve problems, and to increase individual and mutual satisfaction, fulfillment, and productivity.

The *expresser mode* is designed to help an individual be more conscious of and alert to his own feelings and desires and his expectations and wishes with respect to the behavior of others. It helps him to be more realistic in a number of ways: It helps him to recognize that the judgments he makes about the behavior, character, and motivations of himself and of others are based on his own internalized norms and values, rather than on inherent goodness or badness, appropriateness or inappropriateness. It helps him to link his conclusions more firmly to specific observed events, and thus to avoid overgeneralizations. It encourages him to check his own perceptions against the perceptions of others. Adherence to the requirement that every significant statement be made from an explicitly subjective stance guarantees the expresser that he will be the world's leading authority on everything he says. This can eliminate countless inevitable arguments that might otherwise significantly reduce or destroy chances of improving the relationship or resolving conflict.

In addition to helping him to be more sensitive to his emotions and desires, to be more realistic in his thought processes, and to avoid much needless controversy, the expresser mode simultaneously helps the individual to communicate his ideas, perceptions, feelings, and conclusions in such a way as to decrease the probability that others will respond to

his statements with hostility and defensiveness. This in turn makes it more likely that they will get a better grasp of his wants and perceptions and will be more likely to respond to them in a helpful and constructive way. For these reasons, and because the expresser mode encourages the individual to be specific about his interpersonal wishes and empathic in his communication of them, the expresser mode greatly facilitates the individual's ability to resolve conflict and increase pleasure in his interactions with others.

As the expresser learns his skills well, he can expect more favorable responses from those with whom he communicates. Over time, the more favorable the responses he receives from others, the less likely he is to store up his grievances and the more likely he is to raise issues directly, immediately, and constructively. And the more he can do that, the less likely he is to initiate conflicts explosively or to exacerbate matters by bringing in irrelevances and pseudoissues.

The *empathic responder mode* is based in large measure on the behaviors (and their underlying attitudes) of the traditional Rogerian psychotherapist. When adopting this mode, the participant endeavors to show unconditional positive regard to the person with whom he is interacting. He momentarily suspends all of his own ideas and feelings, especially judgmental ones, and endeavors to enter, with all the sympathy he can muster, the phenomenological world of the other person, in order to see and experience the world and emotions as the other does. He then conveys his empathic, compassionate understanding to the other person.

Sensitivity to the feelings of the other person is especially important, because such sensitivity is a sure sign that there has been empathic understanding. The avoidance of interpretations or anything else that may threaten the other person's self-perception is critical, because criticism conveys a lack of empathic understanding. Both positive and negative judgments are to be avoided; even positive judgments connote the idea that what the person says is being evaluated, and, once evaluation is perceived to be taking place, the person is put on his guard. Guardedness decreases openness and honesty with oneself and

others. Repetitious phrases such as "I hear you saying" are to be avoided as artificial and mechanical, and thus as detrimental to conveying empathy. Requests for information are to be avoided because they may easily be used to make points that the responder rather than the expresser wishes to make and that may not convey empathic understanding. Such requests generally divert the expresser from following his own thoughts more deeply. Requests for information convey to the expresser that the empathic responder is not completely with him, but is pursuing his own tangents.

All aspects of the empathic responder mode are directed toward one end: *complete acceptance of the other as a valued person.* Each of the components of the mode (including clarification of feelings) is important mainly not in itself, but rather as it contributes toward this end.

The empathic responder mode is designed to accomplish the same things for its recipient, the expresser, as the client-centered therapist seeks for clients: enhancement of the self-concept of the expresser; an increase in the expresser's self-awareness and sensitivity to feelings; more intimate, self-revealing communication toward the empathic responder; and increased expresser self-acceptance and confidence. When these changes are achieved, the expresser is able to gain deeper understanding of his own reactions and wishes with respect to relationship issues, conflicts, and possible alternatives available to resolve conflicts and enhance pleasure. When the expresser receives empathic understanding to a statement, he is more likely to dig progressively deeper toward the root causes of those things that disturb him or that would maximize his satisfactions, instead of using defensive maneuvers or raising tangential issues. Moreover, once the expresser comes to *anticipate* that his statements will be responded to with empathic acceptance, he will be more and more likely to face his true wishes, or to recognize his sources of dissatisfaction early and communicate them quickly. By so doing, he is more likely to avoid transferring negative feelings from their real source to pseudoissues, avoid resenting others for not responding to unstated desires, and, in general, is likely to get more satisfaction out of relationships and life.

We have also added some guidelines especially pertinent to relationships that are consonant with, but that did not specifically derive from, the role of the traditional client-centered therapist. The empathic responder is trained to include in his empathic response, whenever appropriate, certain aspects of the expresser's statements that, although they must be part of the expresser's phenomenological field, may be implicit rather than explicit in any way. One of these is the *interpersonal message*: The responder is asked always to be alert to *the expresser's wish that he, the responder, would behave toward the expresser in a certain way.* This part of the empathic responder's role prescription is designed to be helpful in more quickly clarifying interpersonal problems and simultaneously begin the process of generating ideas (the wished-for behaviors) that are potential solutions to problems, or that are otherwise pleasure enhancing. There is another major aspect of the expresser's statement that often remains implicit and that the responder is asked to look for and (provided it is within the expresser's phenomenological field) to make explicit in his empathic response. We refer to the *positive aspect* that so often lies on the other side of the coin in a statement of anger, frustration, or complaint. By making such positive wishes, expectations, or feelings explicit, the empathic responder can (in addition to often providing proof of the responder's deep empathy and acceptance) move the problem or conflict much more rapidly toward resolution by removing much anger and defensiveness from the exchange.

The empathic responder mode also is designed to accomplish certain things for the responder himself. The empathic responder mode acts to increase the intensity of the responder's concentration on, and thus his capacity to understand, the communication of his partner on both cognitive and affective levels. It promotes his ability to gain a perspective on issues that goes beyond his own. The empathic responder learns to look for the positive features of the relationship that may underly what otherwise would seem to be solely accusations or attacks. The empathic responder mode also alerts the responder to possible specific courses of action on his part that might enhance the

relationship or solve problems. Finally, by stating his understanding of the expresser's feelings and perceptions, the empathic responder sets the stage for receiving feedback on the accuracy of his understanding.

The technique of *mode switching* is a set of skills taught to the participants to enable each of them to use expressive and empathic skills in a free-flowing dialog, while nevertheless maintaining some assurance that: (1) each person's point of view is likely to be well understood and viewed as sympathetically as it can be under the circumstances; (2) the responder will not have to deny himself the opportunity to express his own point of view for more than a very brief while; (3) suggestions for problem solution will not emerge prematurely—that is, before each person has a chance to understand fully his own perceptions, feelings, and wishes, and those of the other; (4) specific, behaviorally oriented suggestions for enhancing the relationship will be forthcoming as soon as such understanding is reached; (5) these suggestions will be ones that are based on full mutual understanding; and (6) these suggestions also will be considered within the same type of constructive framework as has just been described.

The *facilitator mode* is a set of teaching skills described in general terms in the preceding section on leadership. The client is taught to use the same skills in the same fashion as the leader does. He thus serves as an assistant teacher or leader for others within group RE sessions. He uses these facilitator skills at home to help the people who have been trained with him to generalize skills into the home and, wherever it is important, to use them faithfully and consistently. Eventually, it is theoretically possible for him gradually to introduce still other significant persons in his environment to the benefits of those skills, encourage their use and help them to become proficient in their use. The teaching skills are taught to RE program participants in the same manner as those skills prescribe—structuring, demonstrating, modeling, covert rehearsal, behavioral rehearsal, prompting (encouragement), and reinforcement. As always, intensive specific feedback is provided to participants as they attempt to master the skills.

*Broader Implications*

The *generalization and maintenance* of RE skills is regarded as an integral part of skill acquisition. Only after a high-
enough level of skill is attained, and a sufficient apperceptive
mass of satisfaction from using the skills in everyday life has
been reached, does the use of any skill become habitual. Thus,
homework assignments of various kinds are systematically included in the program to encourage generalization into everyday life. Supervision of this homework is designed to improve
and to reinforce generalization and maintenance of skills. Also,
when clients encounter difficulty in applying the skills in their
everyday life, role playing is used in the session to improve the
participants' ability to use the skills in a variety of challenging
situations.

We believe that RE skills are powerful tools to aid people
in rational thinking, communication, problem solving, conflict
resolution, self-development, relationship enrichment, and work
productivity. They contain within themselves the ingredients
for self-perpetuation and propagation. In this book, we have
concentrated mainly on their application to certain family-
related subunits. Within this context, we believe that RE has
greater potential (especially considering its multifaceted purposes, which include prevention and enrichment) than do traditional therapeutic methods for strengthening the family and
promoting socioemotional vigor and satisfaction among the general populace. We also have pointed out the implications of
their use in a variety of other settings—elementary schools, high
schools, business, industry, and indeed any institution in which
people must relate personally to one another and wherein different viewpoints might exist about goal setting or the best
means by which to implement common goals. In effect, this
means every institutional setting.

Thus, we see RE methods, even alone, as having the potential for significant beneficial impact on the way families and
institutions now function and, should the young receive such
skills training, on the general relationship patterns of the next
generation. However, if RE methods were the only program and
the only set of skills available, it is unlikely that this potential

would ever be realized. Fortunately, there are other skills and other skill-training programs that could be used to accomplish similar and additional objectives. The design and successful implementation of each psychosocial skill-training program encourages the design and successful implementation of other skill-training programs. In considering the broader implications of RE methods and programs, we must consider it as a part of what we see as the revolutionary replacement of the clinical medical model by the socioemotional education model. However, before we can consider implications on this broader scale, in discussing the School for Living, it is desirable to summarize and consider the broader implications of the research that has been done on RE programs.

## Research

For this volume, we have reported studies evaluating the efficacy of RE methods. These studies meet high standards of scientific methodology relative to most research that assesses the efficacy of therapeutic methods. Relatively large numbers of subjects have been used, no-treatment control (or own-control) groups have been used, and subjects have been assigned to groups randomly. Efficacy of the RE programs has been assessed with both behavioral and self-report measures. In some instances, the subjects were not aware that their behavior was being evaluated. Variables have been studied to assess both the specific skills taught in the programs, and more general variables such as communication patterns, trust, harmony, satisfaction, and problem solving. With considerable uniformity, the studies have shown that participation in the RE programs has led to significant improvement on communication, problem-solving, and relationship variables. One study that examined self-concept provided some evidence that this variable, too, could be favorably influenced by an RE approach.

### Recent Research

We will now go beyond summarizing to report briefly on some pertinent recent research. All the research previously

reported in this volume dealt with RE in a format of weekly sessions lasting approximately two hours per session, and thus did not address the question of whether the methods were applicable in other time formats. However, there has also been a major piece of research assessing the efficacy of the marathon, or Intensive Relationship Enhancement Program (IREP) format. This format was described in an earlier chapter. The research has been reported in detail elsewhere (Rappaport, 1976), and we will here summarize it only briefly. The research employed an own-control design: The twenty participating married couples were tested, waited two months, were tested again just prior to beginning the two-month, four-session IREP, and were tested a third time just after completing the program. The hypotheses that IREP would result in various kinds of relationship improvement were tested by comparing the change over the waiting period with the comparable period extending over the course of treatment.

In the following summary, the measures used (all of which are described in the appendices of this book) and the probability levels associated with the testing of each hypothesis will be indicated in parentheses.

All of the hypotheses in the study were confirmed. (It should be borne in mind, of course, that the hypotheses involve intercorrelated variables and measures.) It was found that the IREP participants in the treatment period learned to express themselves more appropriately to their partners (SFAS, $p <$ .001); learned to respond more empathically to their partner (AOS, $p < .001$); experienced greater improvement in marital adjustment (MAT, $p < .01$); experienced a greater improvement in marital harmony (FLQ, $p < .001$); showed greater improvement in their general pattern of marital communication (MCI, $p < .001$); demonstrated greater gains in trust and intimacy (IRS, $p < .001$); showed greater improvement in their overall relationship pattern (RCS, $p < .001$); showed greater improvement in their satisfaction with their relationships (SCS, $p < .001$); and showed greater improvement in their ability to resolve relationship problems satisfactorily (MPCS, $p < .001$).

These research findings indicate that the marathon or

IREP format was quite successful in improving the marriage relationships of the participants.

In the research previously reported in this volume, one major shortcoming was that the control groups used did not rule out the possibility that placebo effects, Hawthorne effects, thank you effects, and the like were responsible for positive results. A more recent study (Harrell and Guerney, 1976) involved approximately the same number and types of married couples as were used in the Rappaport and Collins studies. The setting, length, leadership, and all other features of the experimental group (which was trained in negotiation skills) were nearly identical to those of the RE studies and would be expected to yield equally strong placebo, Hawthorne, and thank you effects. Yet on measures similar to those used in the RE studies reported here, no significant improvement over the control group was found on general marital adjustment variables. This very strongly suggests that it was the specific nature of the RE program, and not program-extraneous or generic factors such as thank you effects that were responsible for the significant improvement found in the studies reported here.

In another recent study (Coufal, 1975), a direct comparison was made between the RE Parent Adolescent Relationship Development program (this time with mothers and daughters, rather than fathers and sons) and an alternate program. The attempt was made to equate the nature and potency of the two methods in every way possible except that the alternate method used discussion techniques in the place of the skill training that is the essence of the RE programs. A no-treatment control group also was included. Subjects were assigned randomly to the three groups. On measures very similar to the ones used in the studies reported in this volume, the results were generally as predicted. The treatment group relying on discussion methods was superior to the no-treatment group, and the RE group showed significantly more improvement than both the other groups. Therefore, by inference again, the view that factors extraneous to RE methodology by itself might account for the positive results reported in this book seems to be untenable.

Another deficiency in the research reported in the pres-

ent volume is that it includes no follow-up results. The question of how durable the positive effects of RE programs are remained empirically unanswered in these studies, although there was much qualitative verbal feedback from families to indicate that the effects endured over time. This deficiency has been corrected by two more recent well-controlled studies. A study by Wieman (1973) with married couples showed that the effects of RE treatment maintained their strength in the follow-up testing ten weeks after termination. In addition, a follow-up study by Vogelsong (1975b) to the Coufal study mentioned above showed that after six months, the discussion group tended to revert to pretreatment levels and was no better than the no-treatment group, whereas the specific skills and the improvement in communication and relationship patterns of the RE participants remained at significantly better levels in comparison to their own pretreatment levels and in comparison to both of the other groups.

Another deficiency in the studies reported in this volume was that the clients were mainly middle class. The Coufal and Vogelsong studies were obtained in a sample that included a large population of rural, lower-class individuals. The very positive results obtained in these studies indicated that the value of RE is not limited to middle-class persons.

### Broader Implications

We are not aware of any other family-oriented treatment program that provides a body of such large-sample, carefully controlled, and comprehensive evidence of effectiveness as exists for the RE method. Of course, this first of all is due to the potency of the method. But we believe there is more to it than that alone. We believe it has been possible for us to build this kind of evidence because of the research advantages afforded by the *educational model*.

Offering psychotherapeutic help in the form of a skills-training course affords significant advantages. First of all, one can deal with a standard content delivered in a specified manner. One can easily describe what one does so that others will

know what the treatment is, and can replicate it if they wish. Second, the researcher can deal with large numbers. In following the educational model, the practitioner and researcher can periodically offer courses designed to accomplish certain objectives (for example, elimination of fear, cessation of compulsions, attaining orgasms, enhancing relationships, or whatever). He can make the availability of such courses known through mass media or course catalogs. Instead of waiting for clients to come one at a time, they come in large numbers, practically self-organized into groups that share a specific objective. Thus, the researcher gains easier control over the assignment of subjects to wait-control groups or to an alternate treatment program.

Another great advantage to mental health research that derives from the use of an educational model is the vastly increased specificity of the criteria to be used for evaluation, without restricting them to a narrow range. One great nemesis of traditional psychotherapy research has been the inability of researchers to find viable criteria for evaluation. When you are planning to *teach* something, you must have a pretty clear conception of what you want the student to know, or in the case of psychosocial assessment, not only what you want him to know, but how you want him to be able to perform in a given type of situation after he has learned. Therefore, *any* course designed to teach new behavioral abilities almost simultaneously designs its own criteria and its own methods of assessing their achievement. The evaluation of most such courses could include measures of cognitive and attitudinal changes measured by paper-and-pencil tests. Gains from most psychosocial courses also could be measured more in the manner that one might judge students' performance in laboratory courses (behavioral adequacy) as well. An example of one such set of "laboratory" criteria for a course in interpersonal relationship enhancement might be, for example, an increased ability to state clearly one's feelings and desires in: (1) a role playing or conflict situation; (2) a genuine conflict situation in the classroom setting; and (3) a conflict outside of the class. The last type presents some practical difficulties. (Generalization to the outside world

is generally simply assumed in established cognitive educational courses.) Such performance can be assessed, however, with just a bit more difficulty than exists in assessing the laboratory performance of a student in biology or chemistry at the subsequent place of employment rather than at school.

In short, as good psychosocial courses are designed, we expect good criteria and sound methods of psychological assessment to follow more or less naturally in their wake. The result may be a revolution in the values of personality *assessment* every bit as heuristic, exciting, and advantageous as the revolution in the provision of psychosocial services itself. When courses are designed to teach people to perform in certain ways, test builders will have specific behavioral targets against which to validate and refine their tests. Then, in turn, these tests will help us build more useful courses. It is a two-way process.

In fact, psychological research *in general* has much to gain from broad-scale application of the educational model. It is true that too much research and therefore too much theory is based on the white rat and the college sophomore, and that too much personality-change (that is, therapy) research is based on the middle and upper classes. One of the great potential advantages of the educational model is that it can bring great numbers of willing subjects of a wide variety of ages and social background into the ken of the researcher and the theorists of personality and personality change. The eventual result should be much more valid personality research and theory development.

## The School For Living

The model of mass psychosocial education we advocate is one that seeks to identify the kinds of interpersonal knowledge, emotional skill, and social skill that are necessary to successful functioning in a rapidly changing society; and then seeks to develop effective, efficient, and economical ways of making such knowledge and skill available to as many people as possible.

We believe that now, for the first time, psychosocial knowledge and psychosocial teaching technology (some may

prefer to call it *psychotherapeutic methods*) have reached a stage of sophistication that makes it feasible to offer the general public a real opportunity to acquire much useful information and many valuable life skills to aid realistic perception; rational thinking; sensible ways of dealing with emotions and with other people; ways of eliminating or reducing the harmful effects of many conflicts, frustrations, and derogations of self and others; and ways of increasing individual fulfillment and interpersonal harmony.

Social and psychological scientists and practitioners have now accumulated enough knowledge, and have become sophisticated enough in changing intellectual, emotional, and behavioral patterns, to proceed in accord with the mass educational model. They can, as a result of years of individually oriented practice, identify those psychoemotional problems, goals, and values that are shared by very broad segments of the public. They can identify attitudes, habits of thinking, ways of reacting to one's emotions, ways of validating one's perceptions, ways of sorting values, ways of solving problems, ways of acquiring desired habits and breaking unwanted habits, ways of reducing fears, ways of building courage that nearly everyone would want to know and use. A given set of skills—for example, RE skills; conversational skills (see Goldstein, Sprafkin, and Gershaw, 1976); assertiveness skills (see Smith, 1975); fair fighting (see Bach and Wyden, 1969); more (or less) control over emotions; methods of eating, smoking, or drinking less; having less (or more) sexual inhibition; diminishing fear of flying in planes, public speaking, or whatever—can be organized into a programatic course of cognitive, attitudinal, behavioral instruction and presented to the public on a mass scale. The programatic nature of such service permits the training of instructors in a relatively short time. It permits the development of training aids such as tests, audio- and videotapes, and films. It permits wider use of paraprofessionals, peers, and other volunteers to help in the teaching process.

The educational model would do even more than make available to the general public efficient, effective help in achieving their psychosocial goals. By removing the *stigma* that has so

long been associated with the medical model approach to psychosocial problems, it can free the public from their inhibitions about availing themselves of such help. "Sickness" and "treatment" have almost always been stigmatic, while "accomplishment" and "education" have almost always been regarded as desirable. The imaginary dichotomy between "neurotic" or "maladjusted" people on the one hand and "normal" or "healthy" people on the other is a wall, constructed by followers of the medical model, that has made people avoid psychosocial services. The more psychosocial skill-training courses there are, and the more people begin to avail themselves of them, the more such services will be looked on like any other instructional service—like lessons in foreign language, tennis, dancing, pottery, photography, or whatever—and the more people will avail themselves freely of such programs. This change in the delivery system of psychosocial services, and public responsiveness, has already begun, and it may not be long before taking psychosocial courses becomes a mark of intelligence, sophistication and prestige rather than the mark of shame and defeat that it has hitherto been when it was called *therapy*.[2]

Some components of psychosocial education can be absorbed into the existing cognitive educational system at all levels from preschool through college. Some will doubtless become the work of other existing types of institutions, such as mental health centers. The incorporation of psychosocial

---

[2] Of course, the use of the educational model in no way prevents professionals from giving service to individuals singly. The educational model clearly contains within it the *tutorial* model. Mass educational techniques in other areas have not eliminated those people who prefer to take private lessons, nor those instructors who prefer to work with individuals singly. Personal tutelage exists side by side with mass education in every area of instruction. In fact, the availability of mass instruction so broadens demand that there will probably be more demand for private tutelage among those who can afford it than exists today. Also, especially in small communities, there probably will always be some psychological and interpersonal problems and desires that fall between the boards of what can be offered in organized courses of instruction and that will call for individualized instruction.

courses into both traditional and nontraditional educational settings has already begun. What we will discuss here, however, is the pure institutional form to which the educational model could give birth. Such an institution would be an educational resource for those who wanted to be more successful in shaping their personalities and behaviors to accord with their ideals for themselves. Such an institution would develop unhampered by built-in restraints of the politics and tradition of already existing institutions. It would be, in effect, a School for Living. What form might such an institution take? How might it be formed? Who would be the students? What kinds of courses and programs might it offer? Who would make use of it?

### Form and Financing

A School for Living could have a single physical location and be set up like any other training institution. A fixed facility would have the advantage of making use of teaching aids for training both students and future instructors: one-way vision mirrors, audio- and videotaping, film screens and projectors, library, and so on. But a School for Living could also be a *school-without-walls,* with a staff that takes its programs out into the community, traveling to meet people on their home grounds, at clubs or churches, organizations, interest groups of various kinds, and business and industrial organizations. It could offer specific training programs in widespread communities on a periodic basis, much as (in the cognitive domain) speed-reading courses are now offered. Or the School for Living, like many colleges, could be a combination of these two forms: a school with a fixed location that also offers an "extension" program that reaches a wide geographical area.

Such an institution conceivably could be supported by instructional fees alone. Ideally, it could be supported by a prepayment plan. It could be supported by a forward-looking industry or labor organization. Or, like many other public service agencies, it could be supported by a mix of local and federal tax dollars, private donations, and fees for service.

*Students*

We see such a school as useful to students across the entire life span: Infants would be beneficiaries, one step removed, of courses designed to help their parents to care better for them in terms of their emotional development; those whose age makes facing death a problem of living could benefit from preparation in meeting their final challenge. Appropriate courses could be designed to aid people with the broadest range of assets and liabilities: those who are emotionally or intellectually impoverished—the depressed and retarded, for example—as well as those who have strong emotional and intellectual resources, but who wish to make still greater use of them in accomplishing their personal and interpersonal objectives.

*Types of Programs*

All of the programs envisaged for the School for Living involve cognition, behavior, and values or attitudes in varying degrees. All courses would deal in emotions, with intrapersonal and interpersonal processes, and with change of one kind or another. At least three general areas or types of programs can be envisaged. One type would center around preparing for change, another around coping with change, and a third around creating change.

*Preparing for change.* Programs that prepared for change would teach people about developmental processes across the life span and about what to expect when a certain change takes place in one's life circumstances. An example would be a course for expectant parents. What behavior can a mother expect in her infant from birth to six months? What intellectual and emotional processes are taking place during that time? What influence does the mother's behavior have on these processes? As always, skill training is of the essence; therefore, *what* can the parent *do* to bring about favorable development? Still closer to the central feature of courses in the School for Living is the question of precisely *how* the parent goes about doing this. As

always, demonstration, modeling, and behavior *practice* with instructor feedback, not book learning, would be the major feature of such a program. Similar parent programs could be devised regarding the second six months of life, the first, second, third, fourth, and fifth years, the early school years, and so on. More understanding today about typical stages of adult development such as retirement make such courses applicable in preparing adults for changes throughout the entire life span.

*Coping with change.* Courses centered on coping with change would deal with such topics as How can one deal with grief? With divorce? With widowhood? With retirement? With one's own or another's failure—for example, in school? With failure or change in vocation?

*Creating change.* Courses focused on creating change would teach people how to achieve their personal and interpersonal ambitions: eating less (or more); falling asleep quickly; making do with less sleep; being able to relax; eliminating compulsions; establishing better work or study habits; being more assertive, more cooperative or altruistic, more loving, less hostile, less depressed, and less anxious; acquiring courage (that is, eliminating fears of one kind or another); refraining from alcohol or from other drugs; more sexual control of one kind or another; less sexual inhibition of one kind or another; reorientation of one's sexual preferences; enhancing one's self-esteem; acquiring leadership skills; and so on. Many such courses already exist; many more are in the process of being developed; still others have yet to be developed, although much of the knowledge exists for developing them; and still others probably require much more experience and research before effective courses can be developed. We believe, however, that the skill-training route offers the best potential for helping bring change in all areas of personal growth.

*A beginning.* Centers that offer life education through skill training are beginning to spring up throughout the country. The only one we know of that has aspirations of eventually covering all of these kinds of programs and of being national in scope, is one with which the author is closely associated. It is

the Institute for the Development of Emotional and Life Skills (IDEALS), a nonprofit, tax-exempt educational corporation.

The most immediate objective of IDEALS is to train professionals to administer specific psychosocial skill-training programs of all varieties. In addition to providing training through its own staff, its goal is to bring together under its auspices professionals who have developed, or who have experience in administering, specific skill-training programs with other professionals who want to learn how to use those methods. We hope that this will represent a beginning, not of the educational-model revolution (which is *already* well under way) but of its transformation into the *standard* way of providing psychosocial services.[3]

[3]For information regarding training and certification in Relationship Enhancement and other educational programs, contact IDEALS, P.O. Box 391, State College, PA 16801.

# Appendix:
# Inventories, Tests,
# Questionnaires, and Scales

ᵂᵂᵂᵂᵂᵂᵂᵂᵂ

## A: The Primary Communication Inventory (PCI)

The Primary Communication Inventory or PCI (Locke, Sabagh, and Thomas, 1956) was first used in a study of two aspects of interaction between husbands and wives (primary communication and empathy) and the relationship of these to marital adjustment. Primary communication was defined as the exchange of symbols, including words and gestures, in an intimate, free-flowing, and unrestricted manner.

Samples of the twenty-five questions are: "Do you and your spouse talk about things in which you are both interested?" "Do you and your spouse avoid subjects in conversation?" and "Do you understand the meaning of your spouse's facial expressions?" Possible answers are: "very frequently," "frequently," "occasionally," "seldom," and "never." The items are weighted from 1 to 5, yielding a scoring range of 25 to 125. The higher the score, the better the communication.

Ely (1970) obtained high test-retest reliability ($r = .86$) with an eight-week interval. With such a long interval, this should be considered a minimal estimate of test-retest reliability.

Studies by Navran, Ely, Schlein, and Collins afford evidence of the construct validity of the PCI. Navran (1967), using the Marital Relationship Inventory (MRI) and the PCI, obtained a significant difference ($p < .001$) between a group of twenty-four happily married and a group of twenty-four unhappily married couples. Ely (1970) found the PCI to be sensitive to changes resulting from conjugal therapy. Schlein (1971), using a slightly modified form of the PCI with ninety-six premarital subjects, found significant Pearson Product Moment correlations with the Premarital Communication Inventory (.40, $p < .001$), the Interpersonal Relationship Scale (.55, $p < .001$), the Relationship Scale—Self (.51, $p < .001$), and the Relationship Scale—Partner (.49, $p < .001$). Collins (1971), in the study reported earlier in this book, found correlations between the PCI and the Marital Communication Inventory (.69, $p < .001$), the Marital Adjustment Test (.63, $p < .001$), and the Family Life Questionnaire (.66, $p < .001$).

## B: The Marital Communication Inventory (MCI)

The Marital Communication Inventory or MCI (Bienvenu, 1970) was developed to give spouses a better insight into the degree and patterns of communication in their marriage. The inventory consists of forty-six questions concerning perceptions of different family functions. There are different forms for husbands and wives. Examples of questions are (for the wife): "Does he discuss his work and interests with you?" "Does he pay you compliments and say nice things to you?" and "Does he confide in others rather than in you?" The possible answers are: "usually," "sometimes," "seldom," and "never." Higher scores indicate better communication.

Using the Spearman-Brown Correction formula with sixty subjects, Bienvenu reported a split-half correlation coefficient of .93. In the study summarized in this book, Rappaport (1976) found a Pearson Product Moment test-retest correlation of .94 ($N = 40$) between the prewait scores and postwait scores two months later.

Bienvenu also reports some validity evidence: A group of

couples without apparent marital difficulties had significantly higher scores on the MCI ($p < .01$) than a group of couples receiving counseling for marital problems.

The 1971 study by Collins, described in this book, provides evidence of construct validity for the MCI by confirming hypothesized differences in his experiment via the MCI. Collins' study afforded further evidence of validity in that the MCI correlated with measures of communication, adjustment, and harmony in married life. With ninety married subjects, there were significant Pearson Product Moment correlations between the MCI and the Primary Communication Inventory (.69, $p < .001$); the Marital Adjustment Test (.70, $p < .001$); and the Family Life Questionnaire—Conjugal (.78, $p < .001$).

## C: The Marital Adjustment Test (MAT)

The Marital Adjustment Test or MAT (Locke and Williamson, 1958) consists of twenty-two items divided into five areas relating to marital adjustment. These areas are companionship, consensus or agreement, affectional intimacy, satisfaction with mate, and sexual behavior. Some of the questions are: (1) "Do you and your mate agree on aims, goals, and things believed important in life?" (consensus or agreement); (2) "How frequently do you and your mate get on each other's nerves around the house?" (affectional intimacy); and (3) "Do you and your mate agree on sex relations?" (sexual behavior). The choice of answers differs with different questions. The maximum score is 120 and the minimum is 49. There is one form for both husbands and wives.

The reliability for this specific form of the test was not stated by the authors. But reliability for a similar scale, computed by the split-half technique and corrected by the Spearman-Brown formula, was estimated at .90. Rappaport (1976), in the study summarized earlier in this book, found a Pearson Product Moment correlation of .75 ($N = 40$) between the prewait and the postwait scores obtained two months later. Considering the long interval, this should be considered a minimal estimate of test-retest reliability.

Although no validity studies of this form of the test were mentioned by the authors, Locke, Sabagh, and Thomas (1956) found a significant positive correlation ($p < .01$) between primary communication and marital adjustment as measured respectively by the PCI and a forerunner of the MAT. Hobart and Klausner (1959), while studying the relationships among marital adjustment, communication, and empathy, obtained the expected results on the MAT, which contributes evidence of the test's validity. Collins (1971) found significant Pearson Product Moment correlations between the MAT and measures of marital communication and of marital harmony. The MAT correlated .70 ($p < .001$) with the Marital Communication Inventory, .63 ($p < .001$) with the Primary Communication Inventory, and .78 with the Family Life Questionnaire ($p < .001$). Finally, the confirmation of hypotheses by Collins (1971) and Rappaport (1976) via the MAT in the studies summarized in this book provide evidence of the construct validity of the MAT.

## D: The Family Life Questionnaire (FLQ)

.The Family Life Questionnaire (FLQ) was devised by Bernard Guerney, Jr., as a measure of harmony and satisfaction in family life. It was devised to fill the need for a measure of gains in family therapy through an instrument that could be completed by all the (literate) members of a family, thereby providing comparable assessments from all family members on a single measure. However, it has not yet been used in empirical studies of family therapy in itself. Rather, it has been adapted to make three forms appropriate for three specific dyadic relationships: married couples, fathers and sons, and mothers and daughters. The first, or married couples form, is called the Family Life Questionnaire—Conjugal (FLQ-C). The second is called the Family Life Questionnaire—Father, Son (FLQ-FS) and the third, the Family Life Questionnaire—Mother, Daughter (FLQ-MD). The latter two are identical except for changing *father* and *son* wherever they appear to *mother* and *daughter*. (The FLQ-MD is not used in the studies reported in this book, but is mentioned here because it has been useful in evaluating

other relationship enhancement programs and, in fact, is being used currently in such research.)

The FLQ has twenty-four items and the scores range from 24 to 96. Higher scores indicate more harmony in the relationship.

The Family Life Questionnaire is reproduced below with certain phrases in parentheses to indicate the parts that are interchanged to produce alternate forms in the following order: Family, Conjugal, and Father-Son. A single format can be used for each of the three forms of the test. To accomplish this in the father-son (or mother-daughter) form, the word *son* (or *daughter*) is placed in parentheses after the word *father* (or *mother*) except where the word *and* appears between the two words.

The FLQ is scored as follows: $Y = 4$, $y = 3$, $n = 2$, and $N = 1$ for items 1, 4, 5, 6, 11, 14, 15, 16, 20, 23, and 24. For the remaining thirteen items, $Y = 1$, $y = 2$, $n = 3$, and $N = 4$.

*Family Life Questionnaire*

NAME _____ DATE _____

This is a questionnaire about how you and your family (spouse; father; son) get along together. There are four possible responses to each of the questions. You may answer:

| Y | y | n | N |
|---|---|---|---|
| "YES," strongly agree | "Yes," mildly agree, or "yes," but not so sure | "No," mildly disagree, or "no," not so sure | "NO," strongly disagree |

Put a circle around the letter that shows your feelings. Your feelings may have been different in the past, and may be different later, but we are interested in your feelings right now, at this point in time.

Be sure to put a circle around *one* response for *each* question. Do not spend too much time on any one question. Please answer frankly and honestly.

Remember always to include yourself as part of the family (pair) when thinking of "one of us."

| | YES | yes | no | NO |
|---|:---:|:---:|:---:|:---:|
| 1. It's easy to laugh and have fun when we are together. | Y | y | n | N |
| 2. At least one of us gets angry about very unimportant things. | Y | y | n | N |
| 3. At least one of us doesn't enjoy life enough because he or she is too busy doing what other people want or expect. | Y | y | n | N |
| 4. Except for the kids too young to go to school, there's very little crying that goes on in our house. | Y | y | n | N |
| 5. We are more relaxed when we're together than most families (couples; fathers and sons) I know. | Y | y | n | N |
| 6. At least one of us often says very nice things about others in the family (the other). | Y | y | n | N |
| 7. At least one of us gets things his or her own way too much. | Y | y | n | N |
| 8. At least one person in the family (of us) is picked on too much. | Y | y | n | N |
| 9. Most of the time somebody is arguing with somebody else in our family (one of us is arguing with the other). | Y | y | n | N |
| 10. I don't expect other members of my family (my spouse; father; son) to ever understand the way I feel about certain things. | Y | y | n | N |
| 11. All things considered, I doubt if there are many families (couples; fathers and sons) that are as happy with each other as we are. | Y | y | n | N |

|                                                                                                                                              | YES | yes | no | NO |
|----------------------------------------------------------------------------------------------------------------------------------------------|-----|-----|----|----|
| 12. I have some feelings that I don't want anyone in the family (my spouse; father; son) to know about.                                       | Y   | y   | n  | N  |
| 13. One of us is always criticizing or correcting another (the other).                                                                       | Y   | y   | n  | N  |
| 14. When I've been away from my family (spouse; father; son) most of the day, I feel very good about getting back home.                       | Y   | y   | n  | N  |
| 15. We (my spouse; father, son and I) usually have a pleasant time during supper at our house.                                               | Y   | y   | n  | N  |
| 16. There is very little lying done by anyone in our family (either of us).                                                                   | Y   | y   | n  | N  |
| 17. At least one of us wants other people to do things for him or her too much of the time.                                                   | Y   | y   | n  | N  |
| 18. We find it hard to agree on things to do together.                                                                                        | Y   | y   | n  | N  |
| 19. At least one of us can't stand being criticized even when he or she is wrong.                                                             | Y   | y   | n  | N  |
| 20. I really enjoy being with my family (spouse; father; son) most of the time.                                                              | Y   | y   | n  | N  |
| 21. We should be more like another family (couple; father and son) I know.                                                                    | Y   | y   | n  | N  |
| 22. At least one of us often says things that hurt the feelings of another.                                                                   | Y   | y   | n  | N  |
| 23. Whatever kind of trouble I might be having, I feel I can tell one person or another in my family (my spouse; father; son) about it.       | Y   | y   | n  | N  |
| 24. All in all, we are very nice to each other.                                                                                              | Y   | y   | n  | N  |

Reliability of the FLQ-C was assessed, using twenty-two

married subjects, in a study by Ely (1970) who found a test-retest reliability correlation coefficient of .61. Because of the long time interval (eight weeks) between the two tests, this should be considered a minimal estimate of test-retest reliability. In the study by Rappaport (1976) summarized in this book, test-retest reliability was assessed, using forty husbands and wives, after a two-month interval, with a resulting Pearson Product Moment correlation coefficient of .84.

Grando (1971a), using pretest data from the study by Ginsberg (1971) that is reported in this book, studied the reliability of the FLQ-FS. Item consistency was assessed with a sample of twenty-nine fathers and twenty-nine sons. An alpha of .84 was found for fathers and .91 for sons. A factor analysis (Principal Components Analysis) by Grando confirmed the interval consistency of the FLQ. The factor loading of the total FLQ score on the first factor was high (.99 on the father form, .93 on the son form) indicating that the first factor was the total score. Also, all but one item (4) had factor loadings above .2 on the first factor.

The test-retest reliability of the FLQ-FS was assessed in the Ginsberg study reported in this book. The control group was retested after a ten-week interval, and a test-retest correlation of .77 was found. Again, because of the long interval between tests, this should be considered a minimal estimate of test-retest reliability.

The positive results obtained with various forms of the FLQ by Ely (1970), and by Rappaport (1976) and Ginsberg (1971) in the studies summarized in this book, provide evidence of the construct validity of the FLQ. Further evidence of the validity of the FLQ-C was found by Collins (1971) in the study reported in this book. With ninety subjects, Collins found significant Pearson Product Moment Correlations in the expected direction with other measures of marital adjustment and with measures of marital communication: There were correlations between the FLQ-C and the Marital Adjustment Test (.78, $p <$ .001); the Marital Communication Inventory (.78, $p < .001$); and the Primary Communication Inventory (.69, $p < .001$).

Evidence of the concurrent validity of the FLQ-FS also

was found in the Ginsberg (1971) study. There were significant Pearson Product Moment correlations between the FLQ-FS and: the Parent Adolescent Communication Checklist (.62, $p <$ .001); the Parent Adolescent Communication Inventory (.73, $p$ < .001); the Semantic Differential—Self (.40, $p < .01$); the Semantic Differential—Other (.38, $p < .01$). The FLQ-FS also correlated with measures of observed behavior: Acceptance of Others (.39, $p < .01$) and Unobtrusively Observed Acceptance of Others (.26, $p < .05$).

### E: The Interpersonal Relationship Scale (IRS)

The Interpersonal Relationship Scale (IRS) was devised by Stephen Schlein with the collaboration of Bernard Guerney, Jr., and Lillian Stover. It is intended to measure the quality of interpersonal relationships, particularly trust and intimacy.

An initial pool of 106 items was constructed by the authors of the scale and their colleagues. These were presented to eight judges whose field of study emphasized interpersonal relationships. They were asked to estimate the value of the item as a measure of trust, intimacy, or both. An item was retained when at least 75 percent of the judges rated it as suitable for measuring trust, intimacy, or both. Items were eliminated when 25 percent or more of the judges stated that an item should be rewritten or was weak as an assessment of either trust or intimacy. This process and further minor pruning by the authors eliminated all but 52 items. The measure is shown below.

On the IRS, the following thirty items are scored $SA = 5$, $MA = 4$, $N = 3$, $MD = 2$, $SD = 1$: Items 1 through 3; 5 through 11; 13; 15 through 18; 22; 24; 36; 38 through 43; 47 through 52. The remaining 22 items are scored $SA = 1$, $MA = 2$, $N = 3$, $MD = 4$, $SD = 5$.

### Interpersonal Relationship Scale

This is a questionnaire to determine the attitudes and feelings you have in your relationship with your partner. We are interested in the relationship *as it is, not* in the way you think it

*should be.* Please answer the statements by giving as true a picture of your own feelings and beliefs as possible. Be sure to read each item carefully and show your beliefs by marking an *X* through the appropriate answer for each question.

If you *strongly agree (SA)* with an item, that is you feel it is very true of your relationship, place an *X* through *SA.* If you think an item is *generally more true than untrue,* place an *X* through *MA* (mildly agree). If you feel the item is about *equally true and untrue,* place an *X* through *N* (Neutral). If you feel you *mildly disagree (MD)* with the item, place an *X* through *MD.* If you *strongly disagree (SD)* with an item—that is, you feel it is very untrue of your relationship—place an *X* through *SD.*

Strongly Agree (SA)
Mildly Agree (A)
Neutral (N)
Mildly Disagree (MD)
Strongly Disagree (SD)

Your answers will be held in strictest confidence.

1. When serious disagreements arise between us, I respect my partner's position.                    SA  MA  N  MD  SD

2. I feel comfortable expressing almost anything to my partner.        SA  MA  N  MD  SD

3. In our relationship, I feel I am able to expose my weaknesses.        SA  MA  N  MD  SD

4. In our relationship, I'm cautious and play it safe.                  SA  MA  N  MD  SD

5. I can express deep, strong feelings to my partner.                  SA  MA  N  MD  SD

6. I can accept my partner even when we disagree.                      SA  MA  N  MD  SD

7. I believe most things my partner says.                              SA  MA  N  MD  SD

8. I would like my partner to be with me when I receive bad news.      SA  MA  N  MD  SD

9. I would like my partner to be with me when I'm lonely.  SA  MA  N  MD  SD

10. I seek my partner's attention when I'm facing troubles.  SA  MA  N  MD  SD

11. I feel comfortable when I'm alone with my partner.  SA  MA  N  MD  SD

12. I'm afraid of making mistakes with my partner.  SA  MA  N  MD  SD

13. I feel relaxed when we are together.  SA  MA  N  MD  SD

14. I am afraid my partner will hurt my feelings.  SA  MA  N  MD  SD

15. I face my life with my partner with confidence.  SA  MA  N  MD  SD

16. I share and discuss my problems with my partner.  SA  MA  N  MD  SD

17. I understand my partner and sympathize with his/her feelings.  SA  MA  N  MD  SD

18. I listen carefully to my partner and help him/her solve problems.  SA  MA  N  MD  SD

19. I feel my partner misinterprets what I say.  SA  MA  N  MD  SD

20. My partner would tell a lie if he/she could gain by it.  SA  MA  N  MD  SD

21. In our relationship, I am occasionally distrustful and expect to be exploited.  SA  MA  N  MD  SD

22. I get a lot of sympathy and understanding from my partner.  SA  MA  N  MD  SD

23. There are times when my partner cannot be trusted.  SA  MA  N  MD  SD

24. We are very close to each other.  SA  MA  N  MD  SD

25. My partner doesn't really understand me.  SA  MA  N  MD  SD

26. I'm better off if I don't trust my partner too much.　　SA　MA　N　MD　SD

27. I do not show deep emotions to my partner.　　SA　MA　N　MD　SD

28. It is hard for me to act natural when I'm with my partner.　　SA　MA　N　MD　SD

29. My partner is honest mainly because of a fear of being caught.　　SA　MA　N　MD　SD

30. My partner pretends to care more about me than he/she really does.　　SA　MA　N　MD　SD

31. My way of doing things is apt to be misunderstood by my partner.　　SA　MA　N　MD　SD

32. I wonder how much my partner really cares about me.　　SA　MA　N　MD　SD

33. I sometimes wonder what hidden reason my partner has for doing something nice for me.　　SA　MA　N　MD　SD

34. It is hard for me to tell my partner about myself.　　SA　MA　N　MD　SD

35. I sometimes stay away from my partner because I fear doing or saying something I might regret afterwards.　　SA　MA　N　MD　SD

36. My partner can be relied on to keep his/her promises.　　SA　MA　N　MD　SD

37. The advice my partner gives cannot be regarded as being trustworthy.　　SA　MA　N　MD　SD

38. I don't believe my partner would cheat on me even if he/she were able to get away with it.　　SA　MA　N　MD　SD

39. My partner can be counted on to do what he/she says he/she will do.　　SA　MA　N　MD　SD

40. My partner treats me fairly and justly.　　SA　MA　N　MD　SD

41. My partner is likely to say what he/she really believes, rather than what he/she thinks I want to hear.　　SA　MA　N　MD　SD

42. It is safe to believe that my partner is interested in my welfare.          SA  MA  N  MD  SD

43. My partner is truly sincere in his/her promises.          SA  MA  N  MD  SD

44. There is no simple way of deciding if my partner is telling the truth.          SA  MA  N  MD  SD

45. Even though my partner provides me with many reports and stories, it is hard to get an objective account of things.          SA  MA  N  MD  SD

46. In our relationship, I have to be alert or my partner is likely to take advantage of me.          SA  MA  N  MD  SD

47. My partner is sincere and practices what he/she preaches.          SA  MA  N  MD  SD

48. My partner really cares what happens to me.          SA  MA  N  MD  SD

49. I talk with my partner about why certain people dislike me.          SA  MA  N  MD  SD

50. I discuss with my partner the things I worry about when I'm with a person of the opposite sex.          SA  MA  N  MD  SD

51. I tell my partner some things of which I am very ashamed.          SA  MA  N  MD  SD

52. I touch my partner when I feel warmly toward him/her.          SA  MA  N  MD  SD

Reliability of the IRS was assessed in the Rappaport study summarized in this book. After a two-month interval, with forty subjects (twenty married couples), he found a test-retest Pearson Product Moment correlation of .92. Also, the positive results Rappaport (1976) found in assessing the results of training provide evidence of construct validity for the IRS.

Evidence of validity is afforded by the Schlein (1971) study summarized by Ginsberg and Vogelsong in this book. With ninety-six subjects, he found correlations between the IRS and a number of measures of communication and of the quality

of interpersonal relationships. There were significant correlations in the expected direction between the IRS and the Premarital Communication Inventory (.69, $p < .001$); the (modified) Primary Communication Inventory (.55, $p < .001$); the Relationship Scale–Self (.79, $p < .001$); and the Relationship Scale–Partner (.70, $p < .001$).

### F: Handling Problems Change Scale (HPCS)

The Handling Problems Change Scale (HPCS) is a simple measure devised by Stephen Schlein, Bernard Guerney, Jr., and Lillian Stover to evaluate change in the ability to handle problems in a given relationship over a specified period of time. The measure consists of only two items as shown below.

*Handling Problems Change Scale*

1. How adequately do you feel you were dealing with your relationship problems _____ ago? (a) very inadequately; (b) fairly inadequately; (c) erratically, or don't know; (d) fairly adequately; (e) very adequately.

2. How adequately do you feel you are dealing with your relationship problems now? (a) very inadequately; (b) fairly inadequately; (c) erratically, or don't know; (d) fairly adequately; (e) very adequately.

The dash in the first item is filled in with whatever time interval is desired for a given study. In the studies reported in this book, the time period corresponded to the nearest month with the length of the particular training period being assessed. In scoring, Answers a through e are assigned numbers 1 through 5 respectively for each of the two items. When using a comparison of the answers to both questions to assess change, the number assigned to Item 1 is subtracted from the number assigned to Item 2. Thus, the higher the difference score the greater the improvement. (A constant may be added to these difference scores to eliminate negative numbers, thereby reducing chances of error in statistical analyses.)

Change can be assessed in a number of different ways using this instrument. If posttreatment scores alone are used, a comparison of the score on Item 2 with the score on Item 1 yields a measure of the subject's view of his current ability to handle problems with his retrospective view of his ability to solve relationship problems prior to the experimental intervention.

A number of other comparisons become possible if the two questions are administered both at pretreatment and at posttreatment. With such dual administration, it is possible to compare change as retrospectively judged by the subject over the period from the beginning of the program to its conclusion (Item 2 score minus Item 1 score at posttreatment testing) with the change that the individual had retrospectively perceived for a comparable period of time prior to beginning the program (Item 2 minus Item 1 at pretreatment testing). This provides a type of own-control comparison from a subjective, retrospective point of view. With such repeated testing, it is also possible to assess change in the subject's view of his ability to handle problems at the time the program began (Item 2, pretreatment) with his view of his ability to handle problems at the conclusion of the treatment period (Item 2, posttreatment). Thirdly, one might for some reason wish at the conclusion of treatment to compare the subject's posttreatment recollection of how well he handled problems when treatment began (Item 1 at posttreatment) with his assessment of his ability to handle problems as they were actually reported at that time (Item 2 at pretreatment).

Internal reliability tests would not be appropriate for this simple measure. To provide a meaningful test-retest reliability estimate for a measure designed to be sensitive to short-term change, the retesting interval would have to be very brief: a matter of days or, at most, a week. The retesting of the subjects in the studies using this measure was done after a much longer interval than that, and therefore there is no appropriate estimate of reliability available from these studies. Nor have any independent studies yet been conducted to assess the reliability of the HPCS. However, adequate reliability for purposes of

group testing, as well as construct validity, can be reasonably inferred from the fact that experimental hypotheses that were tested via the HPCS were confirmed in both the Schlein (1971) and Rappaport (1976) studies summarized in this book.

There also is evidence of validity from the Schlein study summarized in this book in terms of correlations with other measures. With ninety-six subjects, Schlein found significant correlations between the HPCS and measures designed to assess relationship change in general and change in satisfaction with the relationship. The HPCS correlated (Schlein, 1971) with the Relationship Change Scale (.29, $p < .01$) and the Satisfaction Change Scale (.43, $p < .001$).

## G: Satisfaction Change Scale (SCS)

The Satisfaction Change Scale or SCS is a simple measure devised by Stephen Schlein, Bernard Guerney, Jr., and Lillian Stover to evaluate change in a subject's satisfaction in a given relationship over a specified period of time. The measure consists of only two items, as shown below.

### Satisfaction Change Scale

1. How would you describe your relationship as of _____ ago? (a) very dissatisfying; (b) fairly dissatisfying; (c) mixed or don't know; (d) fairly satisfying; (e) very satisfying.

2. How would you describe your relationship as it stands today? (a) very dissatisfying; (b) fairly dissatisfying; (c) mixed or don't know; (d) fairly satisfying; (e) very satisfying.

The dash in Item 1 is filled in with whatever time interval is appropriate for a given study. In the studies reported in this book, the time period corresponded to the nearest month with the length of particular training period being assessed. In scoring, Answers a through e are assigned numbers 1 through 5 respectively for each of the two items. When using a comparison of the answers to both questions together to assess

change, the number assigned to Item 1 is subtracted from the number assigned to Item 2. Thus, the higher the difference score, the greater the improvement. (A constant may be added to these difference scores to eliminate negative numbers, thereby reducing chances of error in statistical analyses.)

Change can be assessed in a number of different ways using this instrument. If posttreatment scores alone are being used, the difference between the score on Item 2 and the score on Item 1 yields a measure of the subject's view of his current satisfaction in the relationship with his retrospective view of his satisfaction prior to treatment.

A number of other comparisons become possible if the questions had also been administered at pretreatment. First, it is possible to compare the subject's retrospective view of change over the period from the beginning of the program to its conclusion (Item 2 score minus Item 1 score at posttreatment) with the change that the individual had retrospectively perceived during a comparable time period prior to beginning the program (Item 2 minus Item 1 at pretreatment testing). This provides, from a subjective, retrospective point of view, a type of own-control comparison. Second, it is possible to assess change in the subject's view of his satisfaction in the relationship at the time the experimental treatment began with his view of his satisfaction in the relationship at the conclusion of the experimental treatment period (Item 2 posttreatment versus Item 2 pretreatment). Third, one might for some reason wish to compare the subject's posttreatment recollection of his satisfaction in the relationship when treatment began with his satisfaction as it was actually reported at that time (Item 1 at posttreatment versus Item 2 at pretreatment).

The same statements concerning reliability that were made for the Handling Problems Change Scale apply to the SCS. Construct validity for the measure can be inferred from the confirmation of Rappaport's hypothesis using this measure. A similar hypothesis by Schlein was not confirmed. (Both studies are summarized in this book.) It is believed, in light of the overall pattern of Schlein's (1971) findings and of Rappaport's (1976) results, that this failure resulted from the special characteristics

of the dating population coming to a PRIMES program rather than from a lack of SCS reliability or validity.

The Schlein (1971) study also affords some evidence of concurrent validity in that the SCS correlated with other measures designed to assess change in the relationship. With ninety-six dating subjects, there were significant correlations of the SCS with the Relationship Change Scale (.49, $p < .001$) and the Handling Problems Change Scale (.43, $p < .001$).

### H: The Relationship Change Scale (RCS)

The Relationship Change Scale (RCS) was developed by Stephen Schlein and Bernard Guerney, Jr., as a measure that would be sensitive to change in the quality of a relationship. These questions deal with a variety of areas in relationships such as satisfaction, communication, trust, intimacy, sensitivity, openness, and understanding.

The time interval in the RCS can be altered to suit the needs of' the investigator. In the studies reported in this book, the interval was chosen to correspond approximately with the length of the particular program being investigated. In the form reproduced below, three months is the time interval used.

All twenty-seven items of the Relationship Change Scale are scored as follows: Choice a = 1, b = 2, c = 3, d = 4, and e = 5.

*Relationship Change Scale*

This is a questionnaire to determine whether, and in what ways, your relationship with your partner has changed in the last three months. Please complete the statements by *underlining the phrase that most accurately completes each statement.* Please give as accurate and honest an account of your own feelings and beliefs as possible.

Your answers will be held in strictest confidence.

1. Within the last three months, my satisfaction with myself as a person has become: (a) much less; (b) less; (c) unchanged; (d) greater; (e) much greater.

2. Within the last three months, my satisfaction with my partner as a person has become: (a) much less; (b) less; (c) unchanged; (d) greater; (e) much greater.

3. Within the last three months, I feel my mate views me as a satisfactory partner: (a) much less; (b) less; (c) no change; (d) more; (e) much more.

4. Within the last three months, my mate views herself (himself) with satisfaction as a person: (a) much less; (b) less; (c) no change; (d) more; (e) much more.

5. Within the last three months, our relationship with each other has become: (a) much worse; (b) worse; (c) unchanged; (d) better; (e) much better.

6. In comparison with three months ago, I am clearly aware of my partner's needs and desires: (a) much less; (b) less; (c) no change; (d) more; (e) much more.

7. In comparison with three months ago, I understand my own feelings: (a) much less; (b) less; (c) no differently; (d) more; (e) much more.

8. In comparison with three months ago, I understand my own needs and desires in this relationship: (a) much less; (b) less; (c) no differently; (d) more; (e) much more.

9. In comparison with three months ago, I understand my partner's feelings: (a) much less; (b) less; (c) no differently; (d) more; (e) much more.

10. In comparison with three months ago, our ability to communicate has become: (a) much worse; (b) worse; (c) unchanged; (d) better, (e) much better.

11. In comparison with three months ago, my sensitivity towards my partner as a person is: (a) much less; (b) less; (c) unchanged; (d) more; (e) much more.

12. In comparison with three months ago, my concern and warmth toward my partner has become: (a) much less; (b) less; (c) unchanged; (d) more; (e) much more.

13. In comparison with three months ago, my self-expression and openness in relation to my partner is: (a) much less; (b) less; (c) unchanged; (d) more; (e) much more.

14. In comparison with three months ago, my ability to understand my partner's likes and dislikes is: (a) much less; (b) less; (c) unchanged; (d) more; (e) much more.

15. In comparison with three months ago, my listening abilities with my partner are: (a) much worse; (b) worse; (c) unchanged; (d) better; (e) much better.

16. In comparison with three months ago, my trust in my partner is: (a) much less; (b) less; (c) unchanged; (d) more; (e) much more.

17. In comparison with three months ago, my feelings of intimacy with my partner are: (a) much less; (b) less; (c) unchanged; (d) more; (e) much more.

18. In comparison with three months ago, my confidence in our relationship is: (a) much less; (b) less; (c) no different; (d) greater; (e) much greater.

19. In comparison with three months ago, our ability to handle disagreements constructively is: (a) much less; (b) less; (c) no different; (d) greater; (e) much greater.

20. In comparison with three months ago, our satisfaction with our sexual relationship is: (a) much less; (b) less; (c) unchanged; (d) more; (e) much more.

21. In comparison with three months ago, my difficulty in talking with my partner is: (a) much more; (b) more; (c) unchanged; (d) less; (e) much less.

22. In comparison with three months ago, my ability to express positive feelings toward my partner is: (a) much less; (b) less; (c) unchanged; (d) greater; (e) much greater.

23. In comparison with three months ago, my ability to constructively express negative feelings toward my partner is: (a) much less; (b) less; (c) unchanged; (d) greater; (e) much greater.

24. In comparison with three months ago, my willingness to share my personal concerns with my partner is: (a) much less; (b) less; (c) unchanged; (d) greater; (e) much greater.

25. In comparison with three months ago, my capacity to believe and accept positive feelings my partner expresses toward

me is: (a) much less; (b) less; (c) unchanged; (d) more; (e) much more.

26. In comparison with three months ago, my capacity to deal constructively with negative feelings my partner expresses toward me is: (a) much less; (b) less; (c) unchanged; (d) more; (e) much more.

27. In comparison with three months ago, my understanding of the kind of relationship I want to have in the future with my partner is: (a) much less; (b) less; (c) unchanged; (d) more; (e) much more.

When used to evaluate a treatment program, the measure can be used simply as a postmeasure, or it can be administered pre- and posttreatment. In the latter instance, one compares a retrospective view of change over the course of treatment with a retrospective view of change over a comparable period of time before treatment began.

For reasons similar to those mentioned earlier with respect to the HPCS and SCS, studies of reliability have not been conducted with this instrument. However, adequate reliability for purposes of group testing, as well as construct validity, can be reasonably inferred from the fact that experimental hypotheses tested via the RCS were confirmed in both the Schlein (1971) and Rappaport (1976) studies summarized in this book.

Further evidence of concurrent validity is afforded by the study by Schlein (1971). The RCS correlated with two measures designed to assess specific components of relationship change. With the ninety-six dating couples, there were significant correlations of the RCS with the Handling Problems Change Scale (.29, $p < .01$) and with the Satisfaction Change Scale (.49, $p < .001$).

## I: The Verbal Interaction Task (VIT)

The Verbal Interaction Task or VIT, devised by Bernard Guerney, Jr., consists of two tasks designed to stimulate emotionally meaningful dialog between a pair of intimates. In

essence, the two tasks are: (1) "Discuss something you would like to see changed in yourself"; and (2) "Discuss something you would like to see changed in your partner." The instructions to each person define his role as either openly expressing his feelings about the issue or helping the other person to express his feelings.

The instructions are written out on cards. The examiner gives the appropriate card to each participant, sets a bell-timer for four minutes to limit the duration of each task, and leaves the couple alone to carry out the dialog. The discussants are aware that their dialog is being tape-recorded.

The resulting dialog may be scored according to any coding or rating appropriate for assessing verbal interaction. In the studies in this book, the dialogs were rated on the Acceptance Of Other Scale and the Self-Feeling Awareness Scale.

In the generic instructions presented below, the letters *A* and *B* designate the partners. In actual application, for example, *son* or *husband* would be substituted for *A*, while *father* or *wife* would be substituted for *B* and, of course, genders would be changed as necessary.

### *Verbal Interaction Task*

1a. *For A*—Please discuss with B *something you would like to change in yourself.* Try to be as open and expressive of your feelings as possible. You are asked to discuss this for four minutes. At the end of four minutes, a bell will go off signaling the end of this discussion. I'll be in to give you the next question.

1b. *For B*—Please discuss with A *something he would like to change in himself.* You are to try to help him express his feelings as much as possible. You are asked to discuss this for four minutes. At the end of four minutes, a bell will go off signaling the end of this discussion. I'll be in to give you the next question.

2a. *For B*—Please discuss with A *something you would like to change in yourself.* Try to be as open and expressive of your feelings as possible. You are asked to discuss this for four min-

utes. At the end of four minutes, a bell will go off signaling the end of this discussion. I'll be in to give you the next question.

2b. *For A*—Please discuss with B *something he would like to change in himself.* You are to try to help him express his feelings as much as possible. You are asked to discuss this for four minutes. At the end of four minutes, a bell will go off signaling the end of this discussion. I'll be in to give you the next question.

3a. *For A*—Please discuss with B *something you would like to see changed in him.* You should *not* choose the same thing he chose to discuss about changing himself. Try to be as open and expressive of your feelings as possible. You are asked to discuss this for four minutes. At the end of four minutes, a bell will go off signaling the end of this discussion. I'll be in to give you the next question.

3b. *For B*—Please discuss with A *something he would like to see changed in you.* You are to try to help him express his feelings as much as possible. You are asked to discuss this for four minutes. At the end of four minutes, a bell will go off signaling the end of this discussion. I'll be in to give you the next question.

4a. *For B*—Please discuss with A *something you would like to see changed in him.* You should not choose the same thing he chose to discuss about changing himself. Try to be as open and expressive of your feelings as possible. You are asked to discuss this for four minutes. At the end of four minutes, a bell will go off signaling the end of this discussion. I'll be in to end the session.

4b. *For A*—Please discuss with B *something he would like to see changed in you.* You are to try to help him express his feelings as much as possible. You are asked to discuss this for four minutes. At the end of four minutes, a bell will go off signaling the end of this discussion. I'll be in to end the session.

The task would appear to be a useful one for research when used with an appropriate coding system. The VIT generated material confirming the experimental hypotheses in the

studies by Ginsberg (1971), Rappaport (1976), and Schlein (1971) that are summarized in this book.

With respect to the usefulness of the VIT in family and interpersonal research, it is also encouraging to note that the performance of the participants in the VIT when they realized it would be assessed for research purposes was significantly correlated with their performance immediately afterwards, when they believed that their performance was no longer being assessed. In the Ginsberg study reported in this book, the Acceptance of Other score was correlated (.52, $p < .001$) with the Unobtrusive Acceptance of Other and the Self-Feeling Awareness was correlated (.56, $p < .001$) with the Unobtrusive Self-Feeling Awareness.

### J: The Acceptance of Other Scale (AOS)

The Acceptance of Other Scale or AOS (sometimes referred to as the Listener Acceptance Scale or LAS) was developed by Lillian Stover, Bernard Guerney, Jr., Barry Ginsberg, and Stephen Schlein. It is designed to measure the understanding and acceptance conveyed by one person (the *responder*) in his verbal responses to a communication from another (the *other*).

The scale gives primary weight to empathy as a form of acceptance, and to those responses that encourage the other to follow his own line of thought. It assesses the responder's sensitivity to the other's phenomenological field; his willingness to stay within the boundaries defined by the other's phenomenological field; and his sensitivity to the feelings, needs, and motivations of the other as these have been expressed both by the other's words and manner. The guiding question in its development was "What would be the best and worst responses that could be made to another's statement by a Rogerian psychotherapist?" It is an eight-point scale wherein the lowest level of responses are argumentative and accusative; the middle range of responses are ordinary social conversation; and the highest level of responses are ones that convey complete empathic acceptance of the other person.

The scale can be used with the response unit defined in

two ways: (1) an arbitrary unit of time (we have found one minute of conversation reasonable), or (2) a statement of the person being rated which is made between two statements by another. The latter is our preferred method for most applications.

The scale and guidelines for its use are presented below.

### Acceptance of Other Scale

8. Verbally reflects (states) the deepest feelings expressed by the other. Also, content, if any, accurately reflects the main thrust of the other's meaning. A highly empathic response.

7. Recognizing feelings with full attention to mood, but not conveying sensitivity to level of intensity, or not responding fully to the significant feelings. Also, content, if any, is in accord with main thrust of the other's meaning.

6. A paraphrasing of content that is in accord with the main thrust of the other's meaning. Acceptant, accurate, but not stating any feelings of the other.

5. The attempt to "stay with" the other is clear, but the response goes astray in some way. The following are examples of ways in which the response may stray away from one that focuses fully on the other's own thoughts and momentum: (a) questioning in an attempt to get an elaboration of the other's thoughts; (b) giving a suggestion about the other's intent that has not been implied by the other; or (c) a response that has the effect of infusing ideas different from the other's.

4. Nonaccusative social conversation. Responding with one's own ideas after the fashion of typical social discourse. (A half minute of total verbal silence is scored here. Under certain circumstances, "Yes" or "uhm uhm" and responses of this nature are also scored here—see guidelines.)

3. Directing. Moderately critical in tone, but not abusive. Taking the lead. Giving suggestions. Although statements are not presented as being in direct opposition, the statement has the effect of interjecting thoughts that are in opposition to those expressed by the other. Questioning in order to defend one's own point of view.

2. Open disagreements with content expressed by the other. Contrary statements. Statements suggestive of boredom, incredulity, rejection, disgust, disbelief, and so on.

1. Strongly argumentative. Accusative. Openly rejecting the other person or that person's rights to have the feelings he has expressed. Abusive. Demanding. Angry.

## *Guidelines for Using the Acceptance of Other Scale*

1. The AOS can be divided into two parts. If the responder focuses on the feelings and/or content of the other's message, the response should be placed in the upper part of the scale (5-8). If, instead, the responder "takes over" and offers advice, social conversation, disagreement, and so on, the response falls in the lower part (1-4). The rater then proceeds to make appropriate further differentiation.

2. The responder's statement should be evaluated *primarily* in the light of the other's statement that just preceded it, although he need not completely ignore statements that the other made prior to his most recent statement. Reflections of ambivalent or contradictory thoughts and feelings that the rater judges to be within the other's present field of awareness and that he could readily acknowledge often constitute responder statements of the very highest level. However, it lowers the responder's score if the responder draws on previous statements to bring out feelings or ideas that tend to force the other to *reconcile* current statements or feelings with ones he expressed in the past. Such responses have the effect of being a challenge or a confrontation, are not fully accepting of the other's present communication, and should be rated in the lower half of the scale.

3. All rater judgments are made immediately following the responder's statement and prior to the other's reaction to that response. Ratings should not be changed because of any future statements of agreement or disagreement by the other. That is, the rating should reflect the rater's judgment only. Rating should not be subject to revision on the basis of the other's response to a statement being rated. To do so would open the

ratings to contamination on the basis of variation among subjects
(that is, other-person subjects) on such variables as assertiveness,
agreeableness, defensiveness, and so on. We regard it as appropriate to rely exclusively on the judgment of the rater uncon-
founded by statements that follow the statement of the responder, because the responder cannot be held fully account-
able for statements that follow his own response.

4. In rating compound responses, the main criteria to be considered is the *interpersonal effect* of the response. A restatement of the content of the other's statement (6), followed in
the same response by an extremely accepting empathic response
(8), would be scored 8. On the other hand, a highly empathic
response (8), or a restatement of content (6), followed by a
statement of disagreement (2), would be scored 2. Generally,
but not always, the last part of the response should be given the
most weight, because it generally will have the most influence
on the other.

5. For Level 7 and 8 responses, if a statement contains *both* the
feelings and the content of the other's previous statement, then
the criteria established for each must be met for *both* feelings
and content to qualify the statement for a 7 or 8 rating. However, it is not *necessary* for a response to include content in
order to be scored a 7 or 8.

6. Responses such as "yes," "uhm uhm," and "go on" that are
not accompanied by more substantive statements are not scored
except when preceded by a ten-second pause. In the latter instance it is scored 4.

7. The emotional or tonal qualities of the responder need not
match those of the other for the response to qualify for the
highest scoring levels. The responder has a wide range of lati-
tude in this respect. The rater need not be on the lookout for
concordance and warmth or acceptance in speaking *manner* as
opposed to content. It is only necessary that the emotional
quality and style of delivery of the response not be likely to
make the other feel ignored, rejected, uneasy, or distracted
from pursuing his own line of thought. Such a negative impact
on the other is likely to occur if the responder's mood is in

*marked* contrast to the other's, or if the responder's manner of speech is entirely mechanical or clearly denotes impatience, boredom, incredulity, and so on. When such a negative manner of delivering a statement does *intrude itself* on the rater's awareness, it brings the response down to the same lower level of coding as if an actual verbal statement showing such impatience, boredom, and so on had been made by the responder. In other words, if the manner of speaking seems likely to affect the other more than what has been said, the manner of speaking is rated rather than the words. Where the words seem likely to carry the major impact, the manner of speaking may be ignored.

8. Level 7 and 8 responses must contain a statement of feeling. Expression of feelings by the *other* is not meant to be limited to a direct verbal *statement* of feelings. In fact, the seventh and eighth levels of responses are very often a reflection of thoughts and feelings the other has not yet put into words. Rather, the best type of response often will strike the rater as being the *next* statement the other *would* make *if* he were very sensitive to his own feelings.

9. Responses at the seventh and eighth levels are inferred by the responder from the content, tone, and manner of the other's statement and a straightforward, empathic knowledge of which events generally lead to which kinds of feelings. Such high-level responses must be judged by the rater to be within the present phenomenological field of the other. That is, the response must be one that the rater believes will be *immediately* acceptable to the other—one that is not ego-alien; one that he can recognize as a valid reflection or extension of his just-expressed thoughts and feelings. The rater must be able to anticipate that the other could enthusiastically respond "Yes!" or "Right!" and proceed with the previous flow of his communication. High level responses are not inferred from any complex psychodynamic analysis of unconscious conflicts and cross-currents. To qualify as a high-level response, the response must be one that the rater believes will not give pause to the other for any reason. It must not infuse a *new* perspective (however beneficial the rater may feel this new direction to be). The rater must be able to anticipate that the other will *not* say, "I guess so," or "I'm not sure

about that." When the rater anticipates a comment of this type by the other, the response should be rated as a 5 (has the effect of infusing another idea). When the rater anticipates a rejection of the responder's statement by the other, he needs to consider scoring the response as 5, 4, or 3. The decision of a 3, as opposed to a 4 or 5, would need to be made on the basis of whether the other seems likely to regard the responder's comment as reflecting critically or negatively on him, the other, when the other had not been talking that way about himself. In that case, the score would be a 3. A positive value judgment or statement of agreement, like a negative one, is regarded as judgmental and as infusing an idea of the responder and therefore reduces the score to a 5 or 4 depending on the rest of the content of the statement.

10. Clarification of feeling emotion is regarded as a more empathic and accepting response than restatement or clarification of content or of cognitive processes. This is the dividing line between a Level 6 response and higher-level responses. The use of the term *feel* by the responder is not relevant, since people often use the word *feel* when *think* would be as appropriate, if not more so. If *think* could be substituted for *feel*, it is a Level 6 response. Similarly, the expression, "You feel *that—*" usually is associated with a cognitive rather than an emotional response. A word or phrase denoting an emotional or a physical sensation is required to score above a Level 6. When words like *uncertain, confused, unsure,* and *puzzled* are used in a cognitive sense, they do not qualify for a Level 7 or 8 rating. Other terms, such as *wit's end* and *buffaloed,* often qualify as 7 or 8 responses. The context of the response must be considered in making such decisions: If the response is in the context of an intellectual decision-making process and thus cognitive, it is scored 6; if it is more in an interpersonal or emotional context, a Level 7 or 8 rating would be appropriate.

11. Phrases such as, "It drives you up the wall," "You feel like pulling out your hair," and "That was the last straw," can be highly empathic and have an effect on the other similar to a clarification of feeling even though they do not actually contain a feeling word. Such responses, when they seem to capture

the emotional state of the other, qualify for a Level 7 or 8 rating.

12. Words such as *wish, like, want,* and other words indicating desires, aspirations, or motivational states are in a grey area in terms of whether or not they designate feelings. However, the positive effects in terms of making the other feel understood and accepted when such motivational states are clarified and accepted is very similar to that achieved through acceptance and clarification of feelings. Therefore, recognition and acceptance of the other's desires, wishes, and motivational states should be regarded in the same manner as recognition and acceptance of feelings. Such responses may be rated as high as 8.

Interjudge reliability of the AOS has been studied using four independent judges skilled in empathic responding who each received twelve hours of training in the use of the scale. After training, they rated 14 four-minute interactions taped during the Verbal Interaction Task described in Appendix I. There were several different types of pairs interacting: husband-wife, father-son, and dating couples. The tapes were drawn randomly from pre- and posttesting periods and from experimental and control groups of the Ginsberg (1971), Rappaport (1976), and Schlein (1971) studies summarized in this book.

One rating of the responder was made every minute, and the ratings were averaged to give each responder one score per rater. The following correlations were found among the four raters' scores for the 14 responders: .96, .93, .93, .91, .90, and .89. Another type of interrater reliability check was performed by determining the degree of agreement between the judges on a response-by-response basis. Using 96 responder statements, three or more of the four judges coded the same response with the same numerical rating for 76 percent of the responses, and two or more of the judges gave the same rating for 100 percent of the responses.

Validity of the AOS was studied in terms of correlations with other measures. One would expect some correspondence between the ability to *express* oneself well and the ability to *respond* well to others. This expectation is borne out by the

correlation found by Ginsberg (1971) with 58 subjects in the study reported in this book between the SFAS and the Acceptance of Other Scale (.30, $p < .05$). It is especially encouraging to note that there was a similar correlation (.32, $p < .05$) when the Acceptance of Other Scale was used in a situation where the subjects were unaware that their behavior was under observation.

Unfortunately, research experience in psychology has shown that we often cannot expect correlations between paper-and-pencil measures of interpersonal behavior or adjustment on the one hand and behavioral measures on the other. Generally, significant correlations were not found between the SFAS and paper-and-pencil measures of communication or measures of the quality of the pertinent interpersonal relationships used in the studies reported in this book. Exceptions to this lack of correspondence occurred in the significant correlations between the AOS and the Family Life Questionnaire—Father, Son when the subjects were aware that their behavior was being assessed (.39, $p < .01$) and also when they were not aware that they were being assessed (.26, $p < .01$). Another exception to the general lack of correspondence was found by Schlein (1971) in the study summarized in this book. He found a significant correlation (.23, $p < .05$) between the AOS and the Premarital Communication Inventory.

The positive findings obtained via the use of the AOS in the studies by Ginsberg (1971) and Schlein (1971) summarized in this book also provide some evidence of construct validity for the AOS.

### K: The Self-Feeling Awareness Scale (SFAS)

The Self-Feeling Awareness Scale, or SFAS, was developed by Lillian Stover, Bernard Guerney, Jr., Barry Ginsberg, and Stephen Schlein. The person being rated is referred to as the *self* or *speaker*. (The scale has also been referred to as the Speaker-Feeling Awareness Scale.) The person being spoken to is referred to as the *listener*. If the scale is used in a group context and the speaker addresses more than one person, a separate

score is used for each person spoken to directly. The SFAS is designed to measure the speaker's feeling awareness, stated in subjective terms. It was designed with this question in mind: What kinds of statements are most (and least) likely to lead another to respond in terms of the speaker's phenomenology rather than to some other aspect of his statement? The SFAS is an eight-point scale in which: A high-level statement includes important feelings put in subjective terms; a middle-level statement is ordinary social conversation; and a low-level statement is one that emphasizes the deficiencies of oneself or another without the speaker acknowledging his feelings or the subjective nature of his perceptions. The previous discussion of the unit to be rated with respect to the AOS also applies to the SFAS. The scale and guidelines for its use are presented below.

### Self-Feeling Awareness Scale

8. Directly stating as one's own ("owning") deep or long-standing feelings about self or partner that are positive or negative. The feelings are not expressed indirectly; they are designated by name (for example, angry, happy, depressed).

7. Owning feelings about self or partner at a more guarded level or in less emotional terms.

6. Owning thoughts, interests, values of self or the listener. Feelings are not expressed except inferentially.

5. Making comments or statements about self or the listener of an abstract or descriptive nature (not owning them). Simple agreements or disagreements.

4. Making social conversation not about self or the listener. (A half minute of complete silence is also scored here.)

3. Making suggestions in a negative or positive manner to influence behavior of partner. Rejecting ideas put forth by the listener.

2. Giving directions. Making demands. Being mildly accusative. Mildly attacking or praising self or the listener without owning feelings.

1. Strongly attacking, accusing or praising self or the listener without owning feelings.

### Guidelines for Using Self-Feeling Awareness Scale

1. Speaker statements are rated in the upper range of the scale (6-8) when they are expressions about the self or the listener in which the speaker states his *own* feelings, wishes, desires, concerns or thoughts. In discriminating among these scores, a critical factor to consider is whether the statement is affective or cognitive. The affective area includes expressions of feelings, wants, needs, and desires, and should be rated 7 or 8. The cognitive area includes thoughts, interests, values, and descriptions, and should be rated 6. Distinguishing between ratings of 7 and 8 is a question of degree. A rating of 8 includes statements that directly name specific, deep, or long-standing feelings of a positive or negative nature about the self or the listener. There is no attempt to hide or mask the feelings or needs; they are stated directly and openly. When the speaker guards against a full expression of feelings, the statement is rated 7. Examples of 7 and 8 are:

"I get hurt when I see you flirting." (8)

"It's unpleasant to see you flirting." (7)

"I want you to show me how you feel about me." (8)

"I wish you'd express your emotions more." (7)

2. The use of the word *feel* does not necessarily denote an affective statement. "I feel that you are away from home too much" is a cognitive statement, because no feeling is directly expressed even though the word *feel* is used. If the word *think* can be easily substituted for the word *feel,* the expression is one of cognition and should be rated 6. Examples of 6 and 8 statements are:

"I feel sad when I have to say good-bye to you." (affective: 8)

"I feel that we are drifting further and further apart and will never get back together." (cognitive: 6)

3. A statement of feeling is rated 7 or 8 whether it is an expression of positive or negative regard for the listener. Expressions of a cognitive nature (rated 6) also are made without regard to whether they are positive or negative statements. Examples are:

"I love you very much." (8)

"I hate you when I see you doing that." (8)

"I believe we have a wonderful relationship." (6)

"I don't really think our marriage has much of a chance anymore." (6)

It is obvious that these statements will have a very different effect on the listener. The main criterion, however, is that in each of the above statements the speaker is taking the responsibility for the thoughts and feelings expressed. He is stating the nature of the world as he sees it and is not placing the responsibility for his perceptions on the listener. The following examples further illustrate this point:

"I hate you." (8)

"I have little regard left for you." (6)

"You're a no good bum!" (1)

4. Deciding whether a cognitive statement should be rated 6 or 5 is determined by assessing whether the statement is acknowledged by the speaker to be his own opinion (6) or whether there is general authorship for the thoughts that may or may not belong to the speaker (5). For example:

"I think we have an excellent marriage." (6)

"People have said we make the ideal pair." (5)

"I've often wondered about the way I handle the children." (6)

"My mother appears to be critical of the way in which I handle the children." (5)

5. Level 5 also includes statements that convey simple, direct agreement or disagreement with the listener. For example:

"Yes, that's right." (5)

"No, that's not it." (5)

6. A Level 4 statement is one of neutral impact in which subjects of a social nature are discussed in a general, superficial manner. For example:

"The weather is nice tonight." (4)

"I wonder if Jane went out with Bill." (4)

7. The focus of statements in the lower part of the scale (1-3) focuses only on the listener rather than being a statement of self perceptions. The listener is therefore less likely to be able to respond to the speaker empathically and more likely to respond to the content of the message by itself.

8. A statement is rated 3 when the speaker places the responsibility on the listener for making behavioral changes. The speaker can do this by making suggestions about the listener's behavior and also by attempting to influence the listener to make changes. For example:

"You could try spending more time with the children." (3)

"It might be a good idea to try being more considerate." (3)

9. A 3-rated statement also includes the rejection of an idea put forth by the partner. This would not be a simple disagreement (a 5), but rather an argumentative rejection of the listener's statement. An example of the difference is:

"No, it's not like that." (5)

"You're wrong. That's not anything like what I've said." (3)

10. Statements rated 1 and 2 are direct verbal accusations, demands, attacks and/or labeling of the listener with no attempt by the speaker to own his thoughts or feelings. It is not necessary for the labeling to be negative to qualify for a 1 or 2. The criterion is whether the speaker is owning the sentiments or whether he is making statements of an objective nature about the listener. Examples are:

"You're so sweet." (1)

"You're a real bum." (1)

"You acted foolishly at the party." (2)

11. The main distinction between 2 and 1 is the *degree* to which

the listener is being accused, attacked, or praised. This discrimination is comparable to the judgments made in differentiating between 7 and 8. Strong and vehement attacks and/or accusations and/or praise are rated 1. Attacks and/or praise that have a less powerful effect, or that somehow lessen the impact of the accusation, are rated 2. For example:

"You're being somewhat silly about this. (2)

"You're a complete fool!" (1)

"You don't pay enough attention to your family." (2)

"You ignore your family and treat us like chattel." (1)

12. In rating compound speaker statements, the main criterion to consider is the interpersonal effect of the statement. When it is not clear just what effect the speaker's statement is likely to have on the listener, the following guidelines should be used:

a. Rate each part of the statement independently. If the ratings all fall within the 3-8 range, assign the highest rating to the entire statement, because the positive interpersonal effect of the higher rating will usually offset the negative effect of the lower rating in this range. For example, a statement that contained two parts that could be rated 7 and 5, would be assigned a 7. If a statement was comprised of three parts that could be rated 3, 6, and 8, the entire statement would be rated 8.

b. When any part of the statement is rated 1 or 2, assign the lowest rating. Thus, a compound statement that included the owning of deep feelings (8), a rejection of the partner's ideas (3), and labeling (1) would be rated 1.

The same tapes, judges, and procedures earlier described with respect to assessing interjudge reliability of the Acceptance of Other Scale were used to assess interrater reliability for the SFAS. The following correlations were found among the scores of four independent raters rating 14 speakers: .97, .93, .93, .89, .88. Using 96 speaker statements, precise agreement of scale designation (1 to 8) occurred among three of the four judges on 79 percent of the ratings, and precise agreement between two or more judges occurred on 100 percent of the ratings.

Validity of the SFAS was studied in terms of correlations with other measures. One would expect a correspondence between good expressive communication skills and good responding skills as we have defined them. Ginsberg, in the study reported in this book, found such a correlation between the SFAS and the Acceptance of Other Scale (.30, $p < .05$). Unfortunately, psychological research often finds little correspondence between measures of overt behavior and paper-and-pencil measures. This scale proved no exception. Neither Ginsberg (1971) nor Schlein (1971), who investigated this question in the studies summarized in this book, found significant relationships between the SFAS and the paper-and-pencil measures used to assess general communication or the quality of the relationship.

However, the studies by Ginsberg (1971), Rappaport (1976), and Schlein (1971) summarized in this book do provide evidence of the construct validity of the SFAS.

## L: Relationship Questionnaire (RQ)

Date_____                    Identification _____

The purpose of this questionnaire is to encourage you to think about your relationship—how you get along with each other, and what improvements you would like to see. We would like you to be able to respond to each item as openly and honestly as possible, therefore, we ask that you do not show this to anyone, including each other. Feel free to use the other side of the page if needed.

1. In order of importance, list below the three most important things about your relationship that please you now or that you have valued highly in the past. (Indicate whether this still exists or has existed only in the past.)

   1.

   2.

   3.

2. In order of importance list below the three most important things about your relationship that you would like to see developed or enhanced.

1.
2.
3.

3. If there are important problems or aspects of your relationship that seem very important to discuss but that are not presented in clear form in your answers to the above questions, please list them here in order of importance.

1.
2.
3.

4. Place either an A, B, or C beside all of the above items in accord with the following guideline.

A. You would feel comfortable talking about it in the group meetings at the present time.

B. It would be difficult, but not impossible, to talk about it in the group meetings at the present time.

C. You could not talk about it in the group meetings at the present time.

### M: Practice Home Session

Name: _____ Date: _____

Topics discussed in this practice session:

My perception of:

1. Feelings expressed by my partner:


2. Feelings I expressed:


3. I feel my partner understood me: (a) very well; (b) pretty well; (c) rather poorly.

4. I feel that, as a result of this conversation, I understand myself: (a) no more; (b) somewhat more; (3) much more.


5. I feel that, as a result of this conversation, I understand my partner: (a) no more; (b) somewhat more; (c) much more.

# References

‸‸‸‸‸‸‸‸‸‸‸‸‸‸‸‸‸‸‸‸‸‸‸‸‸‸‸‸

Andronico, M. P., Fidler, J., Guerney, B., Jr., and Guerney, L. "The Combination of Didactic and Dynamic Elements in Filial Therapy." *International Journal of Group Psychotherapy,* 1967, *17,* 10-17.

Ard, B., Jr., and Ard, C. *Handbook of Marriage Counseling.* Palo Alto, Calif.: Science and Behavior, 1969.

Ashby, J. D., Ford, D. H., Guerney, B., Jr., and Guerney, L. F. "Effects on Clients of a Reflective and a Leading Type of Psychotherapy." *Psychological Monographs,* 1957, *71,* 24.

Authier, J., Gustafson, K., Guerney, B., Jr., and Kasdorf, J. "The Psychological Practitioner as a Teacher: A Theoretical-Historical and Practical Review." *The Counseling Psychologist,* 1975, *5,* 31-50.

Bach, G. R., and Wyden, P. *The Intimate Enemy.* New York: Avon, 1969.

Bandura, A., and Walters, R. H. *Social Learning and Personality Development.* New York: Holt, Rinehart and Winston, 1963.

Beaubien, Clare Olivia, O. P. "Adolescent-Parent Communication Styles." Unpublished doctoral dissertation, The Pennsylvania State University, 1970.

Berenson, B. G. Carkhuff, R. R., and Myrus, P. "An Investigation of Training Effects Upon Interpersonal Functioning of Undergraduate College Students." *Journal of Counseling Psychology,* 1966, *13,* 441-446.

Bergin, A. E., and Solomon, S. *Personality and Performance Correlates of Empathic Understanding in Psychotherapy.* Paper presented at the 71st annual meeting of the American Psychological Association, Philadelphia, Pa., September 1963.

Bernard, J. "The Adjustments of Married Mates." In H. T. Christensen (Ed.), *Handbook of Marriage and the Family.* Chicago: Rand McNally, 1964.

Bessell, H., and Palomaris, U. *Methods in Human Development.* San Diego, Calif.: The Human Development Training Institute, 1969.

Bettelheim, B. "The Problem of Generations." *Daedalus,* 1962, *91,* 68-96.

Betz, B. "Bases of Therapeutic Leadership in Psychotherapy with the Schizophrenic Patient." *American Journal of Psychotherapy,* 1963a, *17,* 196-212.

Betz, B. "Differential Success Rates of Psychotherapists with 'Process' and 'Non-Process' Schizophrenic Patients." *American Journal of Psychiatry,* 1963b, *11,* 1090-1091.

Bienvenu, M. J. *A Counselor's Guide to Accompany a Marital Communication Inventory.* Durham, N.C.: Family Life Publications, 1968.

Bienvenu, M. J. *A Parent-Adolescent Communication Inventory, Form A.* Durham, N.C.: Family Life Publications, 1969.

Bienvenu, M. J. "Measurement of Marital Communication." *The Family Coordinator,* 1970, *19,* 26-30.

Box, G. E. "Some Theorems on Quadratic Forms Applied in the

Study of Analysis of Variance Problems. I. Effects of Inequality of Variance." *Annals of Math and Statistics,* 1954, *25,* 484-498.

Brammer, L. M., and Shostrom, E. L. *Therapeutic Psychology: Fundamentals of Counseling and Psychotherapy.* Englewood Cliffs, N.J.: Prentice-Hall, 1960.

Broderick, C. *Individual, Sex and Society.* Baltimore: Johns Hopkins Press, 1969.

Bronfenbrenner, U. "Some Familiar Antecedents of Responsibility and Leadership in Adolescents." In L. Petrillo and B. L. Bass (Eds.), *Leadership and Interpersonal Behavior.* New York: Holt, Rinehart and Winston, 1961.

Burgess, E., and Wallin, P. *Engagement and Marriage.* New York: Lippincott, 1953.

Carkhuff, R. R., and Berenson, B. G. *Beyond Counseling and Therapy.* New York: Holt, Rinehart and Winston, 1967.

Carkhuff, R. R., and Truax, C. B. "Training in Counseling and Psychotherapy: An Evaluation of an Integrated Didactic and Experimental Approach." *Journal of Consulting Psychology,* 1965a, *29,* 333-336.

Carkhuff, R. R., and Truax, C. B. "Lay Mental Health Counseling: The Effects of Lay Group Counseling." *Journal of Consulting Psychology,* 1965b, *29,* 426-431.

Clarke, C. "Group Procedures for Increasing Positive Feedback Between Married Couples." *The Family Coordinator,* 1970, *19,* 324-328.

Collins, J. D. "The Effects of the Conjugal Relationship Modification Method on Marital Communication and Adjustment." Unpublished doctoral dissertation, The Pennsylvania State University, 1971.

Combs, A. W., and Soper, D. W. "The Perceptual Organization of Effective Counselors." *Journal of Counseling Psychology,* 1963, *10,* 222-226.

Coufal, J. D. "Preventative-Therapeutic Programs for Mothers and Adolescent Daughters: Skill Training versus Discussion Methods." Unpublished doctoral dissertation, The Pennsylvania State University, 1975.

Cutler, B. R., and Dyer, W. G. "Initial Adjustment Processes in

Young Married Couples." *Social Forces,* 1965, *44,* 195-201.

Dickinson, W. A., and Truax, C. B. "Group Counseling with College and Underachievers: Comparisons with a Central Group and Relationship to Empathy, Warmth, and Genuineness." *Personnel Guidance Journal,* 1966, *45,* 243-247.

Endler, N. S. "Changes in Meaning During Psychotherapy as Measured by the Semantic Differential." *Journal of Counseling Psychology,* 1961, *8,* 105-111.

Ely, A. L. "Efficacy of Training in Conjugal Therapy." Unpublished doctoral dissertation, Rutgers University, 1970.

Ely, A. L., Guerney, B. G., and Stover, L. "Efficacy of the Training Phase of Conjugal Therapy." *Psychotherapy: Theory, Research and Practice,* 1973, *10,* 201-207.

Erikson, E. *Identity: Youth and Crisis.* New York: Norton, 1968.

Ginsberg, B. G. "Parent-Adolescent Relationship Development: A Therapeutic and Preventive Mental Health Program." Unpublished doctoral dissertation, The Pennsylvania State University, 1971.

Goldstein, A. P., Sprafkin, R. P., and Gershaw, N. J. *Skill Training for Community Living.* Elmsford, N.Y.: Pergamon Press, 1976.

Gordon, T. *P.E.T.: Parent Effectiveness Training.* New York: Wyden, 1972.

Grando, R. "Interrelationships Between Pretraining Variables, Role Performance and Improvement in Relationship in the Parent-Adolescent Relationship Development Program." Unpublished doctoral dissertation, The Pennsylvania State University, 1971a.

Grando, R. Unpublished research, Kansas State University, Manhattan, Kansas, 1971b.

Greenberg, I. A. (Ed.). *Psychodrama: Theory and Therapy.* New York: Behavioral Publications, 1974.

Grinker, R. R., Sr., Grinker, R. R., Jr., and John Timberlake. " 'Mentally Healthy' Young Males (Homoclites)." *Archives of General Psychiatry,* 1962, *6,* 405-453.

Guerney, B., Jr. "Filial Therapy: Description and Rationale." *Journal of Consulting Psychology,* 1964, *28,* 303-310.

Guerney, B., Jr. (Ed.). *Psychotherapeutic Agents: New Roles for Non-Professionals, Parents and Teachers.* New York: Holt, Rinehart and Winston, 1969.

Guerney, B., Jr., and Hatch, E. J. "Singles Training in Interpersonal Relations." Unpublished manuscript, University Park, The Pennsylvania State University, 1974.

Guerney, B., Jr., Guerney, L., and Andronico, M. P. "Filial Therapy." *Yale Scientific Magazine,* 1966, *40,* 6-14.

Guerney, B., Jr., Guerney, L., and Stollak, G. "The Potential Advantages of Changing From a Medical to an Educational Model in Practicing Psychology." *Interpersonal Development,* 1971/1972, *2,* 238-246.

Guerney, B., Jr., Guerney, L., and Stover, L. "Facilitative Therapist Attitudes in Training Parents as Psychotherapeutic Agents." *The Family Coordinator,* 1972, *21,* 275-278.

Guerney, B., Jr., Stollak, G., and Guerney, L. "A Format for a New Mode of Psychological Practice: Or, How to Escape a Zombie." *Counseling Psychologist,* 1970, *2,* 97-105.

Guerney, B., Jr., Stollak, G., and Guerney, L. "The Practicing Psychologist as Educator—an Alternative to the Medical Practitioner Model." *Professional Psychology,* 1971, *2,* 276-282.

Guerney, B., Jr., Stover, L., and Andronico, M. P. "On Educating the Disadvantaged Parent to Motivate Children for Learning: A Filial Approach." *Community Mental Health Journal,* 1967, *3,* 66-72.

Haley, J. "Marriage Therapy." *Archives of General Psychiatry,* 1963, *8,* 213-234.

Harrell, J., and Guerney, B., Jr. "Training Married Couples in Conflict Negotiation Skills." In D. Olson (Ed.), *Treating Relationships.* Lake Mills, Iowa: Graphic Publishing, 1976.

Hatch, E., and Guerney, B., Jr. "A Pupil Relationship Enhancement Program." *The Personnel and Guidance Journal,* 1975, *54,* 102-105.

Hess, S. "Listening to Youth: A Less-Traveled Road and on

Being Young, Down and Out in the American System."
*Congressional Record,* April 22, 1970, pp. 13512-13515.

Hickman, M., and Baldwin, B. "Use of Programmed Instruction to Improve Communication in Marriage." *The Family Coordinator,* 1971, *20,* 121-126.

Hinkle, J. E., and Moore, M. "A Student Couples Program." *The Family Coordinator,* 1971, *20,* 153-158.

Hobart, C. W., and Klausner, W. J. "Some Social Interactional Correlates of Marital Role Disagreements, and Marital Adjustment." *Marriage and Family Living,* 1959, *21,* 256-263.

Hollingshead, A. B. *Two Factor Index of Social Position.* Unpublished manuscript, 1965 Yale Station, New Haven, Connecticut, 1957.

Human Development Institute. *General Relationship Improvement Program* (4th ed.). Atlanta, Ga.: Author, 1964.

Human Development Institute. *Improving Communication in Marriage* (4th ed.). Atlanta, Ga.: Author, 1970.

Jackson, D. "Family Interaction, Family Homeostasis, and Some Implications for Conjoint Family Psychotherapy." In J. H. Masserman (Ed.), *Individual and Family Dynamics.* New York: Grune & Stratton, 1959.

Jackson, D. "The Study of the Family." *Family Process,* 1965, *4,* 1-20.

Kagan, J. "The Concept of Identification." *Psychological Review,* 1958, *65,* 296-305.

Karlsson, G. *Adaptability and Communication in Marriage.* Totowa, N.J.: The Bedminster Press, 1963.

Keniston, K. "Social Change and Youth in America." *Daedalus,* 1962, *91,* 145-171.

Kind, J. "The Relation of Communication-Efficiency to Marital Happiness and an Evaluation of Short-Term Training in Interpersonal Communication with Married Couples." Unpublished doctoral dissertation, University of Oregon, 1968.

Knox, D. *Marriage Happiness: A Behavioral Approach to Counseling.* Champaign, Ill.: Research Press, 1971.

Lederer, W., and Jackson, D. *Mirages of Marriage.* New York: Norton, 1968.

Levinger, G., and Senn, D. J. "Disclosure of Feelings in Marriage." *Merrill-Palmer Quarterly,* 1967, *13,* 237-249.

Levitt, E. E. "The Results of Psychotherapy with Children: An Evaluation." *Journal of Consulting Psychology,* 1957, *21,* 189-196.

Lewis, R. "A Developmental Framework for the Analysis of Premarital Dyadic Formation." *Family Process,* 1972, *11,* 17-48.

Lindquist, E. F. *Design and Analysis of Experiments in Psychology and Education.* Boston: Houghton Mifflin, 1953.

Locke, H. J. *Predicting Adjustment in Marriage: A Comparison of a Divorced and Happily Married Group.* New York: Holt, 1951.

Locke, H. J., and Williamson, R. C. "Marital Adjustment: A Factor Analysis Study." *American Sociological Review,* 1958, *23,* 562-569.

Locke, H. J., Sabagh, G., and Thomas, M. "Correlates of Primary Communication and Empathy." *Research Studies of the State College of Washington,* 1956, *24,* 116-124.

McCandless, B. R. *Children: Behavior and Development.* (2nd ed.) New York: Morrow, 1967.

Marcus, D., Offer, D., Blatt, S., and Gratch, G. "A Clinical Approach to the Understanding of Normal and Pathologic Adolescence." *Archives of General Psychiatry,* 1966, *15,* 569-576.

Masters, W., and Johnson, V. *Human Sexual Inadequacy.* Boston: Little Brown, 1970.

Miller, G. A. "Psychology as a Means of Promoting Human Welfare." *American Psychologist,* 1969, *24,* 1063-1075.

Miller, S. L. "The Effects of Communication Training in Small Groups Upon Self-disclosure and Openness in Engaged Couples' Systems of Interaction: A Field Experiment." *Dissertation Abstracts International,* 1971, *32,* 2819. University of Minnesota, 1971. (University Microfilms No. 71-28, 263).

Moreno, Z. T. "A Survey of Psychodramatic Techniques." *Group Psychotherapy,* 1959, *12,* 5-14.

Moss, J. J., Apolonio, F., and Jensen, M. "The Premarital Dyad During the Sixties." *Journal of Marriage and the Family,* 1971, *33,* 50-69.

Mussen, P. "Some Antecedents and Consequences of Masculine Sex Typing in Adolescent Boys." *Psychological Monographs,* 1961, *75* (2), 1-24.

Navran, L. "Communication and Adjustment in Marriage." *Family Process,* 1967, *6,* 173-184.

Nunnally, E. W. "Effects of Communication Training Upon Interaction Awareness and Empathic Accuracy of Engaged Couples: A Field Experiment." *Dissertation Abstracts International,* 1971, *32,* 4736. University of Minnesota, 1971. (University Microfilms No. 72-5561).

Offer, D. *The Psychological World of the Teenager.* New York: Basic Books, 1969.

Osgood, C. E., Tannenbaum, P. H., and Succi, G. J. *The Measurement of Meaning.* Urbana, Ill.: University of Illinois Press, 1957.

Payne, D. E., and Mussen, P. H. "Parent-Child Relations and Father Identification Among Adolescent Boys." *Journal of Abnormal and Social Psychology,* 1956, *52,* 358-362.

Pierce, R., Carkhuff, R. R., and Berenson, B. "The Differential Effects of High and Low Functioning Counselors Upon Counselors-In-Training." *Journal of Clinical Psychology,* 1967, *23,* 212-215.

Randolph, N., and Howe, W. *Self-Enhancing Education.* Stanford, Calif.: Stanford University Press, 1966.

Rappaport, A. F. "Conjugal Relationship Enhancement Program." In D. H. L. Olson (Ed.), *Treating Relationships.* Lake Mills, Iowa: Graphic Publishing, 1976.

Rappaport, A. F., and Harrell, J. "A Behavioral Exchange Model for Marital Counseling." *Family Coordinator,* 1972, *21,* 203-212.

Rogers, C. R. *Client-Centered Therapy.* Boston: Houghton Mifflin, 1951.

Rogers, C. R. "The Necessary and Sufficient Conditions of

Therapeutic Personality Change." *Journal of Consulting Psychology,* 1957, *22,* 95-103.

Sanford, F. H. "Creative Health and the Principle of *Habeas Mentem." American Psychologist,* 1955, *10,* 829-835.

Satir, V. M. *"Conjoint Marital Therapy."* Paper presented at the 41st meeting of the American Orthopsychiatric Association. Chicago, March 1964.

Satir, V. M. "Conjoint Marital Therapy." In B. L. Green (Ed.), *The Psychotherapies of Marital Disharmony.* New York: Free Press, 1965.

Satir, V. M. *Conjoint Family Therapy.* Palo Alto, Calif.: Science and Behavior, 1967.

Schlein, S. P. "Training Dating Couples in Empathic and Open Communication: An Experimental Evaluation of a Potential Mental Health Program." Unpublished doctoral dissertation, The Pennsylvania State University, 1971.

Shapiro, J., Krauss, H., and Truax, C. "Therapeutic Conditions and Disclosure Beyond the Therapeutic Encounter." *Journal of Counseling Psychology,* 1969, *16,* 290-294.

Shipman, G. "Speech Thresholds and Voice Tolerance in Marital Interaction." *Marriage and Family Living,* 1960, *22,* 203-209.

Smith, M. J. *When I Say No, I Feel Guilty.* New York: Dial Press, 1975.

Stover, L., and Guerney, B., Jr. "Efficacy of Training Procedures for Mothers in Filial Therapy." *Psychotherapy, Research and Practice,* 1967, *4,* 110-115.

Strupp, H. H. *Psychotherapies in Action.* New York: Grune & Stratton, 1960.

Strupp, H. H., Wallach, M. S., and Wogan, M. "Psychotherapy Experience in Retrospect: Questionnaire Survey of Former Patients and Their Therapists." *Psychological Monographs,* 1964, *78* (11, Whole No. 588).

Targow, J., and Zweber, R. "Participants' Reactions to Treatment in a Married Couples Group." *International Journal of Group Psychotherapy,* 1969, *19,* 221-225.

Terman, L. M. *Psychological Factors in Marital Happiness.* New York: McGraw-Hill, 1938.

Truax, C. B. "Effective Ingredients in Psychotherapy: An Approach to Unravelling the Patient-Therapist Interaction." *Journal of Counseling Psychology,* 1963, *10,* 256-263.

Truax, C. B. "Therapist Empathy, Warmth, and Genuineness and Patient Personality Change in Group Psychotherapy: A Comparison Between Interaction Unit Measures, and Patient Perception Measures." *Journal of Clinical Psychology,* 1966, *22,* 225-229.

Truax, C. B., and Carkhuff, R. R. "The Experimental Manipulation of Therapeutic Conditions." *Journal of Consulting Psychology,* 1965, *29,* 119-124.

Truax, C. B., Carkhuff, R. R., and Kodman, F., Jr. "Relationships Between Therapist-Offered Conditions and Patient Change in Group Psychotherapy." *Journal of Clinical Psychology,* 1965, *21,* 327-329.

Truax, C. B., and Mitchell, K. M. "The Psychotherapuetic and the Psychonoxious: Human Encounters That Change Behavior." *Buffalo Studies,* 1968, *4,* 55-92.

Truax, C. B., and Wargo, D. G. "Antecedents to Outcome in Group Psychotherapy with Hospitalized Mental Patients: Effects of Therapeutic Conditions, Alternate Sessions, Vicarious Therapy Pre-Training and Patient Self-Exploration." Unpublished manuscript, University of Arkansas, Arkansas Rehabilitation Research and Training Center, Fayetteville, Ark., 1967.

Truax, C. B., Wargo, D. G., Frank, K. D., Imber, S. D., Battle, C. C., Hoehn-Saric, N., and Stone, A. R. "Therapist Empathy, Genuineness, and Warmth, and Patient Therapeutic Outcome." *Journal of Consulting Psychology,* 1966, *30,* 395-401.

Udry, J. R. *The Social Context of Marriage.* New York: Lippincott, 1966.

Vogelsong, E. L. "Empathy Training for Preadolescents in Public Schools." Unpublished manuscript, University Park: Pennsylvania State University, 1974.

Vogelsong, E. L. "Homework Exercises for Relationship Enhancement Programs." Unpublished manuscript, University Park: Pennsylvania State University, 1975a.

Vogelsong, E. L. "Preventative-Therapeutic Programs for Mothers and Adolescent Daughters: A Follow-up of Relationship Enhancement versus Discussion and Booster versus No-Booster Methods." Unpublished doctoral dissertation, The Pennsylvania State University, 1975b.

Watson, A. S. "The Conjoint Psychotherapy of Marriage Partners." *American Journal of Orthopsychiatry,* 1963, *33,* 912-923.

Wieman, R. J. "Conjugal Relationship Modification and Reciprocal Reinforcement: A Comparison of Treatments for Marital Discord." Unpublished doctoral dissertation, The Pennsylvania State University, 1973.

# Index

▶◀▶◀▶◀▶◀▶◀▶◀▶◀▶◀▶◀▶◀▶◀▶◀▶◀

392